A Micro Handbook for
Small Libraries and Media Centers

Second Edition

A MICRO HANDBOOK
for
SMALL LIBRARIES
and
MEDIA CENTERS

BETTY COSTA and MARIE COSTA
Illustrated by W. Y. Regan

LIBRARIES UNLIMITED, INC.
Littleton, Colorado
1986

LIBRARIES UNLIMITED, INC.
P.O. Box 263
Littleton, Colorado 80160-0263

Throughout this book the following products that have trade names and trademarks have been mentioned. No such mention is intended to convey endorsements by or other affiliations with this book.

AppleDOS, Apple Computer, Inc.; Apple III, Apple Computer, Inc.; Apple II, Apple Computer, Inc.; Appleworks, Apple Computer, Inc.; Bernoulli Box, Iomega Corp.; Centronics, Centronics Data Computer Corp.; Commodore Amiga, Commodore Electronics, Ltd.; CompuServe, CompuServe, Inc.; Computer Cat, Colorado Computer Systems, Inc.; Concurrent DOS, Digital Research, Inc.; Corvus, Corvus Systems, Inc.; CP/M, Digital Research, Inc.; CP/M-86, Digital Research, Inc.; DIALOG, Dialog Information Service, Inc.; DIF, Software Arts; IBM AT, International Business Machines Corp.; IBM PC, International Business Machines Corp.; IBM Selectric, International Business Machines Corp.; IBM XT, International Business Machines Corp.; Lotus 1-2-3, Lotus Development Corp.; MacIntosh, Apple Computer, Inc.; MITINET, Transform, Inc.; MS-DOS, Microsoft Corp.; Omnidrive, Corvus Systems, Inc.; Omninet, Corvus Systems, Inc.; Overdue Writer, Follett Software Co.; PC-DOS, International Business Machines Corp.; ProDOS, Apple Computer, Inc.; Telemarc, Catalog Card Corp.; The Source, Source Telecomputing Corp.; Topview, International Business Machines Corp.; TRSDOS, Tandy/Radio Shack Corp.; UNIX, AT&T Bell Laboratories; VisiCalc, Visicorp; Windows, Microsoft Corp.; Wordstar, MicroPro International Corp.; Xenix, Microsoft Corp.; Z80, Zilog.

Library of Congress Cataloging-in-Publication Data

Costa, Betty, 1931-
    A micro handbook for small libraries and media centers.

    Includes bibliographies and index.
    1. Libraries--Automation--Handbooks, manuals, etc.
2. Instructional materials centers--Automation--
Handbooks, manuals, etc. 3. Microcomputers--
Library applications--Handbooks, manuals, etc.
4. Small libraries--Automation--Handbooks, manuals,
etc. 5. Library science--Data processing--Handbooks,
manuals, etc. I. Costa, Marie, 1951- . II. Title.
Z678.9.C64 1986   025'.0028'5   86-15387
ISBN 0-87287-525-3

This book is gratefully,
respectfully, and
lovingly dedicated
to
Larry Costa

Contents

List of Illustrations

Preface

You are about to enter a largely uncharted, mysterious, and challenging territory, one which, furthermore, is constantly changing, so that literally no one knows what might appear around the next bend. It is a territory full of exciting possibilities and opportunities for learning, for growth, and for a new kind of freedom from the routine and tedious chores that, until now, have consumed so much of our time and energy. It is a land of dramatic achievements, and small but significant accomplishments. It can also be a land of tremendous disappointment for someone who ventures into it unprepared and unwary.

This book is intended as a guide for the novice traveler in that section of the vast microcomputer territory which relates specifically to small libraries and media centers. Although the landscape is changing too rapidly to provide an actual map, we have tried to provide the necessary equipment, as well as certain rules of navigation, for a successful and productive journey. We suggest you read the book all the way through before planning your own course, then keep it as a handbook to use for future reference. We hope you will find it interesting as well as informative and useful.

Readers of the first edition of *Micro Handbook* will notice some substantial changes in this edition. These changes reflect not only differences in the microcomputer industry, but our own growth in knowledge and experience. We have taken out some information that is outdated or just unnecessary, and added a great deal, including two new chapters. This necessitated some reorganization of the original text.

Chapter 1, which surveys the history of computers and their role in society, particularly in libraries, has been updated to reflect the changes of the last few years. Chapters 2 and 3, which cover the basics of software and hardware, respectively, have been almost completely rewritten, since both these areas have changed dramatically in the last three years. These are the most technical chapters in the book, which we believe provide essential background knowledge for anyone buying and/or using computers.

The remaining chapters deal more specifically with computers in libraries. Chapter 4 discusses in detail a variety of specific types of software and the ways microcomputers may be used in libraries. Chapter 5 is a discussion of the library/media center's growing role as a computer resource center. Chapter 6 is a new chapter which discusses networking and other ways of using micros to connect with the world outside. Chapter 7, on how to choose and implement a computer system, is an updated and expanded version of the original chapter 6, and now includes selection and implementation checklists. Chapter 8 addresses computer ethics. Chapter 9 expands a discussion of one librarian's "micro-conversion" to include comments by two other micro-converts. Further readings sections have been added to each chapter and to some of the appendices. (Some annotations in these sections are direct quotes from the publications themselves.) The five appendices include an expanded glossary, a completely updated and expanded resource section, advice on caring for your computer, suggestions for funding possibilities, and sample evaluation charts.

Writing this book was a highly rewarding experience for both of us. We can't begin to list all of the people who responded to our letters and phone calls regarding their activities with microcomputers and libraries. Many of their names are listed in the resource section. We are grateful to all of them for taking time to write to or talk with us, and to the software vendors who willingly answered questions about their products. We would especially like to thank our families, who patiently listened to "When the book is done . . ."; our editor, Heather Cameron, for believing we could do it, and for her patience; and most of all, our technical consultant, who read patiently through endless drafts with a remarkable attention to detail, the person who got us into this whole computer business in the first place — our respective husband and father, Larry Costa.

More than ever, we are convinced that microcomputers offer marvelous opportunities for libraries, their staffs, and their patrons. We hope that *Micro Handbook* will help you to exploit those opportunities as fully as possible.

1 Libraries in a Computer-Dependent Society

Our society in the twentieth century has shown a pronounced tendency to "progress" headlong into the future, with little regard for the sanity, health, and happiness of its members, most of whom are struggling to keep up in an increasingly confusing, complex world that is at once too large to grasp and too small for comfort. The key word for the 1980s is "information" — piles of data and statistics and facts and speculations and premises and deductions and concepts and observations. Technology is simultaneously racing ahead of our ability to use its wonders, and stumbling behind the tremendous obstacles created by both natural and man-made problems. People today are faced with an "information overload" which, though it threatens to overwhelm them, could, if somehow tamed, managed, and understood, hold the secrets to an exciting and marvelous future.

As educators and information specialists, librarians, particularly school librarians, are faced with the responsibility not only of managing a vast supply of resources, but of giving children and other community members the tools, skills, and confidence to function in today's — and tomorrow's — ever-changing environment. The thought is at once challenging and terrifying, stimulating and exhausting.

Libraries today are evolving into sophisticated resource centers, responsible for gathering, sorting, and dispersing a huge variety of information in all forms, including not only books and magazines, but films, recordings, and, increasingly, computerized data, whether received online via special communications devices and procedures, or printed and distributed as hard copy. School libraries not only select and distribute resource materials and equipment, but also provide instruction and practice in using library services.

Libraries by their very nature are the logical institutions to provide both the method and the means for coping with the information overload we are all beginning to experience. But doing so will mean profound changes in both the image and the functions of libraries — and in the people who run them. Essentially, libraries have *always* been in the business of information storage and retrieval. What makes things so different now?

In a word, computers. Thirty, even twenty, years ago, computers were the stuff of science fiction, alien and mysterious machines attended by an elite and not entirely trusted class of professionals and technicians. Today they form an integral part of daily life, affecting numerous small and large facets of what we do, see, hear, think, produce, and consume. Computers have made both subtle and dramatic changes in the ways that society and individuals cope with the events and problems of business, science, government, even art. Some large-scale computer applications have been accepted, if sometimes annoying, facts of life for at least a generation (computerized billing and junk mail address lists, for example), but the recent trend toward individualized or personal applications will almost certainly have far more profound and direct effects on our thoughts, perceptions, and actions. As computers become simultaneously smaller, more powerful, and more pervasive in our society, those who possess the skills to take advantage of them will be better able to function as productive and aware individuals in what might otherwise be an overwhelming and unmanageable world, while those who do not will be left further and further behind.

So what exactly is a computer? At its most basic, a computer is a machine that computes, or performs mathematical processes. Today "computer" means an electronically powered machine that is capable of performing complex series of computations, known as algorithms, at very high rates of speed. It is both amazing and reassuring to realize that all of the marvelous, complicated things that computers do derive from one very small, singular feature—the ability to tell if a switch is ON or OFF. Is that space on a Hollerith (key-punched) card light (from light shining through a hole) or dark? Is that tiny area on a disk or tape magnetized or not? ON or OFF. YES or NO. ONE or ZERO. This is why computers are so exasperatingly, unerringly literal minded. Unlike humans, they exist in a world of absolutes where each action is based on whether a given switch is ON or OFF at a particular instant. Every computation, no matter how complex, consists of a series of ON/OFF-based actions, which are predetermined by a programmer. Before a computer can do anything, somewhere a human being, or more likely several human beings, must painstakingly spell out all of the steps necessary to perform each function.

When thinking about this process, it is helpful to picture yourself going through some very basic, everyday routine, one step at a time. For example, suppose you are sitting at your desk reading this book and you wish to look up the word "computer" in the dictionary. What is the first step you would take? The second? The third? If you describe the process as follows: "Get the dictionary, find the Cs, find 'computer,' read the definition," you would still have left out most of the steps. A programmer would describe it something like this:

```
100   Stand up.
110   Push back chair.
120   Move out from between desk and chair.
130   If you are facing in the direction of the dictionary, go to 190.
140   If the dictionary is to your left, go to 170.
150   Rotate 15 degrees right.
160   Go to 130.
170   Rotate 15 degrees left.
180   Go to 130.
190   Take one step forward.
200   If you are in front of the dictionary, go to 220.
210   Go to 190.
```

220 Open the dictionary.
230 If the word at the top of the page begins with "co-" go to 270.
240 Open to a different page.
250 Go to 230.
260 Look at the first word.
270 If the word is computer, go to 300.
280 Look at the next word.
290 Go to 270.
300 Read the definition.

And this is what a higher-level program, one several levels above the ON/OFF of machine language, would look like. Several steps are left out. (Lower your hands to the sides of the chair. Push down with your hands. Raise your body up from the chair. Push the chair back. Take your hands off the chair, etc., etc.)

Fortunately for those of us who are inclined to say "Get the dictionary," a lot of those steps, in fact the great majority of them, are built in when we acquire a computer system. And there are many programmers seeking ways to free us from executing even more steps, making computers speak and understand languages that are very close to human ones. Their work makes it possible for the majority of people to operate microcomputers without ever learning a programming language, although some knowledge of programming may be useful and even fun.

A BRIEF HISTORY OF COMPUTERS

Actually, computers are not such a recent phenomenon. People have been devising calculating tools since they discovered the value of fingers for counting. They carved notches in sticks, drew lines in the dirt, piled pebbles in heaps. Eventually, about 3000 B.C., the first computing device appeared in China. The abacus, which consists of beads strung on wires and uses a base 5 system, was practical enough to have stayed in use five thousand years, up to and including the present. School children use it as an aid to comprehending the principles of addition, subtraction, and place value, and merchants in some countries still use it as a practical everyday calculator. The base 5 system and the awkward Roman numeral system used in Western society eventually gave way to the Hindu-Arabic numerical system, and the mechanical abacus was replaced by the equivalent of pencil and paper algorithms. Knowledge of and ability to perform arithmetic, like reading and writing, were esoteric and reserved to the priesthood and other learned types, much as computers have until very recently been the province of a select, knowledgeable few.

Forty-five hundred years or so after the development of the abacus, an Englishman named William Oughtred produced the slide rule, the most durable of a number of mechanical calculators invented during the seventeenth century. The slide rule incorporated the logarithms developed a short time before by a Scotsman, John Napier, and remained a popular tool up until the first battery-powered calculators came on the market. Not long after

Oughtred's invention of the slide rule a gear-driven machine capable of performing addition and subtraction was built by an 18-year-old Frenchman, Blaise Pascal, to help his administrator father deal with taxation and other financial matters. His machine was the precursor of automobile odometers. Pascal patented his machine in 1642. Soon after that German philosopher and mathematician Gottfried Wilhelm von Leibniz went Pascal one better and devised the stepped-wheel calculator, which also multiplied, divided, and found numerical roots.

Even before Oughtred and Pascal and their successors, other inventive people had introduced such useful items as clocks and compasses, and there is evidence that a four-function calculator already existed by the time Pascal was born. As with most inventions, there was much parallel development, and the credits are hazy. Nonetheless, functional mechanical calculators gained wide use in government and business, though not in education, during the seventeenth and eighteenth centuries.

The next step was to automate tools, beginning with the weaving loom, automation of which took three-quarters of a century to develop. Joseph-Marie Jacquard exhibited his loom, which used large punched hole cards to regulate the finished design, at the 1801 World's Fair in Paris. The concept was very similar to that used with punched paper rolls that manipulate the keys of a player piano.

Other technological and mathematical developments were occurring which would eventually lead to modern computers. These developments included George Boole's system of algebraic logic, which became the basis for machine computations; the discovery of the Edison effect, which made possible the invention of the vacuum tube; and the invention by Charles Xavier Thomas of a commercially successful calculating machine. But the technology was not yet far enough advanced to activate the "Analytical Engine" envisioned by Charles Babbage. This was to be a programmable machine with a memory and punched cards, powered by a steam engine and capable of carrying out sequences of calculations automatically. Though he died before engineering technology could catch up with his ideas, Babbage contributed substantially to the principles used later in functioning computers. While he was working on his "Difference Engine," Babbage met Ada Byron, Countess of Lovelace, who became the first computer programmer. Though her gender prevented her from making her identity public, Ada Byron gave the world a clear and concise explanation of Babbage's engines. At the same time she wrote operating instructions that were the precursors of today's programming languages, one of which is named in her honor.

Necessity as a stimulus to invention stepped in again when the U.S. Census Bureau found itself in a bind. The 1890 census was imminent, and information collected in 1880 was still being processed. The bureau needed a faster way to process data. In the American tradition, the Census Bureau held a contest to find a new system. The winner, a statistician from Buffalo, New York, was Herman Hollerith, whose tabulating machine processed data fed into it in the form of punched cards (the familiar "do not fold, spindle or mutilate" Hollerith cards of a now-vanishing era). The first machines were hand operated. Operators processed an average of 8,000 cards a day, recording, compiling, and tabulating data on some 63 million Americans. Later the card feeding was done automatically. In the early 1900s a new industry sprang up around tabulating and comparing machinery, giving birth to companies such as the Computing-Tabulating-Recording Company (later known as IBM), the Powers Tabulating Machine Company (which became the UNIVAC Division of Sperry Rand), and National Cash Register.

During the late nineteenth century and the early twentieth century inventors and researchers in other fields such as radio and electronics made technological contributions beyond the wildest dreams of Charles Babbage and others. It wasn't until the 1930s, however, that serious development of general purpose digital computers began. The Mark I, an electromechanical "automated sequence controlled calculator," was developed by Howard Aiken of Harvard University during the late 1930s and early 1940s. The Mark I could be thought of as a link between the "prehistoric" mechanical calculating devices and the first generation of true electronic computers (the bulky, light-flashing, temperamental "electronic brains"). The Mark I, consisting of almost 80 adding machines and calculators controlled by a roll of punched paper, was a considerable improvement on its predecessors, performing up to three additions per second. Operational in 1944, it was quickly and dramatically outpaced by the first generation of modern computers.

The development of the first electronic general purpose computer in the United States, ENIAC (the Electronic Numerical Integrator and Calculator), was financed by the U.S. Army at a cost of some $400,000 during World War II. Operational in 1946, ENIAC, built by J. Presper Eckert and John W. Mauchly at the University of Pennsylvania, is generally considered to be the world's first general purpose digital computer. (Recent evidence, just released from classification by the British government, indicates that England had in operation in late 1943 a computer called COLOSSUS, developed by a group of mathematicians, engineers, and linguists for the purpose of deciphering German codes. Other rumors have it that the Germans had developed a computer or two of their own.) ENIAC and the first generation computers that followed it were large, bulky machines that used vacuum tubes and electronic relays to process and store information which they received via punched cards. They gave off large amounts of heat, consumed a great deal of electricity, and were maddeningly slow by today's standards. Even with their attendant teams of engineers and technicians, the machines tended to be unreliable and difficult to operate. Their memories were quite small. (ENIAC could not store programs and actually had to be partially rewired for each new problem it was given to solve). Early computers responded only to machine language programs, which were exacting and time-consuming to produce. Even so, ENIAC could perform calculations at a rate a thousand times faster than a human with a desk calculator — an astonishing feat.

The first commercially available computer, UNIVAC I (UNIVersal Automatic Computer), also developed by Eckert and Mauchly, was installed at the U.S. Census Bureau in 1951. UNIVAC used magnetic tape instead of punched cards, and was considerably faster than ENIAC, but presented similar problems of unreliability, difficult maintenance, small memory, and programming difficulties. Most of the computers produced in the 1950s conformed to these early prototypes. During that decade high-level programming languages such as FORTRAN, COBOL, and ALGOL were developed. A computer market began to develop, though it was limited to governments and large corporations that could afford the tremendous expense of owning and operating machines that cost hundreds of dollars an hour to run. Even with these limitations, computers began to exert an influence over people's daily lives. The new age had begun.

The second generation of computers, which appeared during the early 1960s, was made possible by a 1947 invention of Bell Laboratories, the transistor. Transistors performed much more reliably than vacuum tubes on a tiny fraction of the power, took up an even smaller amount of space, and gave off far less heat. Computers, along with televisions, radios, and other electronic devices, became much more efficient and less costly in terms of energy and size. The second-generation computers also used very small electromagnets for primary memory storage. Software (programming) developments kept pace with technology, and other companies like Honeywell, General Electric, and Burroughs joined IBM and Sperry-Rand in what was becoming a billion-dollar industry.

The third generation of computers, based on solid-state circuitry, became commercially available around 1965. Increases in memory capacity and speed were matched by corresponding decreases in size, price, and difficulty of operation. Minicomputers came into the public realm, in reach of universities, researchers, and small businesses. Programming was taught in colleges, high schools, and even junior high schools. In 1971, the Intel Corporation announced the invention of the 4004, the first microprocessor.

The microprocessor incorporated thousands of transistors on a silicon chip a fraction of an inch across. In the past fifteen years, chip technology has advanced to the point where an entire computer — faster, more powerful, and with much greater storage capacity than the computers of the 1950s — fits onto an area less than a quarter inch wide. The advent of the microprocessor led to the developments which have made computerization so pervasive in the 1980s — the first decade of true computer dependency. Besides functioning in a variety of devices from traffic lights to microwave ovens, microprocessors have made it possible for individuals to have the resources and capabilities of computers at home.

During the last few years, microprocessors have grown in capabilities while shrinking in size and price. Amazing advances have been made in memory and storage, printing, communications, and software development. Among the most exciting new technologies are optical disks, or CD ROMs, which make it possible to store vast amounts of information in a very small space and to retrieve any of it at will. Printers, once among the most expensive and unreliable components of microcomputer systems, are now faster and considerably cheaper, and may produce more attractive, readable copy. Communications devices provide rapid, affordable electronic transmission of information, including complete documents.

Software development, meanwhile, has expanded into a wide range of applications. Work is being done on systems which will enable people to communicate with computers using languages such as English or French. The controversial quest for so-called artificial intelligence—the effort to make computers "think" and "learn" as people do—has led to programs known as "expert systems." Expert systems consist of information and heuristics, or "rules of thumb," painstakingly gleaned from human experts and programmed into computers. Expert systems are used to analyze and aid decisions about a wide variety of human problems, from medical diagnosis to space flight engineering. Lacking common sense, imagination, and the type of knowledge that comes from experience, expert systems cannot replace humans, but they can provide invaluable assistance, vastly increasing our abilities to fight disease or launch ourselves into space.

Also in varying stages of development are voice recognition and speech synthesis, "flat" screens using liquid crystal displays instead of cathode ray tubes, new types of memory storage, robot servants—the list grows daily. Not all of the new technologies will prove practical or beneficial. Many will never get much beyond conception; others may be developed only to fade into obscurity because there are no practical applications for them.

The implications of this rapid advance are profound, exciting, and disturbing all at once. Four (some say five) generations of computers have emerged in one and a half human generations. The effects on society are more far-reaching than we could expect to cover in a lengthy book, much less this brief overview. We will look at the effects of the computer age on libraries in general and small libraries in particular.

Until the introduction of the microcomputer, few libraries were in a position to take advantage of computer technology. Those that could were primarily large university libraries which shared computer time with other departments. A number of dreamers recognized the potential for library computerization, but the size and cost of computers were prohibitive until the late 1970s, when minicomputers and turnkey software enabled large and medium-sized public and academic libraries to use circulation, acquisition, and cataloging systems without having to employ staff programmers. During the late 1960s and early 1970s the Library of Congress and the Ohio College Library Center began offering cataloging services which made it possible for libraries to enjoy some of the benefits of computers without owning individual systems. Still, as the flood of information increased, funds diminished, and labor costs rose, manual systems became less effective and more expensive to operate.

At first microcomputers were used in libraries mostly to supplement larger computer systems, as in the use of light pens in circulation control, or intelligent terminals connected directly or by telephone to a mini or mainframe computer (for an explanation of the different classifications of computers, see chapter 3). Now, thanks to increased capabilities and falling prices, microcomputers have become a viable means of library automation for nearly everyone. It is now feasible for even a small library to have a computerized system that is at once independent and interactive, individually tailored to the community being served and able to access the resources of surrounding larger communities, including national and even international institutions and services.

Automating a library does not mean that computers will replace teachers, librarians, or administrators. Computerization is not really the same thing as automation, though the two words are often used interchangeably.

Automatic means self-regulating, operating independently of external control. Though they are used in automation, automation is not what computers, particularly microcomputers, are all about. There is nothing independent about a computer, perverse as it may seem at any moment. Computers are powerful electronic tools for carrying out actions, according to *human* wishes and instructions, which if performed by the people themselves would consume large, sometimes prohibitive, amounts of time and energy. Computers do only what people tell them to do, but, given proper instructions, they can do wonderful things, thus freeing the people they serve to do other wonderful things that only people can do.

Some of these wonderful things are happening right now, in libraries of all types and sizes. Since the business of a library is information—collecting it, processing (or sorting) it, and making it available to patrons—it follows that the more knowledge a librarian has about what types and amounts of information are available, and the more easily that information can be accessed, the better the service the library can provide. And since the business of computers is information—collecting it, processing it, and making it available to users—libraries are places where computers are fast becoming *necessary*.

It is wise to approach the idea of computerization with some wariness and skepticism. Simply buying and installing a computer will not cause miracles to happen in your library or anywhere. In order to participate in the "computer revolution" and not be swept away or passed up by it, librarians must make full use of their special skills—analysis, research, and awareness and anticipation of patron needs. They must learn to evaluate and use the capabilities of computers, and to understand the limitations as well as the possibilities of computerization. Knowledge, planning, and foresight will mean the difference between increased efficiency, service, and creativity, and frustration, hostility, and wasted money. Many a system sits gathering dust and resentment alongside less esoteric equipment.

The object of computerization is to free people to work with people (and books, and films, and ideas) by taking over the routine tasks that they are better at doing anyway, and by giving people access to all kinds of information that might otherwise be difficult or impossible to locate. Computers are becoming easier and easier to use (user friendly in computerese), and the necessary skills do not include math ability—logic, perhaps, and attention to detail, and patience, but not math. As for not being able to afford it—in real cost, it is very likely that quite soon not having a computer system will be more expensive than having one, *if* the system is carefully chosen and fully used.

This is where a little knowledge (such as the kind available in this book) can save a lot of grief. It is true that there are (some) turnkey systems available which you can bring home and use with almost no knowledge of computers. ("Almost" is an important word here. Even with the most automatic of systems, you need to know such mundane but mysterious skills as turning the computer on, loading a program, and backing up data. The days of "plug it in and let it rip" have yet to arrive.) If you get very lucky, you might find a vendor who will magically intuit your needs and sell you just the right turnkey system, and if you are even luckier, that vendor will hold your hand and continue to answer the phone whenever a problem comes up (which is virtually guaranteed to happen, even with the best of systems).

Such luck, however, is rare. What is more, as every media specialist is aware, there is more involved than simply choosing and implementing a system. The purchase must be explained and justified not only to the purchasing department, but to the school or library board, parent-teacher associations, and other community members. Once the system is in use, the library staff must be prepared to deal with questions and problems of patrons, teachers, and parents. As the coordinator of library services, you are knowledgeable about the resources of your library. If those resources include a computer or two, you had better be knowledgeable about that, too.

This doesn't mean you have to rush out and take a class in BASIC or Pascal, or start reading up on Boolean algebra. It just means it's useful to have some idea of where computers came from, what they do and how they do it, and how to make them do what you want. This book will give you the background you need to get started, and probably enough to keep you going indefinitely, unless you happen to develop a passion for programming. And once you have your own system, you'll pick up a lot just by using it, through accomplishments and mistakes—yours and other people's.

Wondrous as microcomputers can be, they can't perform miracles. A computerized "dream library," with a completely integrated system including circulation, catalog, acquisitions, etc., is not impossible to achieve using microcomputers, although the reality might not match your imagination. But it would be expensive, impractical, and probably foolish to try to implement such a system all at once. The best way to approach computerization is slowly, a function or two at a time, starting with a single microcomputer and one or two software packages and building from there. There are several advantages to this approach. In addition to the expense, planning and implementing computerization takes considerable staff time. Limiting the size and number of changes under way at any one time minimizes disruption of library services and lessens staff anxiety. Also, when the changes are small, your mistakes are smaller, less drastic, and more easily corrected. Best of all, you have a chance to tailor your system as it grows, taking into account the reactions of the patrons, the staff, and the community, rather than attempting the impossible task of tailoring the users to a system that may have very little to do with their needs.

We suggest reading the following chapters to gain an overview of what micros are and what possibilities they offer. Then take the time to do some careful planning. Shop around, ask questions, be skeptical and visionary at the same time. Computerization does not offer automatic answers to all of your problems. Carefully planned and implemented, it can, however, help you place information literally at patrons' fingertips, while freeing you and your staff from time- and energy-consuming routine chores. The effects can go even further, resulting in more creative and innovative services, and more personal interaction with patrons and staff. Even with a limited budget, you and your library can enjoy the benefits of computers as *humanizing* tools.

CHRONOLOGY

Prehistory	People count on fingers and toes, pile rocks, make scratches, etc.
ca. 3000 B.C.	The abacus comes into use in China
1614	John Napier (inventor of logarithms) produces a device for arithmetic computations using rods or "bones"
1630	William Oughtred invents the slide rule
1642	Blaise Pascal invents a gear-driven adding machine
ca. 1694	Gottfried Wilhelm von Leibniz invents the stepped-wheel calculator.
1801	Joseph-Marie Jacquard exhibits his punched-card weaving loom at the Paris World's Fair
ca. 1810	Charles Thomas begins mass production of calculators
1812	Charles Babbage builds the "Difference Engine"
1834	Charles Babbage builds the "Analytical Engine"
ca. 1830	Ada Byron, Countess of Lovelace explains Babbage's engines and writes operating instructions—the first computer programs
1854	George Boole develops a system of algebraic logic
1868	The first practical typewriter is patented
1884	John Patterson introduces the commercial cash register
1887	Herman Hollerith invents a punched-card tabulating machine for the 1890 census
1920	James Smathers invents the electric typewriter
1937	Howard Aiken begins work on the Mark I Clause Shannon designs electrical switching circuits using symbolic logic to perform addition using relays and switches
1944	Mark I is up and running
1945	John von Neumann introduces the concept of a stored program
1943-1946	J. Presper Eckert and John Mauchly build ENIAC
1947	Bell Laboratories produces the first transistor
1949	Maurice Wilks of England designs and builds EDSAC, the first computer to use an internally stored program
1951	UNIVAC is installed at the U.S. Census Bureau
1955	IBM introduces the first large-scale business computer John Backus invents FORTRAN
ca. 1956	Grace Murray Hopper invents FLOMATIC (which later becomes COBOL)

1959	Transistors are incorporated in computer circuitry (second generation)
1963	John Kemeny and Thomas Kurtz develop BASIC Introduction of time sharing
1964	Use of integrated circuits in computers (third generation)
1965	Minicomputers enter wide use
1971	Intel develops the microprocessor
1975	Microcomputers enter the marketplace
1975-1976	CP/M, first standardized operating system for microcomputers, is developed
1982-1986	Numerous developments, including

- Introduction of CD ROM/optical disk technology.

- Introduction of multi-user, multitask micros.

- Entry of IBM into microcomputer marketplace helps gain widespread acceptance for micros and establishes MS-DOS as standard 16-bit operating system.

- Development of fifth-generation computers (expert systems).

- Fast, affordable facsimile transmission of documents becomes possible.

Projections	Possibilities include

- Read/write optical disk technololgy.

- Cathode-ray tube screens replaced by "flat" liquid crystal displays.

- Electronic journals.

- A "paperless" society.

- Robotic servants.

- Artificial intelligence.

- Local, national, and international networks.

FURTHER READINGS

Monographs

Videodisc & Optical Digital Disk Technologies/Applications/Libraries. By Information Systems Consultants, Inc. n.p., n.d. unpaged. $6.00 (prepaid) (Council on Library Resources, 1785 Massachusetts Ave., NW, Washington, DC 20036).
Looks at optical disk technology, production, and economics, as well as possible library applications.

Periodicals

Aveney, Brian. "Online Catalogs: The Transformation Continues." *Wilson Library Bulletin* 58, no. 6 (February 1984): 406-10.

Desroches, Richard A. "Systems Librarian in the 1980s." *Library HiTech News* 1, no. 3 (March 1984): 1, 8-9.
"Systems librarianship is a relatively new aspect of the information management field. . . . A systems librarian is the library staff member in charge of computers and automation."

Green, John O. "Making Computers Smarter—A Look at . . . Artificial Intelligence." *Popular Computing* 3, no. 3 (January 1984): 97-100.
Includes a chart, "Some Key Dates in the History of AI," as well as further readings.

Herther, Nancy. "Artificial Intelligence—New Technology for Library Microcomputers." *Small Computers in Libraries* 5, no. 6 (June 1985): 12-15.

Horny, Karen L. "Managing Change: Technology & the Profession." *Library Journal* 110, no. 16 (1 October 1985). No pages available.

Immel, A. Richard. "Innovation, Where Are You?" *Popular Computing* 4, no. 3 (January 1985): 43-45.
"New packaging hardly disguises old technology."

Lancaster, F. W. "The Paperless Society Revisited." *American Libraries* 16, no. 8 (September 1985): 553-55.
"Ten years after his famous prophecy, the prophet takes stock of changes."

Melin, Nancy. "Artificial Intelligence: Coming Soon to a Library Near You! " *Information Today* 2, no. 11 (December 1985): 15, 27.

Parker, Elizabeth Betz. "Library of Congress Non-Print Optical Disk Pilot Program." *Information Technology & Libraries* 4, no. 4 (December 1985): 289-99.

"A variety of visual media have been recorded on analog laser videodisc, in order to test the ability of this technology to help preserve pictorial material and to help improve researchers' access to pictorial collections."

Roszak, Theodore. "Partners for Democracy: Public Libraries & Information Technology." *Wilson Library Bulletin* 60, no. 6 (February 1986): 14-17.

Excerpted from *The Cult of Information,* published in May 1986 by Pantheon.

Savage, Noelle. "New Technology in Libraries: A Report." *Wilson Library Bulletin* 58, no. 6 (February 1984): 411-16.

Report on conference with theme, "Technology in Libraries: The Impact on Publishers."

Suprenant, Tom. "Future Libraries." *Wilson Library Bulletin* 58, no. 3 (November 1983): 206ff.

Discusses how "fifth generation" artificial intelligence computers will affect future libraries.

"10th Anniversary of the Personal Computer." *Popular Computing* 4, no. 3 (January 1985): 72-90ff., 177-79.

This is a special report, including part 1, "Ed Roberts: The Father of the Personal Computer"; part 2, "Ten Years After: The Micro's Imprint on Society"; and part 3, "The Future of the Micro: Looking Ahead at the Next Decade."

2 An Introduction to Computer Software

FIRST THINGS FIRST

You might think it strange that we are discussing software—the programs—before hardware, the physical components of a computer system. The reason is that software availability ideally should be your *first* consideration in choosing a system. You have probably realized by now that buying a microcomputer is not like buying other types of equipment, such as movie projectors or tape recorders. When you purchase the latter, you assume that films or tapes in your existing collection, plus any new ones you acquire, will work with the equipment regardless of brand. You cannot make the same assumption when buying a microcomputer. The computer industry is notorious for its lack of standardization, the result of which is that a given piece of software will not run on just any computer. Since the software is the portion of the system that will actually perform the tasks you are computerizing, it pays to locate the software first, then find the hardware needed to run it.

Admittedly this is not always possible. You may be reading this book because you are wondering what to do with one or more microcomputers already in your library. If so, you will in a sense be working backward, and you will have to make your software decisions within the limitations presented by the type of hardware you happen to have. Although you may not be able to computerize your preferred application right away, you should be able to choose from several useful functions, any of which can serve as a starting point. Also, when considering future additions and expansions, you need not be bound into the same brand (which may no longer be available). Micro-based systems are by nature modular. There is no reason why you can't employ two or more different kinds of machines in the same system, if your software requirements call for them.

By themselves, computers are incredibly stupid. Even the most sophisticated, technologically advanced computer is useless without the detailed sets of instructions, or programs, which control every hardware function from displaying characters on the screen to printing text to performing complex calculations. Collectively, these programs are known as software. In the early days of micros (about ten years ago) users made their own software, which required some programming knowledge. Now you can use micros for all kinds of purposes without ever writing a line of program code, thanks to the abundance of commercial software available.

The amount, quality, and diversity of software have increased dramatically in the short time since the first appearance of *Micro Handbook*. At that

14

time, it appeared that some standards might be emerging to simplify the choices facing microcomputer users and potential users. Such, however, has not been the case. The continuing rapid growth of computer technology, combined with the intense and sometimes self-destructive competition among both software and hardware manufacturers, has increased the confusion along with the options, and the situation does not seem likely to improve.

WHAT IS SOFTWARE?

Basically, there are two types of software—systems and applications. Systems software works directly with the components of a computer system, enabling it to function or to run more efficiently. Types of systems software include operating systems (see below), sorting packages, programming aids, and debugging tools. Applications software is the category which most concerns you as an end user. It consists of programs designed to perform specific tasks such as word processing, inventory control, accounting functions, etc. Since applications software is designed to run with specific operating systems and/or hardware, your hardware and operating system needs will depend on your choice of applications software.

Software is written in a variety of programming languages. High-level languages, such as BASIC or Pascal, are usually based on English, with vocabularies, syntax, and rules of usage that make them relatively simple for people to understand and use. Low-level languages include machine language—the ones and zeros that the computer can understand directly—and assembly language, which resembles machine language but uses mnemonic instead of numeric instructions.

Most applications programs, and some systems programs, are written in high-level languages. The high-level instructions for a program make up its source code. Through special programs called compilers and interpreters, the source code is translated into object code, which consists of instructions that the computer can use. The object code is what you receive when you buy a piece of software. Each kind of computer uses its own object code. Software portability means that the same source code can be recompiled into different object codes to run on different computers.

Software which is permanently stored in hardware is called firmware. Microcomputer firmware is, by necessity, limited in function. Its main component is usually a program whose primary task is to read the first track of a floppy or hard disk and follow the instructions there—to load, or read, the operating system from the disk into the computer's RAM, or random access memory (a process known as "booting" the system). The firmware may also contain portions of the basic input output system (BIOS), which controls functions such as displaying characters on the screen or transmitting them to the printer. In a few computers, including the Apple II and the IBM PC, the firmware also includes portions of BASIC or another language, allowing for some rudimentary programming.

UNDERSTANDING OPERATING SYSTEMS

Originally developed to free programmers from having to constantly rewrite the routines for basic tasks such as decoding keyboard signals or sending output to the printer, operating systems are essential elements of all computer systems. Without the operating system, all other parts of the system are useless. The operating system acts as an interface between the computer and the applications program or user, transmitting information between them in a way each can understand. It also coordinates all the hardware components, regulating the input and output functions of each device, and causing each to respond properly to signals from the user and the applications software. For example, when you press a key on the keyboard (input), the operating system directs a program in firmware called the monitor to display the character on the screen (output). Similarly, when you type the command that tells your word processor to print a page, the program passes the command along to the operating system, which directs and regulates the flow of characters to the printer.

Operating systems make using and programming for computers much simpler, since a single instruction to the operating system from a user or an applications program activates a whole series of instructions which are sent directly to the hardware. The operating system also acts as a file manager, keeping track of where data are stored in the system and how much storage is available for additional data, and provides for the loading and execution of applications software. Included with the operating system are a number of utilities, programs used to perform specific "housekeeping" tasks such as copying files or formatting disks.

The operating system may also be responsible for handling concurrency and multitasking. Originally, microcomputers were all single-task machines—that is, they could perform only one task (such as word processing) at a time, and for a single user. With the introduction of more powerful microprocessors and more sophisticated operating systems, it became possible for microcomputers to do several tasks concurrently, sometimes even for several users. For example, a user might be working simultaneously with a word processing program and a spreadsheet. In actuality, however, the computer is not performing the tasks at the same time. Instead, it is switching back and forth between them so rapidly that both appear to be active at once.

A more limited type of concurrency is called spooling. In spooling, the computer stores characters in a temporary storage area called a buffer until an input or output device, such as the printer or the CRT screen, is ready for them. This allows you, for example, to queue up several files for printing while you work on something else. In both types of concurrency, the operating system serves as a traffic controller, switching the processor back and forth between tasks, or controlling the flow of characters to the printer or the screen.

Disk Operating Systems

The acronym DOS stands for the generic term disk operating system. The first operating systems were built directly into the hardware, and were thus limited by the small amount of available storage space. Placing the operating system on a floppy or hard disk (see chapter 3) greatly increases the amount of available storage, allowing a more complex, powerful, and extensive system. Now all but the least sophisticated microcomputers use some form of DOS.

Operating systems for early mainframe computers were *all* machine-specific, that is, meant to run on only one type of computer. With the advent of micros, people began to realize the advantages of a portable operating system, primarily the ability to run each other's applications software. Unfortunately, the rapid and chaotic growth of the industry spawned not one but many operating systems, most of them completely incompatible with one another. *It is critical to understand how this lack of standardization affects you as a computer user or would-be user.* A program designed for CP/M will not run on AppleDOS; one designed for MS-DOS will not run on UNIX. Some operating systems are even incompatible with different versions of themselves — programs written for AppleDOS, for example, may not run on its upgraded version, ProDOS. If an operating system will run programs written for its earlier versions, it is said to be upward compatible. Without upward compatibility, simply upgrading your operating system means replacing all of your applications software.

A few operating systems have gained some prominence in recent years, creating de facto standards which apply to sizable portions, though not all, of the industry. Notably, the successful operating system manufacturers have pursued an open architecture policy, as opposed to keeping their systems proprietary. Open architecture means that the source code and technical specifications are made available, free or for a fee, by the manufacturer. Proprietary means that the code and specifications are kept secret. In the case of operating systems, the availability of source code and other technical specifications determines whether or not any third party development of applications software will take place. It is difficult to sell computers for which little or no software exists. Therefore, with rare exception, those manufacturers who attempted to isolate their users by maintaining proprietary operating systems usually ended up converting to another, open operating system, or fading from view.

The following is a list of the operating systems which you are most likely to encounter:

CP/M — the first portable operating system, developed by Digital Research in 1975 for computers using the 8080 and Z-80 "family" of 8-bit microprocessors (for an explanation of microprocessors, see chapter 3). When we wrote the first edition of *Micro Handbook,* it appeared that CP/M had a good grip on the micro market, particularly for business applications. Thousands of software packages were written for it. Even competitors such as Apple, with their own operating systems, offered plug-in boards enabling their users to run CP/M.

The original version of CP/M used only a tiny amount of memory (which at that time was very expensive), and was oriented toward skilled users,

i.e., programmers. It was decidedly not user friendly, although subsequent versions have made it slightly more so. The documentation (user
manuals) for CP/M was notoriously bad, but a large number of books
have been written to aid befuddled users.

When the more powerful 16-bit machines were introduced, Digital
Research developed a 16-bit version, CP/M-86. There are several stories,
most if not all of them apocryphal, explaining how MS-DOS took the
16-bit market away from CP/M (see below). Digital Research may make a
comeback, however, with its Concurrent DOS, which has the ability to
run MS-DOS, CP/M, and CP/M-86 programs, plus a number of other
features. Meanwhile, CP/M maintains a large and diverse software base
for users of 8-bit systems, including a wide assortment of public domain
programs.

MS-DOS/PC-DOS—the current "standard" for microcomputers with
8088/8086 16-bit microprocessors, MS-DOS owes its prominence to
IBM's decision to use the system for its PC. Originally developed by
Seattle Computer Products as a stopgap system while awaiting a 16-bit
version of CP/M, QDOS (for quick and dirty operating system) was acquired in 1981 by Microsoft, manufacturers of a popular version of
BASIC. Microsoft upgraded the operating system and renamed it MS-
DOS (for MicroSoft-DOS). Among hardware manufacturers licensing the
new system was IBM, which christened its virtually identical version PC-
DOS. As IBM sales began to mount, a sort of strange fever overcame
software manufacturers. Figuring (with some reason) that "everyone"
would buy IBM, they decided to play it safe by developing their products
to run on MS/PC-DOS, and a standard was born. The number of MS-
DOS/PC-DOS applications, particularly in business, is growing daily.

In many ways, MS/PC-DOS is like an improved version of CP/M, which
it closely resembles in appearance and commands. It makes use of increased memory and is more powerful and flexible, offering advanced
features such as windows and graphics capabilities not available under
CP/M. Versions above 2.0 contain special provisions for using a hard
disk, and 2.1 provides for multiple file access in networks. MS-DOS is
somewhat easier to use than CP/M, although mastering its more complex
functions is difficult (and unnecessary for most users). Like CP/M, MS-
DOS has spawned a number of "how-to" books and articles on its use.

With the use of add-on programs such as IBM's Top View or Microsoft's
Windows, MS-DOS can even handle multitasking, which should ensure
its competitiveness with Concurrent CP/M and even with UNIX (see
below).

AppleDOS/ProDOS—AppleDOS is a relatively simple and easy to use disk
operating system designed to run on the Apple II family of computers
with one or two floppy disk drives. Its more powerful relative, ProDOS,
was created to cope with the added capabilities of hard disks. As with

most software, the tradeoff for ease of use is limited capabilities, but AppleDOS and ProDOS are sufficient for a wide range of purposes. Except for its Apple III, which has since gone out of production, Apple has also strongly encouraged third-party software development, and the list of applications, particularly in education, is impressive. AppleDOS also boasts an enormous selection of public domain software.

Unfortunately, AppleDOS is not completely upward compatible with ProDOS—that is, many AppleDOS programs will not work under ProDOS, so a user with a large investment in AppleDOS software will have to sacrifice the software library to upgrade, or use both DOS 3.3 and ProDOS on the same machine, which can be confusing. Also, ProDOS will not work with some non-Apple manufactured hard disks.

TRSDOS—a simple, easy-to-use and well-documented disk operating system designed by Tandy Radio Shack for its TRS-80 line of 8-bit home and small business computers. The original TRSDOS was slow and clumsy, but the system was considerably improved upon by a number of third party versions, of which most, though not all, are mutually compatible. In order to keep more memory available, TRSDOS relies on a greater than average amount of input from the operating system disk, which requires keeping the DOS disk in the first disk drive all the time, instead of freeing up the drive for applications programs.

In 1983, Tandy introduced a CP/M-compatible machine, and more recently has entered the MS-DOS-compatible market. A large number of good TRSDOS programs, including many educational programs and CP/M conversions, are currently available, although not as many as for Apple, CP/M, or MS-DOS.

MacIntosh/Lisa Operating System—Considered by many to be the most user-friendly operating system available, the "Mac" relies heavily on icons, windows and the use of a mouse to choose task options and manipulate objects and text on the screen. Developed by Apple for its Motorola 68000 microprocessor-based computers, the operating system and its accompanying software packages represent an estimated 200 programmer years' worth of work (as compared to months for the original CP/M and MS-DOS systems). Apple's original intention to keep the system proprietary and the fact that the system is very hardware specific in order to make full use of the "Mac's" special capabilities severely hampered early software development. By opening up the MacIntosh architecture and releasing technical specifications, Apple has remedied the situation, and an abundance of "Mac" software is now available.

The MacIntosh/Lisa system has both fans and detractors. It's easy and even fun to use, but the price of "friendliness" is reduced power and speed, and some find the mouse more of a nuisance than an advantage. (The newer MacIntosh versions have arrow keys for "mouse-haters.")

Perhaps the major effect of the MacIntosh/Lisa system will be an increased emphasis throughout the industry on the human component of computer systems.

UNIX — a large, complex operating system developed primarily for multi-user, multitask operations by Bell Laboratories. Now being marketed vigorously by AT&T, UNIX is thought by many in the industry to be the system of the future, at least for business applications. Written in a high-level language called C, UNIX is more easily transported to different computers, including mainframes and minicomputers, than any of the above systems, which are written for specific types of hardware systems.

On the minus side, UNIX exists in several incompatible versions. Extremely powerful, with a large collection of utilities, it is not especially easy to use or maintain. Its current usefulness is mainly limited to expensive multi-user systems, and the amount of UNIX-based applications software is relatively limited. UNIX faces its stiffest competition from Microsoft, which has moved down several UNIX-like features to MS-DOS, and released its own UNIX-like operating system called Xenix. Still, AT&T recently announced its intention to go after the educational market, so you may be hearing more about UNIX.

It is quite likely that you will end up using two or more of the above systems, and/or others, perhaps even on the same computer. All of them have advantages and disadvantages, and the success of one or the other seems to have as much or more to do with the foibles of the marketplace as with features and capabilities. In any case, in shopping for applications software, you need to be aware of operating system, as well as hardware, requirements. They will affect not only the efficiency, power, and ease of use of your system, but its possibilities for future expansion. Chapter 7, on implementing your system, explains what you need to know about whatever operating system(s) you acquire in order to use your computer effectively.

THE IMPORTANCE OF DATA FORMAT

"Format" refers to the way a computer stores and arranges information. Physical format refers to the way information is physically arranged on a floppy or hard disk (see chapter 3). Logical format is the way the computer stores information within a file. A file consists of a collection of related information which the computer treats as a single unit. A letter created with a word processing program, student records from a database management program, or monthly budget figures from a spreadsheet — all are contained in files, as are the programs themselves.

Depending on the program you are using, the information you enter will be stored in files either in ASCII (pronounced ass-key) or machine language format. ASCII stands for American Standard Code for Information Interchange, one of the few standards in the microcomputer industry. If a file has been written in machine language, it can only be read and interpreted through the program and by the type of computer that created it. But ASCII files can be read and understood by a variety of computers and programs—and by humans.

The purpose of a computer system is to receive information, process it, and output the results. To do this, it must exchange information among its various components, such as the keyboard, the display screen, and the printer. It must also communicate with various applications software and, of course, with the operator. Computers also frequently need to communicate with other computers.

The only information a computer component can understand is electrical impulses, each of which it interprets as being in one of two states—ON or OFF, YES or NO, ONE or ZERO. Each of these ON or OFF, ONE or ZERO impulses is called a bit. In ASCII, bits are grouped together in units of eight. Each of these units, called a byte, represents one character, such as the upper-case letter A, or the digit 3. By agreeing on the bit arrangement, or code, for each character, microcomputer manufacturers and programmers have made it possible for their machines and software to communicate among themselves and with humans.

There are 256 ASCII codes. The first 128 are agreed-upon standards; for example, everyone uses the same code to represent an uppercase A or to tell a printer to move the paper up one line (see figure 2.1). Files using only the first 128 codes are called "pure ASCII" files. The second 128 codes are used by hardware and software manufacturers for a variety of nonstandardized functions. If a file has been created using only the standard codes, the information in it is transportable to other programs—even a human can read and understand it. If the file contains individualized codes from the second 128, it must be converted to pure ASCII if other programs are to use it. Then, if the second program uses different specialized codes, the data must be reconverted to the new format. Such conversions are accomplished through special utility programs.

These are critical concepts, especially important when you wish to transfer data between programs. For instance, you may want to use information already entered into a circulation program for your new online catalog software. Whether you will be able to do so depends on the types of files both programs create and use, and whether there are conversion programs available if either program creates nonpure ASCII files.

CHOOSING APPLICATIONS SOFTWARE

Applications software is divided into two types: general purpose or "horizontal" packages, for tasks such as word processing, spreadsheets, or database management; and specific or "vertical" packages, aimed at special markets such as medical offices, construction companies, and libraries. Depending on what you want to do, you may end up with one or more general purpose packages, and one or more library-specific packages. Chapter 4 covers specific types of horizontal and vertical software and their possible

Decimal	Hex	CHR	Decimal	Hex	CHR	Decimal	Hex	CHR	Decimal	Hex	CHR
000	00	NUL	032	20	SPACE	064	40	@	096	60	`
001	01	SOH	033	21	!	065	41	A	097	61	a
002	02	STX	034	22	"	066	42	B	098	62	b
003	03	ETX	035	23	#	067	43	C	099	63	c
004	04	EOT	036	24	$	068	44	D	100	64	d
005	05	ENQ	037	25	%	069	45	E	101	65	e
006	06	ACK	038	26	&	070	46	F	102	66	f
007	07	BEL	039	27	'	071	47	G	103	67	g
008	08	BS	040	28	(	072	48	H	104	68	h
009	09	HT	041	29	)	073	49	I	105	69	i
010	0A	LF	042	2A	*	074	4A	J	106	6A	j
011	0B	VT	043	2B	+	075	4B	K	107	6B	k
012	0C	FF	044	2C	,	076	4C	L	108	6C	l
013	0D	CR	045	2D	-	077	4D	M	109	6D	m
014	0E	SO	046	2E	.	078	4E	N	110	6E	n
015	0F	SI	047	2F	/	079	4F	O	111	6F	o
016	10	DLE	048	30	0	080	50	P	112	70	p
017	11	DC1	049	31	1	081	51	Q	113	71	q
018	12	DC2	050	32	2	082	52	R	114	72	r
019	13	DC3	051	33	3	083	53	S	115	73	s
020	14	DC4	052	34	4	084	54	T	116	74	t
021	15	NAK	053	35	5	085	55	U	117	75	u
022	16	SYN	054	36	6	086	56	V	118	76	v
023	17	ETB	055	37	7	087	57	W	119	77	w
024	18	CAN	056	38	8	088	58	X	120	78	x
025	19	EM	057	39	9	089	59	Y	121	79	y
026	1A	SUB	058	3A	:	090	5A	Z	122	7A	z
027	1B	ESCAPE	059	3B	;	091	5B	[	123	7B	{
028	1C	FS	060	3C	<	092	5C	\	124	7C	¦
029	1D	GS	061	3D	=	093	5D	]	125	7D	}
030	1E	RS	062	3E	>	094	5E	^	126	7E	~
031	1F	US	063	3F	?	095	5F	_	127	7F	DEL

Fig. 2.1. ASCII character codes.

applications in small libraries, and chapter 7 explains how to go about determining the requirements for your particular library or media center. For the present we are concerned with general techniques and criteria for finding and evaluating software packages.

In the first edition of *A Micro Handbook,* we listed four ways to obtain software for a specific purpose: in-house development, custom development, purchased services, and purchased software. The first two methods can be prohibitive in cost, not only in money but in time, energy, and staff resources, while the third is impractical for most small libraries. For these reasons, and because of the wide selection of both general purpose and library-specific commercial software, basing a system around one or more "ready-made" programs is the most popular, affordable, and practical method, and the one we shall discuss most in this and the following chapters. (For a detailed breakdown of the advantages and disadvantages of the four methods, see appendix E.)

In choosing software, your primary concern should be the goal you intend to meet by using the program. *If you do not yet have a specific objective in mind, you are not ready to begin shopping for a computer system.* Once you have a purpose for purchasing a system, you can establish criteria for evaluating possible selections. You will also be able to develop some specifications, in order to describe to a vendor what capabilities your system should have. *You must be able to describe your needs in detail.* For example, if you intend to produce computerized bibliographies or implement a computerized "card" catalog, you should be able to estimate the number of records you expect to have, the number of characters (including spaces) in each record, the number of ways you wish to sort or retrieve the information, and so on. A program that works marvelously with 500 records could become hopelessly bogged down if asked to deal with 3,000.

If your computerization list includes bibliographic lists, form letters, inventory records, community files, statistical reports, and patron files, you may be able to find a software company that has packages to handle several or all of these functions. There are several companies that offer a word processing program, a file management program, a spreadsheet program, and a mailing program, all similarly structured. Once you are proficient with one, the subsequent programs are easier to learn. Also, it may be possible to integrate, or combine, the packages for some functions, increasing the usefulness of the individual programs.

One of the best ways to begin researching the types and quality of software is to read reviews. A growing number of publications, both books and periodicals, are partially or wholly devoted to reviewing various hardware and software packages for both general and specific markets, including several geared toward educators and/or librarians. We have included the most helpful of the current publications in appendix B in the back of this book. We strongly recommend reading at least one or two of the periodicals on a regular basis, not only for software reviews but for information on technological hardware and software developments, for helpful advice, and for advertisements, which can serve as a starting point in your software search. (Beware "vaporware" — software which is announced long before it is developed. Protect yourself by using the criteria list at the end of this chapter when buying any software package.)

As it would be impossible for a mere human to keep up with the volume of material covered in periodicals each month, we suggest you examine sample copies and choose several to subscribe to and read regularly. Depending on the size and location of your library, the ages of your patrons, whether or not you are responsible for choosing educational software for classrooms, and so on, different publications will be better suited to your needs. If you are in a school district with a cooperative library system, you might consider having members subscribe to different periodicals, possibly on a yearly rotation basis, or according to special staff interests. Pertinent information or review sources, curriculum developments, and so on could be shared with less time and money expended by everyone.

Don't neglect the wide selection of public domain software, especially for the Apple II family and CP/M and MS-DOS-based computers. Although you may not find what you need for your primary application, this is a great way to add to your software library with very little cash investment. Public domain software is available through local users' groups, through online bulletin board services, through periodicals and books, and through clubs created for the purpose of obtaining and distributing it. Often the cost is no more than that of blank disks and postage or long-distance telephone charges. Some clubs do charge for membership and/or copying.

Public domain software includes a large number of new packages whose creators want to test them out with real users before launching them in the marketplace. Quite a few good programs have gotten their start as "freebies," graduating into the paying market after the bugs have been ironed out, using considerable user feedback. In the further reading list at the end of this chapter, you will find sources of public domain software, including users' organizations, books, and magazine articles. Also, a number of smaller software manufacturers are now offering what they call "freeware." This means that they send you the program on disk, for free, without the manual. If you like what you see, you send them money and they send you the manual. It's a good way to try before you buy.

A Software Checklist

The following criteria apply no matter what you plan to do with your system. Unless the software meets basic requirements, it doesn't matter what the vendor or the brochure says it can do, or that it sounds like the realization of your dreams. Some questions to keep in mind:

Does the program accomplish the objective(s) you have established for it?
To answer this question, you must have a clear concept of what you want to accomplish and be able to translate it into terms of size and speed capabilities, specific functions, and so on. Chapter 4 discusses criteria for choosing specific types of general purpose and library-specific packages. Chapter 5 includes criteria for educational software, and chapter 7 includes methods and criteria for evaluating software in terms of specific needs.

In evaluating systems, and particularly in reading accounts of others' successes and failures, remember that the workability of a system depends upon the basis for judging it. A system designed for the high school level could be disastrous in an elementary school, and vice versa. How relevant to you is another librarian's experience with a particular system?

One question to ask yourself is whether the program does *more* than you need it to, or ever will need it to. Don't buy a powerful, complex, expensive, and hard-to-learn program (usually requiring more expensive hardware) if a simpler one will do. If you will not really be taking advantage of the capabilities of a program, look for one that is closer to your actual needs.

What are the hardware and operating system requirements?
If you already have a computer, will the software run on it? If not, do the hardware requirements fit your criteria, such as price, storage capabilities, support availability, etc.? How much memory does it require? (The availability of cheap memory has caused programmers to be more liberal in using it, so this is an important question.) Are there special requirements, such as a color monitor, an 80-column screen, or a hard disk?

What operating system does the program require? Is it available for more than one operating system? Will it run on different versions of the same operating system? Do you have to know a lot about the operating system to use it?

Has it been used successfully by someone else? For how long?

This is an especially important question for vertical (i.e., library-specific) programs. The longer a system has been up and running, the more time its creators have had to iron out the "bugs," to streamline it and make it do what it is intended to do. To avoid problems, look for software that has been on the market a year or more. Ask the vendor or manufacturer for a list of users and contact several of them. People are usually happy to share their experiences, and may even be able to give you some tips about using the program should you decide to buy it. If possible, try to visit one or two sites so you can actually see the program in use.

If you are adventurous and have the time, energy, and patience, you might save some money by purchasing a program as a test user. Sometimes manufacturers will offer programs at a substantial discount to those willing to put up with frequent updates and a few bugs. Being a test user also gives you an opportunity to have some input into the program itself. Caution—this is not an alternative for the fainthearted.

How user friendly is it?

Are the screen directions clear and easy to understand? Is the response time reasonable, or is it so slow users will become impatient, or so fast they will get flustered? How does it respond to operator mistakes—does a misplaced keystroke spell disaster? Are the error messages easy to understand and respond to? Do color and sound, if used, serve a useful purpose, or are they gratuitous or even annoying?

Beware of programs that are too user friendly. For example, "Help" screens make the program easier for the novice, but they take up memory and/or disk space, and slow a program down. If a program uses "Help" screens, users should be able to turn them off once they are familiar with the program.

How easy is it to learn and use?

It is a truism that the easier a program is to learn and use, the more limited it is. However, in many cases ease of use is a stronger consideration, and many limited programs serve their users well for years. In considering ease of use versus power, the major factors are who will be using the program, and how much? If the answer is staff members, will they have the time necessary to master and use a complex, sophisticated program? If the answer is patrons, how often will they use it, and for what?

There are two main ways in which software is controlled by the user. A menu-driven program displays lists of options or possible tasks on the computer screen. The operator selects an option, either by placing the cursor over it or by typing the number(s) or letter(s) corresponding to his choice, then the computer carries out the selection. Menus are often hierarchical — a narrowing-down process takes the operator through increasingly specific menus until the actual task is selected. Menu-driven programs are especially useful for novices and operators who have no knowledge of (or interest in) programming. If the system is going to be used by patrons, as in an online catalog or information service, a menu-driven program is probably a good choice.

A command-driven program is one in which the computer responds to specific commands, usually consisting of one or two keystrokes. The operator must memorize or have easy access to the list of commands, and the skill to know which ones to use. Command-driven programs are generally more difficult to learn, but once mastered are faster and more convenient than menu-driven programs. Some programs have a built-in flexibility that allows the user to choose whether to use menus, commands, or even a combination, displaying partial or complete menus upon operator request and otherwise responding directly to commands. If you and/or members of your staff are willing to take the time and effort to learn to use it, a command-driven program may prove more efficient for administrative applications.

How good is the documentation?

Documentation, consisting of the users' manuals and written technical specifications, has long been the weakest point of the computer industry. Most manuals were written by programmers, usually as an afterthought, and were uniformly terrible. Recently this has begun to change (a little). Many dealers will let you borrow a manual or at least look through one; some manufacturers will ship a manual for a small amount which is applicable to the purchase price if you buy the program. Features to look for: a detailed index and table of contents, a list of terms and conventions used in the manual and program, a glossary, chapter summaries, explicit step-by-step numbered directions, consistency and simplicity of language, and helpful (not just decorative) graphics.

The documentation for many programs now includes tutorials in either book or disk form. These can be very helpful for self-directed learners, who can then teach others how to use the software. Also useful are quick-reference cards, key templates or key labels showing the program's most commonly used commands. For some of the more popular programs, such as Lotus 1-2-3 or Wordstar, third-party companies offer quick-reference books and/or interchangeable key templates (see appendix B). The templates, which are made of plastic and fit over the keyboard, are especially helpful when you are switching between different programs with different commands. The computer sections of many bookstores also include books intended to help you decipher the screens and manuals of some of the bigger selling programs.

What are the possibilities for expansion and/or data conversion?

A system that fits your needs and budget now may not fit them in the future. What will happen if and when you outgrow the system? What if new budget allotments enable you to expand your circulation system into a full online catalog next year? What if you decide to merge your holdings with a union catalog in your district or state?

Expansion possibilities are especially important when you are computerizing functions involving data entry, such as a circulation or cataloging program. If you change systems in the future, you will want to convert data already entered to the new program format without having to re-enter them. Some software producers provide conversion programs—for example, to convert circulation data from a floppy disk to a hard disk system, or to transfer relevant circulation information into a catalog system. A number of third-party manufacturers also sell conversion utilities. These are special programs which can convert the files produced by a program into standard ASCII or DIF files which may be understood by another program. Ask the dealer about the possibility of later expansion or conversion to a more extensive and/or sophisticated program before you purchase the program and start entering information into it.

Is there support and/or training available?

Nearly all reputable software companies and vendors provide some kind of support, often in the form of an 800 number you can call if you have problems. Since even experienced programmers and operators run into difficulties with new software acquisitions, someone who knows the software and is there to respond to your cry for help is more of a necessity than a luxury. The need for support is a major reason to buy from a local, reliable dealer. Although software purchased locally may initially seem more expensive than, for example, mail order, it's worth the extra cost.

For some of the more sophisticated and expensive vertical systems, the manufacturer and/or the dealer may provide actual hands-on training for one or more staff members. If this is offered, take advantage of it; it can save days or even weeks of frustration. Even if the training is extra, you may wish to invest in it, as it may be cheaper in the long run.

What are the manufacturer's policies on backup?

This is the first, but far from the last time we will talk about the importance of backing up your programs and data. Because of the vulnerability of floppy disks, backup copies are essential, particularly if a program is in daily use. Unfortunately, and not without reason, software manufacturers are very sensitive about unauthorized copying of their products (more on this later). Some companies trust users to honor the copyright laws and to make copies only as a safeguard, and therefore do not copy-protect their software. Other companies, however, go to great lengths to make their programs uncopyable, or almost so. If you purchase copy-protected software, you will have to obtain backup copies. Some companies send backups when they receive your signed registration. Other companies require more money for backups. Nearly all companies require some sort of licensing agreement in which you agree not to copy the software for use on more than one computer without paying an additional licensing fee.

If the program will be used on more than one computer, find out if site licensing is available. With site licensing, you pay the manufacturer a set fee which enables you to make copies of the software and documentation for in-house use. Site licensing agreements vary widely; some include features such as updates and support. Even manufacturers who have not done site licensing before may be receptive to a well-thought-out proposal that is fair to both parties.

What are the manufacturer's policies on updates?

Usually, when you load a commercial program into a computer's memory, the first thing that appears on the screen is the name of the program, followed by a number such as 3.2. This number indicates the version of the program. Software versions are similar to book editions, except that they are issued much more frequently. The first version is numbered 1.0 and is usually distributed only to test users. As the program is improved and debugged, updated versions are issued. Smaller changes are called revisions and are indicated by the number to the right of the decimal point.

Since most working programs are constantly being updated and improved, it is helpful to have the option of updating your copy of a program when a better version comes out. Some manufacturers will replace an old copy with a new version simply for the return of the old disk (this is usually true for test users of new programs); others charge a fee which may range anywhere from a few dollars to the entire price of the program. Sometimes updating an applications program requires updating your version of the operating system as well, since the program may take advantage of features offered by the updated operating system. In almost all cases, you are not eligible to receive updates unless you send a signed license agreement back to the manufacturer when you purchase the software.

Have you tried it?

If at all possible, get a hands-on preview before you buy. Many manufacturers supply dealers or even customers with demos, limited versions of their software that allow you to try different functions and get a general feel for the program. The dealer may let you try the actual program in the store. Some manufacturers offer preview privileges: you try the software for a month, and if you don't like it you get a full refund. Others offer the "freeware" option mentioned above: if you like the program, you pay for it and receive the manual. For some types of software, you may be able to obtain a 30-day review, though this is not common practice (for obvious reasons).

Like dresses or suits, software that looks great "on the rack" can be a big disappointment when you "try it on." This is also an opportunity to find out if the program actually does what it is supposed to do, something you cannot take for granted.

After you answer these general questions, you are ready to look at the more specific criteria determined by the type of package you are looking for (see chapters 4-6). Informed, direct questions such as these will let you hold your own with jargon-spouting vendors, and enable you to choose the best possible software to meet your goals.

FURTHER READINGS

Sources of Free or Inexpensive Software

Berglund, Patricia. "School Library Technology Column." *Wilson Library Bulletin* 59, no. 1 (September 1984): 48-49, 79.
Berglund and Ann Lathrop discuss sources of public domain software and selection aids for commercial software.

Eckhardt, Robert. "Penny-Wise Programs: Public-domain Software for the MacIntosh." *A+ Magazine* 3, no. 7 (July 1985): 101-16.

Fawcette, James E. "Free Software: Is It Any Good?" *Personal Computing* 8, no. 1 (January 1984): 243-47.
"There are some powerful programs that are yours for the asking—if you know who to ask."

"FrEdWRITER (Free Education Writer)." *The Computing Teacher* 13, no. 5 (February 1986): 53-54.
Review of public domain word processor available through SOFTSWAP, San Mateo County Office of Education.

Glossbrenner, Alfred. "Free Software." *Popular Computing* 4, no. 4 (February 1985): 82ff.

McGrath, Lindsay. "Software on a Shoestring." *A+ Magazine* 3, no. 1 (January 1985): 71-78.
Includes list of sources, including two or three public libraries.

Michels, F., N. Harrison, and D. Smith. "User-Supported Software for the IBM PC." *Library HiTech* 3, no. 2 (February 1985): 97-106.
User-supported software is also called "freeware"; users are asked to contribute to the author if satisfied. Four programs are evaluated: PC-File, PC-CALC, PC-File III, and PC-Talk III.

Milone, Michael N., Jr. "Public Domain Software: The Ultimate Bargain?" *Classroom Computer Learning* 6, no. 3 (November/December 1985): 20.

"Public Domain Software Listings." *The Computing Teacher* 11, no. 7 (March 1984): 46-59.
Softswap update and information about offerings of other software exchange organizations.

Reck, Lawrence R. "Why Pay More? A Guide to Free—Or Almost Free—
    Educational Materials." *Tech Trends* 30, no. 7 (October 1985): 31-35, 39.
    Catalog listings for public-domain software.

Starshine, Dorothy. "Free or Inexpensive Software for Teaching the Language
    Arts." *The Computing Teacher* 13, no. 3 (November 1985): 19-21.
    Discusses public domain software, shareware, libraries, user groups,
books and magazines with software listings, and educational resources. Included is information about Freewriter, a public domain word processing program written by Paul Lutus, the author of Apple Writer.

Operating Systems

Cook, Rick. "Whenever You Use a Computer, You Are Using a Thing Called
    an Operating System." *Popular Computing* 3, no. 10 (August 1984):
    111-14, 135-38, 140, 142-43, 146-48.

Deacon, Jim. "CPU and DOS." *CMC News* 4, no. 2 (Winter 1984): 3-4.

Foster, Edward. "Microsoft, IBM Sign Pact for Operating System Systems."
    InfoWorld 7, no. 36 (2 September 1985). No pages available.
    IBM representative Buddy Price states, "We are committed to an open ar-
chitecture concept with DOS and plan to continue using it on IBM's family of
personal computers."

Freedman, Mary, and Larry Carlin. "Warm Boot Cannot Be Ordered from
    L. L. Bean." *Library Journal* 110, no. 16 (1 October 1985): 76-77.
    Includes good descriptions of the most common microcomputer
operating systems.

"How to Choose an Operating System." *Popular Computing* 3, no. 3
    (January 1984): 148-50.

O'Malley, Christopher. "What You Need to Know about UNIX." *Personal
    Computing* 9, no. 7 (July 1985): 120-25.

_____. "What You Should Know about MS-DOS." *Personal Computing* 9,
    no. 8 (August 1985): 43-51.

Pournelle, Jerry. "Micro Revolution" (columns). *Popular Computing* 3, nos.
    8, 9 (June and July 1984). No pages available.
    June: "The Operating System Jungle—Finding a Common Path Keeps
Getting More Difficult." July: "Clearing a Path—The 16-bit Operating System
Jungle Offers Confusion, Not Standardization."

Rosenthal, Steve, and Ken Kashmarek. "Understanding ProDOS." *A +
Magazine* 13, no. 5 (May 1985). No pages available.
The first of several articles.

Tucker, D. M. "Understanding Operating Systems." *PC World* 2, no. 5 (May
1984): 192-99.

Selecting Software

Deacon, Jim. "Reviews Are No Substitute for Personal Evaluation." *CMC
NEWS* 5, no. 2 (Winter 1985): 5.

Jacobson, Bill. "Choosing and Using a Data Base Management Program."
Creative Computing 10, no. 9 (September 1984): S2-S16.

Rappaport, Susan. "Software Collecting: Method for Madness (Computers
for the Public)." *Library Journal* 110, no. 6 (1 April 1985): 56-57.
Compares and contrasts selection criteria and methodology of public
libraries with those of schools.

Summers, Tan S. "Taking Software for a Spin." *Popular Computing* 4, no. 10
(August 1985): 67-70.
"The only way is to test-drive it yourself." Summers includes specific
selection criteria for four basic types of programs: word-processing, spreadsheet, file-management, and graphics.

Tenopir, Carol. "Identification and Evaluation of Software." *Information
Technology & Libraries* 3, no. 1 (March 1984): 21-33.

3 An Introduction to Computer Hardware

Although Charles Babbage had the right idea when he began work on his "Difference Engine" over 150 years ago, the limited technology of his time doomed his efforts to failure. Computerization would still be mere theory without the machinery that has been developed in the past few decades. This machinery performs functions that are too voluminous, repetitive, or complex for people to do efficiently. In this chapter we will introduce the workers of the computer system, the infinitely patient, infinitely stupid drudges that actually carry out the tasks specified by the programs and the operator—the hardware.

Computers are generally referred to as mainframes, minicomputers (minis), or microcomputers (micros), based on size, capabilities, and cost. The categories, however, are difficult to define. Today's microcomputers outperform the mainframes of ten or even five years ago, and will be outpaced by the micros of next year (or even next month). The line between minis and micros is particularly hazy, and becoming more so all the time. Basically, a mainframe can handle more information more rapidly than a mini, which can handle more information more rapidly than a micro. Mainframes are large, filling one or more rooms, while a mini may fill a wall, or only a desk. A micro fits on a desktop or even, in some cases, a lap. Mainframes and minis often serve as host computers to systems that include several smaller computers and/or dumb terminals. But it is now possible to have a "supermicro" as the central player in a network made up of other micros and/or dumb terminals.

Another distinguishing factor between these types of computers used to be the number of tasks and users they could handle at one time. Mainframes and minis support multiple tasks and several users simultaneously, while micros used to be limited to performing one task at a time for a single user. Changes in hardware and software, however, have resulted in micros with multitasking, multi-user capabilities, though they are less extensive than those of the bigger machines.

Perhaps the easiest way to distinguish among the types is in terms of cost. Mainframe and minicomputer systems are still outside the reach of individuals and most small businesses and libraries. Most minis, and some mainframes, are sold as part of vertical packages including software, hardware, and maintenance. Mini-systems range between $20,000 and $100,000, and mainframes start around $100,000 and go as high as many millions of dollars. Supermicros are only slightly less expensive than minis. Mainframes require full-time, specialized staff and controlled environments, while minis and supermicros require considerable technical support.

Microcomputers, also popularly called personal computers, may be had for less than $2,000, with vertical systems, *including* software and peripherals such as printers and modems, ranging from just under $10,000 to around $20,000. They may be operated by noncomputer professionals and can function in nearly any physical environment that is comfortable for people.

The ability of computers to communicate with one another, even over great distances, opens up possibilities for users of all types of systems. Access to a microcomputer equipped with a modem may also mean access to the resources and power of a huge mainframe computer system, as well as to other small computers in remote locations. The process of intercomputer communications is called networking, and is the subject of chapter 6.

All computers, from the least sophisticated micro to the most powerful mainframe, have five basic functions:

- Input of information

- Storage of information

- Processing of information

- Output of information

- Control of information.

The first four functions are handled, respectively, by input devices such as a keyboard or bar code reader, storage components such as internal memory and floppy or hard disk drives, the central processing unit (CPU), and output devices such as monitors and printers. All of these are coordinated and controlled by an operating system. The computer proper consists of a central processing unit and its associated read only and random access memory (sometimes called primary memory). The other devices mentioned are known as peripherals.

CENTRAL PROCESSING UNIT

The heart of any computer, from a mainframe to a micro, is the CPU, or central processing unit. In a microcomputer the CPU consists of one or more microprocessors, tiny silicon chips etched with sophisticated electronic circuitry. The terms microcomputer and microprocessor are sometimes (incorrectly) used interchangeably. A microprocessor by itself is not a computer. Preprogrammed, unalterable microprocessors and memory chips are found in all kinds of devices, from digital gas pumps and automatic cash registers to traffic lights, sewing machines, and electronic typewriters. In fact, many computer peripherals, including printers, monitors, bar code readers, and modems, may contain their own microprocessors. None of these devices are in themselves computers, since they function only within a specific, limited set of instructions.

A computer's CPU has two main parts, the control unit and the arithmetic logic unit. The control unit interprets program commands stored in the primary memory and coordinates their execution. It keeps track of the locations and identification of operations and data, moving data to and from the arithmetic logic unit, which performs the actual computer operations — addition, subtraction, multiplication, division, numerical comparisons, and logical functions. Such a sequence of relatively simple operations used to solve a complex problem is known as an algorithm. Microprocessors perform such sequences extremely rapidly, running through several million program cycles (getting an instruction, executing it, incrementing the program counter, getting the next instruction, etc.) per second.

In addition to the control and arithmetic logic units, the CPU contains several kinds of registers, which are used as temporary holding areas for information currently being used by the processor. Accumulator registers, for example, store the results of arithmetic calculations, while address registers hold the memory location of various data items being used in the current program.

The first microcomputers processed one byte (8 bits) at a time — thus the term "8-bit." Newer machines process 16 or even 32 bits at one time. The primary difference between 8-bit, 16-bit, and 32-bit computers does not have so much to do with processing speed (in fact the higher bit machines may actually be slower) as with the amount of memory the CPU is able to "address," or directly access. Without getting overly technical, an 8-bit machine uses a 16-bit address path and can directly address a maximum of 64 kilobytes (1024 bytes, abbreviated "K") of memory. A 16-bit micro uses 20- or 24-bit address paths and can address up to 8 megabytes, or over 8 million bytes, of memory. The additional memory, not the processing speed, is what gives 16- and 32-bit micros their extra capabilities and power.

Because of the "bigger is better" mentality of most of our society, there is a tendency to assume that the more powerful machines are the only way to go. However, an 8-bit machine may be perfectly capable of doing what you need it to do, and for less money. This brings us to a fundamental point — *a computer system is not obsolete as long as it meets your needs.* Developments in computer technology occur so quickly that virtually every computer on the market is technically obsolete as soon as it hits the shelves. Functional obsolescence, in most cases, takes much longer. This is why we advise you to determine what your needs actually are before you start to shop, and to choose your software first, then find the equipment to run it.

Another reason for choosing software first is that even within the categories of 8-bit, 16-bit, etc., all CPUs are not the same. There are several different "families" within each category. Two of the more popular 8-bit families are the Z80 and the 65xx. The former includes 8080/8085 and Z80 processors, and is the family for which CP/M was written. The 65xx series, including the 6502 and 6509, is used in popular home computers such as the Apple II series. MS-DOS and PC-DOS run on the 8088/8086 family of 16-bit processors, while MacIntosh and Lisa are based on the Motorola 68000. As a rule, programs written for one operating system and one processor family will not run on a processor from a different family. In fact, software is not necessarily interchangeable within a family, because of the tendency of many applications programs to "go around" the operating system and work directly with the processor in the interests of speed, efficiency, or proprietary ownership.

THE PROBLEM OF COMPATIBILITY

As of this writing, the term "IBM-compatible" is featured in a large number of computer advertisements and articles. The Franklin is an example of an "Apple-compatible" computer, and at least one system, the Commodore Amiga, claims to be "Mac-compatible." The term "compatible" refers to the ability of one machine to run software and use peripherals or interfaces designed for another. The compatibility issue is one more result of the overall lack of standardization within the industry, and of the natural tendency of software developers to design their products for the largest perceived market. This problem makes obvious the necessity for an open architecture policy on the part of hardware and operating system manufacturers. As we explained in the previous chapter, open architecture means that the technical specifications for the hardware or software are made available. Open architecture is a necessary prerequisite for third-party software development, which can increase computer sales. It also makes it possible for the competition to mimic your product in hopes of getting in on the success.

There are basically three levels of compatibility: operational, data, and operating system. Operational compatibility is the highest level. If two computers are operationally compatible, they can run virtually all the same software, accept plug-in expansion boards designed for one another, and read disks written by each other. Operational compatibility requires that the machines use the same microprocessor, operating system, and disk format. Data-compatible machines can read data on disks written by each other, so that you can transfer data between them easily. Data-compatible computers use similar (but not identical) microprocessors and the same operating system, and can read, though not necessarily write, each other's disk format. (Sometimes this only goes one way, i.e., the "copycat" computer can read the model's disks, but not vice versa.) They cannot accept each other's plug-in cards, and they may use different interfaces, or ways of connecting to and communicating with peripherals such as the keyboard and monitor. Operating-system-compatible computers use similar microprocessors and the same operating system, but different interfaces and disk formats. Each can run programs written for the same operating system, but only if the program has been translated to its own disk format.

How important is compatibility? Again, it depends primarily on your software needs. If you absolutely must be able to run all the software written for the IBM PC or the MacIntosh, for example, you need a computer that is operationally compatible with the original IBM PC or MacIntosh, especially since many software manufacturers are deciding that converting their programs to run on other machines is not worth the expense. If the software you need is available only for a particular machine, however, compatibility may not be as important to you as other factors. A number of less well known manufacturers offer other features in place of compatibility, such as faster processing speed, better graphics, or increased storage. There may be definite advantages to buying a little-known, compatible computer as opposed to a well-known brand, including price, expansion capabilities, screen display, keyboard, bundled (included) software, and other extras. It all depends on what your needs are. A lesser-known company may offer excellent quality, and their "we try harder" attitude often means better support as well. If you do decide to buy a compatible, spend some time researching it. Check periodical reviews, ask around, try to talk to other users. Also, make sure that it contains "off-the-shelf" standard parts, those you can buy at any reputable electronics store rather than only from the original manufacturer. This will ensure your ability to get service and replacement parts even if the company goes out of business.

COMPUTER MEMORY

With the CPU inside the computer are two types of semiconductor memory which the CPU may directly address: ROM (read only memory) and RAM (random access memory). The ROM is permanently imprinted on a chip; it can be read by the computer but not altered. This type of memory is called nonvolatile because it is not erased when the power is turned off. The ROM usually contains the program whose main job is to boot the operating system. When the computer is first turned on, or when the operator presses a reset button or special key combination, the ROM program activates the disk drive and reads the first sector of the disk that it finds there. If the disk contains the disk operating system, the first sector instructs the system to load, or read, the rest of the operating system into RAM. If the disk does not contain the operating system, or if the drive door is not shut, another ROM program displays a message such as "boot error" on the screen.

In some inexpensive computers, the ROM also contains a low-level BASIC interpreter, so that the computer can respond directly to commands typed in the BASIC programming language. Since storage space within the computer itself is limited, however, general applications microcomputers have smaller ROMs and rely on disk operating systems (DOS) for most operating and other systems functions. (One exception is the Apple MacIntosh, which contains a large set of ROM routines.)

Another type of nonvolatile memory is EPROM (or EEPROM) — erasable programmable read only memory. EPROMs are erasable and programmable only by the manufacturer, not by the user. The capacity of EPROMs has increased dramatically, to 256K or more. This has led to some speculation that software producers, especially operating system manufacturers, may begin to offer software on plug-in "memory cartridges," freeing up the RAM for other purposes.

Random access memory may be changed as well as read (in fact, some people refer to it as read alterable memory). The RAM serves as a temporary holding area for programs that are being executed, including operating and other systems software and applications programs. It also holds data files being worked on, such as a letter being edited with word processing software. Most RAM is volatile, meaning its contents are destroyed when the power is turned off or lost, or when the system is rebooted. This is why it is important to save your work—i.e., have the program store the file on the floppy or hard disk—often whenever you are entering or editing information. If something happens to your power, the disk holds everything up until the last "save"; otherwise you risk losing a whole session's work.

Computer memory size is usually measured in kilobytes (K). In practical terms, a single character of information, whether it is a letter, number, space, or a "control character," uses one byte of memory. Two kilobytes hold the approximate equivalent of one double-spaced, typewritten page of information. Memory is one of the areas that has seen the most dramatic increases in capability, accompanied by drastic price decreases. Since memory is cheap, the newer programs use a lot of it. Some vertical programs may require a megabyte or more of RAM. In shopping for a system, be sure you know the memory requirements of your chosen software.

Expandability—the ability to add more memory—is important. To expand memory in 16-bit and higher machines, you add chips—but the computer must have a place for them to go. As a rule, 8-bit computers are limited to 64K of primary memory, although a technique called bank switching can be used to "trick" the microprocessor into addressing 128K or more. This requires additional hardware and software, but is cheaper than getting a new system. Be sure to ask the dealer how much memory is possible for your machine, and how much it costs to acquire it. Some programs limit their capacity to information that can be held in memory; others keep supplementary program files on disk and access them only as needed. You may be able to increase the capacity of the first type by adding more memory. *Find out before you buy.*

AUXILIARY STORAGE DEVICES

Auxiliary devices store data and programs not in current use by RAM. The first microcomputers used cassette tapes and tape recorders for auxiliary storage, but tape proved extremely limited in its usefulness. The advent of floppy disks and disk drives has made cassette tapes virtually obsolete except for some games and limited educational applications. For all practical purposes, and especially for library applications, a microcomputer system is incomplete without at least one floppy disk drive. For any applications involving a database of any size, such as an online catalog, a hard disk will be necessary as well. In the near future, CD-ROM drives will probably also become important components of many library microcomputer systems.

If you already have a microcomputer that uses cassette tapes, you should consider purchasing one or more disk drives for it. Such an investment (probably only a few hundred dollars) could vastly increase the usefulness of your current system. Or you could purchase a different system altogether for administrative applications and use the existing system with the cassette recorder for computer literacy and other types of instruction.

Floppy Disks

A floppy disk, also called a diskette, is a technologically advanced version of the once-familiar Hollerith punched card. Instead of holes, the bits of information consist of magnetized spots on the disk surface. The disk drive read/write assembly, which looks somewhat like the arm of a record player and operates like the head of a tape recorder, can rapidly access stored information from anywhere on the disk. A double-sided disk drive has two read/write assemblies, one for each side of the disk. On a single-sided drive, a felt pad on the opposite side of the disk holds the read/write head against the disk surface (see figure 3.1).

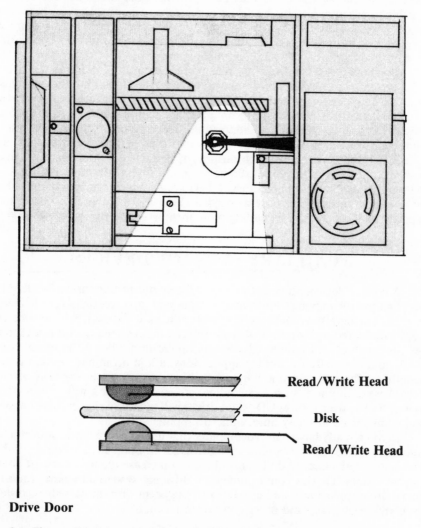

Read/Write Head

Disk

Read/Write Head

Drive Door

Fig. 3.1. Floppy disk drive and closeup of read/write assembly and a disk.

The disk itself is a thin, flexible sheet of mylar material coated with a magnetic oxide. (Some high density disks use slightly different types of magnetic media.) It is encased inside a protective square jacket with an access slot for the read/write assembly, a center hole or disk hub, and an index hole (see figure 3.2). The index hole is used, like a timing light for a car engine, to determine which sector on the disk is being written to or read. Depending on whether it is hard-sectored or soft-sectored, the disk itself has one or more holes. As the read/write assembly moves back and forth across the surface of the rapidly spinning disk, the disk holes pass beneath the jacket hole, and the computer can determine where it is on the disk.

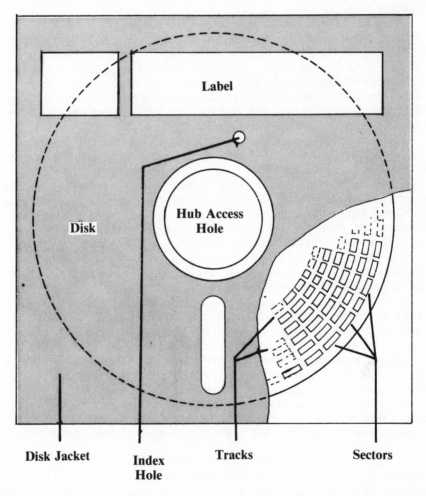

Fig. 3.2. A floppy disk. Data are written onto circular tracks which are divided into sectors.

Whether a disk is hard or soft sectored is one of its four main distinguishing characteristics, the others being size, density, and number of usable sides. A fifth distinguishing characteristic is added when the disk is initialized, or formatted, for a given disk operating system and computer. Like software, disks, once formatted, are not interchangeable between computers, unless the computers are data or operationally compatible. It is now possible, using specialized software (and sometimes hardware) to convert data (though not programs) from one disk format to another. It is probably not practical to do disk format conversions yourself, especially as a number of dealers and/or independent computer consultants offer this service for a reasonable fee. Caution: transferring data to a different disk format only makes sense if you are going to use a version of the same program that was used to create the files in the first place, unless the files are either pure ASCII to begin with or go through a conversion process.

Floppy disks presently come in three sizes: 8-inch, 5¼-inch, or 3½-inch diameter. These used to be categorized as standard, mini, and micro floppies, respectively, but the 8-inch size is now relatively uncommon. 5¼-inch is currently the most popular, but 3½-inch disks may eventually become standard. The amount of information a disk will hold is related to its size, number of usable sides, and density. The latter is determined by the disk drive capacity, the process used to make the disk, and the logical disk format imposed by the individual computer and operating system.

The range of disk capacities is tremendous, from about 90 kilobytes on single-sided, single-density, 5¼-inch disks formatted for the no-longer-manufactured (but still popular) Osborne, to an anticipated 1.6 to 2.0 or higher megabytes on new 3½-inch disks formatted for computers like the IBM AT or the MacIntosh. As of this writing, drive technology is lagging somewhat behind disk technology, but availability of such drives is only a matter of time. Of course, the newer the technology the less reliable the product, so a drive that has been around long enough to prove itself, even at a lower capacity, is a better buy than the latest state-of-the-art equipment. If you do get a system with high-density drives, it will require special disks; to be safe, obtain a list of suitable brands from the computer manufacturer.

The other physical disk characteristic does not concern storage capacity, but determines the method used to locate information on the disk. Data are stored on a floppy in binary format (ON or OFF, ONE or ZERO) by means of magnetic patterns arranged along concentric circles or tracks. Each track is divided into segments called sectors. The tracks and sectors have identifying numbers used to locate data on the disk. A hard-sector disk has a ring of holes punched around its center to mark the sectors, with an index hole to indicate the beginning of the first sector. A soft-sector disk uses only one index hole. For practical purposes, you don't really need to be concerned with the whys and wherefores of sectoring. Just make sure to purchase the type of disk required by your system.

You should *write protect* all valuable program and data disks as soon as you make them, to prevent accidents. Different types of disks use different write-protect methods. For example, on 5¼-inch disks, the disk jacket has a write-protect notch on one edge. When this notch is covered (with stick-on covers provided in the disk box), the computer cannot write to or erase the disk.

The size, type, and number of disk drives a computer uses depends on the disk controller, which may be either a circuit board plugged into the computer motherboard or a box connected to it with a cable. Controllers are designed for single, double, or high density disks; a dual disk controller can handle both single and double density. Drives are equipped to handle either single-sided or double-sided disks.

Most micro disk controllers are equipped for up to four disk drive units. It is possible to get by with a single drive, but for most serious applications at least two, one of which may be a hard disk drive, are necessary. Two disk drives make backing up fast and easy (and more likely to become a habit), and also provide increased data capacity for such purposes as word processing, where the primary drive contains the disk with the software and the second is free for data files.

For tips on care and handling of floppy disks, see appendix C.

Hard Disks

Although they are a considerable improvement over cassette tape, floppies do not have the capacity to handle large databases (such as those called for in many library applications). They are also quite susceptible to damage (and lost data) from dust, fingerprints, improper handling, etc. The entry of the hard disk into the micro market opened a whole realm of new possibilities for microcomputer applications. Hard disks offer many times the storage space of floppies, operate at a higher speed, are less fragile, and spare users the headaches of constant disk switching and file hunting. They are also considerably cheaper now than they were just two or three years ago.

The type of hard disk used with most microcomputer systems is the Winchester drive. Winchester is a generic name, supposedly derived from the sealed cartridge Winchester rifle. Going back to the record player analogy, a Winchester drive is rather like taking the turntable and stylus of the record player, complete with a permanent "record" or disk, and enclosing it in an airtight, hermetically sealed protective chamber. Some hard disks contain several platters, each with its own set of read/write assemblies. Each disk is made of a hard but light material, such as aluminum, coated on both sides with magnetic oxide. It rotates at a very high rate of speed (average: 3000 to 3600 revolutions per minute). The read/write stylus "flies" on a very thin cushion of air above the surface of the rapidly spinning disk. The distance between the recording head and the disk surface, though less than the width of a molecule of cigarette smoke, prevents wear and tear on both the disk and the head, except in the event of a crash (see below).

Hard disk storage space ranges from about 5 megabytes to over 200 megabytes at last count, and data access speed averages ten times faster than with floppies. Hard disk sizes range from 3½ inches to 14 inches; many of them fit into the same space required for a floppy drive. Many computer systems are now available with built-in hard disks ranging from 5 to 20 megabytes, combined with a floppy drive. An entire computer system of this type costs less than a 5-megabyte hard drive cost when we first wrote *Micro Handbook*.

It is also becoming increasingly easy and inexpensive to add a hard disk to an existing system. Add-on hard disks may be either internal, i.e., installed in the chassis of the computer itself, perhaps replacing a floppy drive, or external, connected to the computer by means of a controller card and a cable. External hard drives are also called "standalone," and may serve as central storage for two or more microcomputers connected to a network (see chapter 6). Internal drives offer space and power savings, but require caution—you must be sure that the drive does not generate more heat or require more power than your computer can handle. Also, internal drives are currently limited to about 20 megabytes. You can add additional hard drives, but "chaining" more than two can lead to the same sort of disk switching problems presented by floppies. Therefore, a general rule in hard disk buying is to start with at least twice as much storage as you'll need.

In addition to fixed hard disks, a number of manufacturers now offer removable hard disks. These are five- or ten-megabyte cartridges which are slipped in and out of the drive, much like floppies. They offer the advantage of portability and security (you can take them out and lock them in a drawer). You can store any amount of data, but only in five- or ten-megabyte chunks, making removable disks inappropriate for large-scale databases such as catalogs or circulation systems. Some people use removable cartridges for backup.

Calculating the amount of storage needed can be tricky. Once again, you need to know what software you'll be using. For instance, if you plan to have an online catalog, you must know how your software stores records, and the maximum number of bytes each record will use. Multiply that by the number of records you expect to have eventually. Add the amount of space needed for the program files themselves. If you plan to be using other types of applications programs, such as word processing, add the amount of space needed for the programs, along with room for active data files such as letters and bibliographies. Throw in another 25 percent for formatting, indexing, temporary work files, etc. Double the total, and get the closest size above that.

Software is an important consideration in using hard disks. Although most of the newer programs run with hard disks (and some require one), older software, especially that written for Apple IIs, may not. Hard disk operating system requirements are also greater. The more recent versions of operating systems, such as ProDOS and MS-DOS 2.2 and above, contain special provisions for hard disks, including file structures that allow you to create multiple directories (or "volumes") and subdirectories. This has the effect of dividing the disk into manageable chunks, so that you don't have to search through several hundred files looking for the one you need. Most hard disks may even be partitioned so that you can run two or more operating systems on the same computer. Copy-protected software may also present special problems with a hard disk. Some companies provide special hard disk versions, or utilities for upgrading floppy software to run on a hard disk. Even so, the transition may mean giving up some programs.

With hard disks, backup becomes a crucial consideration. The data on your hard disk are more precious than the disk itself. Including the price of a backup system in the cost of the disk itself, and purchasing both at the same time, will save you endless grief. Hard disk backup systems are getting a lot of attention in the industry right now. Although you can back up a hard disk on floppies, the process is slow and clumsy, leading to neglect, which can be disastrous. (If you are running MS-DOS, there are several software packages available for high-speed hard-disk-to-floppy backups). Tape cartridge backup systems currently offer the greatest capacity at the best price, and are mechanically reliable and much faster and easier than floppy backups. A good tape system should allow you to do either selective file by file backup or to back up the entire disk contents. Also, due to the nature of hard disks, it is wise to ask whether the tape system backs up in such a way that you can restore its contents to a different hard disk if necessary. Some tapes make "image backups." If for any reason you change disks, restoring an image backup to the new disk will almost certainly result in lost data.

One alternative to a hard disk drive is the Bernoulli box, a flexible disk in a sealed removable cartridge. Each cartridge holds 10 to 20 megabytes. Bernoulli box systems offer more flexibility than a hard disk, but are, at this writing, quite expensive. Other possible future alternatives include stretched surface recording (SSR), which may allow as many as 100 megabytes to squeeze onto a 5¼-inch flexible disk, and perpendicular magnetic recording (PMR) which allows up to five or six times as many bits per inch as current recording methods.

A major advantage of a flexible disk system is the protection against head crashes, the major enemy of hard disks. If a hard disk is bumped, or if the power fails, or if a piece of dust or even cigarette smoke gets in the way when the head is in motion, the head can fall, or crash, onto the disk. At the least, this can destroy the data on the disk. At worst, it can actually gouge the disk and damage the head. If only data are lost, you can recover by reformatting the disk and restoring the data from your backups. If the disk drive is damaged, it will have to go in for repair or replacement.

In purchasing a hard disk, there are several things to watch for. First and most critical, it must be compatible with your system. It should have firmware capable of detecting and fixing errors in data transmission and storage. Find out how fast it can locate data on the disk (data access) and transfer them to your computer. Data access averages 30 to 100 thousandths of a second. Data transfer ranges from 400 to 1250 K per second, but can be increased by means of direct memory access, where the drive is "hard-wired" to the computer's central memory. Other important factors, especially for internal drives, are how effectively the disk dissipates heat and how much power it uses. Another consideration is whether the drive meets FCC standards for radio frequency emissions (many don't). For all these reasons, we suggest you choose your dealer carefully, and ask for guarantees that the drive meets the necessary criteria. The dealer should also install and check the drive to make sure it is compatible with your hardware and software. The dealer may also show you how to format the drive, following the procedure in the manual. It is important that you be able to format the drive yourself. In the event of a crash or other problem, you need to be able to bring the disk back up without having to resort to outside help.

If you are reasonably brave, you may even decide to install the drive yourself. It is now possible to buy a "disk on a card" that you simply plug into the motherboard of the computer. Although relatively new, these drives are proving to be quite reliable. Just be sure to do your homework regarding quality, reliability, and the all-important compatibility with your system. (See "A Hardware Checklist" at the end of this chapter for buying tips.)

Optical Disk Technology

Some of the most exciting recent mass storage developments have been in the area of optical disk technology, used to produce compact disk read only memory (CD ROM) and videodiscs. On an optical disk, the ONs and OFFs of binary data are created by burning tiny pits, or blisters, into the surface with a laser. Currently there is no way to erase the blisters, so these disks are read only once produced. Optical disks can store vast amounts of data — as many as 600 megabytes on one side of a 4¾-inch disk 1/16 of an inch thick. Since the laser reading device in a CD ROM drive does not touch the disk, scratches, dirt, and other surface imperfections have no effect on data quality. Compact disks take up very little room, are nearly indestructible, and are relatively easy to reproduce once encoded. All of this makes them a wonderful medium for storing all kinds of information, including moving pictures and sound.

CD ROMs have important implications for libraries, which, along with the medical and legal professions, represent the largest potential market for optical disks. The entire Library of Congress MARC database fits on a single disk, as does the Grolier American Academic Encyclopedia, now available on disk for under $200. Several services offer databases on compact disk, with subscriptions that include periodic updates. Such databases can serve as a supplement to online services, thus decreasing connection time and cost.

In addition to a special drive, CD ROMs require special search software. The cost of drives, software, and disks, while not unreasonable now, should drop rapidly as technology develops. Some libraries may want to consider a write once read mostly (WORM) CD drive, which can encode but not change data on optical disks. WORM drives can prove useful for archiving valuable but rarely updated information, such as a base catalog or internal records.

Wide consumer acceptance of audio compact disks and players, which use the laser process and digitally recorded music to produce marvelous clear sound, has had a positive impact on both the technology and costs of computer compact disks. As with the rest of the industry, the greatest obstacle to rapid optical disk technology developments is a lack of standardization, which has caused many manufacturers to adopt a wait-and-see attitude. Some serious efforts are under way to establish standards as soon as possible, however, and we should see great strides in this field within the next few years.

INPUT DEVICES

Before a computer can do anything, it must have a way of receiving information and commands. When the operator types a command on a keyboard, passes a bar code reader over a label, or moves a joystick, the operating system, acting as "traffic cop," directs the information to the various other components. For example, an input command may be simultaneously displayed on the screen and relayed to the CPU and other relevant peripherals such as the modem or printer. The two most important input devices for libraries are keyboards and bar code scanners.

Keyboards

The most common means of input for microcomputers in business and personal applications (other than games) is through a keyboard. A computer keyboard resembles a typewriter keyboard, with the addition of special control and function keys which serve a variety of purposes, depending on the software in use.

Keyboards vary surprisingly, and it pays to check out this part of your system before you buy to make sure it meets some minimum standards.

- It should contain cursor movement keys, including arrow keys, a < HOME > and < END > key, and page up and page down keys. These are used to move the cursor, or marker, around the screen. The cursor keys may be combined with a numeric keypad used for calculator functions.

- Other special keys, such as < CTRL > ("Control"), < ALT > , < ESC > ("Escape"), and especially the < ENTER > or < RETURN > key, should be plainly marked and easy to locate.

- It should include < INSERT > and < DELETE > keys.

- If you will be running MS-DOS or UNIX, the keyboard should contain at least ten easily located function keys. These programmable keys are used by applications programs to activate program commands and otherwise make life easier for microcomputer operators.

- Keys should actually move, with audible feedback that indicates a stroke is complete, but that is not so loud as to be annoying or distracting.

- Keys should auto-repeat when held down for more than a second.

- Key rows should be staggered slightly.

- Keys should be clearly labeled and a neutral color.

Nice extras include adjustable height and slant, lights to indicate when the <CAPS> lock or <NUMBER> lock keys are on, and separate arithmetic function signs such as + and −.

Some keyboards are detachable, connecting to the computer via a plug-in cord; others are built into the monitor or computer chassis. Detachable keyboards are more flexible and allow individual users more control. Unless security is a problem they are probably preferable.

Some people in the industry have advocated the use of the Dvorak keyboard over the standard QWERTY arrangement. Although it may be more efficient for nontypists, the Dvorak keyboard has not exactly caught on in a big way. Still, if nontyping patrons will be using the system, you may want to consider one.

Beyond the basics listed above, differences in keyboards are largely subjective and have mainly to do with "feel." The best way to decide whether you like a keyboard is to try it out in the store.

Bar Code Readers

Bar code readers are especially applicable to library functions such as circulation and inventory. Like so many other computer devices, bar code scanners and their accompanying software are continuing to get cheaper, more reliable, and easier to use.

Bar code readers work by focusing visible red or infrared light from a light-emitting diode (LED) on the stripes of a bar code. The dark stripes absorb the light, while the white spaces reflect it back, generating a sequence of high and low voltage signals which the computer interprets as—you guessed it—ONES and ZEROS. Translated into ASCII code, the signals represent numbers, letters, or special characters. Bar code readers vary in size and type, ranging from portable, handheld systems to large stationary scanners such as those used in many supermarkets, which use lasers rather than LEDs to detect the bar code.

Visible light bar code wands can scan both carbon- and alcohol-based inks, while infrared wands read only the carbon-based inks. For this reason, if you use a program which requires you to print your own labels, make sure that the ink is the proper type for your wand. You must also have a printer that is capable of printing good quality labels.

The Book Industry Study Group recently endorsed the use by publishers of an internationally standardized code that incorporates the ISBN number. If implemented, it will make librarians' and booksellers' lives simpler. Nevertheless, implementing a bar code system requires a major time investment for coding and labeling book jackets, card pockets, and patron cards. Therefore, if you choose to use bar codes, you should plan on a commitment of at least five years to the same system. It may be possible, down the road, to convert your labels to a different code using special conversion software, but even that would require relabeling everything.

A good source of current information on bar code hardware and software is *Bar Code News.* For more information, see the resources section, appendix B, under "Periodicals."

Other Input Devices

There are a number of other input devices available as substitutes or supplements for the standard keyboard. Optical character recognition (OCR) devices "read" printed or typed information by converting reflected light patterns into binary data. Although they are still quite expensive and limited in what they can read, OCRs may someday play a useful role in many libraries. Voice recognition devices are another area of intense research, along with speech synthesizers for output. These devices, while still imperfect and quite expensive, hold wonderful promise, especially for disabled users.

Still other input devices include joysticks and paddles, which are used primarily for games. Light pens, which are used to "draw" directly on the screen, and graphics pads, where the user draws with a finger on a touch-sensitized surface, are valued by artists, engineers, designers, draftspeople, and young children. Touch-sensitive screens allow users to select menu choices and move text and pictures around on the screen without using a keyboard. A mouse, a little control box atop a rubber or stainless steel ball, can be rolled around on a desktop; its motions are duplicated on the screen.

OUTPUT DEVICES

Once the computer has received, stored, and processed information, it needs a way to get the results of its work back to the user. This is accomplished through output devices. In most microcomputer systems, the primary output devices are the video display unit, or monitor, and the printer.

Monitors

The monitor, or video display unit (not to be confused with the monitor program in firmware), provides immediate feedback to the computer operator by means of screen displays on a cathode-ray tube (CRT). Screen display characteristics depend on the combination of the monitor quality and the types of signals sent by the video generator. Like the CRT in a television set, the video monitor forms images with dots of light. The image quality and definition of a CRT screen display depend on its ability to follow the modulation frequency of the signal being received. The higher the frequency, the greater the number of dots, and the sharper the image that can be produced. The degree of image sharpness is called resolution.

High-resolution screen displays suitable for general text purposes such as word processing require a signal of 15 megahertz or greater. To prevent interference between television stations, television sets are designed with a wave trap that cuts out any signal above 3.57 megahertz. Even if the wave trap is bypassed, few television sets can handle a signal over 5 megahertz. This means that even though popular home and personal computers are advertised as be-ing suitable for hookup via a modulator with a regular television set, such a combination has only limited applications.

A variety of specialized monitors capable of receiving the higher-frequency signals is available for computer systems. Composite video, or NTSC, monitors are capable of receiving signals averaging 18 megahertz or better from a video generator inside the computer. Such signals provide full-resolution black-and-white information on a monochrome monitor, or lower-resolution information on a color monitor. Another type of monochrome monitor has separate video and synchronization signals. These monitors pro-vide a much sharper display than composite monitors. The type of monochrome monitor you choose depends on your computer, since it will re-quire either one or the other (which may be a factor in your computer choice).

Monitors capable of producing high-resolution color graphics are called RGB (for red-green-blue) or direct drive monitors. The higher resolution and color intensity are possible because the monitor receives the signals broken down into the three primary colors of light: red, green, and blue. RGB monitors are considerably more expensive than composite monitors. Also, though their resolution is higher than that of composite color monitors, RGB monitors cannot compare with the clarity of a good monochromatic monitor. While color is not likely to be a consideration in library applications, resolu-tion and price are, and a monochromatic monitor is probably the better choice. Also, although television sets are not practical for displaying text, a television set and modulator (which converts video signals to a form suitable for television set antenna terminals) will be sufficient for educational and game programs using low-resolution color graphics. Television sets also have the advantage of being standard equipment in many libraries.

Besides resolution, other factors to consider in CRT performance include the ability to display both upper- and lowercase letters, the use of descenders (i.e., the tails of y, g, etc. descending below the line), and the number of characters per screen line, along with such niceties as the ability to display reverse and different intensity characters, underlines, and graphics. These are features that may be hardware or software dependent or both.

Monochromatic monitors may display characters as green on black, amber on black, or white on black. A few monitors allow you to reverse this arrangement, although this makes for a bright screen which can be hard on the eyes. There is some debate as to which is easier to read and less strain for the eyes; green tends to be the most popular in the United States, while Europeans opt for amber. Depending on the type of monitor you buy and where you buy it, you may or may not have a choice of color.

Other physical factors to consider are size of display, glare control, and video controls, which may range from a simple brightness knob to contrast and horizontal and vertical placement controls. The angle of the monitor is also important. Some monitors swivel for individual comfort control.

As with everything else, the type of monitor you choose should depend on how you plan to use your system. And of course the first requirement is that it be compatible with your computer. Caution: monitors are limited by the hard-ware's capabilities. Don't buy a monitor that is capable of doing more than your computer can handle. Such overkill can lead to disappointment as well as wasted funds. If you have not yet chosen a system, the monitor should be a factor in your choice—you're going to spend a lot of time staring at that screen.

Once you have narrowed your choices to monitors that suit both your purpose and your computer, the best way to decide which one you like best is with your eyes. Look closely at the characters on the screen, perhaps even with a magnifying glass. Fill up the screen with one or two characters and check the edges of the screen for blurring. Scroll through a page or two of text (press the PgUp and/or PgDn key) and watch the screen to see if it blurs or leaves a "ghost" trail. If you intend to use graphics, ask the dealer to put the monitor through its paces with a graphics program.

To prolong the life of your monitor, turn down the brightness and/or contrast as far as possible whenever you are not actually using the display. This prevents the dots from burning a permanent image into the screen.

Printers

Useful as information displayed on a computer screen may be, it is helpful to have the ability to create hard copy at will. Therefore, whatever your plans for a computer system, they will almost certainly include at least one printer. Because they are more complex mechanically and have more moving parts, printers have been among the more costly and failure-prone microcomputer peripherals. We are happy to report, however, that printers offer much more in terms of reliability, quality, and features, for much less money, than when we wrote the first edition of *Micro Handbook* in 1983. At that time, if you had $1,000 to spend on a printer, you could get a good quality dot matrix printer and have some money (not a lot) left over. A letter quality printer was out of the question. It is now possible to spend that same $1,000 and acquire *one of each,* both of which are better in terms of speed, features, and often print quality, than the printers that were available then. And you might still have some money left over. Of course, if you have more money, a hankering for typeset quality print, and the desire to do some desk top publishing, you can go a step up and get a laser jet printer (around $3,000 and up, as of this writing). If you have quite a bit less to spend, you can still get a printer that will do very nicely, either letter quality or dot matrix.

Printers are basically classified by two criteria—the way the characters are imprinted on the paper, and the manner in which the characters are formed. The two main categories of imprint method are impact and nonimpact. Impact printers fall mainly into two types, dot matrix and daisy wheel or letter quality (see figure 3.3). The nonimpact category includes thermal, ink-jet, and laser-jet printers. Within these categories there are wide variations in print quality and versatility, speed, noise, and price, including operating expense.

Dot Matrix Printers

Like a CRT screen, dot matrix printers form characters by arranging dots in a close pattern. The dots are made by a print head containing several fine wires, each of which acts as a tiny print hammer. The arrangement, or matrix, of the wires forms the pattern of the character. The number of wires in the print head can vary from a 5x7 matrix to as many as 18x18, with a corresponding variation in image quality. Dot matrix are faster, quieter, more versatile, and generally less expensive than daisy wheel printers. The primary objection most people have to dot matrix printers is that the print looks like it came from a computer and not from a typewriter. Some people feel that dot matrix print is more difficult to read, particularly in a long document. However, dot matrix printers have shown a steady improvement in quality. By using more and smaller wires and using overprinting to create a denser pattern, they can produce very acceptable copy. A number of them, in fact, produce print that is almost indistinguishable from letter quality.

Dot matrix printers average 150 to 200 characters per second (cps) in draft, or basic, mode. Setting the printer to correspondence, enhanced, or near-letter-quality mode, so that it uses a second pass to overprint and create denser characters, will slow it down considerably, but it will still be faster than most daisy wheels. With the appropriate software, dot matrix printers can also

Letter Quality

Dot Matrix

Fig. 3.3. A printer sampler.

be used to print graphics designs, including bar codes. They are capable of varying the size and shape of characters for emphasis and special creative effects and to create international character sets. A reasonably good dot matrix printer can be had for less than $300 as of this writing, though prices for near-letter-quality printers are quite a bit higher.

Daisy Wheel Printers

Daisy wheel printers produce letter quality characters that appear to be the work of a prolific and accurate typist. Their name comes from the shape of the print element, which has petal shaped spokes radiating from a central hub. At the ends of the "petals" are embossed characters. The daisy wheel rotates on a driveshaft between the typewriter-style ribbon and a print hammer. When the proper character is in position, an electrical signal causes the hammer to fire against the petal, which strikes the ribbon, pressing it against the paper to produce an image of the character. Thimble printers, less common than daisy wheels, also produce letter-quality characters using a similar print element, except that the wheel is folded in on itself so that it looks like a cup or thimble, with the characters embossed around the rim. As with most dot matrix printers, boldfacing and underlining are produced by making a second pass on the original character. Daisy wheel elements are interchangeable so that a wide variety of typestyles and characters may be produced, including international character sets and even, in some cases, limited graphics. Some daisy wheel printers include a keyboard so that they may be used independently as an electric typewriter.

Daisy wheel printers have shown one of the most dramatic price drops in the industry. For around $500, you can have a printer comparable to one that cost over $2,000 a couple of years ago. Daisy wheels are considerably slower than dot matrix printers, averaging anywhere from 10 to 50 characters per second. This may seem fast compared to a human typist, but when you are printing an inventory list or a series of bibliographies it can be maddeningly slow. Although daisy wheels are generally quieter than they used to be, the "ratatatat" of the petals striking the paper can be distracting, especially when two or more printers are in use. In fact, if you buy a letter-quality printer for use inside the library, you may find a noise muffler (a plastic cover which fits over the printer and absorbs the worst of the noise) a useful investment as well.

Another method for obtaining letter-quality printouts is to purchase equipment and software to convert an electric typewriter, such as an IBM Selectric, to work as a printer. Electric typewriters are not as sturdy as printers built for that purpose, nor is the setup very fast, making this arrangement impractical for extensive use. An even bigger problem is the lack of service and support for a system that is the product of at least two manufacturers, neither of which wants to be responsible for breakdowns or difficulties.

Nonimpact Printers

The least expensive type of nonimpact printer is a thermal printer, which forms characters using heat or electric sparks. Though inexpensive initially, many thermal printers require specially treated paper and thus have a high operating cost. The quality of print produced by earlier models also left quite a bit to be desired. Since dot matrix and letter-quality printers are so much less expensive than they used to be, thermal printers currently don't offer much of an advantage, except perhaps in noise level. Some improved models are beginning to appear, however, and thermal printers may become a viable alternative to other types. If you are considering buying a thermal printer, be sure to find out whether it uses special paper, and if so, whether the print quality warrants the extra expense.

Ink-jet printers propel ink onto the paper in a highly concentrated pattern using tiny jets. Ink-jet printers are quiet, relatively fast, and produce acceptable type, which, however, has a tendency to smudge. Low-end ink-jet printers are available for a few hundred dollars.

The queen of printers is the laser jet, which uses a variation on photocopier technology to produce commercial-quality print. Although the characters are formed using dots, the pattern is so dense and the dots so small that they cannot be distinguished. Laser-jet printers are extremely fast, producing several pages a minute, and extremely quiet. They can produce a wide variety of fonts, graphics, and special effects. They are also expensive, ranging from about $3,000 to $9,000 or more, which nevertheless represents a sizable drop from the cost of the first commercial laser-jet printer, available in 1977 for $350,000. Some of the more expensive models are computing systems in themselves, with powerful microprocessors, extensive memory, disk drives, expansion slots, and resident operating systems. Industry competition is spurring the production of lower-priced, lower-performance machines that may eventually replace both dot matrix and daisy wheel printers as standard microcomputer accessories.

Plotters are actually not printers at all, but computer-driven drawing machines. They are used primarily for drafting and scientific applications, are relatively expensive, and are unlikely to be of much use in a library, unless it is a high school or college library with a high proportion of patrons interested in science.

Choosing a Printer

It is important to be certain that the printer(s) you intend to buy is compatible with your system. Printers are described as either parallel or serial depending on how they interface with the computer. (Interfaces are explained later in this chapter.) Some printers may be either parallel or serial. Parallel interfaces have managed to achieve a high degree of standardization; also, most computers have at least one parallel port which is intended for the printer (with some notable exceptions, such as the MacIntosh, which requires a serial printer). Although serial printers generally use what is known as an RS232 interface, RS232 means different things to different people. Therefore a parallel printer is more likely to work with a wide assortment of computers. Communication between a computer and a printer is also faster via a parallel port, but since both types of interfaces tend to communicate faster than a printer can print, this is of minor importance. Serial printers do have one advantage: they can be a greater physical distance from the computer (up to 100 feet, as opposed to 15 feet for a parallel connection). Serial interfaces often require special cables, as well, while parallel cables are standard (and therefore probably cheaper, as well). The cable, by the way, is extra, as are any interface cards required to make your computer and your printer talk to one another. If you buy two printers, such as a dot matrix and a daisy wheel, you might want to invest in a special cable that plugs into both, with a switch so that you can change printers without unplugging and plugging in cables.

Your printer must also be compatible with your software (one more reason for choosing software first). Software communicates with printers through special programs called drivers. Many programs include an assortment of drivers for popular printers, and many of the less well known printer brands are compatible enough with the big names to use their drivers. Some programs also allow you to install a custom driver; for this you need to be familiar with the printer (or handy with a printer manual) and to learn to use the install program.

You will need to consider a number of other factors when choosing a printer, including the following:

Number of Characters per Line. The printer should have the ability to print either pica (10 characters/inch) or elite (12 characters/inch), or 80-96 characters per line on standard 8-inch-wide paper. Also useful are condensed mode, which prints as many as 200 characters to a standard line, and expanded mode, which elongates characters so that there are anywhere from 20 to 40 on a line. On a dot matrix or laser printer, you set the number of characters per inch through the software; some printers also have an external control for setting this. On a daisy wheel, you change character size by changing the print wheel. Proportionately spaced characters (where an "m" takes twice as much space as an "l", for example) are available with all three types of printers, and are generally considered more attractive. Proportional spacing is also software dependent—if your software can't do it, it doesn't matter if the printer can.

For most library applications you will need a printer that can print at least 80 characters per line; for spreadsheets and inventories, etc., you may need as many as 132. If you do a lot of this sort of printing, you may want to get a printer with a wide carriage, rather than using compressed print.

Ribbons. The type of ribbon (spool or cartridge, nylon or carbon) will affect the cost of operation and print quality. Spool ribbons can be refilled, for example, with refills costing quite a bit less than new ribbons, but they will gradually fade. Cartridge ribbons, on the other hand, provide the same quality print throughout and are also easier and less messy to replace. However, they cost more and may not last as long. If you plan to print bar codes, make sure your bar code reader can read the printer ink.

Paper Feed Method and Paper Requirements. In a pin or tractor feed system, special continuous paper with holds on both sides is pulled or pushed through the printer on pins. In a pin feed system, the pins are affixed to the ends of the platen, or roller, and are therefore of a fixed width, while tractor feeds are adjustable for different paper widths. Computer paper quality has improved a great deal. "Microperf" continuous feed paper, once you have detached the hole strips on either side and separated the sheets, looks much like standard-quality typing paper. Single sheet feeding uses a friction method like that on a standard typewriter. The paper is held tightly against the platen; as the platen turns, the paper moves. Laser printers feed paper like a photocopy machine, from a stack of single sheets.

The main considerations in paper feeding methods are ease of loading, speed, and registration (positioning of the paper so that the dots or characters strike in the right place). Ideally, a printer should accept either single sheets or continuous paper. (You may have to buy an optional tractor feed attachment.)

Ability to Print Card Stock. If you intend to print cards, be especially careful in choosing your printer. Many dot matrix printers cannot handle card stock, which requires a bottom feed. Ask to see the printer work with card stock before you buy.

Number of Copies Possible. If you will be making multiple copies, the printer should be able to handle the extra layers or thickness of paper. Again, ask to see it work.

Size and Weight. Some printers are easily portable, others are anything but. Generally, letter-quality and laser printers tend to be larger and heavier than dot matrix printers. Another consideration is storage room for paper.

Durability and Reliability. A great deal of delicate timing and mechanical precision are involved in getting those hammers and wires to strike in the right places at the right times, to keep the platen turning smoothly and the paper feeding steadily, etc. Also, some parts wear out faster than others. Daisy wheels are available in plastic or metal. Platens can be rubber, steel, or plastic. Look for the sturdiest printer available to fit your needs.

Available Character Sets. If you buy a daisy wheel printer, it should accept standard daisy wheels, so that you have a wide selection of typestyles. A dot matrix printer should be able to print italics and foreign character sets without a lot of special programming.

Special Features. Again, these will depend on your specific needs and budget. Features such as color graphics are expensive luxuries, and other features such as descenders (those tails on *g*s and *y*s) may be options, not standards. A detailed checklist is important. Options may add to the speed and capabilities of a printer, but they also add to the price, including the cost of the accessories and software needed to make the printer work with your computer.

Service. Service and support are vital considerations in printer choice. Find out who is responsible for service, the dealer or the manufacturer (if it's neither, find a different printer). Service calls range from $50 to $200 initially, with parts and time over an hour or two costing extra. For these reasons, an extended (12- to 18-month) warranty is an especially nice feature for a printer.

Once again, one of the best ways to judge printers is by watching, and listening to, them print. Most printer manufacturers supply sample sheets showing all the fancy tricks their printers can do (many of which require special software to accomplish). Even so, before buying, it's best to have the vendor hook the printer up, preferably to a computer like yours, so you can see and hear it for yourself.

OTHER PERIPHERAL DEVICES

Two other types of peripheral devices that libraries are likely to need are modems and power protection and backup devices.

Modems

A modem is a telecommunications device used to transfer communication between computers using ordinary telephone lines. "Modem" is short for MOdulator-DEModulator, for the way the device modulates the ON/OFF signals from a computer into two different tones, or frequencies, which can be transmitted over a phone line and demodulated back to computer signals on the receiving end. Modems enable computers of different types and in different places to talk to one another.

Intercomputer communications offer some of the most exciting possibilities for microcomputer users, from access to large databases to electronic communities linked by computer bulletin boards. However, don't let advertisements mislead you into thinking that once you own a modem, you can plug one end into a phone line and the other into your computer and carry on a conversation with the computer in the district media center or your local university. The rules governing the exchange of information between computers (or between a computer and its peripherals) are called protocol. Like the rest of the industry, communications protocols are plagued by a lack of standardization. A number of major and minor manufacturers are actually working together to develop industrywide communications standards; if they succeed, it will make at least one facet of computer selection easier. In the meantime, if you plan to access another system or systems with your computer, either by modem or directly by means of a dedicated line, protocol compatibility with the other computers should be one of the important criteria for your hardware and software purchases.

Most modems on the market today are direct connect, that is, they plug directly into a phone line, bypassing the need to convert the digital data from the computer into sound that can be detected by a telephone headset. It is even possible to buy telephones with built-in direct-connect modems. Auto-dial modems allow the phone number to be input from the computer itself, either through the keyboard or from previously entered disk files; some auto-dial modems have internal memory for storing phone numbers and communications software. Modems are also either originate-only or originate-answer. Originate-answer modems can automatically answer the phone and hook callers into the computer.

Beyond compatibility, probably the most important consideration in buying a modem is the speed at which it transmits information. The term "baud rate" is commonly used to measure the data transmission speed. Some people prefer the more accurate "bits per second" (bps), but baud is likely to remain popular for some time. (Bits, remember, are the ONES and ZEROS transmitted by the computer to and from its memory and peripherals. ONES represent one frequency; ZEROS represent another. Baud rate is actually a measure of the number of times per second a signal changes from one frequency to the other.) Modem transmission speeds range from 300 bps to as high as 9600, with a corresponding range in price.

The data are sent across phone lines in ASCII code. Each ASCII character takes seven bits. Additional bits are used for marking the beginning and end of characters and for error checking, so it actually requires about ten or eleven bits to send one character. Therefore a modem that sends data at 300 bps can transmit about 30 characters per second—about the speed of most letter-quality printers. For uses involving much transmission, particularly if you are paying for connect time, 1200 bps is about the slowest acceptable speed. Generally, the faster the modem, the more it costs; also, some online services charge higher rates for the higher bps modems.

Another factor affecting transmission speed and price is whether the modem is full or half duplex. Full-duplex modems can transmit and receive information simultaneously; half-duplex modems can only do one at a time. Some communications services, such as The Source, *require* full-duplex communications.

Modems may be either internal or external. An internal modem plugs directly into the computer's motherboard. An external modem connects to the computer via an RS232 serial port and a cable. Many computers come with serial ports. However, since RS232 ports are not standardized, you must make sure the port and the modem can connect. This may mean buying an additional serial interface card and connecting cable when you buy your modem, in which case you must make sure your computer has a slot for the new card. (See "Putting it All Together," later in this chapter.) External modems have the advantage of being adaptable to different computers. Internal modems can be customized to take advantage of the attributes of a specific machine, and are slightly less expensive. Which type is best for you depends on your needs, the availability of modems that are compatible with your system, and your budget.

A modem will not be much use without one or more types of communications software. Many modems include bundled communications software, perhaps even in the firmware in the modem itself. There is also an abundance of public domain communications software available. Some communications software is very friendly, while other programs are meant for programmers only. When shopping for a modem, make sure you find out what software is included and/or available, what it will do, and how easy it is to use. Like other microcomputer products, modems are increasing in number and capabilities while decreasing in price, and are frequent topics for review in periodicals. We'll have more to say about intercomputer communications in chapter 6. In order to use a modem with your system, you *must* have a single phone line to your library—that is, one not run through a switchboard.

Power Protection and Backup

"Glitch" is a term you may come across often in computer talk. Originally used to indicate a short, low-magnitude electrical disturbance, it has come to mean any unexpected and inexplicable problem. Glitches range from blackouts due to power failures to the electrical noise caused by small appliances, hand tools, powerline switching equipment, etc. In between are voltage dips caused by such events as an office building's air conditioning switching on or off, and spikes, or power surges, which are usually caused by equipment failures or changes in the utility distribution network. Even small disturbances can do harm to sensitive computer circuitry, from turning data into garbage to actually melting components. Database damage caused by power fluctuations may not become apparent for weeks or months—one reason to keep archival backups. (See chapter 7.)

Powerline conditioners, or surge protectors, and backup power supplies are two ways of protecting your precious data and equipment from disaster. A surge protector acts as a shock absorber to suppress voltage shocks and noise. Voltage regulators can offer further protection against longer and more drastic power drops or surges. Many surge protectors provide multiple outlets for your computer and peripherals, along with an on/off switch. By leaving your equipment switched on and using the switch on the protector, you prolong the life of switches on your components. Incidentally, don't turn your computer on or off more than necessary. The abrupt changes in power cause more wear and tear than leaving the equipment running. Some experts even recommend turning the computer on Monday morning and leaving it running until Friday afternoon. (Do remember, however, to turn down the monitor brightness when the computer isn't in use.)

Backup power supplies provide auxiliary power in case of a complete power loss, by means of a battery which may be built in or supplemental. The backup power gives you time to shut your system down normally during a blackout. This type of protection is more expensive than a surge protector, but may be worthwhile if you live in an area prone to electrical storms or other power loss. Backup power supplies may be either standby or uninterruptible. In a standby system, the battery is kept charged by the AC line but does not switch on unless there is an actual power failure, causing a delay of up to a hundred milliseconds—generally not enough to damage most computers. The battery for an uninterruptible system is always switched in to the circuit so that there is no gap in power at all in the event of a power failure.

Another frequent cause of damage is static electricity. Even a minor jolt can be harmful. Antistatic mats and sprays are inexpensive ways to protect your system against static. If you live in a dry climate, you may want to invest in a humidifier.

Surge protectors, backup power supplies, and antistatic protection offer reasonably priced insurance for your computer system. We strongly recommend including some type of power protection in your purchase. Chapter 7, "Choosing and Implementing Your Computer System," offers more advice on how to protect yourself against computer catastrophes.

PUTTING IT ALL TOGETHER

Buying a computer system is similar to buying a stereo system: it may be purchased as a complete package, as a customized set of individual components, or as a combination of the two. There are some significant differences, however. Stereo units such as amplifiers, speakers, and turntables are essentially interchangeable. You can mix and match brands and models with nothing more complicated than some jacks and speaker wire. Getting computer components to work together is considerably more complicated, if they can be made to work together at all.

In order to function as a system, the various components must be able to communicate with one another in forms each can understand. This is accomplished through ports, which send and receive bits between the computer proper and the various input and output devices. The computer ports are connected to corresponding ports in external components by means of plug-in cables. Within the computer itself, a bus structure consisting of a set of electrical conductors transmits signals between the internal components of the system, such as the CPU and memory. An interface converts the signals coming through a port to signals that may be transmitted through the bus structure, and vice versa.

The bus structure and other circuitry and mechanical elements are supported and connected by the motherboard. An interface may be built into the motherboard, or added to it by means of a circuit card that plugs into a slot on the bus structure itself. One requirement for system expandability is a provision for adding new or different plug-in cards to the bus. These plug-in cards may range from serial or parallel interfaces, to additional microprocessors and/or memory, to entire peripherals such as a hard disk drive or an internal modem.

Interfaces and ports may be either serial or parallel. A parallel port handles 8 bits of data at once, while a serial port handles only one bit at a time. Most modems and other peripheral devices such as bar code readers use serial ports. Printers, as mentioned before, may be either parallel or serial, although parallel printers are more common. The most common parallel type, Centronics compatible, has actually become a widely accepted standard (a rarity in the industry). Computers themselves may include either or both types of ports as standard equipment. If your computer has only one port, and you want to connect more than one peripheral, you will have to use a slot and an interface card for each additional device. To conserve slots, you may be able to use multifunction cards, which combine various components such as RAM, ports, clock/calendars, etc. on a single card.

Though the packaging may vary, each microcomputer system will include some form of each of the basic components: CPU and primary memory (ROM and RAM); a keyboard (or other primary input device); a display screen; one or more auxiliary storage units; a printer; and interfaces, ports, and cables to connect all of the components together. One system might include in one lightweight desktop unit everything but the printer. (Some systems even include a small printer in the main unit.) Another may include the keyboard in the unit housing the CPU and memory, matched with one or two disk drives and a monitor. Still another may have the CPU, memory, and one or two disk drives in a box that interfaces to a separate terminal which includes a CRT, keyboard, and video generator (see figure 3.4).

Terminals themselves may be either "intelligent" or "dumb." Earlier definitions of terminal intelligence had to do with functions such as cursor addressing and sensing (being able to tell where a character is on the screen), ability to use special function keys, and graphics capabilities. The current definition refers to a terminal's ability to function as a standalone computer in addition to its role as a communications device linking the user and a separate computer via a cable or a telecommunications link. An intelligent terminal contains user-programmable memory; a dumb terminal, though it probably contains a microprocessor, cannot be programmed by the user. Any microcomputer system with the necessary equipment and software can function as an intelligent terminal. A dumb terminal can never function as a microcomputer system.

The microcomputer industry has thus far achieved little standardization in the makeup (except in some aspects of physical structure) of bus structures, peripheral devices, interfaces, ports, and the cables and cards used to connect them. There is little conformity as far as which pins and wires carry which signals, which slots hold which interface cards, and which ports can receive signals from which peripherals. Therefore, whenever you make any additions or expansions to your system, you must acquire not only the components themselves but the correct cables and interface cards for connecting them to your computer. You may also need additional software in the form of device drivers, the programs that enable your computer to talk with a given peripheral.

All of these extras can run into considerable expense, especially if a specialized cable or card is required, or worse, if a peripheral cannot be made to work with your computer at all. This is what makes compatibility between computers and peripherals such a problem, and why compatibility must always be your first consideration in choosing any peripheral device. Even relatively standard configurations, such as RS232 ports or S100 buses, can vary enough to cause problems. Make sure your dealer includes *everything* in the price quotation *and* shows you how to hook the system up correctly; it is possible to plug a computer component in the wrong way, a potentially damaging situation that you may not discover until it is too late. If you are

A

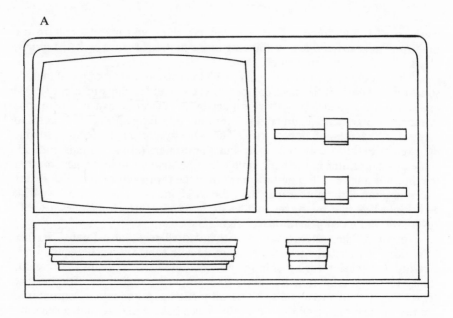

B

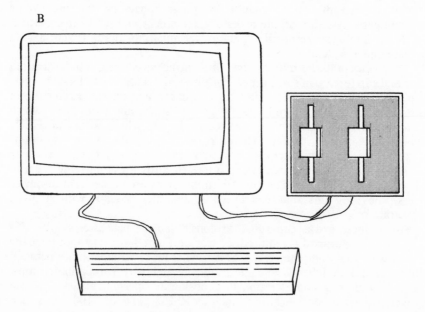

Figure 3.4. Two types of microcomputer systems.
Figure A is an all-in-one system with built-in monitor, keyboard and disk drives; Figure B consists of separate components. The CPU is housed in the unit with the disk drives.

installing components yourself, follow instructions and diagrams carefully. If the instructions aren't clear, call the support line for advice. If there isn't a support line through the manufacturer or a trusted expert, don't buy the product.

DECIDING WHAT TO BUY

With all of the options available, narrowing the choices down to one appropriate system may seem a formidable task, but there are things you can do to make it easier. Before you even begin shopping, you should conduct a needs analysis and decide as closely as possible what you want the system to do. Make a detailed shopping list, with "must-haves" at the top, followed by "would-like-to-haves," and take it with you as you shop. (For more information on determining your needs and wants, see chapter 7.)

It is also very helpful to read several periodicals covering at least two or three months. The microcomputer industry is incredibly volatile. Books such as this one can give you the background knowledge you need to get started, but the only way to get current information is through periodicals. Appendix B includes a list of good computer-oriented periodicals, both general audience and library specific, some of them free. They include reviews of both hardware and software, general information, and state-of-the-industry analyses. Many newspapers also carry regular computer columns in their business sections. One caution in using periodicals as a source of information: the computer industry is plagued by a tendency for manufacturers to announce products well in advance of their completion. In fact, many of these phantom products, or "vaporware," never make it to market. Make sure a product is actually available, and working, before you set your heart on it.

Another source of information is users, although you should be wary of making crucial decisions based on the starry eyed enthusiasm or angry regrets of one or two people. Talk to several users, and try to get them to be specific about what they like or dislike.

One option available now that wasn't three years ago is used equipment. A lot of perfectly good systems, especially Apple II and CP/M-based systems, have been discarded by people anxious to acquire the newer machines. They are being offered at bargain basement prices through personal ads or through dealers who specialize in used equipment. What's more, many of them include large libraries of software. As a starter system for a limited budget, or as a supplement to your main system, used computers can be a great buy. (The one type of used equipment we don't recommend, because of its tendency to wear out, is a printer.)

A Hardware Checklist

Following are some general criteria to aid you in your search for hardware:

Will your software run on it?
This is the primary consideration in buying hardware. It may be the

niftiest little computer system on the market, and on sale besides, but if you can't find software for it that suits your needs, there's no point in having it.

This is where the issue of intercomputer compatibility comes in. Depending on your software choices, you may need a computer that is operationally compatible with a given brand, or you may decide that data or operating system compatibility is sufficient, especially given the advantages offered by a different system. If you decide operational compatibility is important, here are some tests you can use to determine the compatibility of a "lookalike" with a "model":

- Will the lookalike boot the model's operating system, either from a floppy or a hard disk? Many so-called compatible computers require their own operating system, which is similar but not identical to the original.

- Will the lookalike run a graphics program designed for the model? Graphics is one area in which programmers are likely to circumvent the operating system and work directly with a machine's BIOS and interfaces. Ask to see the program run. Games and simulator programs are good choices for this test.

- Can the lookalike use keyboard enhancement programs and/or pop-up window programs designed for the model? Such programs are designed to stay resident in the computer's memory while you run other programs, so they can be called on at will, and usually bypass the operating system to get to the hardware itself.

- Most important, can it run the specific program(s) you want to use? This is, after all, the real test. You may want to get a guarantee from the vendor, in writing. It's even better if you can actually see the program run.

Is the dealer reliable, and is he giving you a fair price?

Especially if you are a novice, you need to choose your dealer very carefully. Many retail dealers and salespeople are woefully uninformed about the products they sell, and some of them have a tendency to play on your (supposed) ignorance besides. A recent *InfoWorld* survey showed an astonishing range of system recommendations and prices—from just under $4000 to almost $14,000—among retail dealers trying to meet the identically stated needs of "first-time buyers" looking for a basic small office system.

Your chosen dealer should sell a variety of hardware and software, so that your choices are not too limited. If you have read about software that sounds appealing, get a list of local dealers from the manufacturer rather than trying to rely on long-distance support. Call and/or visit several different dealers. How willing are they to answer questions? What kind of warranties do they provide? Can you understand what they say, or do they seem to be doing their best to confuse you with jargon? Do they provide training, free or at a reasonable cost? What about installation? And—this is crucial—what about follow-up support? Even if you have a private computer expert available, dealer and manufacturer support is essential. In this area, surprisingly, mail order vendors are becoming quite competitive with retailers, offering support lines and warranties. For a beginner, though, nothing beats reliable local support.

In the computer shopping game, knowledge is your best weapon, along with a willingness to comparison shop. This book should give you a basic computer vocabulary for talking on an even basis with any dealer willing to make the effort to meet your needs. Along with the information gleaned from periodicals, it should also enable you to detect ignorance or deliberate misinformation on the part of a salesman.

Finally, if you are shopping for a school library, look for a dealer who is aware of and sympathetic to the special needs of educators—and do right by him. Educators have acquired an unfortunate reputation among dealers, who feel, not unjustifiably, that the educational market requires more service and is less willing to pay for it than small business or private users.

Does the hardware offer some degree of standardization?

What sort of interfaces does it include? A Centronics compatible parallel port will give you a wide range of printers to choose from, and a relatively standard serial port will increase the range of peripherals you can use easily. Does the computer use a standard microprocessor? What kind(s) of operating system will it run? What kinds of plug-in cards does the computer accept? It doesn't help to have ten slots for expandability if you can't find anything to connect to them.

Over and above compatibility, it's useful to have a machine that contains standard, easily replaceable parts. This is especially true with lesser known and "generic" makes. With standard parts, even if the dealer and/or manufacturer go out of business, you have a machine that is still serviceable and repairable.

What does it include?

Do you have to buy a separate monitor, keyboard, or disk drive? If peripheral devices are included, are they good quality? How many ports does the computer have? How much memory is standard? What about cables, interfaces, and device drivers? Is an operating system included, or extra? Does the system include any bundled software, and if so, how useful will it be to you? Does it have a warranty or warranties, and what do they cover? For how long?

Is the system expandable?

Can you add memory, and if so, how much and at what cost? Will it take up extra slots to do so? Can you add another microprocessor? How many slots are there for adding interfaces or peripherals? If you anticipate needing a multi-user system, can the computer expand to accommodate it, or at least be incorporated into it?

Expandability is a major consideration. If you start with the right system, you will be able to upgrade it and use it for a long time, even as your needs grow. Upgrading is nearly always cheaper than a whole new system. Don't lock yourself into a computer that is too limited.

Is the system durable and reliable?

How does it fare in review publications and with other users (your dealer should be able to furnish names). Has it been on the market long enough for bugs to appear and be solved? Or is it still in the experimental stages?

Is the system physically comfortable to use?

The physical relationship between a person and a machine is called ergonomics. This is basically a subjective rating. How does the keyboard feel? Is it in an awkward place? Is the monitor screen at a good height and a comfortable angle? Is it wide enough, and easy to read, with good resolution? How large is the system, including peripherals? Will it fit easily into your library, so that everything is easy to reach (including the printer)? Does it need to be portable, or fit onto a cart, so that classrooms can check it out? How noisy is it?

How good is the documentation?

This includes all the manuals, instructions, and guides that come with the hardware. Are both a technical/programming manual and user's manual included? Is the user's manual written in a language you can understand, or is it highly technical, or worse, just plain garbled? As with software, hardware documentation is often a weak point. One good test is to use the manual to guide yourself through some sample procedures (such as initializing a disk) while examining the equipment in the store.

One final comment is in order here. Whether a given piece of equipment is "state of the art" should not be a criterion. In fact, because computers are changing so fast, it is better to buy products that have had some time to prove themselves. Also, because of the continuing pace of developments, many people are tempted to wait for the ultimate micro. Don't. As we said before, technical obsolescence and functional obsolescence are not synonymous. The fact that any system that you purchase now is almost certain to be outclassed by an equally priced or less expensive system six months or a year from now does not in any way decrease its value. Computer evolution may slow down in the next few years, but it will continue for a long time. If you insist on waiting for the perfect system, you will miss out on the wonderful things you could be doing right now. The object of your search is to find the best currently available system to suit your present needs.

For information on caring for your system, see appendix C.

FURTHER READINGS

General Information

Beiser, Karl. "Microcomputing." *Wilson Library Bulletin* 60, no. 4 (December 1985): 42-43.
"The commodity trends discussed here have broadened the range of safe and satisfactory choices for those who would put computers to good use in libraries."

Bosak, Steven. "Harnessing the White Elephant." *Popular Computing* 5, no. 3 (December 1985): 15-16.
"That outmoded 8-bit business computer can still carry a respectable load."

Deacon, Jim. "CPU and DOS." *CMC News* 4, no. 2 (Winter 1984): 3-4.
Discusses 8-bit and 16-bit CPUs.

Levin, Will. "Interactive Video: The State-of-the-Art Teaching Machine." *The Computing Teacher* 11, no. 2 (September 1983): 11-17.
Includes bibliography for further reading.

"Microcomputer Hardware Policy for Libraries." *ONLINE Libraries and Microcomputers* 3, no. 12 (December 1985): 1-3.
Article focuses on "considerations for hardware acquisition, training, scheduling, and security."

Rubin, Charles. "How to Buy a Personal Computer." *Personal Computing* 8, no. 8 (August 1984): 108-20.

Simonsen, Redmond, and Brad Hessel. "Report from the Nation's Computer Owners." *Popular Computing* 5, no. 1 (November 1985): 67-72.

Smith, Richard Allen. "Computer Demonstrations for Your Benefit." *The Computing Teacher* 11, no. 7 (March 1984): 14-17.
Article includes questions to ask vendor, guidelines for product demonstration and a sample "Hardware Demonstration Comment Form."

Welch, Mark J. "Interest Grows in Generic Computers." *InfoWorld* 8, no. 4 (27 January 1986): 24-27.
"Long ignored by serious business users, no-name PC compatibles are gaining support as legitimate alternatives to systems from major manufacturers."

"Your Rapidly Appreciating Micro Investment." *Technicalities* 4, no. 9 (September 1984): 1-2.

Communications

Bonner, Paul, and James Keogh. "Connected! A Buyer's Guide on Modems." *Personal Computing* 8, no. 4 (April 1984): 146-95.

"Competition for 2400 Baud Modem Marketplace Begins." *ONLINE Libraries and Microcomputers* 2, no. 12 (December 1984): 8.

Cowan, Les, and Larry McClain. "Talking with Your Computer." *Popular Computing* 3, no. 4 (February 1984): 142-50.

Friedlander, Brian, and Allan Page. "Get Your Class in Line and On-line with a Modem." *Electronic Education* 5, no. 3 (November/December 1985): 14-15, 23.
Includes comparison of different modems for variety of microcomputers.

Gabel, David. "Modem Mistakes You Don't Have to Make." *Personal Computing* 8, no. 6 (June 1984): 120-25.
"Careful planning and expert advice can help you avoid pitfalls on the road to successful computer communications."

_____. "Modems — Buyer's Guide." *Personal Computing* 9, no. 1 (January 1985): 109-19.
"Modems allow you to communicate across the hall or around the globe. To ensure a good connection, the prudent buyer needs to know the choices available in a crowded market."

Gold, Jordan. "How Fast Are You Really Communicating?" *Personal Computing* 8, No. 7 (July 1984): 149-59.
"Speed and reliability of communications software vary widely; understanding the argot can help you define your needs." Includes glossary.

Jordan, Larry. "What Makes Modems Run?" *PC World* 3, no. 5 (May 1985): 267-74.

McMullen, John, and Barbara McMullen. "Review: 2400-bps Modems Arrive, Price Differs." *InfoWorld* 7, no. 32 (12 August 1985): 44-45.

"Modems: A Vital Link for Online Library Applications." *ONLINE Libraries and Microcomputers* 2, no. 10 (October 1984): 1-4.

Compatibility

Cook, Rick. "More Bytes per Disk Means Incompatibility." *Popular Computing* 3, no. 12 (October 1984): 198.

Miller, Michael J., and Tom McMillan. "IBM Compatibility." *Popular Computing* 3, no. 12 (April 1984): 104-6, 108, 110-13, 115-18.

Input Devices

Adams, Russ. "The Ultimate Bar Code." *Bar Code News* 5, no. 6 (November 1985): 4.
"CD-ROMs . . . fit the definition of a bar code. . . . Not only is the CD-ROM the ultimate in bar code — it may be the ultimate in keyless data entry."

Anderson, Eric. "You Really Can Talk to Your Apple . . ." *Electronic Education* 3, no. 4 (January 1984): 38.
Review of the Apple Voice Input Module.

"Bar Code and the IBM PC." *Bar Code News* 5, no. 4 (July/August 1985): 6-7, 9, 12-14, 71.

Bravman, Richard. "Hand-Held Scanners: The Latest in Scanning Technology." *Bar Code News* 5, no. 3 (May/June 1985): 8-12.

Dirksen, J. Anthony. "Mouse-Driven Software for Apple II Computers." *A + Magazine* 3, no. 3 (March 1985): 38.

Dyrli, Odvard Egil. "Input Devices — Joysticks, Mice and Lightpens." *Classroom Computer Learning* 6, no. 3 (November/December 1985): 10-13.

"Keyless Data Entry Products. . . ." *Bar Code News* 5, no. 5 (September/October 1985): 22, 24, 27-28, 30.

Melin, Nancy Jean. "Bar Code Readers and OCR: The Old and the New." *Information Today* 2, no. 9 (October 1985): 10-11.

O'Brien, David. "New Scanner Bridges Gap." *Electronic Education* 4, no. 7 (May/June 1985): 22-23.

Pilgrim, Aubrey. "Bar Code Bonanza." *PC World* 3, no. 3 (March 1985): 198-207.

"Portable Bar Code Readers: An Overview." *Bar Code News* 4, no. 3 (May/June 1984): 12-14.

Robinson, Dan. "Scanning Pages for Less Scratch." *InfoWorld* 7, no. 30 (29 July 1985): 48-49.
Review of the Omni-Reader.

Summers, Tan A. "Low-Cost Light Pens." *Popular Computing* 3, no. 12 (October 1984): 127-34.

Worthington, Hall. "Part II: OCR Today." *Bar Code News* 4, no. 3 (May/June 1984): 46-60.
Part I appears in the January/February issue.

Zarley, Craig. "Wide World of Alternative Input Devices." *Personal Computing* 8, no. 2 (February 1984): 129-37.
Covers the mouse, touch tablets, light pens, and voice command.

Output Devices

Bell, Jack. "Letter-Quality Printers—Buyer's Guide." *Personal Computing* 9, no. 8 (August 1985): 119-29.

Casey, Jean M. "Making Micros Talk—Innovations Are Making Speech Easier and Cheaper." *Electronic Learning* 5, no. 3 (October 1985): 16, 21-22, 62.

Crawford, Walt. "Common Sense and Low-Cost Printers; or, Does Your System Have Impact?" *Library HiTech* (Issue 10) 3, no. 2 (2nd quarter 1985): 29-38.

Freedman, Mary, and Larry Carlin. "There's No Copy Like Hard Copy." *Library Journal* 110, no. 10 (1 June 1985): 100-101.

Hewes, Jeremy Joan. "Dot Matrix Triple Play." *PC World* 3, no. 11 (November 1985): 178-85.

Simonsen, Redmond, and Brad Hessel. "Choosing Your Second Printer." *Personal Computing* 9, no. 5 (May 1985): 231-39.

Washington, Curtis. "Printer Pointers." *Small Computers in Libraries* 5, no. 7 (July/August 1985): 13-16.

White, Ron. "Tale of Three Printers." *Popular Computing* 4, no. 2 (December 1984): 84-86, 208.
"Reveals the sordid truth about printers: I. Don't Compromise; II. There Is No Such Thing as Too Much Printer; III. Printers Can't Be Trusted out of Your Sight; IV. If Something Serious Goes Wrong You're in Trouble; V. Nothing Is Simple."

Other Peripherals

Cook, Rick. "Power-Line Protection." *Popular Computing* 4, no. 1 (November 1984): 126-32.
"Keep your computer and your data safe when power problems strike."

Emmett, Arielle. "RS-232C Run Around." *Popular Computing* 5, no. 2 (December 1985): 111.

Jones, Edward. "Computer Peripherals: What to Buy." *School Library Journal* 31, no. 3 (November 1984): 50-54.

Storage Devices and Memory

Beiser, Karl. "Can't Ever Get Enough—Some Words about Memory." *Small Computers in Libraries* 5, no. 8 (September 1985): 6-7.

Dewey, Patrick. "Apple Sider: Affordable Hard Disk Storage for Small Libraries." *Library HiTech* (Issue 9) 3, no. 1 (1st quarter 1985): 79ff.

Fersko-Weiss, Henry. "Data Storage—How Much Do You Need?" *Personal Computing* 9, no. 6 (June 1985): 63-71.
"Accommodating data is only the first step in picking a storage system; you also have to consider access speed and program integration."

Freund, Alfred L. "Regional Bibliographic Database on Videodisc." *Library HiTech* (Issue 10) 3, no. 2 (2nd quarter 1985): 7-9.
"The initial creation of a union catalog containing 600,000 unique titles and 1.8 million physical items; the conversion of this database to interactive laserdisc; and the resulting advantages are described. The application of laserdisc technology (described in this article) is thought to be the first of its kind."

Gabel, David. "Creating a Fail-Safe Hard Disk System." *Personal Computing* 8, no. 8 (August 1984): 137-44.
"A hard disk gives you more storage and higher access speed. But how do you get the most from it? And how do you make sure its data is safe?"

Herther, Nancy K. "CD ROM Technology: A New Era for Information Storage and Retrieval?" *ONLINE* (November 1985): 17-28.

"Mass Storage—Special Report." *Popular Computing* 3, no. 7 (May 1984): 113-18, 120-21, 122-27, 131-34, 146-47.
Includes "Hard-Disk Buyer's Guide: The Latest Technology. . . ."; "How to Organize Hard-Disk Data"; "How a Hard Disk Works"; "Hard-Disk Comparison Chart"; "Hard-Disk Backup"; "Introducing the Bernoulli Box."

Murphy, Brower. "CD-ROM and Libraries." *Library HiTech* (ISsue 10) 3, no. 2 (2nd quarter 1985): 21-26.
"Compact Disc-Read Only Memory data format is explained and illustrated, as are current and potential applications."

Schwerin, Julie B. "Importance of CD-ROM Standardization." *Information Today* 2, no. 11 (December 1985): 5, 23.

The', Lee. "Hard Disks." *Personal Computing* 9, no. 7 (July 1985): 197-209.
"Even those who don't need a hard disk's speed or capacity can appreciate the floppy-free ease a Winchester brings to computing. And now it's affordable."

_____. "Floppy Disks Keep Evolving." *Personal Computing* 9, no. 9 (September 1985): 179.

Video Display Units/Monitors

Blake Randolph. "Choosing a Color for Monochrome CRTs." *Popular Computing* 3, no. 11 (September 1984): 175-78.

Crawford, Walt. "VDT Checklist: Another Look at Terminals." *Information Technology and Libraries* 3, no. 4 (December 1984): 343-54.
    "This checklist prepared on behalf of TESLA, the Technical Standards for Library Automation Committee of the Library and Information Technology Association (LITA)."

"Monitors—Buyer's Guide." *Popular Computing* 3, no. 4 (February 1984): 123-29.

O'Malley, Christopher. "Monitors—Buyer's Guide." *Personal Computing* 9, no. 6 (June 1985): 223-234.
    Includes glossary of video terms.

4   Applications of Microcomputers in Library Services and Management

Before 1979, microcomputers appeared in libraries only in supporting roles to mini- or mainframe-based systems. But during the 1980s, the micro has been emerging as a potent library tool in its own right. Even a single microcomputer and some inexpensive software can make a significant difference in the quality and quantity of services a library is able to provide.

The first part of this chapter describes four types of general purpose software that might be used in libraries: word processing packages, including specialized packages for "desktop publishing"; file or database management systems; spreadsheet programs; and integrated packages which combine two or more of the above functions, and which may include graphing capabilities as well. (A fifth type of general purpose software, networking and telecommunications packages, is discussed in chapter 6.) The second part of the chapter explores some possible applications of micros, using both general and special purpose software, in the various library subsystems: acquisitions, cataloging, circulation, serials, reference, administration, and, to a limited degree, instruction.

GENERAL PURPOSE SOFTWARE PACKAGES

Word Processing

Word processing is perhaps the single most popular use for microcomputers, both on a personal and business level. Besides being one of the easiest kinds of programs to use, word processing offers features that have a way of transforming even computerphobes into dedicated believers of the "how did I ever live without it" variety. Anyone who knows the frustration of typing an entire page, only to find an error in the middle of it, who equates "updating" bibliographies and inventory lists with redoing them, or who spends hours doing laborious "cut and paste" editing, will quickly learn to appreciate a word processor. Word processing saves time and improves quality, making it easy to produce error-free copy and revise text quickly and easily. The result is more freedom to concentrate on form and content.

It is now possible for a microcomputer costing under $2,000 and a software package costing a few hundred dollars to offer features equivalent to those of a "dedicated" word processor costing several times as much. Due to its numerous applications, ease of use, and relatively low cost, word processing software is an excellent starting point for anyone—including a library staff—venturing into microcomputerization. It also provides novices an opportunity to gain confidence in the computer as a familiar, simple-to-use yet powerful tool, easing the approach to other, less verbally oriented functions.

Most word processing software does not require any programming skills. You do need to know the basics of using your operating system in order to format or initialize disks and backup files (see chapter 7). Some of the more powerful programs allow you to use programming-like skills to control printer or keyboard functions for special effects or tasks. For example, you might instruct the program to type the word "microcomputer" whenever you press the "M" key in conjunction with one of the computer's special keys. While confusing for the novice, who may safely ignore them, such features are a boon for the experienced user.

Word processing commands are generally concerned with cursor movement (the cursor is the little rectangle or line of light on the screen that marks your position in the text), and with such editing functions as inserting and deleting sections of text. Often the commands are mnemonic, such as ⟨CTRL⟩ S for "Save" (a very important command). Most word processing programs are menu-driven, i.e., the various commands are chosen from a menu displayed in the screen. The commands are very brief, usually consisting of one or two keystrokes. Some programs allow you to regulate the extent of the menu display as you become more familiar with the commands, leaving more of the screen free for text display (see figure 4.1).

With most word processors, you can learn enough to produce a simple document, such as a letter, in a few hours, and become reasonably proficient within a few days. Mastering the more complex functions may take considerably longer. Generally, the more powerful a program is (i.e., the more features and flexibility it offers), the more difficult it is to learn. Accordingly, the easier a program is to learn, the more limited its capabilities. If you don't do a lot of document production, and the documents are relatively simple, you might be contented with a more limited but easy-to-use program. On the other hand, willingness to invest the time to learn a more powerful program could mean extensive time savings and better results in the long run.

Word processing programs are available for almost every kind of microcomputer. Capabilities and prices vary considerably, so it is helpful to have a specific list of features in mind when shopping, based on what you will actually be using the program for. The computer-oriented periodicals mentioned in appendix B carry frequent reviews of word processing packages, and most vendors have access to demonstration copies you may use to try out the program in the store before you buy. Word processing evaluations seem to be largely a matter of personal preference—the more popular packages all have advocates who will swear that whichever program they use is the best.

Since there are so many good packages available, word processing programs are not as hardware restrictive as other types of software. If you want to use word processing in addition to a more specialized function, locate software and hardware for that function first, then find out which word processing packages are compatible with the hardware (including the printer) and

```
        B:SAMPLE  PAGE 1 LINE 21 COL 67              INSERT ON
               < < <       M A I N  M E N U      > > >
       --Cursor Movement--    ! -Delete- !  -Miscellaneous-  !  -Other Menus-
      ^S char left ^D char right !^G char   !  ^I Tab  ^B Reform ! (from Main only)
      ^A word left ^F word right !DEL chr lf! ^V INSERT ON/OFF  !^J Help  ^K Block
      ^E line up   ^X line down  !^T word rt!^L Find/Replce again!^Q Quick ^P Print
         --Scrolling--          !^Y  line  !RETURN End paragraph!^O Onscreen
      ^Z line up   ^W line down  !          ! ^N Insert a RETURN !
      ^C screen up ^R screen down!          ! ^U Stop a comman   !
      L----!----!----!----!----!----!----!----!----!----!----!--------R
          Word processing commands are generally concerned with cursor

      movement (the cursor is the little rectangle or line of light  on

      the  screen that marks your position in the text),  and with such

      editing  functions  as inserting and deleting sections  of  text.

      Often  the commands are mnemonic,  such as ^BCTRL S^B for  "Save" (a

      very  important  command!).  Most word processing  programs  are

      "menu-driven" -- that is,  you choose the various commands from a
```

Fig. 4.1. A sample screen, with menu, from the word processing program Wordstar. Reprinted by permission of MicroPro. Wordstar is a registered trademark of MicroPro International Corporation, 33 San Pablo Avenue, San Rafael, CA 94903.

operating system. Unless you have a very unusual and unpopular type of system, or have some special word processing needs such as the ability to do sorting operations, you should have little trouble finding a program to satisfy you.

Following are some features to look for in word processing software.

Cursor Movement. Some programs allow you to move the cursor in any direction and in varying increments; others are less versatile. Being able to move the cursor up, down, left, or right a character, word, line, or even screen length at a time streamlines editing. Many programs use the arrow keys to move the cursor; some of the older (8-bit) programs use special key combinations for cursor movement. Also useful is a "go to page #" command that lets you move the cursor to the beginning of a specific page.

Word Wrap. This feature frees you from having to press the ‹RETURN› key at the end of each line. The software automatically begins a new line each time a word is typed that will not fit inside the right margin. The ‹RETURN› key is used only at the end of a paragraph.

Some programs have a right-justifying feature, which adjusts the spacing between words and/or letters to produce a straight right margin like those in books and magazines. If this feature is included, it is useful to be able to turn it off in order to produce a ragged edge for documents such as letters. Some programs also include automatic hyphenization of words at the end of a line. Another useful feature is a paragraph formatter, which automatically indents text to fit a temporary left margin.

Insert and Delete Functions. "Insert" mode allows the insertion of new characters (or of blank lines) without erasing the characters already entered. Some word processors use an insert key to place the computer in insert mode for one key stroke and then return it to standard mode (in which new characters "type over" existing characters). "Dynamic insert" causes the computer to "push" existing words ahead of the new text as it is entered, returning to standard mode only when given the proper command. This type of command is called a toggle because the same stroke or combination of strokes turns the function on if it is off and vice versa.

Programs also vary in deletion capabilities. More powerful programs allow the operator to delete a character, word, line, part of a line, or even a block (an operator-defined section of text) at a time.

Search or **Search and Replace.** The search function enables the operator to search a file for a given "string of characters," which may range from part of a word to several words. Search and replace causes the identified string to be replaced with a different character string, either automatically or at operator discretion. These features have many uses, including correcting recurring spelling or punctuation errors, changing abbreviations to whole words, and customizing "boiler plate" documents, such as replacing every occurrence of "John Jones" in a document with "Sally Smith."

Scrolling. Scrolling allows the operator to move through a file one line or screen at a time, often in either direction. This feature allows rapid movement through a text as it is being edited.

Block Movement. Block moves allow text to be maneuvered within or even between files. Special commands are used to mark blocks of text, which, depending on software capability, may range in size from a few words to all of the text currently in the computer's RAM. The blocks may then be moved to a different location in the text. If, for example, the contents of paragraph 12 of a document would be more appropriate as paragraph 3, a few commands will accomplish the move.

Some programs allow a block to be copied as well as moved, which is useful where a line or paragraph is repeated several times. It is even possible with some packages to copy a block to or from another file on the disk (or even a different disk). Uses for this feature include easy production of "boiler plate" documents or standardized letters.

Another highly useful feature included in a few programs and available as supplemental software for others is the ability to merge files while printing. A common use for the merge function is printing customized form letters using a separate file of names and addresses.

On-Screen Formatting. The format is the appearance of the printed document, including line spacing, paragraph indentations, boldfacing, underlining, centering, and so on. Not all word processing programs allow you to see a document's format on the screen. Instead "imbedded commands" format the material as it is printed. Even with a screen that does not display a full page (and most of them don't), being able to see the text more or less as it will appear in print is very helpful for editing.

Column Mode. This feature allows easy formatting of text in columns rather than paragraphs. Some packages allow columns to be shifted around in block moves.

Footers, Headers, and Page Numbering. Most good word processing programs have provisions for headings (e.g., "Chapter IV"), footers (e.g., "Computer Nut Magazine, Vol. 3, No. 2"), and automatic page numbering. Some will even alternate page numbers on the right and left sides of the page.

Spelling Checks. These are usually separate programs, which may be included with word processors as part of a package. A spelling checker will search through a document and locate misspellings using its own dictionary. Some programs simply flag errors for later correction by you, others will allow you to choose from a list of alternative spellings or change the word yourself. A spelling checker should allow you to easily build supplemental dictionaries, including commonly used names and special terminology. Some programs even include a thesaurus. The nature of the English language places some limitations on spelling checks (Miss steak would pass for mistake, for example), but they can be very useful for correcting recurring typographical errors or misspellings of common words.

Page/Line/Column Display. Especially for long documents, it is useful if the screen displays the current location of the cursor.

Type of Files Created. The format in which your files are stored determines whether you will be able to use the data with different programs or communicate with other computers. If the program does not create standard ASCII files, find out if there is a way to convert the files to ASCII easily.

The following features may be hardware as well as software dependent:

Upper and Lower Case Display. Any serious use of word processing will require that the CRT, printer, and software all be capable of displaying lowercase letters. Sometimes this will mean purchasing additional interfaces.

Number of Characters per Line. It is possible to do word processing with a screen display of 40 characters per line, but working with a full 80-character display is easier. This also may require an additional interface.

File Limitations. The size limits of files depend on the amount of memory available in RAM and on disk, and also on the software. Some programs limit the size of files to the size of the RAM; others will leave the file on disk, calling it up as needed. For practical purposes, you will probably want to limit the size of your files to around 20K (about 10 double-spaced pages), simply because of the amount of time needed to scroll through or save a lengthy file. Documents longer than 20K can be combined after printout. Also remember that in judging disk capacity you must allow enough space for automatically created backup files and editing. A "disk full" message in the middle of an edit can be devastating.

Text and/or Printer Buffer. A buffer is a temporary storage place for characters being fed to the screen or printer. This relates to the baud rate explained in chapter 3. If the characters are being fed to the printer faster than it can print, it stores them in a buffer until it can catch up. In the same way, a fast typist may outpace the characters appearing on the CRT screen. Software and hardware with inadequate buffering may "lose" keystrokes. Since a side effect of word processing is increased typing speed, this feature should not be overlooked.

Simultaneous Editing/Printing. Some software packages allow one file to be printing as another is being edited. This capability also depends on the printer.

Print Enhancements. These include underlining, boldfacing, super- and subscripting, double-width characters, and other techniques for emphasizing text. A number of programs also offer proportional spacing, where *is*, for example, takes up less space than *ms*. Sometimes software adjustments (called "patches") must be made so that the special print commands can be understood by the printer. You may be able to have the dealer set up the printer controls for you.

Highlighting/Reverse Video. This is a combined feature of the software and CRT that sets off portions of text (such as a block to be moved) either by changing their intensity (brightness) or by reversing the text so that it appears as black on white (or green or amber). Some programs and CRTs can also display underlined or even italicized text on the screen.

Function Keys. Most recent word processing programs use the computer's function keys for a variety of commands and special features. These save keystrokes and increase the program's power and flexibility.

Electronic Mail. Some word processing packages, when combined with a modem, will transmit formatted or unformatted text directly to a receiving computer, bypassing physical transportation. If you plan to transmit documents to other computers, you will need a program that stores files in ASCII code rather than binary.

Special Capabilities. Word processors may include a wide variety of special features, including automatic footnoting, indexing and table of contents compilation, windows for manipulating text between files, arithmetic functions, automatic date and time insertion, and more. Some word processors and computers allow you to manipulate text with a mouse or touch screen. Whether such features matter to you depends on how you plan to use the program and whether you are willing to spend the extra time needed to master them.

You can use word processing in almost every aspect of library management, from compiling easily updated bibliographies and inventory lists to printing cards and writing reports and proposals. Though some of these functions may be accomplished even more readily with specialty software, word processing still represents a considerable improvement over manual methods. Specific library word processing applications are covered later in this chapter.

Specialized Word Processing (Desktop Publishing) Programs

A number of programs combine word processing with graphics and/or special formatting capabilities for producing newsletters, signs, banners, and even books. When combined with a laser printer, some of these programs can produce commercial quality documents. With an inexpensive dot matrix graphics-capable printer, an Apple II and a program such as The Print Shop, you can produce in-house signs, posters, greeting cards, bulletin board materials, newspapers, and whatever else your imagination can come up with. It may not be commercial quality, but it's lots of fun!

Database Management Systems

Database management systems form another category of software with a wide range of potential library applications. A database management system is to a filing cabinet what a word processing system is to a typewriter. Just as the word processor streamlines the mechanics of typing and editing documents, a good DBMS streamlines the mechanics of information storage and retrieval, freeing the user to concentrate on form, content, and data relationships.

If the DBMS is compared to a file cabinet, each data file is equivalent to a file drawer containing a set of records, each of which uses the same format and contains the same categories, or fields, of information. An example in a manual system would be a file of student health records, with preprinted forms filled out with information on each student's childhood diseases, vaccinations, etc. The difference is that in a computerized version of the file, records could be retrieved not only by the student name, but by any other field (or piece of information) on the form. This means that during a measles epidemic, for example, it would be possible to obtain within a few minutes a printed list of all students according to whether they had or had not been vaccinated for measles — a process that might take days if done manually.

The effect of this multiple retrieval feature is that in a DBMS one record, for all practical purposes, counts as multiple records. A card catalog, for example, requires as many as eight different cards for a single book, with one card being filed under one or more subject headings, a title heading, one or more author headings, and so on. The same catalog on a computer would require only *one* entry per book, but that entry could be retrieved by any one of several different keys — such as subject, author, or title (or publisher, copyright date, etc., for management purposes). A computer "card" catalog is a complex, specialized version of a database management system, which, because of its large storage needs, requires a hard disk system. A simpler, "generic," DBMS may be used with floppy and/or hard disks for a variety of library applications, including equipment inventory, acquisition files, teacher or student records, mailing lists (including printed labels), curriculum catalogs, and more.

In a DBMS, files, records, and keys are all user-defined. Most systems let you design your own forms, tailoring them to suit the particular record type (see figure 4.2). Once the record format has been designed and saved, the programs allow you to enter, change, or delete data by filling in the form on the CRT screen. The information may then be sorted and retrieved in a variety of different ways. Since each record is entered only once, the chance of errors is considerably reduced.

The user selects the criteria for sorting and displaying records, and for generating reports. Many systems will perform calculations according to user-defined formulas, using the data from one or more fields and storing the results in another field. A business inventory control package, for example, may keep track of the amount on hand of a particular item by subtracting daily sales, flagging the item for reorder when the amount reaches a certain level. More sophisticated systems allow manipulation and cross-referencing of data between files. Some systems may even be used to create files for use with other programs, such as mailing or spreadsheet programs.

Database management systems are more variable than word processing systems in terms of programming skill requirements. In fact, a number of them were designed with programmers in mind, and are used as the basis for more complex applications programs, such as accounting packages and online catalogs. Others require no more skills than those needed for word

```
       => DB MASTER MAIN MENU <=

  FILE NAME :  MT. VIEW INVENT

  CHOOSE FROM:

     (1) DISPLAY/EDIT/DELETE RECORDS

     (2) ADD RECORDS

     (3) LIST RECORDS TO PRINTER

     (4) LOAD OR CREATE SHORT FORM

     (5) SET UP OR PRINT REPORT

     (6) FILE MAINTENANCE

     (7) LOAD OR CREATE NEW FILE

     (8) CLOSE FILES & EXIT

   ENTER  YOUR CHOICE (1 TO 8):
```

Fig. 4.2. A sample menu screen from the database management program for the Apple computer, DB Master, a registered trademark of DB Master Associates. Reproduced by permission of Stoneware, Inc.

processing—basically disk formatting and backup procedures, and mastery of the specific program's commands (DBMS may be either menu- or command-driven). DBMSs also vary considerably in flexibility and capabilities. As with word processing, the more powerful programs take longer to learn, but can be well worth the initial time investment.

Many library-specific programs, including catalogs and circulation systems, are versions of DBMS. You may be able to find a specific package which already handles the functions you are thinking of handling with a general purpose DBMS. Alternatively, you may be able to find templates created by other people to use with a specific DBMS program. If you decide to design your own DBMS applications, the type of system you will need depends on how you want to use it and how much time you are willing to invest. Some general features to consider in choosing a database management system include:

Ease of Data Editing. The system should allow for changes in data within individual fields in a record. Some systems require deletion and reentry of the entire record, even if only one item needs changing.

Ease and Flexibility of Screen Design. Some systems allow you to design screen layouts using your keyboard, then simply save the final version. With others, you are required to visualize the screen as a grid, specifying the coordinates for each field. Many file managers simply follow a vertical format, with each field on a separate line.

Flexibility of Record Size. The system may allow records of any length up to a given maximum, or it may have rigid size requirements. It also helps to know how records are physically stored on the disk. One program, for example, may store records in 128-byte blocks, so that any amount over 128 bytes requires an entire block, resulting in a lot of wasted disk space. Also, some programs compress data by eliminating unused spaces during storage. The way records are stored will determine how many records will fit on a disk.

File Storage. Some systems will allow only one file per disk; others permit multiple files. Some systems even require two disks per file—one for storing program utilities and record formats and one for data, thus increasing the amount of information that can be stored on each disk. Of course, this method also requires two disk drives.

If your proposed application includes files large enough to require multiple data disks, and you will be searching for records by keys other than the primary key (see below), you will probably want a hard disk. Otherwise you will spend a lot of time during searches changing disks.

Ease and Flexibility of Searches. In a DBMS, records are searched according to user-defined search keys. When the record form is designed and data are entered, one field—usually the field most likely to be considered in data retrieval—is generally designated as the *primary* key. Most systems store and search records using the indexed sequential access method (ISAM)—that is, the records are stored in alphanumeric order in the file according to the primary key. For example, a file of student health records would probably have students' last names as the primary key field. The records would then be stored in alphabetical order according to last names. When the user asks for a search according to either the primary or another key, the computer would "look" at each of the records in primary key order. (In a SAM, or sequential access method system, the records are searched in reverse entry order.)

Some systems allow the establishment of permanent or temporary secondary keys. Defining a secondary key causes a second ISAM file of the same records to be set up according to the secondary key order. In the example above, teacher names might be used as a secondary key field. The more ISAM files on a disk, the less space you will have for records, so a program that allows temporary keys offers some real advantages. Relational databases allow the most flexible searches, since almost any field can serve as a key, depending on the number and types of sets in the databases.

A DBMS retrieves information in file records by one or more keys, according to user-defined criteria. In the measles example above, you may wish to find all students in the fourth grade who have not been vaccinated against measles. The search keys would include student names, grade, and vaccination information. The computer would select and display or print the names of all students in grade four whose vaccination record did not include measles.

Most programs will search on a whole or partial match of an alphanumeric character string, but the search capabilities vary. One program, for instance, might allow a search for all records with a city field that includes the letters "glen." This would mean the records for Forest Glen, Glendale, and Northglenn would all be included. Other programs have more definite requirements—a search for the last name of Smith (where the last name is defined as the last word in the field) would not pick up John Smith, Jr., since "Jr.' is the last word in that field. Other search options include ranges of values (such as all the names which begin with the letters M through S), or values with a certain relationship to a defined criterion (such as greater than, less than, equal to, equal to or less than, etc.). A search that includes multiple descriptors or asks for a range of values is called a Boolean search.

Flexibility of Report Design. Some systems will simply print out each entire record; others enable the user to design the form (including enhancements such as page numbering, headings, etc.) and determine the content of each report—all fields, one, or several. Reports can therefore be customized for a particular purpose.

Data Security. A number of systems enable you to use passwords to block access to certain information depending on the assigned level of each operator. For instance, a clerk might not be given access to the salary figure on an employee record. Some passwords allow the operator to read/only—that is, he or she can view data but not change it. Other levels might include read/write access to certain fields and no access at all to others.

Type of Files Created. The format in which your files are stored determines whether you will be able to use the data with different programs or communicate with other computers. Does the program create standard ASCII files, or does it use a unique format that will be difficult or impossible to convert? Many databases create files that can be transported to other DBMSs or even to spreadsheets.

There are numerous possible applications for database management systems within libraries. Several will be covered later in this chapter.

Spreadsheet Programs

The third general purpose program to consider for library use is the electronic spreadsheet, or "calc" program. Spreadsheet programs replace the familiar green ledger sheets just as word processing replaces typewriters and database management systems replace file cabinets—that is, they go far beyond automating everyday spreadsheet functions. They can be used not only for tallying and figure analysis, but for forecasting and "what-if" planning, since changing one variable automatically changes all the related variables. The results of calculations that would take hours and days if done manually are available in seconds.

Though frequently associated with financial planning and budgeting, spreadsheets are not limited to money-related functions. Circulation statistics, collection usage, staff time distribution, service analysis—these are just a few of the areas you could investigate using a spreadsheet program.

As the name implies, spreadsheet programs basically consist of rows and columns, which intersect to form "cells," or memory locations, the contents of which are user-defined. There are literally thousands of locations available. Each location may be filled with one of three types of data: labels, which describe column and/or row contents and are nonfunctional; values, which are variables input by the operator; and formulas or functions, which are calculated automatically from values and/or other formulas in one or more different cells.

To get an idea of how a calc program works, imagine a computerized check register, with columns for the check number, date, payee, amount, and running balance. So far it's nothing special, except perhaps for the automatic calculation of the balance. But now add additional columns for check distribution—categories such as rent, groceries, car expenses, clothing, etc., along with a row that automatically calculates the percentage of income going to each category. You could also add "what-if" and projection columns, calculating, for instance, the practical consequences of buying a new car, or the time needed to save for a Caribbean vacation. Since another feature of spreadsheet columns is the ability to replicate values across a row or down a column, you could view several alternatives at once—how does the picture change if your income increases by 10% each year, or if you save $50 or $100 more each month?

The programs allow you to set up templates for various functions, such as the check register example above, or for a monthly budget report, and then use the template indefinitely with only minor modifications (see figure 4.3).

```
              PURCHASE ORDER RECORD

    A       B      C     D          M        N

  P.O.#   DATE   VEND  AMT        BUDG.   BALANCE

                                          4000.00
    1      1/3    BTSB 120.00       3%     3880.00

    2      1/10

    3      1/10

    4      1/12

    5      1/15



    21     4/3

    22     4/4
```

Fig. 4.3. A sample screen for handling purchase orders, done with a typical spreadsheet program. Columns E through L would be labeled with amount breakdowns for supplies, equipment, books, etc., possibly further broken down by categories (e.g., fiction, nonfiction, media). Columns M and N show the percentage of the budget used for each purchase and the budget balance.

Specific data input is simple and fast, and reports which were odious chores or even unthinkable are easily produced.

Like word processing and database management systems, spreadsheet programs are not turnkey, that is, they require some time to learn. They are usually menu-driven and require virtually no programming knowledge. Mastering the basic functions takes only a few hours; exploring the more complex capabilities takes considerably longer. The more commands you master, and the more adept you become at manipulating data, the more flexible and useful your spreadsheets will be.

There are a number of spreadsheet programs available. For the most part they are comparable in terms of price and capabilities. Therefore, your choice may depend to a large extent on previously chosen hardware and software. Another consideration in choosing spreadsheet software will be the amount of memory available in your system. If this is your first software purchase and you plan to use it extensively with large files and/or complex formula operations, you will need to choose hardware with a fairly large amount of memory to take advantage of all the potential cell locations. A 64K computer effectively limits the number of cells to about 3,000, no matter what the capabilities of the software. For most uses this should be sufficient — one large library keeps its entire $1.7 million budget in a single spreadsheet file, with room left over.[1]

Some spreadsheet features to look for include:

Screen Viewing Capabilities. Since any spreadsheet will be too large to fit onto the screen, the CRT acts as a "window" through which you view different portions of the sheet at a time. Useful viewing features include split-screen capability, which allows you to work on one portion of the spreadsheet while simultaneously viewing another portion that would normally be off the screen. Another feature allows you to "lock" certain rows or columns, such as those containing labels, on the screen while scrolling other portions of the spreadsheet.

Number of Memory Locations. Some programs are restricted only by the amount of available memory; others have a fixed number of locations which cannot be exceeded.

Formatting. Flexibility may be useful here. For example, some programs let you define a column width and then automatically make all the columns the same width, while others allow varying widths within a spreadsheet. The program may also allow you to specify the number of decimal places to be displayed.

Ease of Cursor Movement. The cursor may be controlled by using the < CTRL > key and/or by various function keys; a "GOTO" command allows the user to specify a cell using screen coordinates and send the cursor directly to it. Other commands allow rows and columns to be inserted, deleted, or moved to another position.

Replication. This function allows a value or values to be copied to another part of the spreadsheet, such as across a row or down a column.

Recalculation. This is the feature that lets you play "what-if" by recalculating all entries that are functions of a value or values that have been changed.

Built-in Functions. These include the arithmetic, logarithmic, trigonometric, and logic functions that are used as formulas for manipulating data. One

---

[1]Michael Schuyler, "Visicalc: Library Uses for a Business Standard," *ACCESS: Microcomputers in Libraries* 2 (January 1982): 9, 17, 27.

useful feature not found in all calc programs is an "if-then-else" function, which allows you to set different conditions for calculating the contents of a cell. For example, *if* the age of an item is less than two years, *then* use the purchase price as its value, *else* subtract N (from another cell) dollars for each year. Other built-ins you may want to look for are: averaging, selecting the highest and lowest values in a row or column, counting, calculating absolute or net present values, and search functions.

File Merging Capabilities. Some programs allow data from one file to be merged onto another worksheet, which allows you to assemble very complex worksheets one portion at a time.

Print Capabilities. Printout flexibility of spreadsheet programs varies. Some spreadsheet programs are compatible with other types of programs, so that the calc files may be accessed by word processing and/or database management systems and vice versa. This makes it possible to produce printed customized reports. Some systems manage this more easily than others, however—you may need some special programming skills.

Type of Files Created. As with database managers, this is an important concern. Many spreadsheet programs create a type of ASCII format, called DIF, which pinpoints the cell location of each piece of data, so that it can be transported to other spreadsheets. Another type of file, SYLK, can transfer spreadsheet formulas as well as data. You may also want to be able to transfer data into a program that can display them in graph form.

Integrated Packages

Integrated packages provide two or more basic functions in one package. Lotus 1-2-3, one of the most popular of all business programs, combines a spreadsheet with a database manager and graphing capabilities. Another integrated package is Appleworks, which includes all three basic functions: file management, spreadsheet, and word processing. Some integrated packages keep the entire program, along with any data being processed, in memory; their data handling capabilities are limited by the amount of RAM in your system. Other packages keep data and program portions not in use on disk. Integrated packages often have one function which is considered primary and is therefore stronger than the other components. This may cause problems if your main need is one of the lesser functions.

An alternative to all-in-one packages is a group of individual packages designed to interact with one another. Such a series may include a word processor, a file manager, a spreadsheet, and a graphics package. One advantage of such programs is that they tend to be similar in commands and appearance; having mastered one, you'll find it relatively easy to learn the others.

MICROCOMPUTERS IN LIBRARIES

In addition to the general purpose software described above, the number of special purpose packages designed specifically for libraries continues to grow. These include online catalogs, catalog card printing programs, circulation programs, and more. There are also a number of "total system" library packages on the market. These have the advantage of being turnkey and relatively easy to use; however, they present several disadvantages, including high initial cost, a lack of flexibility—you have to adapt to the system, rather than building a system that adapts to you—a great deal of room for error, and the trauma to patrons and staff of changing your entire library system at one time.

The concepts presented in this book are aimed at building a flexible, modular system customized to the needs of your library. In the following sections, we will discuss both general and special purpose software as applied to specific library functions and services. The possibilities are of course not limited to the ideas discussed here; new applications are being tried all the time, with varying degrees of success. The aim is not to be comprehensive, but to offer a wide sampling of microcomputer potential in library management and services. Further information on specific projects and programs, including review citations, can be found in appendix B.

Acquisitions

One major aspect of the acquisitions process, selection, is to a large extent subjective. The remainder of the process consists of routine, repetitive functions such as checking lists, preparing and placing purchase orders, checking for duplications, verifying deliveries, keeping track of back orders, accounting, and so on. Many of these functions could be partially or wholly computerized with a micro, and even the subjective selection process could be aided by access to the sort of information a computer can make available. Computerizing the routine chores of acquiring library materials would make it much easier to concentrate on the content of the collection, due to time savings and control of information.

The acquisitions process begins with idea-generating activities such as reading reviews, processing student and staff requests, conducting patron surveys, and previewing materials. These sources are used to build a consideration file, something that varies widely in form and content from one library to the next, from a folder full of notes, flyers, and clippings marked by highlighting, to an organized card file.

Any type of manual file, no matter how well organized, is limited by the method for filing, unless you take the time to make multiple cards for each record. There are any number of valid, but necessarily limited, ways to "key" the file—by subject area, author, title, format, publisher, distributor, etc. So what happens when, for example, you have an author-ordered file and the jobber wants the request in title order? Or by ISBN? Or suppose, as happens occasionally, you suddenly find yourself on Monday with a chunk of funds that must be spent by Friday? To obtain a higher rate of fill, you could order direct from one publisher. Your consideration file, however, is organized by subject, and what's more, you haven't had time to update it since the last order was received.

Now suppose, instead, that your consideration file is on a floppy disk, organized with a database management program according to a screen you designed yourself. You would simply print out a list of items in the file to be ordered from a given publisher, listed according to the priority rating you previously assigned to each item. Instead of settling for rushed, nearly random selection, you use the budget windfall to order the items you need and want most. Sound appealing? It gets better.

As items are ordered and received, you can update the records in the file, so that it is always current. With a moderately sophisticated database management system, you could even transfer the relevant information into a different file of outstanding orders, and then into another of new arrivals, without having to reenter it. Since the data entry screen is your design, it is tailored to fit the requirements for your own library and district. Depending on the way you currently keep your consideration file, the screen might look something like figure 4.4.

```
                CONSIDERATION/ORDER FILE
       AUTHOR_____ CAT_____

       TITLE_____PRIOR. _____

         PUB. _____YR. ___COST_____

         JOBBER_____ COST_____

         OTHER_____

         REQ. BY_____DATE_____

         REC/REVS_____


         _____

         ORDERED___/___  REC__/___ BO__/___

         COMMENT_____ CAN___/____

         _____ DATE__/__/__
```

Fig. 4.4. A sample screen for keeping a consideration/ordering file.

By computerizing this file, you may obtain printouts by any category you wish, such as science, biography, 500s, poetry, filmstrips, back orders, publisher or jobber, and so on—quite an improvement over folders of clippings or boxes of 3x5 cards.

Caution: When you computerize any function, you will have to become very conscientious about procedures. In this case, for instance, it would be a good idea to keep a category list to ensure that you are consistent, because the computer will be.

If your first software purchase is a word processing rather than a database management package, you could use a word processing template form to print pertinent information directly onto preprinted continuous forms. Purchase order information could be typed into the template form and printed out as multiple copies or replicated with a copier. The resulting forms could serve not only as purchase orders but as check-in forms for receiving orders and reordering, and even as cataloging aids. A different template could be used to print file records for a manual consideration file—complete with duplicate records for different access keys. These applications would require a word processing program capable of reading text from one file to another, along with some time to set up the original templates. An even simpler word processing application would be compiling easily updated lists for recent or proposed orders, new arrivals, back orders, and so on. Alternatively, a spreadsheet program might be used to enter orders by categories for budget reports and projections, comparing, for example, circulation statistics with ordering patterns.

You might consider banding together with other libraries to set up a centralized ordering system, as has been done in some districts. A single microcomputer with a hard disk and appropriate software could provide complete ordering services, including simple-to-use check-off order lists and batch ordering for cost savings. A spreadsheet could also be used to organize a centralized ordering system, calculating such information as discount variables and handling time along with making "what-if" projections according to orders and reports submitted by individual member libraries. With careful and cooperative organization, orders for various publishers or jobbers could be coordinated to obtain maximum discounts and minimum confusion, while ensuring that individual libraries retain selection control.

Some jobbers are now offering computerized ordering systems, which might be used on a district level once you have developed the batch ordering process. Other possibilities include a networking system using a district mainframe and individual microcomputers equipped with modems and communications software for centralized systems, including acquisitions. (For more information on networking, see chapter 6.)

Cataloging

Cataloging is a high-visibility, labor-intensive function that provides the main means of access to library resources. It also involves several features that make it particularly suited to computerization: large numbers of records containing standardized information that must be accessed by at least three routes (subject, author, and title); repetition; high volume; and continual changes due to acquisitions, losses, damage, and normal circulation. The relatively recent acceptance of a standardized machine readable bibliographic format (MARC, or machine readable cataloging) for cataloging materials, along with technological advances in both individual and network computer systems, is changing not only the methods but the objectives of library cataloging services. Functions that might be wholly or partially computerized include: patron access catalogs; printed catalogs, including complete collections, special collections, specialized bibliographies or inventory records; catalog card production; and equipment inventories. An increasing amount of commercial software is becoming available for cataloging applications, but much may be accomplished using word processing and database management packages as well.

Library catalogs have two primary functions: to document each item in a library collection with a valid, standardized bibliographic record, and to provide patrons with a means for locating information about specific items. Because they are relatively easy to manipulate, cards and card files have been the accepted format for library catalogs for many years. However, as collections grow and information changes, the disadvantages of card catalogs become more and more apparent. They are bulky, unwieldy, intimidating to patrons, and virtually impossible to keep current—except with the aid of a computer (see "Catalog Card Production," page 93).

During the past decade, libraries of all sizes have begun computerizing certain aspects of cataloging via such centralized, large-scale organizations as OCLC (Online Computer Library Center, formerly known as Ohio College Library Center) and RLIN (Research Libraries Information Network), which provide such services as shared cataloging databases, catalog card production, centralized ordering, and interlibrary loan systems. One widely adopted practice is the use of computer-output microfilm (COM) cataloging, which may be purchased through vendors and updated as needed. These services, while making it easier to manage the volume of data, have not really changed the *nature* of cataloging. Micros, however, may have significant impact on the methods by which collection information is made available to both staff and patrons, particularly with the advent of CD ROMs and optical disk technology (see chapter 6).

Online Catalogs

Perhaps the optimum computer application for a library is an online patron access catalog, and for a growing number of libraries, this dream is becoming a reality. The advantages of an online catalog over a card catalog include not only increased access speed and ease of update (thus eliminating or at least reducing backlogs), but benefits such as access to information on nonprint items (including community resources), wider ranges of subject headings and cross-references, and more successful searches by patrons, resulting in increased use of library resources.

In the early 1980s only 3 of the 20 to 30 online catalog systems were microcomputer-based. As of late 1985, there were almost a dozen microcomputer systems available, ranging in price from $5,000 to $10,000, including hardware and software. For a new school without an existing catalog, the set-up cost is comparable to that of a card catalog—and the ongoing operational costs are less. Along with the increased software choices, improved hardware capabilities and lowered prices (especially for hard disks, a necessary component for an online catalog) have broadened the range of choices for small libraries seeking to put their collections online.

The primary criterion for an online catalog, particularly in a school setting, is ease of use. Studies of traditional catalogs have shown that the user success rate declines in proportion to the size of the catalog and increases in proportion to the number of "see" and "see also" references.[2] Another obstacle to catalog use is lack of necessary skills, including spelling and alphabetization as well as understanding of the concepts of subject, author, and title headings. This problem is not helped by the tendency for catalog headings to be other than colloquial, that is, a search for "Cars" will be unsuccessful if no cross-reference is provided to direct the searcher to "Automobiles."

A computerized catalog, if it is well designed and has a fast response time, will not be any more difficult to use with a large collection than with a small one. The only effect might be a barely noticeable (to the user) increase in response time. Further, the multiple retrieval feature of a computerized catalog makes it possible to include as many cross-references as necessary, with new references added according to expressed patron needs. At least one of the current programs was designed for elementary schools and specifically addresses the lack-of-skills problem; it is designed to search on parts of words or even a single letter, and to reinforce subject, author, and title concepts as well as encouraging the students to seek help from the library staff when they are having difficulty with a search. This patron-staff interaction is invaluable in building the *see* and *see also* references in the catalog and in evaluating library materials needs. (See chapter 9 for details on this system.)

Along with ease of use, a catalog program needs extensive search capabilities. Patrons must be able to search by subject, author, or title, just as in a card catalog; the entry screen should also include fields for additional subject headings to increase access and facilitate cross-referencing. In addition, it is extremely useful for the library staff to be able to define temporary search keys in order to locate items by publisher, call number, copyright dates, shelf numbers, etc., in order to streamline activities such as inventory, weeding, and ordering. The program should be able to generate reports by any combination of criteria, for both management and patron use. For example, it should be able to generate bibliographies for class projects, or produce a printout of 500s for an inventory.

Editing capabilities are also important. You should be able to make changes as needed, while protecting records from accidental or intentional tampering. Another potential advantage of an online catalog is the ability to receive status information, such as whether a particular item is missing, out for repair, or checked out for a long term project. If the program has "canned fields," that is, a predesigned entry screen, it should include several extra fields for status and other comments, as well as cross-references, extra subject

[2]Joseph R. Matthews, "Online Public Access Catalogs: Assessing the Potential," *Library Journal* 107 (1 June, 1982): 1068-69.

headings, and any special codes or sort keys that might be needed to customize the form for your library. It is possible to introduce variations into a present screen, as long as you keep records and are consistent. For example, if you purchase most of your books through jobbers instead of direct from the publisher, and a vendor field is not included, you could incorporate the vendor name into the publisher field, placing it at the beginning of the field so that the program will sort according to jobber rather than publisher.

If you are interacting in any way with a larger system, such as a district or regional catalog, or OCLC, the format of the catalog records becomes an important criterion. A standardized format will make it easier to exchange records. Some programs, for example, may be able to use OCLC records directly, saving hours of data entry time.

Another factor in deciding to acquire an online catalog, if you are not in a new library, is what will be done with the old catalog. If the collection is not large, you may be able to transfer all of the entries to the computer catalog within the implementation period. If, however, the catalog has many entries and/or staff time is at a premium, it might be simpler to freeze the old catalog and continue to use it in conjunction with the computerized portion, phasing it out gradually as old entries are either weeded out or entered into the database. (See the further readings at the end of chapter 7 for several articles on library experiences with retrospective conversions.) It is also helpful to use the transition period to instruct patrons in the differences and similarities between the two methods, strengthening both manual and computer search skills and concepts.

5. Backup is another important consideration. Though you *will* have a computer backup on either floppy disks or another medium such as tape cartridges, you should also have a hard-copy backup. This could take the form of a printed catalog or a stripped down (one entry per item) card catalog/shelflist.

If you do decide to implement a patron-access catalog, pay special attention to the location and appearance of the lookup station. The station should be visible and easily accessible, with appropriate lighting (bright lights make it difficult to read the screen), space for taking notes, and an attractive setting. Another way to enhance and increase usage is to keep reference aids such as posters, pamphlets, or flashcards nearby. And you will need to devote time to planning and carrying out user orientation, with introductory classes and demonstrations on how to use the catalog.

An online catalog could also be incorporated on a district level. This would necessitate a mainframe or minicomputer, which could be accessed via modems either in conjunction with in-house catalogs or through separate lookup stations in each library. As funds become scarcer, more interlibrary cooperation will be necessary to make maximum resources available to patrons. Such practices as interlibrary loans, the development of union catalogs, and centralized ordering systems may all be facilitated by computerization. It is important to note that programs that might be impossible on a building level may be accomplished collectively for the benefit of all involved.

Many smaller libraries — school, public, and special — are already participating in some type of larger online catalog system, with each library's holdings entered into the "union" catalog. Although it may not be continuously online to the main catalog, each library has access to the holdings of other participating members via a microcomputer used as a terminal, or via a COM or microfiche catalog of the union holdings. Libraries participating in such arrangements may still wish to have "in-house" computerized catalogs for their patrons, thus separating on-site resources from those available at some other location. In the near future, the union catalog could be stored on CD ROMs and periodically updated, with each member library receiving its own copies of the updates.

Printed Catalogs

For primary cataloging purposes (i.e., replacing a card catalog), printed catalogs are simply not cost effective. Paper and binding costs are high, limiting the ability to make updates. Also, printed catalogs are not convenient for patron use. However, for special purposes, printed catalogs can be highly useful. They may be produced using either a word processor or database management program, or a combination of the two.

To produce a catalog with a word processor, staff members would have to manually compile bibliographic and catalog lists. Once entered, however, the catalogs could be easily updated using insertion and deletion capabilities. Possible applications include producing book catalogs, such as one of nonprint materials, or another of community resources for staff and interlibrary use, or providing bibliographies for special projects or annual class units.

A good database management package is an excellent tool for cataloging. To a limited extent, such a catalog might be used online, though only for staff purposes and only by trained personnel. This is because the search capabilities are relatively limited in a general purpose DBMS program as compared to a specific cataloging program. Searches not only take longer but are more difficult to perform. However, for gaining control of collection information, and for producing printed catalogs for general use, a DBMS is quite practical. For collections of any size, you will need a hard disk and software that is capable of using it. Therefore, you might start by cataloging a specific part of your collection, such as nonprint, using floppy disks, and add the hard disk components at a later time. If you plan to do this, make sure that whatever hardware and software you buy is not only expandable, but that any files entered on floppy will be easily transferable to a hard disk system.

A DBMS will allow you to set up your files and define records according to field types and lengths, as well as sort and display records by different criteria. If you will be using the system to produce printed catalogs and bibliographies, make sure that it includes a flexible report generator, allowing you to sort and print using specified fields.

Database management systems vary widely in capability, cost, and ease of use. There are even some public domain programs, suitable for use with small files, that would give you an opportunity to work with small-scale, low-pressure projects. For example, a simple project bibliography form might be used to create materials bibliographies for different grade levels and subject disciplines from the same data file. This might also be a way to increase use of certain materials such as records or study prints, or to correlate your fiction collection with specific study units; for example, a bibliography of historical fiction for the Revolutionary period.

Other possible ideas include a file of important events for each month, gleaned from the back calendars of periodicals; a bibliography of birthdays of important people and the areas of interest related to them; a catalog of your vertical file or poster file; and an inventory of bulletin board materials. These and numerous other creative projects are inexpensive and simple to implement, yet can increase both the quantity and quality of patron and staff services in your library — while demonstrating the value of your microcomputer.

Catalog Card Production

Another easily computerized function that can result in both time and cost savings is catalog card printing. A number of programs are available for this purpose, ranging from simple public domain programs you key in yourself to packages that not only print complete card sets and book labels, but store the data for possible later use in an online catalog or circulation system. It is even possible to print cards using a word processing package, though it may take some time to set up a template, and the printing process will be slower since cards will have to be edited to conform to the different headings.

Specialized card printing programs may be purchased to work with most of the popular hardware types. Printer configurations are somewhat trickier, and you will have to ensure first that the software you purchase can be made compatible with your printer, and second, that the printer itself is capable of handling card stock. Although a letter-quality printer will produce the best-looking cards, it is possible to get very acceptable results with a good dot matrix printer.

A special purpose commercial card printing program may be extremely cost effective if you are currently typing and copying your own cards. Since each item is entered only once, staff time will be significantly reduced, along with copy machine rental or use costs. In addition to cards, most programs will also print card, pocket, and spine labels, and some will print shelflists as well (see figure 4.5). Some even have sort capabilities, such as alphabetically by call letters or numerically by call number; several include built-in or optional AV format modules. If you are using a card printing program as a starter project and plan to implement a circulation system and/or online catalog at a later date, it would be advisable to spend a little more now for a program that stores data in the MARC format or at least includes the ISBN and/or Library of Congress card number; it will save hours of data entry time in the future. See appendix B for information on some currently available card printing programs.

Figure 4.6 is a sample chart prepared by a librarian for evaluating card printing programs. This is an excellent method for evaluating any type of software. To determine your criteria, do a thorough needs assessment (chapter 7). To determine how each program meets the criteria, read through manuals and reviews and talk to current users — don't rely only on salespeople.

```
PART OF MENU FROM TELEMARC III

  CARD PRINTING PROGRAM DEMO DISK

PRESS KEY FOR OPTION:

1)ALIGN PRINTER      E) EDIT

2)MAKE A CARD        P) PRINT CARD SET

3)EXIT PROGRAM       R) RECONSTRUCT A CARD


     B) BATCH PRINT CARDS OR LABELS

     M) PRINT MAIN ENTRY CARD ONLY

     S) PRINT SHELF LIST CARD ONLY

     C) SORT AND PRINT MAIN ENTRY CARDS
```

Fig. 4.5. An option/menu screen from the card printing program Telemarc. Reprinted from Telemarc operator's manual, copyright 1983 by Catalog Card Corporation.

✻Equipment Inventory

✻ ———>An equipment inventory using basic hardware and a file or database management system is a relatively inexpensive and low-pressure starting project for the computer novice. There are even some public domain programs available that would be suitable for working with small files. If you are among the many library media specialists who have found themselves with prepurchased hardware and little available funding, this might be a practical and useful way to familiarize yourself with the computer while you figure out what to do next.

```
==============================================================================
The numbers 1, 2, and 3 at the left of each item indicate the
importance of each feature to the chart designer, with 1 being very
important, 2 of moderate importance, and 3 of little importance (your
own criteria may be different).  In addition, a few idiosyncrasies of
each program are noted.
```

Program:	A	B	C	D	E
1 Batch Print option	Y	Y	N	Y	N
1 Automatic formatting of added entries	Y	Y	Y	N	Y
1 Flexibility of indentations	Y	N	N	Y	N
1 Capable of using two disk drives	Y	Y	N	N	N
1 AACR2 format can be used	Y	Y	N	Y	Y
1 Fast and easy editing	Y	N	Y	N	Y
1 Menu driven ("User friendly")	Y	Y	Y	Y	Y
1 Adequate length of fields	Y	Y	Y	Y	Y
1 Hardware compatibility (esp. printer)	Y	N	Y	Y	?
1 Prints around card hole automatically	Y	Y	N	N	N
1 Displays card as it will print out	Y	Y	N	Y	?
1 Flexibility of field placements on card	Y	N	N	N	N
1 Call number length and placement flexible	Y	Y	N	?	?
1 Temporary interruption of batch printing	Y	N	?	?	?
1 Customization of sftwre to your hdwre	Y	N	?	?	Y
2 Well-written, understandable manual	Y	Y	Y	N	Y
2 Test-print to align cards	Y	Y	Y	Y	N
2 Shelf list information printed	Y	Y	N	Y	?
2 Prints second cards automatically	Y	N	Y	N	Y
2 Technical expertise of vendor	Y	N	?	?	Y
2 Price (for comparison only)	199	599	149	70	50
2 Auto. hanging indent for title main entry	Y	Y	Y	N	Y
2 Subj headings auto. print all caps	Y	Y	Y	Y	N
2 Can access an 80-column board	Y	N	N	?	?
3 Bibliography printout	Y	Y	N	Y	N
3 Prints labels	Y	Y	N	Y	Y
3 Alphabetical sort capability	N	Y	N	Y	N
3 Utilizes MARC tags to create database	N	Y	N	N	N
3 Retrieval of original data after editing	Y	N	N	N	N

```
==============================================================================
```

Fig. 4.6. Chart for evaluating card printing programs. Reprinted by permission of Susan Rosenthal, Technical Services Librarian, Oakland Park Library, Oakland Park, Florida.

If you currently keep your equipment inventory on file cards, you can use the card format as a basis for designing a data entry screen (see figure 4.7). With a database management system, you would then be able to retrieve records and produce reports according to any field. If, for example, you now file records according to equipment description, e.g., projector, overhead; projector, filmstrip, you would still be able to obtain reports organized by descriptions—as well as by other criteria, such as district identification numbers—very useful for coordinating building and district inventories.

In setting up database management systems such as this one, it is best to design a form and enter a variety of items—not over 50—and then evaluate the form before continuing data entry. For example, the most-used fields should be at the beginning of the form for easier data entry. Try out several report formats as well. You may want to keep a separate practice file specifically for

```
┌─────────────────────────────────────────────────────────┐
│                                                         │
│   DIST ID_____  CLASS/SUB_____           │
│                                                         │
│   DESC 1 _____                   │
│                                                         │
│        DESCR 2 _____                │
│                                                         │
│   BLD ID _____  MAKE_____           │
│                                                         │
│   MODEL_____  SERIAL_____           │
│                                                         │
│   PURCH __ /__ /__       COST _____ . __             │
│                                                         │
│   QTY_____  FUND _____  P.O.#_____           │
│                                                         │
│                                                         │
│   VENDOR_____LAMP_____            │
│                                                         │
│   COMMENTS_____           │
│                                                         │
│                                                         │
│   _____           │
│                                                         │
│                                                         │
│              EQUIPMENT INVENTORY                        │
│                                                         │
└─────────────────────────────────────────────────────────┘
```

Fig. 4.7. A sample screen, prepared on DB Master, for keeping an equipment inventory. DB Master is a registered trademark of DB Master Associates. Reprinted by permission of Stoneware, Inc.

testing different formats before trying them on your actual inventory files. Remember that sort time will increase as the volume of records grows, and that cassette tapes and floppy disks are limited as to the amount of data they will store.

Some of the ways this file might be used include: looking up lamp or other part types for replacement; looking up vendors for repairs or warranty replacement; looking up purchase dates for replacement planning; locating purchase order numbers for bookkeeping purposes; locating district identification numbers for comparison with district computer printouts; listing equipment to be serviced during the summer by equipment maintenance staff; and compiling lists of available equipment for staff use.

Another way to computerize equipment inventory is to set up a file using a word processing template. Equipment lists stored on disks would be easy to update using insertion and deletion capabilities, thereby saving retyping the whole list. Even though a word processing program will not sort, rearranging material on a word processor to correspond to specific requirements is much easier than using a typewriter and/or the cut and paste method. Part of an equipment list prepared on a DBMS and printed out might look something like figure 4.8.

Alternatively, you could format the list to print on labels to be placed on file cards for a manual equipment file.

With either a DBMS or word processing equipment file, you could catalog equipment as you receive it, making the data entry part of the processing routine. The information could then be updated easily for missing or damaged equipment or long-term checkouts. Yet another possibility is using a spreadsheet program to plan replacement schedules based on life expectancy and budget allocations.

```
02-02-83                          TEST LMC REPORT                      PAGE 9

LOCATION    DESCRIPTION                  BLD ID      MAKE
     MODEL        SERIAL #        LAMP               DIST I.D. #

- - - - -  FILMSTRIP - - - - - - - - - - - - - - - - - - - - - - - - - -
- - - - - - - - - - - - - - - - - - - - - - - - - - - - - - - - - - - - -

LMC-EQUIP      PROJECTOR  OPAQUE        1-80        SQUIBBTAYLOR
               7800045           ELC                31000129-X

LMC-EQUIP      PROJECTOR  OPAQUE        1-80        TAYLOR
     TS-7      7800045           DRS                31000289-X


- - - - -  OPAQUE - - - - - - - - - - - - - - - - - - - - - - - - - - -
- - - - - - - - - - - - - - - - - - - - - - - - - - - - - - - - - - - - -

LMC-EQUIP      PROJECTOR  OVERHEAD      1-80        3M
     213       422580            ENX                31000072

LMC-EQUIP      PROJECTOR  OVERHEAD      7-80        3M
     213       422566            ENX                31000073

LMC-EQUIP      PROJECTOR  OVERHEAD      2-80        3M
     213       422495            ENX                31000074

LMC-EQUIP      PROJECTOR  OVERHEAD      8-80        3M
     213       422584            ENX                31000075

LMC-EQUIP      PROJECTOR  OVERHEAD      5-80        3M
     213       422565            ENX                31000076

LMC-EQUIP      PROJECTOR  OVERHEAD      3-80        3M
     213       422567            ENX                31000077

LMC-EQUIP      PROJECTOR  OVERHEAD      4-80        3M
     213       422568            ENX                31000078

LMC-EQUIP      PROJECTOR  OVERHEAD      6-80        3M
     213       422574            ENX                31000079


- - - - -  OVERHEAD - - - - - - - - - - - - - - - - - - - - - - - - - -
- - - - - - - - - - - - - - - - - - - - - - - - - - - - - - - - - - - - -

LMC-EQUIP      PROJECTOR  SND FS VR     1-80        DUKANE
     28A63     895696            DDK                31000102


- - - - -  SND FS VR - - - - - - - - - - - - - - - - - - - - - - - - - -
- - - - - - - - - - - - - - - - - - - - - - - - - - - - - - - - - - - - -

LMC-EQUIP      PROJECTOR  VIEW/SLIDE    1-80        BELL&HOWELL
     799B      0028187           DDM                31000130


- - - - - - - - - - - - - - - - - - - - - - - - - - - - - - - - - - - - -
```

Fig. 4.8. Sample equipment printout using DB Master, a registered trademark of DB Master Associates. Reprinted by permission of Stoneware, Inc.

```
02-02-83                       TEST LMC REPORT                    PAGE 11

LOCATION     DESCRIPTION           BLD ID      MAKE
    MODEL        SERIAL #     LAMP          DIST I.D. #

LMC-EQUIP      RECORDER   TAPE,CAS   CL 4-81      SHARP
    EDUCATOR     10500510                         B-136

LMC-EQUIP      RECORDER   TAPE,CAS   CL 5-81      SHARP
    EDUCATOR     10500594                         B-137

LMC-EQUIP      RECORDER   TAPE,CAS   CL 6-81      SHARP
    EDUCATOR     10500595                         B-138

LMC-EQUIP      RECORDER   TAPE,CAS   CL 7-81      SHARP
    EDUCATOR     10500596                         B-139

LMC-EQUIP      RECORDER   TAPE,CAS   CL 8-81      SHARP
    EDUCATOR     10500597                         B-140


- - - - -  TAPE,CAS - - - - - - - - - - - - - - - - - - - - - - - - - - - - -
- - - - - - - - - - - - - - - - - - - - - - - - - - - - - - - - - - - - - - -

LMC-EQUIP      RECORDER   VIDEO      1-80         PANASONIC
    NV9300       GOHA60089                        31000105


- - - - -  VIDEO - - - - - - - - - - - - - - - - - - - - - - - - - - - - - -
- - - - - - - - - - - - - - - - - - - - - - - - - - - - - - - - - - - - - - -

LMC-EQUIP      RECORDER   VIDEO/VHS  VTR 2-80     QUASAR
               01820079                           31000110


- - - - -  VIDEO/VHS - - - - - - - - - - - - - - - - - - - - - - - - - - - - -
- - - - -  RECORDER - - - - - - - - - - - - - - - - - - - - - - - - - - - - -
- - - - - - - - - - - - - - - - - - - - - - - - - - - - - - - - - - - - - - -

LMC-EQUIP      STATIONS   LISTENING  1-12, -80    TELEX
    753-01                                        B-007-1

LMC-EQUIP      STATIONS   LISTENING  13-10,-81
                                                  B-007-2


- - - - -  LISTENING - - - - - - - - - - - - - - - - - - - - - - - - - - - - -
- - - - -  STATIONS - - - - - - - - - - - - - - - - - - - - - - - - - - - - -
- - - - - - - - - - - - - - - - - - - - - - - - - - - - - - - - - - - - - - -

LMC-EQUIP      SYSTEM 80             1            BORG WARNER
    SYSTEM 80    618126       DNF                 B-101

LMC-EQUIP      SYSTEM 80             2            BORG WARNER
    SYSTEM 80    615723       DNF                 B-102

LMC-EQUIP      SYSTEM 80             3            BORG WARNER
    SYSTEM 80    615723       DNF                 B-103


- - - - - - - - - - - - - - - - - - - - - - - - - - - - - - - - - - - - - - -
```

Fig. 4.8—*Continued*

Circulation

A quick analysis of your current circulation system will, if your library is at all typical, indicate that checkouts, check-ins, and especially overdues, are among the most labor-intensive, least rewarding, and most difficult to maintain of library functions. This, along with the inherent suitability of such tasks to computer capabilities, probably explains why microcomputers are presently being used more for circulation systems and subsystems than for any other library application. Numerous circulation programs are available for most of the popular types of micros, including Apple II series, CP/M, and MS-DOS-based systems.

The actual range of price and capability is considerable, from a very simple overdue program for about $30 to a complex and sophisticated multiple station program costing more than $30,000 (which does include hardware). Most of the programs are clustered toward the lower end of the scale, and are capable of taking on a large part of the circulation burden using basic hardware (a disk drive and a printer are necessary). Another option is designing a circulation system in-house with a database management system — perhaps using the expertise and enthusiasm of one or more students.

"Standalone" circulation systems, that is, those that do not include a cataloging component, are generally absence-based systems, tracking only items that are checked out. Depending on the program's sort, screen-search, and print capabilities, field and record lengths and quantities, and the amount of staff and/or volunteer time available for data entry, circulation computerization may range from producing regularly updated overdue lists and notices to keeping track of collection activity according to any number of criteria, including titles, patron names, dates due, classroom numbers, and teachers' names. A number of programs will print not only overdue notices, but letters and bills for appropriate distribution (see figure 4.9). If the circulation system is part of or includes at least a basic catalog component, it may also provide a means for amassing statistics on collection usage (by grade, class, season, subject, etc.), for ordering, unit planning, inventory, and other purposes. In addition, anyone looking up an item using the catalog component would immediately know its status — checked out, missing, in for repairs, etc.

Although circulation data may be entered via keyboard, bar code readers have become inexpensive and reliable enough to be used in small libraries. Bar code readers are easier to operate as well as being faster and more accurate than keyboard entry. A bar code system, however, takes more time and costs more to implement, since you must encode and label your entire collection, including book spines, card pockets, and cards. If you are printing your own labels, you must be sure that the printer and software produce labels of sufficient quality. There is also the problem of determining a numbering system. If you already use accession numbers or another type of unique identification number, you could use those; you would have to special order or print each set of labels and match them to each item. Alternatively, you could use sequential labels and attach them as items are checked out. This would necessitate creating a new cross-reference file in your database, which would consume more storage space. Also, if the number were to be used as a search key, you

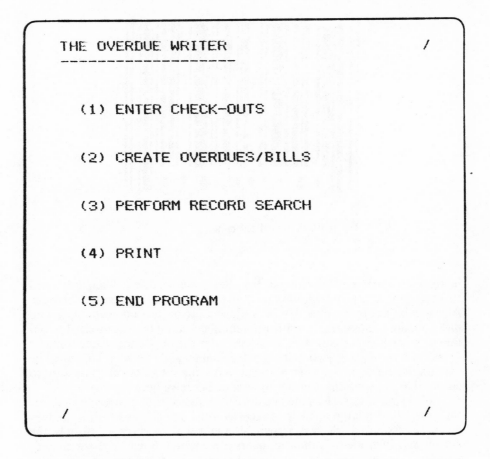

```
THE OVERDUE WRITER                        /
--------------------


    (1) ENTER CHECK-OUTS


    (2) CREATE OVERDUES/BILLS


    (3) PERFORM RECORD SEARCH


    (4) PRINT


    (5) END PROGRAM




  /                                       /
```

Fig. 4.9. Sample option/menu screen from the Overdue Writer. Reproduced by permission of Follett Software Co.

would need a separate record for *each* copy of multiple items. For patrons, however, sequential labels, possibly on library cards, would be an efficient method of identification.

One thing to consider in deciding on a numbering system is the recent decision of the Book Industry Study Group to support the inclusion of the ISBN in bar codes printed on new books. The ISBN will be incorporated into the International Article Number system, thus creating an international standard which is expected to be accepted throughout the industry. Using the same system, while it won't help with your current collection, will save you having to label new acquisitions.

A standalone circulation system that tracks only absent items will not require a hard disk; some systems use different disk storage arrangements to

Fig. 4.10. A typical bar code.

increase the number of records per disk. For example, one disk might be used to store only item identification numbers and patron identification numbers. A search by patron number would produce a list of item numbers. A second disk containing titles and identification numbers could then be inserted to obtain a list of titles currently held by a particular patron—whose name could be found by inserting a disk containing patron names and numbers. This could be very useful, for example, when a student is leaving the school and you want to ensure that all items checked out by him or her have been returned.

While methods such as the one described above involve more disk switching, they allow a large number of records to be stored on each disk, and increase access speed. Such a system also makes data entry easy—only the patron and item identification numbers are entered. Such a system should, however, contain some sort of safeguard against errors, such as requiring double keying of numbers which are then tested to see if they match.

Whatever the method used, volunteers or student aides could handle data entry either as items are checked out or in batch form. This is one application which might be used by a library that has to share its computer with other departments, or as a secondary application, since batch data entry, and even printing overdue lists and notices, can be managed in an hour or less per day. To save even more time on circulation procedures, many libraries are adopting a system whereby items are due only one day a week, or even one day a month.

In choosing a circulation system, you will have to consider such factors as the amount of staff/volunteer time available for data entry, the number of titles the system should be able to handle, and the type and amount of information you will need. A system could function quite well with as few as four or five fields: patron, author, title, date due, and, for a school, teacher. One "canned" program using these fields, for example, only allows screen searches by student, title, and teacher, and printouts only by teacher. There are ways around such limitations, however. By placing the date due in the "teacher" field, the author in the "date due" field, and the teacher in the "author" field, you could search by patron, date due, or teacher, and obtain printouts by date due (an automatic overdue list).

Using a database management program, an in-house system could be designed using the above fields, perhaps using numbers to identify patrons and items, thus decreasing data entry and access time and increasing the number of records per disk. If item cards are then filed in numerical order by date due, a title disk is not even necessary, since the title can be found in the card file as quickly as by disk switching. Overdue notices may be printed and sent out by item number as many times as necessary without reentering the information, except for the addition of a fine the second or third time the notice is sent. Libraries that have tried variations of this system report a much higher rate of return — for whatever reason, patrons seem to respond more quickly to computerized notices.

The more fields per record, and the more search keys that are allowed, the more flexible and informative a circulation system will be. However, more fields also means more data entry time and more disk space used. If you have the staff or volunteer time available, you may find the extra statistical information well worth the software and time investment. For instance, it would be useful to have fields for indicating reserved items, along with the next borrower in line.

Other considerations are whether the program allows record editing (many programs require complete reentry for changes or renewals), printout capabilities (while classroom lists might be suitable for an elementary school, they would not work in a secondary school where students change rooms and teachers, and where their library selections sometimes involve sensitive subjects such as drugs or pregnancy and therefore should be confidential), and flexibility to adapt to your particular system.

An ideal system would combine an online catalog with an online circulation system, with the status of every item and every patron constantly updated by fast, easy, and accurate data entry, and reports obtainable by a wide range of criteria. Even though such a dream system may be outside your present financial and time budget, it is a goal that may be approached in steps. At the very least, you can save considerable time, increase the rate of item return, and decrease the amount of paperwork involved with both regular circulation and interlibrary loans by computerizing the most burdensome of your circulation tasks.

Serials Control

Serials control is yet another library function that is high volume, routine, repetitious, and difficult to maintain. Computerization may be applied to any or all of the following serials control activities: check-in or inventory; circulation statistics; interlibrary loan; union catalogs and periodicals lists; subject bibliographies; routing slips/comments; subscription maintenance; and financial record keeping. These functions are available in several turnkey systems, or you may design your own system using database or file management programs and/or, to a lesser extent, word processing and spreadsheet software.

In considering whether to automate some part of serials control, you should consider the staff time that will be needed to maintain data entry on a daily or weekly basis. (Once the system is implemented, this could be accomplished with student or parent volunteer aides.) Timing is more critical with periodicals than with equipment, books, or nonprint media. Therefore, if you handle many periodicals, you may want to wait to implement any extensive computerization of serials control until after you have successfully computerized other library functions. You could, however, begin by putting a list of periodicals received by your library in a word processing file to be printed and distributed to staff members and interested patrons. The list could then be easily updated as subscriptions are added or expire.

Check-in

A file management or database program could be used for keeping track of periodical check-in and inventory using an entry screen similar to standard check-in cards (see figure 4.11).

As with any file or database management project, you should set up a trial screen, enter several items, and try some different report formats to evaluate your screen. (Remember that when designing a screen you should decide which fields will be used most and put them at the beginning for easier data entry.) The record format in figure 4.11 could be used to generate reports for inventory, weeding of outdated issues, subscription renewals, and missing issues. It could also be used to produce printed individual library and union catalogs of periodicals for staff use and interlibrary loan programs.

Other fields could be added for routing purposes, so that as soon as an issue is checked in it may be sent to the first person or department on the routing list. Routing slips could be printed either from the data file or using word processing, with space included for comments—a good way to increase staff communications.

Another file could be used for circulation control, either according to borrower name or by the name of the periodical. For example, a record form might contain fields for the name of the periodical, the issue date, volume and number, the name of the borrower, and the due date. Reports could then be printed to determine overdues, current locations of specific issues, circulation statistics (a big aid in ordering), and other useful information.

Other possibilities include the production of topical bibliographies using either a file or database management program or a word processing program, and using a spreadsheet program to compare last cost, current cost, and circulation statistics for doing budget projections and ordering, or simply to keep records of expenditures for periodicals.

The approach you take to computerizing your serials control will depend to a large extent on your current methods. Some of these systems will be relatively time-consuming to set up, but could result in considerable time savings for the staff and increased cost effectiveness in periodicals expense and usage.

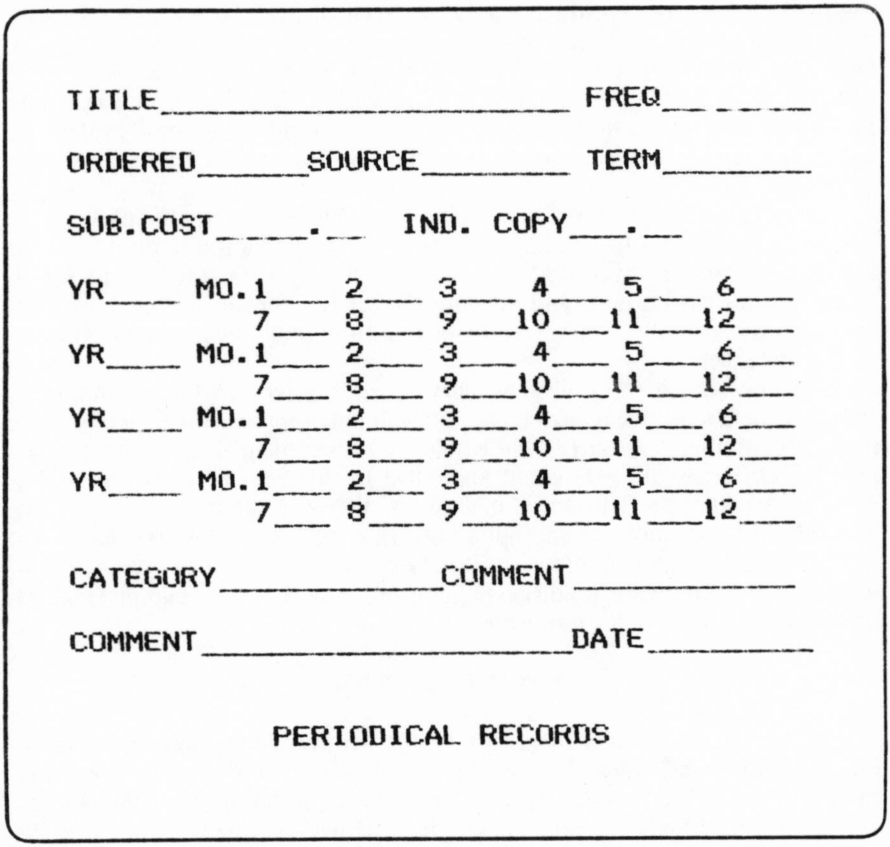

```
TITLE_____  FREQ___ __ __ __

ORDERED_____SOURCE_____  TERM_____

SUB.COST_____.__   IND.  COPY___.__

YR_____  MO.1____   2____  3____  4____  5____  6____
          7____  8____  9____10____11____12____
YR_____  MO.1____   2____  3____  4____  5____  6____
          7____  8____  9____10____11____12____
YR_____  MO.1____   2____  3____  4____  5____  6____
          7____  8____  9____10____11____12____
YR_____  MO.1____   2____  3____  4____  5____  6____
          7____  8____  9____10____11____12____

CATEGORY_____COMMENT_____

COMMENT_____DATE_____


            PERIODICAL  RECORDS
```

Fig. 4.11. A sample screen for managing periodicals.

Reference

The bulk of our discussion on reference will be covered in the next two chapters, "The Library as a Computer Resource Center" and "Networking—Connecting with the World Outside." Within an individual library, however, there are several ways in which micros and one or more general purpose software packages can aid the media specialist's role as a reference librarian. Particularly in a school setting, many questions tend to come up again and again. (No doubt you can think of several with little effort.) These questions and the answers could be computerized using either a word processing or a file management program. The material could then be retrieved either through periodically updated printouts or even through searches performed by

the patrons themselves = which would be excellent practice for later development of more sophisticated searching skills. If you are fortunate enough to
have an online catalog, it could incorporate many reference ques-
tions/answers. Setting up a computerized reference file will take some skill and
familiarity with the computer; therefore, this would be a good project to
undertake after you are somewhat familiar with both the hardware and the
software.

One reference tool familiar to media specialists but largely unknown to
patrons is the *Sears List of Subject Headings.* The guide is a natural tool for
locating *see* and *see also* headings; patrons should be taught how to use it
along with the card catalog and *Readers' Guide.* If a copy is then kept near the
catalog (card or online), many reference questions could be answered without
staff assistance.

Outside sources may also be part of your reference file. Community
speakers, field trips, local media, etc., are valuable supplements to your collection. A community resources file would be an excellent district cooperative
project. Different libraries could specialize in different types of resources,
such as speakers or field trips, and/or in different subject areas, such as
ecology, history, and oceanography. Information could then be shared by
means of periodically circulated printouts or even, if the same type of hardware is used districtwide, on disks. Other useful possibilities are union catalogs
of serials and community resources.

Administration

By administrative tasks we mean report writing, budgeting, record keeping, and any other task that does not fall clearly into one of the other
categories described in this chapter. Every media specialist must deal to some
extent with externally oriented functions, whether they have to do with accountability = to a school principal, district media center and district purchasing committee, parents and others = or, as in the case of a small rural or
specialized library, with more autonomous management tasks such as payroll.
By acquiring one or more of the three types of general purpose software, you
will be able to accomplish more in less time, provided you do not become so
enamored of data accumulation that you bog down in a pile of useless information. Many of the applications of general purpose software have already
been covered in the sections on each type, so this section will give just a brief
overview of specific computerization possibilities.

Letter Writing. Form letters, in particular, are virtually painless to produce if
you have a word processing package. Add a mailing list program and you
can customize each letter with the appropriate name and address, as well
as print envelopes and/or mailing labels. Parent and/or teacher or patron
newsletters, announcements, overdue notices, equipment requests = all
these and more may be kept in template files and modified or updated as
needed. Incidentally, a letter=quality printer is *not* a requirement. More
and more missives are being sent out with the telltale serrated edges and
instantly recognizable characters of dot matrix printers. Actually, since

they let everyone know that their writer has a computer, dot matrix printed letters are beginning to amount to a status symbol.

Reports. The bane of every administrator, report writing, can be streamlined and even enhanced using word processing, database management, or spreadsheet programs singly or in combination. Report writing is directly related to the keeping of statistics.

Statistics. A variety of statistics may be collected and analyzed with the aid of your micro. There is a danger, however, of getting carried away and compiling more data than anyone can possibly use = as a certain relative of ours discovered when he was an assistant postmaster in California. He had assigned a certain monthly report to a clerk to fill out so that he could sign it and send it on. One month he happened to notice that none of the figures had any relation to the columnar headings. A little research showed that about six months before the form had been changed. No one had noticed, from the clerk who continued to put in the figures in the original order to the higher-ups who supposedly used the reports. There is probably no way to avoid doing reports that someone else has ordered and which make little sense. These can be gotten out of the way less painfully with a computer. For your own use, however, stick to data that you can analyze and *use*.

This also holds true within individual records, whether they are part of an overdue system, an equipment inventory, or a patron file. While records must be designed with enough space in each field and enough fields for all the pertinent information (including some "spare" fields for afterthoughts), the space need not be filled just because it is there. The only exception to this is a key field which is needed for sorting. For example, if you are currently sending out overdue lists once each quarter and including prices in the list, computerizing your overdue system would require you to have a price field in each record. With the files on a computer, you would be able to make weekly lists, but there would be no need to include prices except once each quarter. Entering the prices every week would be needless data entry and wasted time.

Budgeting. This is one area in which spreadsheet programs are especially useful. As we stated earlier, there are several comparable programs available, all of which allow you to design your own templates to adapt to your own systems of budget planning, ordering, etc. For an independent library with more complex accounting needs, a general purpose small-business-type accounting package may be more appropriate. Such packages usually include several modules, such as payroll, accounts payable, accounts receivable, and so on, so that you could purchase only the modules that are applicable. Note: Accounting packages are very popular with program writers these days. Be sure to check out any prospective purchase very carefully using the criteria described in chapters 2 and 4.

AV and/or Film Management. Specialized programs are available to aid in AV cataloging and distribution (see appendix B), or you could use word processing and/or DBMS packages to keep records of AV activity (particularly useful where several libraries share materials).

Collection Profiles and Materials Retrieval. There are a number of formulas for testing text "readability" by analyzing such factors as sentence length, word length, number of different words, number of "personal words" ("you," "me," etc.), and number of modifiers. While useful, these formulas require arduous counting and calculating—tasks at which humans balk and computers shine. A number of programs are available that take care of this—some of them free, except for the time involved in typing them into the computer and storing them on tape or disk. These "freebies" are found in a number of computer and/or education magazines (see appendix B). Although many such programs are aimed at helping writers evaluate manuscripts, they are equally useful for evaluating reading levels, and some of them are geared specifically to that purpose. There are also commercial programs available, at least one of which will display the results graphically. Or, if you are at all interested in programming, you might try writing one yourself.

Since evaluating a particular text requires typing a portion of it into the computer, readability programs offer student aides or would-be typists (perhaps recruited from a business class) the opportunity to practice typing and build your collection readability profile at the same time. The profile could then be used as part of a materials retrieval system that includes other criteria such as topic, media type, publisher, and so on, either using a commercial package (see appendix B) or one designed in-house. This could be especially helpful in matching curriculum objectives with library materials and activities, in evaluating collection strengths and weaknesses according to patron needs, and in making purchasing decisions.

These are just some of the ways in which micros can ease the administrative load. Depending on your system and the talents and interests of you and your staff, you will probably discover—or invent—more. Even if you are purchasing a microcomputer system for a specific primary purpose, it would be wise to purchase and become familiar with at least one general purpose software package, even if you must "steal" computer time at lunch or after school to do so. If you are undecided as to which type of package to buy first, we suggest word processing. Virtually any library administrator will be able to discover a number of tasks that can make a word processor indispensable in very short order.

Library Skills Instruction

This section will address only software and applications related specifically to library skills instruction; general educational software will be covered in chapter 5. By library skills we mean not only the traditional skills—how to use a card (or online) catalog, how to locate materials, how to use indexes, etc. — but the newer and increasingly important skills needed to search online databases, particularly the very large and varied databases accessible through services like Dialog and The Source.

The two types of skills have several significant similarities and differences. Sitting down at a microcomputer, logging on to a database, and conducting a search strategy are closely related to tracing a topic through various references and cross-references in encyclopedias, the *Readers' Guide,* and a card catalog, except that the information is much more comprehensive, current, and faster to access.

Online bibliographic searching is becoming an increasingly common method for obtaining information in both the public and private sectors, for business, government, education, and personal use. (The nature of online database searching will be discussed more thoroughly in chapter 6.) In order to search effectively, information seekers will need to know how to develop search strategies, how to use database catalogs to choose databases and descriptors, and how to use search program commands.

These are all skills that can and should be taught alongside traditional library skills. One effective method is hands-on training using an actual database, which might be an online catalog, or a locally administered database on the district or state level. There is also at least one program* that uses diskettes provided by sources such as ERIC — such a program might provide a less expensive alternative for skills acquisition than learning online.

As of this writing, the amount and especially the quality of software aimed at developing traditional library skills is still relatively limited; however, there is quite a bit of work in progress, most of it by professional librarians working in conjunction with programmers or writing programs themselves. Programs that teach and/or reinforce such skills as the use of periodical indexes, almanacs, and card catalogs, and concepts such as classifications are becoming available. Several programs include workbooks or worksheets and many incorporate colorful graphics. The effectiveness of the programs varies considerably; previewing is strongly suggested. Library skills instructional software should be evaluated using many of the same criteria as for other types of instructional programs (see chapter 5). Appendix B contains a list of currently or soon-to-be available programs.

Preparing for the Future

This chapter should have given you some general ideas on how you might put micros to work in your library. There are many possible applications, discussed in magazines and newsletters and materializing in libraries of all types and sizes. This is one area where you can derive vast benefits from the experience of others. For example, rather than spending days or months developing spreadsheet, word processing, or database applications, you can use templates developed and tested by others. Templates exist for many popular general purpose programs. Some of them you key in yourself from a

---

*Microsearch, see appendix B for details.

printed guide; others are available on disk. Some can be had for free in periodicals or through users' groups; others may be had for a fee or the price of a book.

One highly useful resource for both novice and experienced micro users is a local or regional user's directory, which lists various programs along with current users who are nearby. One may already exist in your area; if not, start one! Figure 4.12 is a form which may be copied and circulated to libraries to be filled out and returned. The information collected could then be maintained and distributed at cost to members making specific requests, as for a list of libraries using a particular program and/or machine. (This is a simple use for a database manager = good practice.)

Finally, it is important, even if you think automation for your library is far in the future, to begin preparing for it *now*. A few simple additions and/or changes to your current methods could make automation much faster and simpler in the future. Every catalog or circulation system, for example, demands similar types of information. By using accepted standards to develop this information, you also increase your future ability to interact with other systems, which will become increasingly important as methods of storing and exchanging information change with technology.

Start by thinking of shelf cards as potential data entry forms for printed catalog cards or even an online catalog system. Most shelf cards are too brief to provide adequate data entry information for an automated system. By placing the required information on shelf cards, you will have everything you need in one place. Even if you don't add the information to existing shelf cards, include it for each new purchase/acquisition. Each card should include at least an ISBN or LC number and all subject headings. If you do not already do so, begin using accession numbers, preferably by year (e.g., 86-198). These can serve as an indication that the record has already been updated and is ready for data entry. Most important, practice being consistent. Computers are terribly picky about consistency. They notice *all* the little things = commas, spaces, periods, and articles. It's also helpful to keep written records of your entry methods.

For more information on how to begin preparing for automation, see chapter 7.

OFFICE USE ONLY:
LIBIID NO._____   C_____
SUBDATE_____   R_____
REGION_____   E_____

NAME: _____
TITLE: _____
LIBRARY:_____
TYPE: PUBL._____   ACAD._____   SCHL._____   SPEC._____   OTHER_____
STREET: _____
CITY:_____ TEL. NO.:_____/_____/_____
STATE:_____ (TWO–LETTER POSTAL CODE)   ZIP:_____
LIBRARY/ADMINISTRATIVE USE: YES____ NO____   PUBLIC ACCESS USE: YES____ NO____
ONLINE DATABASE SEARCHING: YES____ NO____   CIRCULATING MICROS: YES____ NO____
                                             CIRCULATING SOFTWARE: YES____ NO____

HARDWARE: (LIST EACH TYPE OF MICROCOMPUTER)
(Please indicate how many of each type you own.)
NAME OF SYSTEM(S):_____
_____
OPERATING   SYSTEM(S):_____
HARD DISK(S): YES_____ NO_____

SOFTWARE: (Specify programs, if you wish)   UTILITIES   YES_____ NO_____
WORD PROCESSING: DATA MANAGEMENT: YES_____ NO_____
SPREADSHEET: COMMUNICATIONS: YES_____ NO_____
GAMES: EDUCATIONAL: YES_____ NO_____
USER-DEVELOPED: INTEGRATED: YES_____ NO_____

IF YOU CAN PROVIDE DETAILED ASSISTANCE TO OTHERS REGARDING *HARDWARE OR SOFT-
WARE USE,* PLEASE INDICATE WHICH BY CIRCLING ANY OF THE CATEGORIES ABOVE THAT
APPLY.

ARE YOU A MEMBER OF A *LIBRARY* USER GROUP? IF SO, PLEASE GIVE NAME, ADDRESS & TEL.
NO. OF CONTACT PERSON FOR USER GROUP (& NAME OF USER GROUP): _____
_____

COMMENTS: _____
_____
_____

Fig. 4.12. Library Microcomputer Users Database Application Form. Reprinted with
permission of PLA Technology in Public Libraries Committee.

FURTHER READINGS

Using General Purpose Software Packages

Services

Apple Library Template Exchange.
>This service, sponsored by LBI and the Apple Library Users Group, has established a method of sharing templates for database programs. For information, send SASE to: Monica Ertel, Apple Library Users Coordinator, 20740 Valley Green Drive, Mail Stop 32AJ, Cupertino, CA 95014 or LBI Library Bureau of Investigation, 1920 Monument Blvd., Suite 540, Concord, CA 94520.

Periodicals

Anderson, Eric S. "Microcomputers and Library Management." *The Book Report* 2, no. 227 (December 1983): 12-14.
>Discusses use of word processors, spreadsheets, database programs, and online applications in the library.

"Appleworks Is Appealing." *The Computing Teacher* 12, no. 6 (March 1985): 61.
>Reactions to and hints for using Appleworks are presented.

Caine, William C. "Spreadsheet Statistics at the LRC." *Apple LUG Newsletter* 2, no. 3 (September 1984): 15.

——. "Producing Information Card for the Card Catalog Using Apple Writer II." *Apple LUG Newsletter* 3, no. 1 (January 1985): 37-40.

Crossfield, Nancy L. "PFS and PFS Report: Adaptable Library Tools." *Small Computers in Libraries* 4, no. 4 (April 1984): 1ff.
>Discusses using an Apple III for acquisitions, budget, bibliographies, and student payroll at the Geology-Geophysics Library at University of Wisconsin-Madison.

D'Anci, Marjorie. "Acquisitions with an Apple." *Technicalities* 4, no. 8 (August 1984): 9, 11.
>Discusses using PFS.

Dewey, Patrick R. "VisiCalc: Templates and Tutorials." *Library Software Review* 3, no. 4 (1985): 532ff.
>A VisiCalc overview with library applications templates is presented.

Diskin, Jill A., and Patricia Fitzgerald. "Library Signage: Applications for the Apple MacIntosh/MacPaint." *Library HiTech* (Issue 8) 2, no. 4 (4th quarter 1984): 71-77.
>Describes use in producing inexpensive signs.

Gillespie, Jim. "Fine Tuning the Book Budget with dBase and Supercalc." *Small Computers in Libraries* 5, no. 5 (May 1985): 6-7.

Justie, Kevin M. "Word Processing Software: Applications." *Apple LUG Newsletter* 2, no. 3 (October 1985): 42-44.

_____. "File Management Software." *Apple LUG Newsletter* 2, no. 3 (September 1984): 10-11.
Discusses ways to use file managers in the library. Part two appears in January 1985 issue.

Lamontagne, Therese. "Using VISICALC to Analyze Collection Use." *Apple LUG Newsletter* 3, no. 3 (July 1985): 35-38.

Mason, Robert M. "Database Management Software." *Library Journal* 110, no. 19 (15 November 1985): 64-65.
Describes some of the differences between "file managers" and "relational" database managers.

_____. "Choosing Spreadsheet and Database Management Software." *Library Journal* 110, no. 17 (15 October 1985): 54-55.

Miller, Bruce. "Key Variable Changes in a Spreadsheet Model of Library Acquisitions." *Library Software Review* (December 1984): 527-31.

ReenstJerna, Fred R. "Public Library Uses Spreadsheets for Statistics." *Apple LUG Newsletter* 2, no. 3 (September 1984): 14.

Tench, R. Terry. "Acquisition Processing with Appleworks." *Apple LUG Newsletter* 3, no. 4 (October 1985): 49-51.

_____. "Catalog Card Production Using Applewriter." *Apple LUG Newsletter* 3, no. 2 (April 1985): 55-63.

Welsch, Erwin. "Computers and Collection Development." *Apple LUG Newsletter* 2, no. 2 (May 1984). No pages available.
Some hints for using word processing and data management software.

Yerkey, A. Neil. "Small Business Microcomputer Programs: Tools for Library Media Management." *School Library Media Quarterly* 12, no. 3 (Spring 1984): 212-16.
A look at the use of general purpose commercial software.

Miscellaneous

Anderson, Eric S. "Cutting Costs with the Micro." *The Book Report* 4, no. 5 (March/April 1985): 60-61.
Includes cost computerization for manual and computerized catalog card production.

Avallone, Susan. "Trial 'by' Error Phase." *Library Computing* (Special supplement to *Library Journal/School Library Journal*) 110, no. 8, pp. 96-97; 31, no. 9 (Supplement to May 1985): 126-27.

Bacsanyi, Thomas, and Karen Bacsanyi. " 'ELL' The Education Library Locator Program." *Apple LUG Newsletter* 3, no. 1 (January 1985): 41-42.
Describes a program that allows patron to enter call numbers and proceed from there to directions for locating desired items.

Berglund, Patricia. "School Library Technology Column." *Wilson Library Bulletin* 58, no. 8 (April 1984): 571.
Discusses various ways school librarians are using microcomputers in their media centers.

Berry, John. "Library Use of Microcomputers: Massive and Growing." *Library Journal* 110, no. 2 (1 February 1985): 48-49.

Cybulski, JoAnne. "Periodicals Management with Appleworks." *Apple LUG Newsletter* 3, no. 3 (July 1985): 29-30.

Ertel, Monica M. "Small Revolution: Microcomputers in Libraries." *Special Libraries* 75, no. 2 (April 1984): 95-101.

Evans, Elizabeth A. "Microcomputers, An Interlibrary Loan Application." *Special Libraries* 75, no. 1 (January 1984): 17-27.

Fletcher, Bonnie. "Cataloging Microcomputer Software: Rules, Guidelines and Trends." *Library Software Review* 3, no. 4 (No date): 486ff.

Fosdick, Howard. "Library Microcomputers: Some Notes Gained from Experience." *Wilson Library Bulletin* 58, no. 8 (April 1984): 558-61.

Frechette, James. "Library Acquisitions on a Micro Scale." *Library Journal/School Library Journal* 110, no. 18, pp. 154-55; 32, no. 3 (November 1985): 142-43.

Kast, John. "Bar Code Handles Books for the Blind." *Bar Code News* 5, no. 5 (September/October 1985). No pages available.

Lathrop, Ann, Curtis May, and Eric S. Anderson. "The Amazing Library Computer — Two Part Series." *Electronic Learning* 2, nos. 5 and 6 (February and March 1983). No pages available.
Part one examines the computer as part of the library's educational media and as a library management tool. Part two looks at software designed specifically for library management tasks.

Lettner, Loretta, comp. "A Library Software Sampler." *Library Journal/ School Library Journal* 110, no. 8, pp. 124, 126-130; 31, no. 9 (May 1985): 154, 156-60.
An annotated (not evaluative) sampler, divided into categories: educational/school aids, information management/retrieval, specific library applications, and multiple library applications.

Lewis, J. Bryn. "Computerized Library Systems: Where They've Been and Where They're Going." *Bar Code News* 4, no. 4 (July/August 1984): 24.

Machovec, George S. "Lapsize Microcomputers for Libraries." *ONLINE Libraries and Microcomputers* 2, nos. 8-9 (September 1984): 1-5.
Applications discussed include circulating hardware, online ready reference, collection development and use in the classroom, and conferences and meetings. Specifically discusses the Apple IIc.

Naumer, Janet Noll. "Microcomputer Software Packages—Choose with Caution." *School Library Journal* 29, no. 7 (March 1983): 116-19.
Description of software is divided into categories: bibliographic management, cataloging, circulation, inventory and purchasing, readability, instruction, miscellaneous.

"Printing Catalog Cards (Some General Guidelines)." *Small Computers in Libraries* 4, no. 5 (May 1984): 2.

Rahn, Erwin. "Bar Codes for Libraries." *Library HiTech* (Issue 6) 2, no. 2 (2nd quarter 1984): 73-77.
Describes two standards most frequently adopted by libraries, Code-a-Bar and CODE 39, including terminology.

"School Librarians Using Computers." *CMC News* 4, no. 2 (Winter 1984): 7-8.
Reprint from the Omaha Public Schools staff newsletter *MFO Staff Communication* . . . information from Connie Champlin, assistant supervisor for computer education.

Steudel, Connie. "Apple Automation on a Limited Budget." *Technicalities* 4, no. 5 (May 1984): 13-14.

Swan, Tom. "Libraries Check Out Bar Codes." *Bar Code News* 5, no. 4 (July/August 1985): 38-43.

Tassia, Margaret. "Impact of Computers on Cataloging Curriculum Materials Using the Dewey Decimal Classification." *School Library Media Quarterly* 12, no. 4 (Summer 1984): 323-25.

Vavrek, Bernard. "Beware of Microcomputeritis." *Library Journal/School Library Journal* 110, no. 18, pp. 164-65; 32, no. 3 (November 1985): 152-53.

Webster, John. "Searching for Ivan Denisovitch . . . Accessing Titles by Keyword." *Personal Computing* 4, no. 7 (July 1980): 68-69.
    Discusses designing a cataloging system for avoiding this sort of accessing problem.

Yarborough, Cynthia Cox. "Library Automation at Presbyterian College." *Small Computers in Libraries* 3, no. 8 (September 1983). No pages available.
    Discusses using an Apple II+ for catalog card production, book labels, news titles listings, periodical holdings, and word processing. For more information, contact James H. Thomason Library, Presbyterian College, Clinton, SC 29325.

5 The Library as a Computer Resource Center

The application of microcomputers in the classroom is no longer coming . . . it is here, and the implementation of microcomputers for instructional purposes should be an integral part of the total instructional program . . . microcomputers, their peripherals, and their software are a part of educational technology and as such should be treated as any other component of educational technology in a school media program. It is understood that computers and their peripherals will be located in, maintained by, and circulated from the media center in the same manner as 16mm projectors, video cassette recorders and other audiovisual equipment.

Computer software . . . and the accompanying documentation will be housed in the media center and catalogued for retrieval by students, teachers and administrators in the same manner as other audiovisual software.

The media professional will be computer literate, have an understanding of computer logic, and be able to demonstrate the use of the microcomputer to students, teachers, guidance counselors, and administrators as they now demonstrate the use of other audiovisual equipment.

— From a position paper by the
Minnesota Educational Media Association[1]

INTRODUCTION

The widespread introduction of microcomputers into schools, homes, and businesses cannot help but influence the role of the library media center. First, as the supply of information grows and budgets shrink, libraries will come to rely more and more on each other and on other sources, such as online databases, to give patrons access to the most complete, current, and reliable information available. Computers offer the only viable and practical means of tapping into that vast information bank and coordinating and managing resources. In addition, as the quotation above points out, media centers and media specialists will be expected to take a leadership role in preparing students and community members for a society in which computers will be an integral part.

Recognition of the growing influence of computers has spawned a new movement in education and the media—the drive to promote computer literacy. Hazily defined, often hastily implemented, and approached with

---

[1]Minnesota Educational Media Association. "Position Paper," *CMC News* 3 (Fall 1982): 4.

everything from enthusiastic abandon to defensive hostility, computer literacy programs have become the educational fad of the 1980s. If computer-related education is not to go the way of new math and other ill-fated experiments, planning, knowledge, and forethought must take precedence over wishful thinking, ignorance, and impetuousness. Computers are here to stay, and some knowledge about them and skill in their use will be requirements for success in many career fields and even in private life.

Those who oppose the idea of computer literacy programs (though not necessarily the idea of computers themselves) have used several analogies meant to illustrate the silliness of learning about computers in order to use them. For instance, in order to use a bicycle, a car, or a telephone, students would have to acquire "bicycle literacy," "automobile literacy," and "telephone literacy." First they would learn the history of the bicycle (car, telephone), then all the parts and how they work, and *then* a few students would be able to try going for a ride or making a call. Actually, some knowledge of the workings of a bicycle or a car is useful for becoming a skilled, responsible, and safe vehicle operator—it is handy to know how to change a tire, or to talk knowledgeably with a mechanic—and driver education and bicycle safety programs bespeak society's recognition of the need for people to learn at least minimal operating skills before venturing out on the road. Also, anyone who has spent much time on the telephone can understand the (mostly unmet) need for teaching telephone skills. It may also be argued that it is very important for people to understand the influence and uses of automobiles, telephones, and even bicycles in society. Similarly, some working knowledge of computers is useful for operating them, and knowledge of computers as they affect society is desirable from both an individual and a societal point of view.

Whether it is called "computer literacy," "computer awareness," or something else altogether, the need to achieve it on a widespread basis is becoming more and more apparent. Perhaps the best definition is the one contained in the Minnesota Educational Media Organization position paper quoted on page 117: "A computer literate person may be defined as one who knows what a computer is—and what it isn't; why computers exist and how they influence people's lives: how computers are being used; what computers do and what they cannot do."[2]

Most definitions seem to concur that computer literacy includes some ability to operate microcomputers, but there is considerable debate on whether it also includes the ability to program. Like drawing, or music, or writing, programming is a specialized skill best performed by people with certain personality characteristics and at least some measure of talent. Though most people can learn programming basics, proportionately few will be interested in pursuing programming further, and fewer still will make it a career. In addition, the costs involved in teaching every student to program would be enormous—one estimate places the equipment bill for the United States alone at a billion dollars, and that figure does not include software or instructor costs.[3]

---

[2]Ibid.

[3]Jerry L. Patterson and Janice H. Patterson, "Teaching Computer Literacy in Schools: The Promise and the Reality," *Educational Computer Magazine* (July/August 1982): 19.

It is equally unrealistic to expect, as some have predicted, that every student will have a microcomputer by 1990, or even 2000, or that computers will replace teachers, or, for that matter, librarians. A realistic approach to the need for education *about* computers and the possibilities of education *using* computers will have to take into account many factors, including the technological, financial, sociological, and even psychological capabilities and limitations of schools, libraries, educators, administrators, and students. It is also crucial that the old-fashioned but still important basics of reading (*especially* reading), writing, arithmetic, history, etc., do not get lost in the rush to become computer literate. Voice capabilities aside, any individual who cannot read will be very limited in his or her ability to use a computer.

COMPUTER-RELATED SERVICES

Given all these considerations, how can media centers promote computer literacy and fulfill their new role as computer resource centers while still providing—perhaps even expanding—the necessary traditional services? Some possibilities were discussed in the last chapter, such as using microcomputers to lighten administrative burdens, leaving more time and energy to devote to patron services, including instruction about and with computers. Chapter 6 discusses the possibilities offered by networking and access to large databases, both online and via optical disk technology. This chapter discusses a variety of computer services libraries can provide directly to patrons. The ideas here are by necessity very general. Since the first edition of *Micro Handbook,* a variety of computer awareness and resource programs have been developed in school and public libraries. The "Further Readings" section at the end of this chapter lists articles about both successful and unsuccessful programs in the areas discussed in this chapter. A few books on computer services are included in appendix B; it would be impossible to cite them all. Columns in periodicals such as *Library Journal/School Library Journal, American Libraries, Wilson Library Bulletin,* and others regularly include descriptions of computer activities and programs that involve libraries as computer resource centers. It is important for library staff members to read and contribute to these journals. Sharing our experiences—both successes and failures—will assist all libraries in their efforts to best use the new technologies for the benefit of their patrons.

The following sections discuss services being provided.

Maintain and Circulate Hardware

Many public and school libraries now offer some level of public access to computer hardware and/or software. Sometimes schools, public libraries, and community organizations work together to develop a means of providing access. On-site availability, either free or with coin-operated machines, is the most common means of getting the public and the computers together, with computers available to anyone who has a library card and has taken a short orientation class on how to use the system. A relatively small number of libraries actually circulate hardware, in some cases requiring only a library card, in others requiring a fee comparable to that charged for VCRs. Many school libraries circulate computers to classrooms just as they would other types of equipment, perhaps allowing teachers to take them home overnight or on weekends.

If only one or two computers are available to serve an entire school or community, schedules and priorities will have to be carefully planned. You certainly could not teach every student to program. The possibilities would then be to limit use of the computer either to gifted and talented students, and/or to remedial or educationally handicapped students, or to find an application such as an online catalog, which would allow everyone to use the computer and gain some idea of its capabilities. Lunch hours and after school time could be used to provide access to those willing and eager to learn more, perhaps through a computer club. If the *primary* purpose in acquiring the computer is to promote computer literacy, you could either incorporate computer awareness classes into regular library instruction or circulate equipment to classrooms for special teacher-conducted units, with the media center acting as a coordinator. (See "Arrange Interlibrary Loans" on page 125.)

Maintain and Circulate Software

Computer software may be cataloged, shelved, and checked out like films, tapes, or other software. However, extra precautions will be necessary due to the special vulnerability of disks. A noncirculating backup collection is essential. Documentation should be circulated with the disks — standard three-ring binders work well, with special plastic pages, obtainable through computer supply catalogs and vendors, for holding disks. It is also a good idea to "write-protect" disks by covering side notches with special tabs made for that purpose (usually included in boxes of new disks). Other considerations in circulating software include precautions against illegal copying and ways of ensuring safe and prompt return of disks. These are problems that are just beginning to be addressed by media specialists, and as yet there are no clear answers. One approach, of course, is to limit software use to library or school premises. Other possibilities include security deposits, or special library cards which can only be obtained by signed agreements to care for disks properly, refrain from copying them, and return them promptly. As more libraries have acquired and begun to circulate software, a variety of methods have been and continue to be developed, providing a popular topic for periodicals and newsletters. One problem with software circulation, that of copyright protection, is discussed in chapter 8, "Computer Ethics."

Provide Evaluations and Information
on Hardware and Software

Just as you now locate filmstrips, records, books, and periodicals to meet specific objectives, you may be expected to locate and evaluate computer equipment and programs, both for library and general use, and to provide instruction. Major sources for descriptions and reviews of computer-related products are periodicals and current users. Caution: Reviews do not always give enough information for you to actually evaluate a program. What they should provide is enough information for you to decide whether you want to investigate a program further. In the case of software, if at all possible, try to obtain preview privileges, either by trying demo programs or by purchasing programs that have some sort of return policy. If you order software for preview and do not purchase it, be sure to include a letter, or even a note, telling the manufacturer *why* you are returning it. Such information will help spur the development of software that does meet your needs.

In the previous chapters, we discussed a number of criteria to consider in choosing hardware and software. See the "Further Readings" and appendix E for more information about developing your own software evaluation criteria and sources for evaluations and review. If, as is likely, you are asked to help evaluate instructional software (also called courseware), you will need to consider some additional factors. Finding quality educational programs can be even more difficult than locating other types of software. It would be a waste of money and hardware to purchase software that is no more effective than an inexpensive workbook or that actually has more negative than positive results. The information below will provide some helpful guidelines for choosing instructional programs.

Computer-assisted instruction, also known as CAI, generally falls into one of four categories: drill and practice, tutorial, simulations, or games. Programs range from what are essentially mechanized workbooks to sophisticated exercises requiring complex problem-solving skills and strategies. In computer-managed instruction (CMI), the programs include some means for evaluating student progress, ranging from displaying a score on-screen for each program session to keeping cumulative records for each pupil by name. Some programs allow the instructor to regulate each student's progress by giving him or her access to certain lessons each time the program is used, or offer some other means of controlling the interaction between the computer and each individual. CMI programs may also provide for printouts of scores and evaluations.

Before beginning to shop for instruction programs the involved teachers and administrators, including the media specialist, should develop a clearly defined set of objectives for computerized instruction. Which students will be involved and to what extent? Is the focus to be remedial, accelerated, standard, or a combination? What will be the program goals? Do they meet an existing curriculum need? Is computerized instruction an appropriate way to achieve them? How will the program be evaluated? Once armed with the answers to these and other questions, you will be able to study periodicals, catalogs, and vendor suggestions for software that might meet your objectives. Remember to consider each program in the context of the way it will be used. What is exciting and appropriate for a fifth grader might be boring and silly to a high school freshman.

A large part of the evaluation process will be subjective, based on the evaluators' perceptions of curriculum objectives, student needs, and computer capabilities. The primary criterion, of course, is whether or not the program achieves the intended objective—that is, does it teach what you want to teach in a way that encourages, motivates, and reinforces learning. Some other features to consider follow:

Error Response. Screen messages such as "That's not it, dummy!" (they do exist) or buzzes, bells, or beeps do not encourage learning. Audible responses have the added disadvantage of advertising to anyone within hearing that the user has made a mistake. A simple message such as "No, that's not it. Try again," is quite sufficient for a drill and practice program. Tutorial programs should allow students to reinforce necessary concepts without belittling them. Any kind of insulting, derogatory, or sarcastic response should automatically eliminate a program from consideration. On the other hand, some programs actually encourage wrong answers with clever graphics or sound effects. These, too, should be avoided.

Feedback and Rewards. Look for programs that give positive reinforcement through screen messages, graphics, or combinations of the two. (Although sound effects can be fun, they can also be extremely distracting to others in the vicinity. If the program does use sound, make sure it can be turned off if necessary.) Many programs can provide personalized responses by having the student type in his or her name at the beginning of the session. Messages such as "That's great, Jeff! Now try this one," are exciting and motivating. Tutorial programs should let the student progress at a rate that is challenging but not frustrating, while games and simulations should give users clear and understandable responses to their actions.

Content Validity and Presentation. An astonishing number of programs contain factual, grammatical, and spelling errors. Watch for them. The manner of presentation also affects a program's effectiveness. The sequence in which information is presented, patterns, etc., should reinforce what is being taught by more traditional methods. This can best be judged by someone accustomed to teaching at the level the program is designed to reach. Programs are more likely to be effective if one or more experienced teachers had a part in their authorship—even the best-intentioned and most creative programmers do not necessarily know what constitutes effective teaching methods. A program may be very clever and creative yet have serious defects which are only apparent to someone with actual classroom experience. Some teachers may prefer to write their own programs, using an "authoring program." These are basically preformatted instructional programs that allow a teacher to write the content, including potential user responses and the appropriate program actions. No programming knowledge is necessary to use authoring programs; the only language needed is English. Another idea that has proven successful for at least one school district is to have older students write programs for younger ones. This is a great way for different students to be learning about computers and with computers at the same time.

Program content should also be evaluated on ethical and "humanizing" grounds. Racial, ethnic, and religious prejudice, whether blatant or subtle, has been known to crop up in programs. If at all possible, the program should encourage cooperative behavior and reinforce positive social skills. At the very least, it should not reinforce negative ones.

Ease of Use. Instructions should be clear and easily understandable. Students should be able to use the program by following screen instructions without having to consult a manual, although accompanying workbooks may be useful. The level of difficulty should be appropriate for the potential users. A program for first graders, for example, should not contain a lot of text.

Documentation. This should be geared to the instructor rather than to the student, and contain instructional objectives, activity suggestions, explanations for teacher use of student evaluation tools, and so on.

Response Time and User Control. Too short a response time can be frustrating and discouraging; too long a time results in boredom and impatience. Also, the user should be able to control such factors as the rate of screen advance rather than trying to match a built-in pace.

Bombproofing. The program should not bomb just because a user inadvertently presses the wrong key. This could be devastating, especially for a first-time or timid user.

Use of the Capabilities of the Computer. Graphics, interactive one-on-one responses, and unending patience are computer fortes and should be used as fully as possible.

Consistency. This should be in all of the above factors. It would probably be helpful to all staff members to set up a software evaluation file, which could range from a simple card file, to a looseleaf notebook, to a database management file using the media center microcomputer. If standardized forms are provided (see appendix E for examples), staff members could be encouraged to evaluate different software packages and contribute their findings to the file.

Provide Computer Reference Material and Resource Information

Whether or not you have a micro in your library or media center, you can provide information about computing for patrons, teachers, and administrators. A "computer corner" could include books, periodicals, pamphlets, video or cassette tapes, and names, addresses, and phone numbers of organizations or individuals to contact for advice and information. These resources can provide general and specific information about computer hardware and software, from background, descriptions, and reviews to how-to's, including not only how to use a computer, but how to find software and hardware. Don't forget to include information about the wealth of public domain software available and about local and national users' groups. These groups, formed around a variety of common computer interests such as profession or the use of a particular program or brand of computer, are a valuable source of information and support. Interlibrary loans are another excellent source of reference material, as are the newsletters being published by a number of national and local educational, library services, or computer-oriented groups.

In the last few years, market "shakeout" has greatly reduced the number of general computer magazines. Most of the computer periodicals are now aimed at specific audiences by profession (libraries, educators, specific businesses) or by a particular type of computer or software application. This makes it more difficult to decide which publications should be offered in a general interest library. Appendix B lists the most enduring and best general periodicals, as well as a number of other types of resources. You may also be able to find local users' groups or individuals who would be willing to donate to your collection subscriptions to periodicals addressing their special interests.

You may also find community members (including local dealers) willing to provide information sessions on a variety of computer-related topics, including demonstrations. Many people are more than willing to talk about their experiences for an interested audience. Interlibrary loans are another excellent source of reference material, as are the newsletters being published by a number of national and local educational, library services, or computer-oriented groups (see appendix B for list).

Another way to serve as a resource center is by distributing information in the form of newsletters, posters, and flyers—produced, naturally, using your new computer system. Newsletters have long been recognized by businesses, and are beginning to be used by large libraries, as an excellent form of public relations. As mentioned in chapter 4, there are a variety of very inexpensive (under $50) combined word processing and graphics packages that may be used to produce attractive and attention-getting documents. If you decide to produce a newsletter, make sure that it is attractive, as well as lively, interesting, and well written. Unlike a staff newsletter, it should be geared to public interests and work toward dispelling the stereotyped images of libraries and librarians as dusty, musty, and intimidating. It should let people know what wonderful things are happening in your library, and encourage them to take advantage of its services. Another way to provide information, and gain free publicity, is by submitting articles, or even a regular column, to a local newspaper.

You don't have to do these projects yourself. Enlist volunteers through Friends of the Library, school or local clubs (especially the computer club), parent and teacher organizations, writing and art classes, and users' groups. You might also join with other libraries in the school district or community to plan for and provide computer-related and public relations services.

Arrange Interlibrary Loans

As rising costs and budget restrictions place more limits on the size and scope of individual library collections, interlibrary loans are becoming more and more essential for providing quality patron service. In addition to the loan assistance provided through information services such as those listed above, many libraries are discovering the rewards of networking on local, state, and national levels. For example, the 1980 *Directory of Library Networks and Cooperative Library Organizations* lists over 600 different groups whose participants are "primarily or exclusively libraries . . . [engaged] in cooperative activities that are beyond the scope of traditional interlibrary loan services . . . [and] extend beyond reciprocal borrowing [and operate] for the mutual benefit of participating libraries."[4] Activities include acquisitions, cataloging, consulting, equipment sharing, research, warehousing, and more. You might begin with small-scale, localized activities such as exchanging (computerized?) bibliographies of special collections or popular topics with other libraries in your area, or "stretching" limited computer equipment and software by having a centrally located computer lab. Such cooperation can potentially expand the quality and quantity of services each library may offer to an almost infinite degree. For more information on interlibrary cooperation and services, see chapter 6.

Provide Patron and Staff Instruction

This could range from simple orientation classes as a prerequisite for using the media center's computer to a complete K-12 computer literacy program. The type and depth of instruction will depend upon who will be using the computers and to what extent, and your community or school district's computer-related educational priorities. You might provide open classes for parents or other community members in the evenings or on weekends, perhaps using some of the more able and enthusiastic students as instructors (See "Sponsor Computer Club," below). Other potential instructors include parents, dealers, or other local computer enthusiasts. By charging nominal fees for such sessions you could even raise money for additional hardware and software purchases. Some topics and skills to cover include the following:

- History, capabilities, and limitations of computers

- Hardware use

- Software use

- Programming

---

[4]*Directory of Library Networks and Cooperative Organizations 1980* (Washington, D.C.: National Center for Education Statistics, 1981), vii.

- Information retrieval via computer, including database searching skills

- Selection of hardware and software.

A great deal of instruction can take place without actually using computers. Keyboarding skills, for example, may be taught using standard electric typewriters, or even cardboard mockups, for all or part of the instruction, at considerably less expense. If typing tutorial programs are used, students could practice on the typewriters and use the computer for taking tests.

Similarly, basic programming skills can be taught using activity books and classroom instruction, with computers, if available, being used only for the final testing of student solutions. Other techniques that have been used successfully include printed practice "keyboards" and exercises in which students act out various computer functions.[5]

The development of full-scale computer literacy curriculums goes considerably beyond the scope of this book. However, since media specialists should be involved in such planning at both school and district levels, we have included a number of resources on the subject in appendix B and in the further readings at the end of this chapter. You will find these particularly useful if budget and staff restrictions cause the media center to do double duty as a computer center.

Sponsor Computer Clubs

Computer clubs are an excellent way not only to increase computer usage and awareness but to enlist volunteers for such projects as holding classes for parents and community members, tutoring, writing programs, and raising money for more equipment and software. Some of the sharpest and most creative programmers around are seventh and eighth grade students who spend every possible moment in front of a microcomputer. Why not use their talents and enthusiasm? It's quite possible that they could write programs for use in the school or library, and then market them. Tutoring programs in which students teach parents, other students both older and younger, and even teachers, have proven enormously successful in several schools and could work equally well in public libraries. In addition, computer club members could use their skills and the library's or school's computer(s) to raise money. Other ideas include public awareness campaigns, with open houses and demonstrations, community newsletters, and career exploration. Some of the larger computer companies, such as Apple and IBM, have personnel and materials available to assist in organizing computer clubs. Community computer groups may also be a viable resource for help with school or library-sponsored activities. Computer enthusiasts tend to be quite self-directed — you might find that the staff time investment for sponsorship could reap some surprising rewards.

---

[5]Barbara Feddern, "Playing Computer, a Computer Literacy Activity for the Elementary Grades," *The Computing Teacher* 9 (October 1981): 57-59.

Provide Computer-Related Services
to the Handicapped

Microcomputers offer special advantages to the physically handicapped. For example, touch sensitive screens and/or keyboards are easier to manipulate than pencil and paper. Voice synthesizers, braille keyboards, and other features may be incorporated into micros to offer new capabilities and open new vistas for those who lack speech, vision, or hearing, or have limited movement. Considerable work is being done now to use the special properties of micros to supplement the abilities of physically and learning disabled children and adults and to teach them the skills they need to become productive and self-sufficient members of society. Information on technology-related (including microcomputer) services, products, and programs for the handicapped is available through a number of sources, including at least one online electronic bulletin board and a semimonthly newsletter (see appendix B for details). Topics range from computer-assisted instruction for the deaf to computer-driven wheelchairs to special computer input devices for quadriplegics. These and related projects represent some of the most exciting and promising applications of micros, and if your library or media center serves disabled students or community members, you should subscribe to one or more of the pertinent information services.

Provide Information on Community Resources

This could be a good computer club or class project. It could be anything from an online community bulletin board to regular printed lists or newsletters giving information on all sorts of resources, including local media, clinics, support groups, museums, business leaders, workshops, jobs, and special events. It could even include a computer user's directory such as that mentioned in chapter 4. Such services could be offered to the public at a slight charge (another fund-raising possibility) or, instead of charging money, why not "charge" a contribution to the resource list?

Although the computer age will place new demands on nearly everyone in our society, it will also open up wonderful opportunities for increasing our knowledge and capabilities to a degree we are just beginning to visualize. Libraries and media centers can and should be leaders in bringing new resources within reach of their patrons, not only by making those resources accessible, but by providing the skills and knowledge necessary to use them.

FURTHER READINGS

Miscellaneous

Atkinson, Hugh C. "It's So Easy to Use, Why Don't I Own It?" *Library Journal* 109, no. 10 (1 June 1984): 1102-3.
Discusses interlibrary loan and resource sharing.

Bardes, D'Ellen. "Video Technology: Conveying Information Visually."
   Wilson Library Bulletin 59, no. 8 (April 1985): 523-26.
   Discusses companies using videotapes for computer training. Includes
sources for tapes, such as "The Video Training Series for Educators on the
IBM-PC."

Boddie, John B. "A Tour of Babel." *The Computing Teacher* (December/
   January 1984-85): 8-11.
   Includes a description of the various computer languages, their strengths
and weaknesses.

"Building a Software Library." *Electronic Learning* 2, no. 2 (October 1983):
   77-85.
   "How do you create a library of software that meets your needs—and
doesn't break your budget?"

BYTE 9, no. 13 (December 1984): Entire issue.
   This issue is dedicated to Apple—history, software and hardware reviews.

Crawford, Walt. "Common Sense and Computer Magazines . . ." *Library
   HiTech* (Issue 8) 2, no. 4 (4th quarter 1984): 61-69.

Dunlap, Dorothy. "Exploring the Use of Microcomputer in the Elementary
   Library." *CMC News* 4, no. 2 (Winter 1984): 5.

Graf, Nancy. "Computers and Media Centers—A Winning Combination."
   The Computing Teacher 11, no. 9 (May 1984): 42-44.

Kayser, Roger, and George King. "7 Steps to Buying Better Software."
   Electronic Education 3, no. 6 (March 1984): 14, 56.

Mojkowski, Charles. "10 Essential Truths to Help You Plan for Technology
   Use." *Tech Trends* 30, no. 7 (October 1985): 18-21.
   Presents ten "truths" to be addressed by educators in order to "realize the
potential of educational technology" while recognizing that computers will not
solve every educational problem.

Collection Development

Baker, Patti R. "Adoption of a Computer Software Cataloging System at an
   Elementary School." *School Library Media Quarterly* 13, nos. 3 and 4
   (Summer 1985): 208-14.

Fisher, Glenn. "Creating a Software Review Collection." *The Computing
Teacher* 12, no. 5 (February 1985): 22.
   Procedures for organizing a central review center are presented.

Johnson, Jerry. "Film Reviews: Beware . . . Read with Caution!" *The Computing Teacher* 11, no. 4 (November 1983): 32-35.
Presents guidelines for reading and writing reviews.

Lathrop, Ann, and Janice Marshall. "Mail-Order Distributors with Liberal On-Approval Policies." *The Computing Teacher* 12, no. 9 (June 1985): 31-33.

Microcomputer Software: A Buyer's Guide to Language Arts Programs." *School Library Journal* 32, no. 6 (February 1986): 42-57.
Contains announcements of new microcomputer programs. To be published three times a year, covering different subject areas. "Many of these items will be critically reviewed during the year in the Computer Software Review section of *SLJ*."

Rappaport, Susan. "Software for the People." *Library Journal* 110, no. 2 (1 February 1985): 56-58.
Article "discusses development of software collection at the New York Public Library for use with public access computing services."

"Selecting Computer Software—We Take It Seriously!" *The Computing Teacher* 12, no. 2 (October 1984): 63.

Circulation of Software and/or Hardware

Armour, Jean. "Software Circulation Success." *Small Computers in Libraries* 4, no. 8 (September 1984): 6.

Berglund, Patricia. "School Library Technology." *Wilson Library Bulletin* 60, no. 6 (February 1986): 39-40.
In this column, how several different libraries handle circulating computer software in the schools and community is discussed.

Bryant, David S. "Circulating Personal Computers." *Library Journal/School Library Journal* 110, no. 18; 32, no. 3 (November 1985): 149-51.

Cohen, Doreen. "Software Library." *Small Computers in Libraries* 5, no. 9 (October 1985): 26-27.
Article includes information about what happened to the ComputerTown project at the Menlo Park Library.

"Computers on Borrowed Time." *Personal Computing* 8, no. 7 (July 1984): 52-56.
Discusses micros for patrons in public library in New Jersey.

Dewey, Patrick R. "Public Access Micros." *American Libraries* 15, no. 10 (November 1984): 704.
"A little equipment can serve scores of walk-in patrons and a whole community of dial-in participants."

Fowler, Bonnie S., and Duncan Smith. "Microcomputers for the Public in the
    Public Library." *Information Technology and Libraries* 2, no. 1 (March
    1983): 46-52.

Hayes, Jack. "The Library That Lends out Its Computer." *Personal
    Computing* 9, no. 10 (October 1985): 15.
    Public library in Andover, Massachusetts lends computers and computer
software.

Julien, Don. "Expanding Service: Public Access Microcomputers." *Wilson
    Library Bulletin* 59, no. 6 (February 1985): 381-85.

"Managing the Library's 'Apples'." *Library Insights, Promotion and Programs*
    (February 1984): 2.
    Article discusses necessity for policy adoption by libraries deciding to in-
corporate computers for public use.

Pearson, Tom. "Public Access Computer in the Small Public Library." *Apple
    LUG Newsletter* 2, no. 3 (September 1984): 18-19.

Rockman, Ilene. "Microcomputer Circulation in Libraries." *Library Software
    Review* (December 1984): 497-500.

Smisek, Thomas. "Circulating Software: A Practical Approach." *Library
    Journal/School Library Journal* 10, no. 8, pp. 108-9; 31, no. 9 (May
    1985): 138-39.

"Software Circulation at Liverpool (New York) Public Library." *Apple LUG
    Newsletter* 2, no. 3 (September 1984): 12-13.

Using Computers to Improve Patron Services

Beserner, Sue, and Randy Gadikian. "Indexing Phone Directories with
    dBase II." *Small Computers in Libraries* 4, no. 6 (June 1984): 1ff.

Emmens, Carol A. "Computer Programs for Video Production." *School
    Library Journal* 32, no. 3 (November 1985): 46.
    Microcomputers assist with video productions: scheduling, budgeting,
and scripting.

Flender, Molly. "A Popular Database." *School Library Journal* 32, no. 2
    (October 1985): 68-69.
    Discusses how one elementary school uses PFS File for "reviews" by
students.

Goldhor, Herbert. "Patrons Use Micros to Answer Library Survey."
    American Libraries 16, no. 9 (October 1985): 668.
    Patrons answered questions directly onto Apple Microcomputers. The
program used is available.

Jacobson, N., N. Sturr, and K. Low. "The Automated Reference Desk."
American Libraries 15, no. 5 (May 1984): 324, 326.
Article describes three ways libraries can use computers to enhance
reference services.

Kane, Matthew J. "Database Management for Interlibrary Loan." *Information Technology and Libraries* 3, no. 3 (September 1984): 297-99.
Describes implementation of ILL system using PFS, Apple III, and 5 MB
hard disk.

Rosenberg, Victor. "Word Processing for Library Patrons." *Library HiTech*
(Issue 6) 2, no. 2 (2nd quarter 1984): 25-26.

Resources for the Handicapped

Baker, Phyllis. "RESOURCE ROUNDUP: What's New for Special Ed
Kids?" *Classroom Computer Learning* 6, no. 2 (October 1985): 50-59.
Some of the newest and best resources about technology in special education are discussed: software, hardware, vendors, and associations. Portions
are reprinted with permission from the February/March edition of *Closing the Gap*. (See page 234 for ordering information.)

Bekiares, Susan E. "Technology for the Handicapped . . ." *Library HiTech*
(Issue 5) 2, no. 1 (1st quarter 1984): 57-61.
Includes citations to recent sources, both books and articles, dealing with
problems of providing library services to the disabled (especially the visually
impaired) and to sources which describe technological equipment in detail.

Training/Instruction

Class/Workshop Materials

International Council for Computers in Education.
ICCE has five complete packets: "Software Selection, Evaluation and
Organizations"; "Ethical Issues in Computer Use"; "Logo"; "Ideas, Reviews
and Resources: A Beginner's Packet"; and "Teaching Process Writing with
Computers." For information, write ICCE, University of Oregon, 1787 Agate
Street, Eugene, OR 97403.

Periodicals

Bitter, Gary. "Computer Labs—Fads?" *Electronic Education* 4, no. 7
(May/June 1985): 17, 35.

Duncan, Carol S. "Compulit: Computer Literacy for Tacoma." *Library
Journal* 109, no. 1 (January 1984): 52-54.
A computer lab in a public library is described.

Elmer-DeWitt, Phillip. "Computers: 'Tools in the Hands of Kids'." *Time*
(16 September 1985): 77.

Freeman, Steve. "The Apple Corps at St. Louis." *Library Journal/School Library Journal* 110, no. 8, pp. 110-12; 31, no. 9 (May 1985): 140-42.
  Describes pilot program using microcomputers for remedial education at St. Louis Public Library branches.

Hoffman, Irwin, Ted Brucker, and Russ Anderson. "Sharing Resources Saves $$$." *Electronic Education* 4, no. 7 (May/June 1985): 8-9, 23.
  How a shared resource computer lab works in high schools.

Miller, John, and William Park. "A Multi-Media Approach to Teaching Computer Operation Skills." *CMC News* 4, no. 1 (Fall 1983): 5.
  Using videotapes in an "operator" licensing program is described.

Naylor, Alice Phoebe. ". . . Addictions to Computer Games." *School Library Media Quarterly* 12, no. 3 (Spring 1984): 233-36.
  Discusses positive ways to use computer games; bibliography of further readings included.

Nicholson, Marilyn. "Library Word Processing Center Enriches Publications Class." *The Computing Teacher* 10, no. 9 (May 1983): 46-47.

Sharp, Peggy Agostino. "Children's Books and Computers—A Perfect Team." *The Computing Teacher* 12, no. 9 (June 1985): 9-12.
  Describes "how to use children's interest in new technology to encourage them to read more—by linking quality children's books with computers!"

Snelson, Pamela. "Library Instruction and the Computer." *Small Computers in Libraries* 5, no. 8 (September 1985): 11-12.
  Reports on ACRL discussion sessions for librarians who offer services related to patron use of micros.

Van Aken, Maxine. "A Computer Lab in Elementary Media Center." *CMC News* 5, no. 2 (Winter 1985): 6.

Wetzel, Keith. "Keyboarding Skills: Elementary, My Dear Teacher?" *The Computing Teacher* 12, no. 9 (June 1985): 15-19.
  This article discusses teaching of keyboarding skills and includes a bibliography of over 25 other related articles.

6 Connecting with the World Outside ⁴/₂₆

The previous two chapters discussed ways you can use microcomputers to simplify the routine, repetitive chores of running a library, or to increase access to and use of your library's resources. This chapter discusses an aspect of computer technology that goes beyond, but is nonetheless a natural extension of, traditional library functions—access to outside information through networking and telecommunications. More and more, libraries will be expected to provide such services for their patrons. Although a detailed investigation of telecommunications is outside the scope of this book, we can offer a general overview, as well as direct you to some resources that can help you to meet its challenges and opportunities.

NETWORKS

When people "network," they share information, resources, and contacts. Librarians and media specialists, for example, network when they exchange books through interlibrary loans, or when they use telephones or mail to locate materials or information requested by patrons. When computers network, they also share information (programs and data); resources (peripherals such as printers and hard disks); and contacts (multiple users). A computer network may consist of any combination of mainframe, mini, and microcomputers, with or without the addition of dumb terminals. The network components may be directly connected with cables or dedicated lines, or they may communicate through ordinary telephone lines using modems and communications software. A network may be confined to a single building, or be regional, statewide, national or even international.

Local Area Networks

In a local area network (LAN), computers are connected directly to one another with cables. Therefore, with rare exceptions, LANs are limited to a single building. LANs differ in the number and types of computers they can accommodate. Some only accept machines of the same model, while others work with different machines from the same company. Some LANs even allow different brands of computers to communicate (software incompatibility is, of course, a separate problem). Other variations include the kind and price of connecting cable required—twisted-pair "telephone" cable, coaxial "cable TV" cable, or expensive but high-quality and noncorrosive fiber optics; the special connecting circuit board necessary for each participating computer; and the system configuration. In a "bus" configuration, the cable runs past each computer in a line, while a "ring" configuration links computers together in a circle. A "tree" chains computers together in separate lines running to a host machine, and a "star," the least used and most difficult system to install, uses separate cables to connect each computer to a central host. All of these factors affect the speed of data transmission through the network, its ability to continue functioning if one unit breaks down, and its expandability.

Most microcomputer LANs consist of independent computers linked together, so that machines may be disconnected and used as individual systems. Only a few microcomputers can support dumb terminals, the use of which may slow response time to an unacceptable level. If you are looking at a network system that purports to support terminals as opposed to potentially self-sufficient stations, be sure you see it running with a database similar in size to your projected database, in order to test the response time when all terminals are in use.

As of this writing, LANs are not without problems, the most significant of which is a lack of standardization, along with a corresponding lack of software. It is also difficult to ensure the security and integrity of a LAN database. Special precautions in the form of extra (and probably expensive) software must be taken in order to protect the database from unauthorized access or accidental modification or erasure. Also, network use of software may amount to copyright infringement (see chapter 8).

LANs are generally difficult to install and require extra training and support for users. Finally, LANs are expensive. Unless you have more than ten workstations, the cost per station remains quite high. With the increased affordability of printers and hard disks, the incentive for sharing peripherals has decreased, and data and software may be shared in other ways than through a physical network. Databases may be duplicated on separate hard disks and updated periodically with floppies. Printers may be shared, if necessary, with relatively inexpensive switch boxes. Computers may be connected with cables and simply exchange data as they would through a modem.

Whether the availability and affordability of LANs will increase is uncertain at this point. The development of UNIX and other similar systems with the ability to link different MS-DOS or other operating-system-based computers may have a positive effect. On the other hand, the lowered prices of hardware, along with the increasing availability of true multi-user, multitasking systems at comparable or less cost than LANs, may make other alternatives more desirable.

This is not meant to discourage you from implementing a LAN if it suits your needs and you can get the necessary support. A LAN may be appropriate, for example, for a combined online catalog and circulation system, where the database is being changed frequently. In deciding whether or not to use a LAN, and if so, which kind, let your software choice be your guide. If the software can support a LAN, the software manufacturer or vendor will be able to give you recommendations (or requirements) for the necessary hardware. The vendor should also be able to provide the extra support that will be needed. Vendor stability and reliability are critical to the successful operation of a LAN.

Regional Networks

A regional or district library network usually consists of a union catalog kept on a large mini or mainframe computer and made accessible to all members. Accessing such a catalog is relatively simple, requiring only a terminal or microcomputer, a modem, a telephone, and communications software, plus the money to pay for any long distance telephone charges. It may even be possible for patrons to search the online catalog from home, or from selected sites within the community, such as shopping centers. If your terminal is a microcomputer, you may not be able to use it for other tasks while you are accessing the catalog.

Entering your own holdings into the union database is more complicated. Most regional systems now catalog through one of the larger bibliographical utilities such as OCLC, RLIN, UTLAS, or WLN. If your acquisitions are cataloged through a regional system using one of these utilities, holdings already on the regional system tapes can be transferred directly into the system catalog. To enter holdings not on such tapes, small libraries may supply ISBNs or LCNs, along with local identification information, and have the bulk of each record transferred to the online catalog from a COM catalog, floppy disks, or CD ROMs. Items that are local, or not found on any of the large bibliographic databases containing Library of Congress records, must be keyed in manually. Unfortunately, many small libraries do not have the funds or staff to cover the clerical cost involved in even this abbreviated entry method. Therefore, you may find yourself in a position of being able to access the catalog, but unable to enter your holdings into it, or having to enter them over a long period of time.

State Networks

As of this writing, a number of states, including Ohio, Illinois, New Jersey, New York, Pennsylvania, and Nebraska, have either already developed networks or are in the process of doing so. In some cases, networking systems are compiling state union catalogs on mainframe equipment with access possible throughout the state via microcomputers. In others, the networking consists of search software which allows libraries throughout the state to search each other's holdings. Such a search might have to be sequential (one library at a time), which could lead to confusion because of the number of responses to a given search. A few states have online catalogs of like libraries, such as that run by the Colorado Alliance of Research Libraries (CARL), which is available for dial-up access at no charge (except any long distance telephone charges). Most states still lack adequate subject access to materials, and the problem has been, and no doubt will continue to be, the subject of much debate and many journal and newsletter articles.

National Networks

The national library networks are the bibliographic utilities used for cataloging by individual libraries and regional systems, such as OCLC, Research Libraries Information Network (RLIN), UTLAS (the Canadian counterpart to OCLC), and Western Library Network (WLN). Until recently, most users obtained access to these systems through company-supplied, dedicated terminals, with a limited number of users gaining dial-up access through other equipment. This is beginning to change; both OCLC and WLN have replaced their dedicated terminals with modified personal computers which may be used for other tasks when not online to OCLC or WLN. Smaller libraries that use such cataloging services usually do so in cooperation with other libraries in order to make the service cost effective. Programs are now available for transferring ("downloading") cataloging information to a microcomputer at the local cataloging site for later editing offline, thus reducing online time charges. The edited records can then be transferred to utility and card sets for local catalogs.

NETWORKING WITHOUT A NETWORK

Nearly all libraries participate in bibliographic networking, exchanging bibliographies of their holdings on particular topics. Individual librarians or media specialists may make up topical bibliographies for patrons, which they then share with other librarians at meetings and conferences. As discussed in chapter 4, microcomputers can be very useful in compiling such bibliographies and keeping them current. Keep the bibliographies on separate diskettes (or hard disk directories) arranged by broad topics such as science, history, sports, etc. for easy access. Newsletters and flyers produced on micros and circulated among other libraries in your district or region are another way of keeping in touch without direct computer hookups.

The development of laser optic technology (CD ROMs) promises to have a major impact on cataloging services from the regional level up. CD ROMs provide a cheaper alternative to expensive online services. Union catalogs on any level could be written and updated using WORM (write once read many) CD ROM drives, with the disks being duplicated and distributed regularly to member libraries, each of which would have its own read-only CD ROM drive.

TELECOMMUNICATIONS SERVICES

In addition to networks, telecommunications make possible a variety of other services which are becoming increasingly important to library staff members and patrons, including bulletin board services (BBS), electronic mail and message services (EMMS), access to online databases, and even telecommuting.

Bulletin Board Services

Computer bulletin boards, like their cork counterparts, provide an easy (and entertaining) way to transfer information and software. The messages "posted" on electronic bulletin boards range from the "ride wanted" or "free puppies to good homes" variety to online "chats" on topics ranging from politics to science. There are bulletin boards for special interest groups (SIGs) on every topic from different types of computer hardware and software to do-it-yourself dating services. Many of the BBS are free (except for long distance telephone charges, which can mount quickly); others require a membership fee and/or connect charges. There are also a number of bulletin board directories and newsletters—all online, of course.

Many libraries are starting their own community calendar/bulletin boards, and/or allowing patrons to call in reference questions and receive answers via the BBS (another way of being a computer resource center). Some school libraries are letting students communicate with students in other schools through bulletin boards, a good computer club or computer literacy class project.

Electronic Mail and Message Services

Electronic mail and message services (EMMS) are used to transfer messages from one computer to one or more other specific computers (unlike bulletin boards, which are open access). More and more business and personal correspondence and memoranda, reports, and other information intended for a specific audience are traveling via telecommunications rather than along the standard postal route. Electronic mail services, including the delivery of hard copy to recipients who lack computers, are now offered by a variety of companies, including telecommunications services such as MCI and online services like The Source and CompuServe.

Some believe that electronic mail is one more step toward a true "paperless society." Computerized mail may also begin to replace many telephone conversations. At least one large corporation provides its field representatives with portable computers and modems for exchanging messages and reports with the home office, a practice the reps claim has saved hours of unsuccessful telephone calls and idle chatter. Newspaper reporters submit stories via modem instead of reading them over the telephone. Many libraries are using EMMS instead of the telephone or regular mail to locate materials for filling interlibrary loan requests. As users become more familiar and comfortable with "paperless mail," its use for other library tasks, such as sending and receiving reports and newsletters, will probably increase.

ACCESSING LARGE DATABASES

This may be one of the most valuable computerized services a secondary school or public library could provide. More and more services are becoming available and affordable not only for small libraries and businesses but for home users as well. Concurrently, the ability to conduct online searches is becoming a valuable skill.

A database consists of related files, abstracts, and other documents collected, updated, and sometimes adapted into a form more suitable for online use by a database producer, which then sells the rights to an online service for a one-time fee and/or royalties. The online service, in turn, keys the information into a mainframe computer and provides search services and instructions to users, who access the database with a modem and a telephone via a telecommunications network or dial-up utility, such as Tymnet or Telenet.

Online services vary widely in the types and amounts of information they make available. We have already discussed the bibliographic utilities such as OCLC and RLIN. The services oriented toward home use, such as The Source and CompuServe, are related mainly to entertainment, travel, and finances, providing airline schedules and reservation confirmations, stock market information, movie reviews, and the like. By contrast, the large information services such as Dialog (a subsidiary of Lockheed Corporation) and BRS offer access to bibliographic, and in some cases statistical and/or factual, information on literally thousands of subjects. Many of the databases include abstracts as well, and for an extra charge you may have entire articles printed offline and sent to you as hard copy. Alternatively, items listed in the database may be obtained through interlibrary loan.

To use a service's databases, you must obtain a membership. This entitles you to an identification number, a password, a user's manual, and regular printed or online publications such as newsletters or database/services updates. Most services charge a one-time membership fee and/or a monthly minimum. For each search, you pay a connect charge, which varies from a few dollars to as much as a few hundred dollars an hour according to the database being searched, plus any long distance phone charges incurred. Although the cost per *hour* sounds high, most searches take only a few minutes, so the cost per *search* may be quite low. Also, if you live in a large city, you may be able to access databases through a dial-up utility with a local call. Some companies charge a higher rate for a 1200 bit per second modem than for 300 bps; most also require you to have a modem that provides full duplex, or bidirectional, information transfer (see chapter 3).

Online database searching advantages over traditional search methods include the following:

The resulting information is much more comprehensive.

There are literally hundreds of databases available, covering a tremendous range of subjects and types of information. Sources include not only books, newspapers, and magazines, but government documents, professional journals, and research reports. Most of the information services will provide database catalogs upon request. Some sample databases include "American Men and Women of Science," "America: History and Life," and the "Foundation Directory."

The information is current.

One of the most up-to-date printed indexes, the *Readers' Guide,* is a good six weeks behind; online databases are updated continuously. In such fast-moving fields as science, medicine, and politics, recent developments can be of major significance. Online databases offer immediate access to information on current thought and events.

More and more sources are going online. Examples include Educational Resources Information Center (ERIC), *Books in Print,* and *MicroSIFT* (an educational software directory and evaluation guide). With so many current reference works available, you may find that providing at least some reference materials to patrons via online searching is more cost effective than annual purchases of the same works in printed form. For example, it may be more economical to access *Books in Print* online when necessary than to purchase the print updates each year.

A number of services are also beginning to provide some of the less changeable databases on CD ROMs, with periodic updates. A combination of CD ROM database subscriptions and online searches of current information may provide more comprehensive, cost-effective, and current access to information than could previously be imagined.

Access to information is very *fast*.

Most online searches may be conducted in 15 minutes or less. The better the search strategy, the less time it takes, and the lower the connect cost, which is one reason good search skills are so important. Using a Boolean search strategy with AND and OR and NOT delimiters takes a fraction of the time needed to sort through printed indexes. For example, you could access all the information in a particular database concerning women in business between 1930 and 1950 in the United States, France, and England with a single command.

Search strategies vary somewhat between services, so it is wise to take advantage of the training sessions many of the services offer; they are likely to be more cost effective than learning online. There are also several software programs, such as MICROsearch (available from ERIC), which provide search practice without the cost of going online. Also, if your staff members or patrons are going to be searching a variety of databases, you should investigate the availability of software that acts as an intermediary or interface between searchers and different databases which may have slightly different searching techniques. The further readings at the end of this chapter include reviews of some of these programs, as well as several articles on the ways different types of libraries are teaching online searching skills and strategies.

The information will be as specific as you want it to be.

The Boolean search strategy mentioned above narrows and refines your search criteria to very distinct and manageable limits.

Information may be multilingual and international.

References will be limited to English only if you specify the limitation.

Online and CD ROM databases, with their rapid access to current and comprehensive information, are already beginning to replace printed resource guides. In the not-so-distant future, many libraries will be expected to provide online access just as they have provided *Readers' Guide* and other printed sources in the past. There is the question, of course, of who will pay for such services and how. If interest is high enough, you might set up a system in which users would pay the connect charge, dial-up charges, and any royalty fee for each search, either at the time of the search or through some sort of regular billing system. A library staff member trained in online database use should interview patrons and conduct the actual searches, perhaps with the patron present. The library would bear the cost of equipment and software, initial membership fees, if any, and administrative costs, which could be defrayed by adding a slight service charge or by using volunteers such as computer club members.

The searching of commercially available databases has brought up the issue of fees and access to information. The National Commission on Libraries and Information Science has compiled an overview of information about this question, entitled *The Role of Fees in Supporting Library and Information Services in Public and Academic Libraries.* No doubt this will continue to be a topic of considerable concern and discussion for some time to come.

CONNECTING WITH THE WORLD OUTSIDE

As with all automation, telecommunications and/or networking implementation must take place in incremental steps. The first requirement for gaining access to information outside your library is a telephone (your own line), *in* the library, not down the hall. You should be able to use the telephone while at the computer that will connect you with the "outside world." Even if you initially intend to use the computer only for organization of and/or access to in-house resources, a telephone lets you talk with your support person(s) while in front of the machine, an advantage you will appreciate with the first call. And for any telecommunications service, whether it be sharing information in a network, communicating with other users via electronic bulletin boards and mail services, or accessing online databases, a telephone line is essential. It is the pathway to the world beyond your library walls.

The world opened by telecommunications is vast and marvelous. In the library of the future, telecommunications and computers will provide gateways to far more knowledge than could be contained within any building. The concept is breathtaking, the challenge tremendous, the changes inevitable.

FURTHER READINGS

Bulletin Board Systems (BBS)
Electronic Mail and Message Services (EMMS)

"Compare TechCentral with Other Services." *Tech Trends* 30, no. 7 (October 1985): 15.
This checklist describes the various features available to users of TechCentral, AECT's telecommunications network; illustrates what to look for in a telecommunications system.

Lamson, Norma. "Microlink Electronic Bulletin Board, San Bernardino Public Library." *Apple LUG Newsletter* 2, no. 3 (September 1984): 16-17.

Lee, Joel. "Information for All: ALANET." *Wilson Library Bulletin* 59, no. 10 (June 1985): 668-72.
Describes the American Library Association's electronic information service which officially started at the January 1984 midwinter meeting.

"Library Electronic Messaging Systems." *LITA Newsletter* no. 19 (Winter 1985): 1-2.
Contains a list of electronic mail systems currently being used by the library community.

"MCI Mail: New Electronic Postal System." *ONLINE Libraries and Microcomputers* 1, no. 3 (November 1983): 7-8.

O'Brien, William G. "Growing Up in the BBS World." *Classroom Computer Learning* 6, no. 3 (November/December 1985): 38-39.
Includes a list of bulletin boards to help you get started.

Oliver, Dennis. "Deciphering Electronic Mail: Connecting and Interconnecting Services." *Library HiTech* 1, no. 2 (Fall 1983): 29-32.

Porter, Peggy. " 'Dear PPO5' Interpersonal Communication . . . Entering the Brave New World." *Library HiTech* (Issue 5) 2, no. 1 (1st quarter 1984): 23-27.
Provides suggestions for using electronic mail systems.

Sievers, Dennis. "Computer Bulletin Boards." *Electronic Education* 3, no. 5 (February 1984): 14ff.

"So You Want to Be a Bulletin-Board Sysop." *Popular Computing* 3, no. 3 (January 1984): 155-56.
A "sysop" (short for "system operator") runs and maintains a computerized bulletin board. Includes a list of BBS software.

Walton, Bob. "Electronic Mail: Choosing a System to Meet Your Library's Needs." *Technicalities* 4, no. 5 (May 1984): 5-7.

_____. "Micro Communications Software: Things to Look For." *Technicalities* (July 1984): 14-15.

Wendland, Mike. "Messaging Systems." *A +* *Magazine* 3, no. 9 (September 1985): 53-57.
"A real bulletin-board service hangs on the wall and presents information to passersby. What we're talking about is an automated information-exchange program."

CD ROM Technology

"CD ROM Revolution for Electronic Publishing." *ONLINE Libraries and Microcomputers* 3, no. 11 (November 1985): 1-5.
Includes history, strengths, and weaknesses of the industry.

Deacon, Jim. "Compact Disks: What These Storage Devices Mean for Libraries." *CMC News* 6, no. 2 (Winter 1986): 9-10.

Foster, Edward. "CD ROM: Megabytes into Minispace." *InfoWorld* (23 September 1985): 27-29.
Discusses "targeting" of libraries as customers for CD-ROM-based systems and software, as data stored on microfilm and microfiche can go on CD ROM.

Goldestein, Mark L. "Libraries on a Platter—Compact Disks Can Record Much More Than Music." *Industry Week 228,* no. 2 (20 January 1986): 59.

Electronic Databases

Anderson, Verl A. "Simultaneous Remote Searching." *Library Journal/ School Library Journal* 110, no. 18, pp. 167-70; 32, no. 3 (November 1985): 155-57.

Dewey, Patrick R. "Professional Librarian Looks at the Consumer Online Services: The Source, CompuServe, Apple Bulletin Board, et al." *ONLINE* (September 1983): 36-41.
Dewey looks at features of consumer online services; includes addresses and additional bibliography.

"Full Text Online Databases: Present and Future" *ONLINE Libraries and Microcomputers* 1, no. 2 (October 1983): 1-5.

Hoover, Ryan. "Microcomputer Literature Online." *Information Today* 2, no. 9 (October 1985): 7-8.

Covers seven online databases devoted entirely or in part to indexing and abstracting published micro literature on three online retrieval services: Business Software Database, Compare Products, The Computer Database, Microcomputer Index, .Menu, Microsearch, and Online Microcomputer Software Guide and Directory.

Johnson, Anne M. "Review of Databases for Education." *Education Libraries* (Spring 1984): 5-9.
Brief descriptions of 17 databases on DIALOG and/or BRS of special interest to educators are provided.

McKnight, Michelynn. "Searching Major Bibliographic Databases with a Microcomputer." *Apple LUG Newsletter* 3, no. 2 (April 1985): 44-48.

Needle, David. "Making On-Line Services Pay Off." *Personal Computing* 9, no. 11 (November 1985): 75-83.
"Many managers and professionals haven't yet figured out the most cost-effective means of getting at crucial on-line information . . . To do adequate on-line searches for business, you don't want a person who just knows how to gather information."

Oser, Fred N. "Free Online Searching (Letters)." *Library Journal* 110, no. 4 (1 March 1985): 6, 8.

Powledge, Fred. "Not So Free Information — An Opinion." *Popular Computing* 4, no. 1 (November 1984): 26.

Roose, Tina. "Public Libraries Online." *Library Journal.*
Sample columns: "A Month of Searches" (1 March 1985); "Online Search Costs" (1 May 1985); "Search Records for Decision Making" (July 1985); "Online or Print: Comparing Costs" (15 September 1985).

Slatta, Richard. "Banquet's Set — an Electronic Banquet for Researchers." *Electronic Education* 4, no. 4 (January 1985): 12-13.

Talab, Rosemary S. "Copyright and Database Downloading." *Library Journal/School Library Journal* 110, no. 18, pp. 144-47; 32, no. 3 (November 1985): 132-35.

_____. "Databases of Microcomputer Software: An Overview." *Library Journal/School Library Journal* 110, no. 8, pp. 101-102, 104; 32, no. 3 (May 1985): 21-22, 24.

"Telecomputing — Discovering a Universe of Data (Special Report)." *Electronic Learning* 4, no. 3 (November/December 1984): 31-34, 39-40, 42-43, 88-90, 92.

Tenopir, Carol. "Online Searching with a Microcomputer." *Library Journal* 110, no. 5 (15 March 1985): 42-43.

_____. "Full-Text and Bibliographic Databases." *Library Journal* 110, no. 19 (15 November 1985): 63.
How does the addition of full-text databases affect document delivery and online searching?

_____. "IAC's Document Delivery and More." *Library Journal* 109, no. 10 (1 June 1984): 1104-5.

Thesing, Jane I. "Online Searching in Perspective; Advantages and Limitations." *Catholic Library World* (February 1983): 258-60.

Local Area Networks (LANs)

Black, Don. "LANs (Local Area Networks)." *Information Today* 2, nos. 7, 8, and 9 (August, September, October 1985). No pages available.
"Televiews" column "examining Local Area Network history and technology with the intent to provide enough detail to allow you, the reader, to gain thorough understanding of LAN technology."

Foster, Edward. "Multiuser System VS LANS" and "New Interest in LAN Alternative." *InfoWorld* 7, no. 31 (19 August 1985): 38-41.
"Multi-user systems run micro software, offer cost-effective way to connect users."

Green, John O. "Straight Talk about Local Networks." *Classroom Computer Learning* 5, no. 2 (September 1984): 73-77.
Discusses both software and hardware.

Hether, Nancy K. "CD ROM Technology: A New Era for Information Storage and Retrieval?" *ONLINE* 2, no. 10 (November 1985): 17-28.

Levert, Virginia M. "Applications of Local Area Networks for Microcomputers in Libraries." *Information Technology and Libraries* 4, no. 1 (March 1985): 9-18.
Important features are reviewed and several microcomputer LANs are described. Some considerations for libraries contemplating automation with a multi-user microcomputer system are addressed.

"Local Area Networks: Expanding Your PC Computing Environment." *M300 and PC Report* 3, no. 1 (January 1986): 1-3.

Micro to Mainframe Communications

Byers, T. J. "Micro-To-Micro Communications." *Popular Computing* 3, no. 4 (February 1984): 113-15, 118, 119.
Includes a data communications glossary.

Emmett, Arielle. "Micro-to Mainframe Links." *Popular Computing* 4, no. 10 (August 1985): 71-73, 126-28.

Feltman, Charles. "Micro-to-Mainframe Connection." *Popular Computing* 3, no. 4 (February 1984): 105-8.
Describes how personal computers unlock the power of mainframes.

Glossbrenner, Alfred. "Fine Art of Data Transfer." *Popular Computing* 4, no. 11 (September 1985): 69-73, 118.
Discusses how to move data out of one program or computer into another.

McGinty, Tony. "Micro-To-Mainframe Links." *Electronic Learning* 5, no. 4 (January 1986): 20-22.

"Transferring Data between Computers." *Popular Computing* 3, no. 5 (March 1984): 149-50.

Networking

"California Conference on Networking." *Library Journal* 110, no. 19 (15 November 1985): 12-14.
Report describes the "first steps taken to mobilize state's library communities to build statewide multitype network."

Clark, Pamela. "Networking: The Promise and the Challenge—An Editorial." *Popular Computing* 4, no. 4 (February 1984): 6.
This issue includes a special report, "Data Communications for Personal Computers."

Colorado Libraries 11, no. 4 (December 1985): 6-17.
Issue theme: networking—local, state, regional, and national. Topics discussed by following authors: local networking, Ward Shaw; state networking, Duane Johnson; regional networking, David Brunnell; national networking, Jim Kennedy.

Culkin, Patricia, and Ward Shaw. "The CARL System." *Library Journal* 110, no. 2 (1 February 1985): 68-70.
Describes the network online system CARL (Colorado Alliance of Research Libraries). Includes discussions on the elements of a network, CARL's purpose, the online and CIRC systems, catalog maintenance, and CARL hardware.

Dunkle, Rebecca, and Catherine McLoughlin. "Automating the Region: A Report on the Seminar." *Library HiTech* (Issue 5) 2, no. 1 (1st quarter 1984): 43-45.

Glazer, Frederick G. "That Bibliographic Highway in the Sky." *Library Journal* 110, no. 2 (1 February 1985): 64-67.
Describes the statewide network in West Virginia.

"IBM PCs and Apples in ILL Net." *Small Computers in Libraries* 4, no. 3 (March 1984): 3-4.
Discusses project of the seven Regional Library Service Systems in Colorado to study and improve interlibrary loan services. Includes an in-depth description of two projects.

"Library Media Practice—Current Research: Studies of Multitype Library Networking with Implications for Schools." *School Library Media Quarterly* 12, no. 2 (Winter 1984): 159-62.

Martin, Susan K. "New Technologies and Library Networks." *Library Journal* 109, no. 11 (15 June 1984): 1194-96.

Rubin, Charles. "Finally . . . Computer Networks that Really Work." *Personal Computing* 9, no. 7 (July 1985): 68-73, 75, 77-78.

Shaw, Ruth Jean. "Alaska's Multilibrary Network: Anchorage School District." *School Library Media Quarterly* 12, no. 4 (Summer 1984): 297-300.
"Anchorage is the first public school system to join WLN as a full participating member."

Walker, H. Thomas. "Networking and School Library Media Centers: Report of Pilot Project—Howard County Public School System and The Maryland Interlibrary Organization." *School Library Media Quarterly* 11, no. 1 (Fall 1983): 20-28.

Role of Libraries and/or Librarians in Telecommunications

"Changing Role of Librarians as End-Users Become More Active Online Searchers." *ONLINE Libraries and Microcomputers* 2, no. 3 (March 1984): 1-3.

Drake, Miriam. "User Fees: Aid or Obstacle to Access?" *Wilson Library Bulletin* 58, no. 9 (May 1984): 632-35.

Drew, Sally. "Online Databases: Some Questions of Ownership." *Wilson Library Bulletin* 59, no. 10 (June 1985): 661-63.
"Questions regarding the handling of copyrighted material can be confusing, especially when copyright is applied to bibliographic records."

Flagg, Gordon. "ONLINE ENCYCLOPEDIAS: Are They Ready for Libraries? Are Libraries Ready for Them?" *American Libraries* 14, no. 3 (March 1983): 134,136.

Huleatt, Richard S. "Variations on the Theme of a Search – An Editorial."
ONLINE Libraries and Microcomputers 3, no. 5 (May 1985): 5-6.
"No two searchers will provide identical results. The best analogy here is
that you can get to New York by different routes and methods, but some are
more efficient and less costly than others. Chalk that up to knowledge and
experience."

Kaplan, Robin. "Online Searching: Introducing the Inevitable." *Library
Journal/School Library Journal* 110, no. 8, pp. 122-23; 31, no. 9 (May
1985): 32-33.

Koenig, Michael E. D., and Stephen T. Kochoff. "Emerging Role for the
Librarian in Data Administration." *Special Libraries* 75, no. 3 (July
1984): 238-46.

Mintz, Anne P. "Information Practice and Malpractice." *Library Journal*
110, no. 14 (1 September 1985): 38-43.
How will the necessity for evaluation by online searchers affect the role of
the reference librarian?

Molholt, Pat. "Nature of Information and Its Influence on Libraries." *Special
Libraries* 75, no. 3 (July 1984): 247-51.

Ojala, Marydee. "End User Searching and Its Implications for Librarians."
Special Libraries 76, no. 2 (Spring 1985): 93-99.
"Is end user searching a threat or a promise for corporate librarians?"

Smith, Jean. "Information: Public or Private?" *Special Libraries* 75, no. 4
(October 1984): 275-82.
Article examines "policies concerning government-generated information,
the trend toward privatization of information and its impact on the public's access to government documents and reports, and the implications for information professionals."

Summit, Roger K., and Charles T. Meadow. "Emerging Trends in the Online
Industry." *Special Libraries* 76, no. 2 (Spring 1985): 88-92.

Search Software

"Gateways to Online Vendors." *ONLINE Libraries and Microcomputers* 2,
no. 3 (March 1985): 1-4.
Advantages and disadvantages of gateways are discussed.

"Is There an End User Market?" *Library Journal* 110, no. 11 (15 June
1985): 41.

Kesselman, Martin. "Front-End/Gateway Software: Availability and Usefulness." *Library Software Review* 4, no. 2 (March/April 1985): 67-70.

Kubik, Kim. "MacIntosh Computer for the Online Searcher/Information Specialist." *Apple LUG Newsletter* 3, no. 4 (October 1985): 45-48.

"Microcomputer Front-End Software for Bibliographic Information System." *ONLINE Libraries and Microcomputers* 2, no. 4 (April 1985): 1-3.

Sloan, Bernard. "The New Age of Linked Systems." *American Libraries* (October 1985): 652-54.
"Now systems suppliers will even help you link with competing systems."

_____. "Weak Links in System Linking." *American Libraries* 16, no. 8 (September 1985): 584-85.

Searching Instruction

Annuals

Dowling, Karen. "Online Searching and the School Media Program." In *School Library Media Annual 1984*. Edited by Shirley L. Aaron and Pat R. Scales. Littleton, Colo.: Libraries Unlimited, 1984. 528p. (Vol. 2). $35.00.

Periodicals

Bennett, Randy E. "Teachers Reach Out and Touch with PCs." *PC Magazine* 3, no. 22 (13 November 1984): No pages available.
Describes how students and teachers use The Source.

Butcher, Diane E. "Online Searching: How to Get Instant Information." *Electronic Learning* 4, no. 3 (November/December 1984): 39-40, 90.
Provides question-and-answer introduction to online searching.

Fiebert, Elyse Evans. "Integration of Online Bibliographic Instruction into High School Library Curriculum." *Learning and Media* (Winter 1984): 4-5, 8.
Online information retrieval now integrated into ninth-grade library unit.
Reprinted in *School Library Media Quarterly* (Spring 1985): 96-99.

Levinson, Michael S., and J. Andrew Walcott. "On-Line Databases – A School Project." *Media and Methods.* (September/October 1985): No pages available.
Describes an eighth-grade project.

Mackey, Kevin. "Electronic Mail in the Writing Class." *Classroom Computer Learning* 4, no. 7 (October 1984): 32-33.
"With one computer and a word processing program, you can set up an electronic mail system that will stimulate your students' writing and hone their communication skills."

Mancall, Jacqueline, and D. Deskins. "Electronic Bibliographic Database Access: Considerations in Offering Services to Students." *School Library Media Activities Monthly* (October 1984): 33-37.

_____. "Teaching Online Searching: Recommendations for School Media Specialists." *School Library Media Quarterly* 13, nos. 3, 4 (Summer 1985): 215-19.

Roose, Tina. "Online Searches for Kids." *Library Journal* 109, no. 18 (1 November 1984): 2010-11.

"Teaching Students to Search Online Databases." *American Libraries* 16, no. 4 (April 1985): 210.

Tennis, Jean. "Telecomputing Diary." *Electronic Learning* 4, no. 1 (September 1985): 28-29.
First of a series of columns recounting Jean Tennis's transformation into a "telecommunicating educator."

Tenopir, Carol. "Online Searching in Schools." *Library Journal* 111, no. 2 (1 February 1986): 60-61.
Includes contact names and article citations.

Ward, Joe. "Online Searching: The Future Is Now with Knowledge Index." *Educational Computer Magazine* 3, no. 3 (May/June 1983): 28-29.

Watt, Dan. "Wired Classroom, a Look at Local Networking in the Schools." *Popular Computing* 2, no. 9 (June 1983): 70-82.

Telecommunications

Andrews, Mark. "Seven Telecommunications Programs for the Apple IIe and IIc." *A + Magazine* 3, no. 3 (March 1985): 48ff.
Discusses pros and cons of seven communications packages. Includes chart of 15 different telecommunications packages.

Bellardo, Trudi. "Telecommunications and Networking." *Library Journal* 110, no. 13 (August 1985): 51-52.
A report of the mid-year conference of the American Society for Information Science.

Fenichel, Caron Hansen. "Using a Microcomputer to Communicate: Part I: The Basics." *Microcomputers for Information Management* 2, no. 2 (April 1985): 59-76.

"General Purpose Communications Software for Microcomputers." *ONLINE Libraries and Microcomputers* 3, nos. 8-9 (September 1985): 1-3.

Hewes, Jeremy, and Joan Hewes. "Gateways to On-Line Services." *PC World* 3, no. 5 (May 1985): 149-56.

Jordan, Larry. "The Communicators." *PC World* 3, no. 5 (May 1985): 277-81.

Keating, Barry. "Choosing and Using Telecommunications Software." *Creative Computing* 11, no. 2 (February 1985): 101-13.
This special report includes brief reviews of 17 communications packages.

Levy, Steven. "Send Me No Abstract — Do Abstracts Tell the Real Story?" *Popular Computing* (December 1985): 32, 34, 37.

_____. "Terminal Software . . . Ticket for Going Online." *Popular Computing* (November 1983): 54-62.

_____. "Touring the Bulletin Boards." *Popular Computing* 3, no. 1 (February 1984): 54-62.

_____. "Who's Got the Data?" *Popular Computing* 3, no. 4 (April 1983): 68-75.

Moursund, Dave. "Modem: Editor's Message." *The Computing Teacher* 2, no. 6 (May 1985): 3-4.
Describes how use of this computer peripheral can expand your world.

Newlin, Barbara. "On-line Search Strategies." *PC World* 3, no. 5 (May 1985): 226-33.

Padgett, Anthony, and Chris Yalonis. "Tapping into On-Line Data Bases." *PC World* 3, no. 5 (May 1985): 120-26.

Miscellaneous

Alexander, Brian. "The Computer Choice: Many or Multi?" *Electronic Education* 4, no. 6 (March/April 1985): 23, 27-28.

Bonk, Sharon C. "Integrating Library and Book Trade Automation." *Information Technology and Libraries* 2, no. 1 (March 1983): 18-25.

Boss, Richard W. "Technology and the Modern Library." *Library Journal* 109, no. 11 (15 June 1984): 1183-89.

Carlson, David H. "Technological Dependency: Who Will Decide for Libraries?" *Library Journal/School Library Journal* 110, no. 18, pp. 128-30; 32, no. 3 (November 1985): 116-18.

Cook, Peter R. "Electronic Encyclopedias." *BYTE* 9, no. 7 (July 1984): 151-70.
Describes using interactive video technologies for exploring encyclopedias.

Everett, John, and Elizabeth Crowe. "Information Brokers—Integral Now." *Electronic Education* (January 1985): 14-15.
Article excerpted from the forthcoming *The Information Broker's Handbook: How to Profit from the Information Age.*

Greh, Deborah. "Technology and Art." *Electronic Learning* 5, no. 4 (January 1986): 29-39.
Feature includes information about input devices, a "graphics bibliography," software directory, and comparison of graphics tablets.

Hlava, Marjorie M. K. "State of the Art 1985: Special Libraries/Online Technologies." *Special Libraries* 76, no. 2 (Spring 1985): 121-27.

McClain, Larry. "Database Business." *Popular Computing* 2, no. 5 (March 1983): 46-50.
Discusses differences between a database producer, an online service, and a telecommunications network.

"Microcomputer Networking in Libraries." *ONLINE Libraries and Microcomputers* 2, no. 1 (January 1984): 1-3.
Describes three types of library networking: local area networks, microcomputer electronic messaging, and timesharing electronic messaging systems.

Miller, Michael J. "Intelligence Databases." *Popular Computing* 5, no. 3 (December 1985): 45-47.
Discusses how AI concepts revolutionize the way we work with database programs.

"Online" issue: *Special Libraries* 76, no. 2 (Spring 1985): Entire issue.
Also see reactions in "Letters" column, *Special Libraries* (Winter 1986): 59-60.

Schwerin, Julie B. "How to Keep Current." *Information Today* 2, no. 8 (September 1985): 6, 28-29.
Describes resources available concerning the optical publishing industry including publications, conferences, and organizations.

Smither, Richard, and Draper Kaufman. "Before You Choose a Network Consider . . ." *Electronic Education* 4, no. 6 (March/April 1985): 23, 25, 27-28.

"T is for Telecommunications—A Special Report." *Popular Computing* 3, no. 9 (July 1984): 105-128, 152-63.
This is a series of articles covering hardware, software, information services, etc.

Tucker, Susan. "Telecommunications Primer." *Tech Trends* 30, no. 7 (October 1985): 12-14.

7 Choosing and Implementing Your Microcomputer System

Implementing a system for your library is a multi-step process, and one you cannot rush through. It requires patience, creativity, resourcefulness, thoroughness, foresightedness, objectivity, curiosity, and above all, a sense of humor. Your approach to the planning, purchasing, and initial implementation stages will to a large extent determine whether your computerization experience is a happy or a tragic one.

Probably the most common — and potentially disastrous — microcomputer mistake is buying a system without knowing how it is going to be used. Before you even begin to shop for software and hardware, you need to decide whether and how computerization will work in *your* library, keeping in mind that your main objective is to provide the most needed services to patrons using available staff, time, and materials. Careful planning at this stage can mean the difference between a computer that sits useless and idle, and one that quickly becomes indispensable. This applies even to any hardware and/or software you may already have — some ways of using it will be more effective than others. In this chapter we will discuss analyzing the needs of your particular library, choosing hardware and software to fit those needs, and incorporating the computer into your present system as smoothly as possible.

DETERMINING YOUR NEEDS

The computerese term for needs assessment is "systems analysis." It starts with a careful examination of current methods with respect to time requirements, efficiency, and appropriateness for computerization. As you analyze your library, you will probably find that some existing manual methods are quite satisfactory, or require only minor reorganization. Other functions, however, will probably stand out as strong candidates for computerization.

To promote user acceptance of the new system and to justify expenditures to the administration, it would be helpful if the initial project(s), at least, offers high visibility and direct user benefits, that is, somehow makes life easier and/or more satisfying for staff and patrons. Therefore a good place to start your analysis is with the people who will be affected by the change. A formal or informal survey of potential users will help you to discover who is most interested in using the computer, for what purpose(s), and how often, the existing degree of familiarity with computers, and the amount of staff and volunteer time that will be available for computer-related activities, such as data entry, orientation classes, or monitoring of users. Besides offering useful information, such a prepurchase survey can contribute to building a higher acceptance level for the coming changes.

In addition to the human factor, you will also have to consider space needs. Is there room in your library or office for a "computer corner"? What about noise? Perhaps some physical reorganization will be necessary. If so, now is the time to start planning for it. Space availability may turn out to be an important factor in your decisions as to who will use the system and for what purpose(s), and it may also affect your choice of hardware.

Yet another primary consideration in deciding what to computerize is the amount of time and energy you will be able to invest in the selection and implementation process, including training time. Although when done properly computerization will save at least some, and probably a great deal, of time once it is in effect, the transition process itself can be very time consuming. Development time can be anywhere from a few days to several months or even years, depending upon the task(s) involved, the availability of suitable software (which may need to be adapted), the degree of difficulty involved in learning to use the system, and the amount of data to be entered.

A good way to begin your analysis is to keep a log of daily activities. How much time do you spend doing what? If you have other staff members or aides, have them keep logs as well. To make log keeping easier, use a tally sheet like the sample log in figure 7.1. It is actually a simple spreadsheet, with various activities labeling the horizontal rows, and 15-minute or half hour blocks forming the columns. Each sheet represents a day. By duplicating the sample or a similar spreadsheet, you can keep a log simply by checking the appropriate boxes. It would also be useful to project a year-long tally sheet, breaking down major activities such as ordering and taking inventory.

As an added indicator, we have placed an extra column near the right edge of the sheet headed "Caught up?" You will probably find that certain tasks (such as filing) always have "No" in the "Caught up?" column. These may be just the tasks that could be handled more efficiently with a computer, leaving your time and conscience free for patrons. There are also two additional columns for subjective ratings of the "reward value" of each activity on a scale of 1 to 10, from both a patron and a staff point of view ("Value-P" and "Value-S").

After two or three weeks, you should be able to tell roughly the relative amounts of staff time spent for each type of activity, which functions are the most difficult to maintain, and which activities are most rewarding for patrons and/or staff. Now you may begin to analyze each activity to determine whether it is a suitable candidate for computerization.

You may want to create another chart at this point, with cells defined by the various activities on one side and computerization criteria on the other. Or make a checklist, with a separate copy for each activity. The questions you should ask about each activity include: whether the task is the sort that computers do well (remember that computers excel at tasks that are repetitive, quantitative, routine, voluminous, simple, logical, and straightforward, and

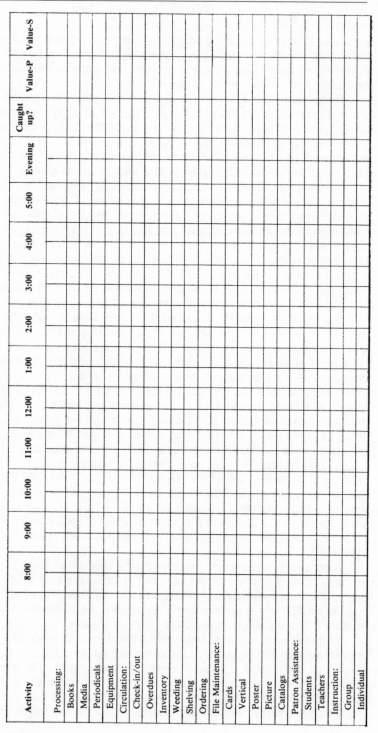

Fig. 7.1. Sample log.

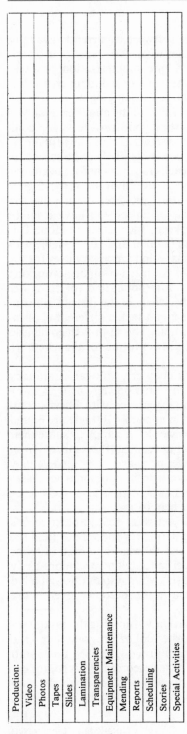

Fig. 7.1—*Continued*

that require accuracy and precision);[1] whether software is currently available to perform it; how visible the system would be; what user benefits it offers, both direct and indirect; time and cost estimates for computerization; how well or how poorly the current method for the task works (including cost effectiveness); and how much resistance there might be to changing it.

Once you have evaluated each activity according to the above criteria, you should be able to list several tasks that look like good prospects for computerization. Now is the time to begin thinking in terms of long-range planning and implementation. As we stated earlier, you are more likely to be successful if you build your system in steps, completing each transition before beginning another. Eventually you may wish to incorporate several or all of the eligible functions into your computer system, but to start, pick one or two that are relatively simple and low pressure. For example, unless you have a lot of assistance, avoid a task that requires daily upkeep, such as circulation. This will give you and everyone else time to become familiar and comfortable with the computer. You may want to designate primary and secondary uses for the system: for example, a computer might be used for instruction or networking in the morning, for administrative tasks in the afternoon, and for computer club projects in the evening. If other media specialists in the district are considering computerization, individuals or teams might tackle different applications, sharing experiences with the group as a whole. This approach could also be used, for example, to develop standardized district forms for the inventory and file management systems.

Besides the ideas offered in the preceding chapters, you can find many suggestions in educational, library, and computer periodicals, as well as by talking to people who have already had some experience with library computerization. (Some possible contacts are listed in appendix B; there are bound to be others in your community or nearby who would be happy to share their experiences.) It is also a good idea to invite input from staff members, from patrons, and from the community. Besides offering suggestions, people may wish to get involved in fund-raising activities to help in computer purchases (see appendix D). The acceptance level for the new system is also likely to be higher if people feel they have had a part in its acquisition.

Once you have decided what function(s) you want to computerize, it's time to get specific. The better you are able to define for the vendor (and the budget committee or purchasing department) exactly what you need in terms of volume, speed, accuracy, response, and specific functions, the more likely you are to get it. If, as is likely, you are purchasing your system through a bid process, knowing how to ask for what you want becomes even more important.

Begin by analyzing the method you are currently using for the task(s) involved. A good way to do this is to use a favorite tool of programmers—the flow chart. A flow chart is simply a diagram of a process, broken down into steps. The steps are placed in different-shaped boxes according to type, for example, rectangular for a definitive action, or diamond-shaped for a decision (always yes or no). Figure 7.2 is a simple flow chart for checking out a book.

---

[1]William T. Cound, *Colonet, Microcomputers in Libraries* (Denver: Colorado State Library Network, 1982), 1-4.

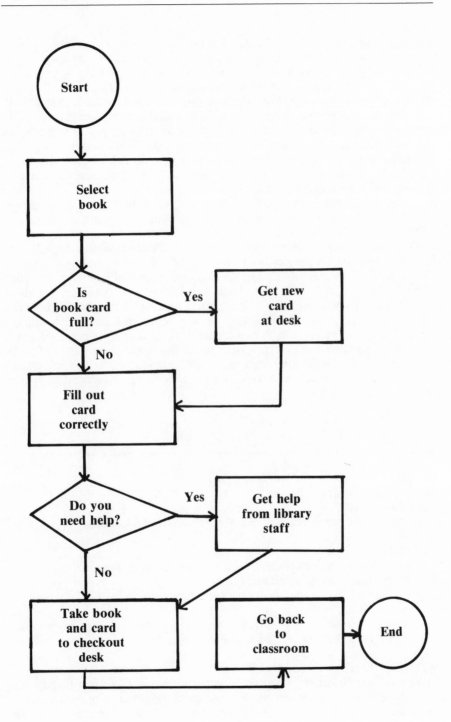

Fig. 7.2. A simple flowchart.

Depending on the outcome of a decision box, the process either returns to an earlier step or skips ahead. Flow charting requires you to be very specific and detailed about the process you are describing, and also provides a graphic illustration of the feasibility of computerizing it. You may find yourself "going to" one of the preliminary selection processes described earlier if the application you chose is not really suitable, or if you discover that making a simple change or two in your current method would actually be just as effective as computerizing it. If the application you wish to implement is something altogether new, such as one of the networking systems described in chapter 5, rather than an automation of a current function, use a flow chart to describe the way the system should work.

The second step, using the flow chart analysis from step 1, is to prepare a written statement describing *exactly* what you want the system to do, how it will be used, and by whom. The object of this statement is to give everyone, including you, the vendor, your administration, and the purchasing department, a precise view of the objectives and goals of the computerization project. Clearly defined, written objectives will also give you a tool for evaluating your progress later. If part of the objective is to become more cost effective (which may include salary savings due to less clerical time, etc.), be specific about the expected savings, some of which may be long term. Include a list of the expected benefits to patrons, such as increased staff availability, increased access to resources, and so on. You may want to include a cost comparison of traditional methods versus computerization. A sample comparison of a card catalog versus an online catalog for a new school, including a list of patron benefits, appears below.

To: Mr. V. I. Person and the Board of Education
From: Meade A. Specialist
Date: May 5, 1983
Regarding: Computerization of the Modernview Card Catalog

PURPOSE:
1 . Developing a more efficient media management system
2 . Promoting student computer literacy
3 . Making the entire media/library collection readily accessible to teachers and students
4 . Saving time for library staff, teachers, and students seeking information (less than 3 seconds to find a title or subject)

WHY LOOK AT A COMPUTER?
Considerable time and resources are required for organizing a new library. Rex O. Mend of the State Library has advised us to computerize our card catalog now, since it would be cost effective, excellent software is available, and the system is working well in Success Elementary in Nexttown. If we were not creating a new library collection this procedure would not be as cost effective.

WHAT ARE THE COSTS OF A COMPUTERIZED CATALOG PROGRAM COMPARED WITH A TRADITIONAL CATALOG?

These costs are for 4,000 library volumes purchased over a four-year period and 1,950 other media, including educational kits, filmstrips, magazines, prints, films, etc. The costs are based on current salaries of a part-time aide and a librarian, and do not reflect inflation. The 1983 summer salary is $7.00 per hour, and the average contracted school time salaries for both people is $11.50 ($7.00 per hour for the aide and $14.00 per hour for the librarian). It would appear that the librarian will be doing more cataloging than the aide due to the limited time the aide would be available on the Modernview Library Program. The $11.50 per hour estimate is therefore low.

	Four-Year Costs for Conventional Card Catalog Setup		**Four-Year Costs for the Computer Catalog Setup**	
Summer 1983 1,000 titles	6 books/hr. @ $7.00/hr. 166 hrs	= $ 1,162.	30 books/hr. @ $7.00/hr. 33 hrs	= $ 231.
750 media	3 media/hr @ $7.00/hr 250 hrs	= $ 1,750.	30 media/hr @ $7.00/hr 5 hrs	= $ 380.
Winter/Spring 1984 1,000 titles	6 books/hr @ $11.50/hr 166 hrs	= $ 1,909.	30 books/hr @ $11.50/hr 33 hrs	= $ 380.
500 media	3 media/hr @ $11.50/hr 167 hrs	= $ 1,920.	30 media/hr @ $11.50/hr 17 hrs	= $ 196.
Winter/Spring 1985 1,000 titles	6 books/hr @ $11.50/hr 166 hrs	= $ 1,909.	30 books/hr @ $11.50/hr 33 hrs	= $ 380.
350 media	3 media/hr @ $11.50/hr 116 hrs	= $ 1,334.	30 media/hr @ $11.50/hr 11 hrs	= $ 127.
Equipment to do Cataloging	Card Catalog Furniture and Cards	= $ 2,000.	Microcomputer, Hard Disk Printer, Training	= $ 9,445.
TOTAL	Conventional System Total	= $15,227.	Computer System Total	= $11,441.

EQUIPMENT NEEDED
1. 48K microcomputer
2. Hard disk drive
3. Floppy disk drive
4. TV monitor
5. Printer
6. Software

UNIQUE ADVANTAGES OF THE COMPUTER CATALOGING PROGRAM
1. Arouses natural curiosity about computers.
2. The computer lists subject/title/author indexes, and provides many more cross-referencing suggestions than do most catalogs.
3. Requires less skill in alphabetizing, spelling, and filing which makes many more opportunities available for research to elementary school children.
4. Computer stores an inventory that can be retrieved as printed lists.
5. The computer system eliminates the need for multiple cards and prevents filing backlogs.
6. In addition to library uses the system can be used to keep track of all school textbooks, workbooks, and other instructional materials in the building.
7. Instant catalog changes are possible.
8. No cards to file or withdraw.
9. All holdings (books and materials) are integrated into a single catalog. Includes articles from periodicals, poster file, and pamphlet file, which is not possible with a card catalog.
10. Cost of maintaining the catalog is more predictable and not as dependent on extra aide time or money available.
11. Makes more time available for helping users, teaching students, and creative use of media instead of tedious typing and filing tasks.

RECOMMENDATION
We purchase necessary equipment to place Modernview Library materials into a computerized program since the program is financially sound, administratively efficient, and educationally beneficial to the entire curricular program.[2]

Next, list your requirements for hardware and peripherals, including any special features, such as color graphics capability or letter-quality printing. The list should be divided into two parts — *must haves* and *would likes*. Do the same for software. Include the number of records the system must be able to

[2]Based on a proposal submitted by Dr. Clark L. Milsom, Principal, Larkspur Elementary, Larkspur, Colo. Used with the permission of Dr. Milsom.

handle, the size of the records, the average frequency of usage for each record, the response time and speeds needed, and the degree of accuracy required. (Refer to chapters 2, 3, and 4 for some general and specific criteria for hardware and software choices.) It may be helpful to prepare comparison charts, using your required and desirable features as criteria to evaluate various hardware and software choices. (Sample comparison charts may be found in appendix E.) If your research (reviews, interviews with experienced users, etc.) and preliminary evaluations indicate specific equipment and programs you think may fit your needs, include them as suggestions. You may feel very strongly that a certain brand of hardware or a specific program is what you want. If so, go ahead and include it as a requirement, but keep in mind that there may be products your dealer knows about that have not surfaced in your research and that might be ideal for your purposes. If a vendor does recommend a product you have not heard of, you can use the comparison charts to evaluate it.

The next section of your specifications is the part that protects you from unpleasant surprises. It spells out the obligations of the prospective vendor with respect to accountability, delivery and installation, experience, references, service and support (including training), system compatibility, and equipment and software guarantees. The list should include:

Demonstrations. The vendor must be able to demonstrate the hardware and software in a school or library setting at your request. In the fast-moving and highly competitive microcomputer industry, many manufacturers have ideas that outpace their capabilities. *See it work before you buy.* Better yet, use it yourself. Also, keep in mind that many demonstration programs are abbreviated versions, and as such handle fewer data but at a faster speed than the actual program. This is especially true in the case of database management systems. If you can, get specific figures on what differences to expect.

References. The dealer should furnish a list, with contact names and phone numbers, of customers in the educational or library field, whose needs are similar to yours. Once you have this list, use it. Most people are quite willing to share their experiences with you, both good and bad. If the vendor is unwilling or unable to furnish references, find a different vendor.

The dealer should also be able to verify that the hardware and software have been in use by at least five educational or library customers for a minimum of three months. The exception to this would be customized software or a test site project for which you are prepared to deal with the debugging process. In the latter case, verifying the dealer qualifications and references is especially important.

Equipment. If you have made any suggestions as to specific brands and models, the vendor should ensure that the equipment named in the actual bid is equal or superior. In any case, it must be capable of running the software (which ideally has been chosen first). Also, any necessary cables, interfaces, or other special equipment must be included in the original bid price. Surprise add-ons could prove very costly.

The above also holds true with respect to delivery and installation costs. State that all necessary services must be included in the package price, whether specified or not. Your specifications should indicate the location or locations and a fixed date for delivery, with a penalty clause for late delivery.

In addition, if you have plans for future expansion, such as to a multi-user system, find out if the dealer is capable of providing those services and products as well. Otherwise, you may find yourself caught in a bind between or among dealers, with no one willing to accept responsibility.

Training and Follow-up Assistance. The dealer should provide a minimum of two hours of on-site staff training in basic use and maintenance of the system, with the cost of further training, if needed, specified in the bid. You should also have telephone access to someone qualified to answer the inevitable questions about the software. (Though this service should be available, and is one of the primary reasons to buy from a local dealer rather than through mail order, it should not be abused. Manuals are included for a purpose.)

If your project is ambitious and/or staff members have little or no experience with computers, you may wish to investigate the option of a short term "handholding contract" providing intensive support during the early stages of implementation.

Service Contracts and Warranties. Accept bids only from authorized dealers, and specify that all equipment must be factory-approved and warrantied for a minimum of 90 days, with free repair or replacement. You may wish to require an extended service contract for up to a year, possibly even including training of district service personnel, and availability of loaner equipment if necessary.

In reviewing the bids, remember that cost is not the most important consideration. For this reason, you must be prepared to defend your vendor choice to the budget committees and/or purchasing department. We hope we have given enough emphasis to the crucial importance of dealer support in purchasing a computer system. Microcomputers are particularly vulnerable to bargain backfires, and what seems like a good deal could become very costly all too soon. One way to help bring costs down is to buy "in bulk," with a district (or even several) ordering en masse. This, of course, would require careful cooperative planning, but could result in considerable savings.

In determining your computer budget, and in negotiations with vendors, don't forget to include the "hidden costs" of a computer system. We have already mentioned the cables, interfaces, and special software needed to make your system work, along with important accessories such as surge protectors.

In addition, you may need to buy special furniture. An older building may require the installation of special wiring or even dedicated lines. The value of productivity lost due to training and implementation time is yet another "hidden cost," as are telephone installation charges. (Remember, if you intend to include a modem in your system, you *must* have a single phone line to your library. A modem will not work with a switchboard line.) You may also need to purchase special insurance for your system, as most general policies do not include computers. And there are the ongoing costs of paper, disks, ribbons, telephone and connect time charges, maintenance contracts, software updates, etc. Planning for all these from the beginning will save you unpleasant surprises later.

Though all of this may seem like a long, complicated process, in the long run (and perhaps sooner) it will save you both time and money, not to mention irritation. If you are working with prepurchased hardware and/or software, use it as a starting point for your specifications, incorporating it into your comparison charts to guide you in choosing potential applications as well as software and peripherals. You may have to use extra thought and imagination in order to turn a potential white elephant into a wise and rewarding investment. It is highly probable that an already-purchased computer will by its very existence be justification for additional purchases, such as disk drives or a printer, if it is of little or no value otherwise. Also, remember that just because your library already possesses a certain type of computer, all future applications are not necessarily limited to that type. The nature of microcomputers can allow for an effective system consisting of several independent subsystems, which may use different types of computers altogether.

IMPLEMENTING YOUR NEW COMPUTER SYSTEM

Now that you have planned for and selected a microcomputer system and outlined one or more proposed uses for it, how can you ensure that it will be used as effectively and beneficially as possible? What are the pitfalls to avoid, and the steps to take to ease the transition for staff and patrons alike? How will you evaluate the progress of your program in terms of cost effectiveness and improved services? And how do you determine the possibilities and directions for growth?

The first thing you should realize is that the implementation process is bound to take longer than you think it will, even if no significant problems develop. Therefore, it would be wise to double or even triple your original estimates for completing each step, at least when setting up time frames for the benefit of administrators, staff members, patrons, and parents. If you purchase a circulation system in September and hope to have your entire collection online by the time school reopens in January, *plan* for a completion date sometime in April. This will prevent a lot of unrealistic expectations and resulting tension. If you should finish by January, consider it a bonus and go on to the next step. You might even set up two timetables, one ideal and one based on everything you can imagine going wrong, and see where you come out.

We *strongly* advise you to keep a computer journal, beginning no later than the date your system is delivered and installed. A day-by-day record of computer events—what you or someone else did and how the computer responded, procedures, problems, accomplishments—will be enormously useful for maintaining consistency, as well as debugging and troubleshooting. Also, in the case of staff turnover, new members will have a basis from which to start. A system that is known by only one person is utterly useless if that person should happen to leave. Keep the journal near the computer and encourage users to make entries in it, including subjective responses. If your computer is being used by both staff and patrons, you might want to keep two journals, one for staff and one for general use. This would be an excellent way to evaluate progress and plan for future computer projects.

Start keeping your computer journal at the very beginning of the implementation phase. Use tabs to index the journal according to subject—hardware notes, software notes, diagnostic testing results, policies, calls to vendors, problems and their solutions, etc. Be sure to write down the exact sequence of events whenever you have a problem. Support personnel will use the sequence to reproduce the problem—if they can't reproduce it, they can't solve it, and you cannot trust your memory not to leave out steps. If several staff members and/or patrons will be using the system, a comment section might be useful, or at least entertaining. If an application involves data entry, make sure the journal contains notes on how items are entered. For instance, how are commas and spaces used? Is an author's name entered "Cleary, Beverly" or "Cleary,Beverly"? What about *a*s, *an*s and *the*s? Such notes help maintain consistency, which is a critical element in successful computerization.

You should do some preparation before the computer's arrival. This includes setting up a "computer corner" in the library or an office, deciding who will be using it and when, and doing some preliminary training and orientation. User preparation is extremely important. You will no doubt encounter a full range of attitudes toward the new acquisition, from enthusiasm to timid curiosity to outright resistance. With luck, at least one staff member will fall into the enthusiastic category; this person or persons will probably be the best choice(s) for getting the project underway. They should attend training sessions offered by or arranged through the vendor, and be given access to manuals and any other information that will help them to feel at ease with the computer when it arrives. If possible, they should take an introductory programming course through a local college or adult education program. Also, try to recruit student, patron, teacher, and/or parent volunteers, either people who have computers at home or at work and therefore have at least some experience with micros, or who are highly motivated to work with them. Don't try to do the whole project yourself if you can get help! Note, however, that at this stage you need people who are self-starters and able to learn a lot on their own. Later they can help everyone else play catch-up.

During the preparation phase you should also give noninvolved patrons and staff members notice that a change is coming. This "publicity campaign" could be anything from printed announcements or newsletter articles to orientation classes giving a brief overview of computers in general and your new system in particular. Include a list of benefits, but don't get carried away.

Unrealistic expectations could mean trouble if the system does not live up to its advance billing.

When the computer first arrives, allow enough time for those staff members who will be primarily responsible for its use to get acquainted with it. Before you can start to implement any applications, someone must know how to connect all of the hardware correctly, how to turn it on and off, how to load the printer, and how to use the operating system(s) to:

- Format disks (including the hard disk, if there is one).

- Copy files.

- Back up and restore files.

- Obtain a listing (directory) of files on the screen and as a printout.

- Rename files.

- Erase files.

- Run simple diagnostics to determine if a problem is in the hardware or software, or with the operator.

- Create and change directories or volumes, if you are using a hard disk.

A number of good books are available on each of the popular operating systems; one of these would be a good supplement to the manuals, which are usually difficult to use, especially for beginners. During this phase it is also very helpful to have someone available to demonstrate and answer questions, either the dealer or volunteers with previous micro experience (make sure the "instructors" know what they are doing—bad advice is worse than none). The primary users should also go through any disk and/or manual tutorials included with the system and/or the applications software.

As soon as one or two people are somewhat comfortable with the system, start implementing the first application, possibly with dealer assistance. Learn how to install the applications software, even if the original installation is done by the vendor. After installation, the next steps will depend on the application. If you are using general purpose software to develop your own applications, the first phase should be one of experimentation. For a database management program, try setting up different record formats, experimenting with the placement and lengths of fields, entering small practice files (about 50 records) and printing some sample reports. For a spreadsheet, try some simple exercises like setting up a checkbook balancing worksheet. For a word processing program, create a "computerized" newsletter announcing the new arrival.

If your primary application is a cataloging and/or circulation system, the initial stages will consist primarily of data entry. However, you should not try to get your whole collection online all at once. Plan your retrospective conversion carefully, with an eye to integrating the computer system into your routine as smoothly as possible. Unless your library is new, you will be computerizing an existing function; do not be in a hurry to retire the old system. In most cases, the transition should be fairly gradual, with the manual method and the computer method running parallel until the new system is "up" and operational and data entry is complete. Besides giving everyone time to become familiar with the new system, this ensures that you have a backup in case something goes wrong. For instance, you might start an online catalog by entering only new acquisitions for the first month or two, keeping the card catalog for your existing collection. Then, once you are sure the system is working, and as time permits, you can begin entering items from the card catalog, taking the opportunity to weed as you go. One method is to enter your collection in subsets, such as reference works, paperbacks, or biographies.

Take small steps. As with anything new, learning is easier in stages. The idea is to start with something simple and low pressure, until you are sure there are no serious hardware or software problems and involved staff members are familiar with basic procedures. Make sure you allow plenty of time for the initial training period. This is liable to be the most frustrating phase of computerization, since everyone is dealing with something new and strange on top of trying to keep up with what is probably already a heavy work load. Patience is the key! Once you get to the "How did we ever live without it?" stage, it will be worth all the frustration. In the meantime, proceeding in steps will make the adjustment easier for both staff and patrons. Publicize each step as you complete it: "We now have all of our reference collection (or paperbacks, or audio visual materials) on the computer." Emphasize what has already been accomplished, at the same time as you look ahead to long range goals.

In the beginning, at least, do not attempt to upgrade your system at the same time you are computerizing it. Get the basics first and add the frills later. For example, if you are computerizing your overdue system, and your present method lets you send out notices two weeks after books are due, don't plan to start sending out notices the *day* books become overdue instead—at least not right away.

If patrons are going to be using the computer, the next step will be some sort of orientation program. Orientation can begin even before the computer is ready to use, with demonstrations, descriptions, and class exercises such as "playing computer." At some point, however, each user should have some hands-on experience in the basics of operation—turning on the computer, inserting a disk or cassette, loading a program, etc. The peer-tutoring method works well here. You or another staff member can instruct two or three especially interested students or patrons who in turn will serve as instructors. Orientation sessions could be held on a class by class basis, or, in the case of a public library, once or twice a week (more often with volunteer tutors). Even though everyone who uses the computer will have to go through the orientation, you will probably want to have staff or volunteer monitors available whenever the computer is in use.

Orientation classes are one way to help overcome "technophobia," which is more likely to afflict staff members than patrons. There are a number of reasons for this fear of computers, ranging from nervousness about breaking the computer to fear of being replaced by it. In the first instance, it may be helpful to draw analogies between computers and more familiar equipment such as movie projectors or tape recorders. Selecting and running a program is not so different from selecting and showing a film. In each case, a specific objective is involved, and a specific process is necessary to achieve the objective. Inserting a disk into a drive is actually less complicated than inserting film into a projector. Demonstrations and hands-on trials help to overcome fears of breaking the computer by striking the wrong key, etc. Fear of replacement, or simply a resistance to change, is harder to deal with, and may, in fact, be manifested as overt hostility. For these people you will need to stress the benefits of the computer as a *tool* while making its limitations very clear. If you have involved people from the beginning, your chances of problems at this stage will be lessened.

If the computer is to be available for general patron use, you will have to decide whether to allow game playing. This is a subject of some debate. Some people feel that games increase the noise and general commotion level and serve no useful purpose, while others believe that they serve as motivation for students to learn more about computers. They may also be used as "rewards" for accomplishing more instructional tasks. If you do decide to allow games, be prepared for more scheduling and noise problems. You might want to limit game playing to lunch or after school hours, or only allow educational and/or user-written games to be played.

In order to cut down on staff time and increase user independence, it is a good idea to have some sort of user's guide at or near the computer station. Include such things as the basics of machine operation, a program catalog, a glossary, and perhaps a bibliography of resource material. Alternatively, you might "decorate" the area around the computer station with posters or flashcards depicting the various steps of operation, such as inserting a disk, along with terminology and things to remember, for example, "Don't touch the shiny part!" captioning a picture of a disk.

Early in the implementation process, make a list of definite rules for using the computer, and keep a copy at the computer station. Include which periods the computer is to be used for each purpose, the number of persons who may be at the computer at any one time, the length of time each person is allowed to use the computer during one session, allowable noise levels, rules for scheduling, and so on. The actual rules structure will depend on your computer priorities and the amount of time available (you will soon find there is never enough). Sign-up sheets are one way to handle scheduling, with limits on the number of times each person may use the computer during a given period of time. Or computer time may be scheduled by class. If you have an online catalog or other type of database searching service, time limits may be set according to whether or not others are waiting to use the computer. You will also need to set rules for disk space usage, printer use, and so on, if these are factors.

The journal you have been keeping should also include backup procedures and logs. You *must* develop a backup routine and follow it from the first day you start to enter data. Your actual procedure will depend on your application and what type of backup media you are using, but it should involve some sort of rotational system. *Never back up onto the most recent backup*. For instance, if you are using tapes to back up an online catalog and circulation system that changes daily, it would be wise to have a tape for each day of the week. On Monday, you would back up over the previous Monday's tape, so if something should happen during the backup, you would lose no more than a day's entries. If you are using a database package, such as a catalog or circulation system, or any type of accounting package, you should also make archival backups on a regular basis, and keep them for a longer period of time (up to a year or more). These provide a known reference point in case of damage that goes undetected for a period. Database damage from a power surge or operator error, for example, may not become apparent for several months. If you do not have any backups over a week old, they would all contain the damaged data, and you would have to start over from scratch. It's also a good idea to keep on hand data entry forms, such as shelflist cards and acquisition forms, in case you need to reconstruct data. And keep hard copy printouts of all your documents (letters, lists, etc.)

We cannot overemphasize the importance of backup. Many people, unfortunately, do not understand the necessity for backups until, through error or mishap, they lose hours, days, or even months or years of work. Perhaps an example from our own experience will help. Not long ago, while one of us was working on the manuscript for this book, a power surge caused the lights to flicker and the image on the screen to waver. Within hours, the computer began to deny that files and even whole directories even existed. A trip to the service department revealed that the hard disk and the disk controller had both been destroyed. Several hundred dollars and a few days later the computer was back at work, with a new disk and controller but quite bare of files. Since all of our work was safely backed onto floppies, within twenty minutes the files were restored and work on the book could continue. Imagine if those floppies hadn't existed! Also, since our computer was covered under a special computer insurance policy which included damage from power surges, much of the expense was reimbursable. Forethought turned a potential horror story into a relatively minor inconvenience.

Sooner or later, something will happen to *your* data. A careless or hurried operator may accidentally erase a disk; lightning may strike a power line and fuse the circuits in your computer; someone may pull the plug on the computer and cause a head crash, or spill a cup of coffee on a floppy disk. Insurance can replace the equipment, but not the data. Don't find out the hard way. *Always, always back up*.

In addition to data and software backups, you need to have a hardware backup. We were lucky; our glitched computer was back up in a few days. It could have taken weeks. It is important to have a contingency plan before disaster strikes. You may be able to include loaner equipment in a maintenance contract or insurance policy, or work out arrangements with other libraries in your area. At the very least, plan a manual backup system that could carry you for several days or longer.

Another consideration is the matter of security. Hardware is best protected with locks (including bolt-down equipment or lockable carrels), sign-up or sign-out sheets, and staff monitors, just as you protect other types of equipment. In the case of software, your best protection is a backup collection, including documentation. If possible, keep master copies of software in a place other than the library.

SELECTION CHECKLIST

Start by learning all you can.
Read at least one general computer periodical over a period of two or three months, along with computer-related articles in library journals and the computer column in your newspaper's business pages. Talk to users, especially librarians. Attend conferences and possibly users' group meetings. If at all possible, get some hands-on experience with a computer, any computer.

Set broad goals.
Why do you want to computerize? Do you want to reduce the burden of routine, repetitive chores in order to spend more time with patrons, increase patron access to information, allow patrons or students an opportunity to acquire computer skills and knowledge?

Analyze your library.
What tasks could be improved with better manual procedures? What tasks are good prospects for computerization now; in two years; in five years? How much staff time is available for implementation? Where will the computer be kept? Who will use it?

Prepare for computerization.
During inventory, update shelf card information for your existing collection to include ISBN and/or LC card numbers and subject tracings. Design and begin using a computer consideration/order form which includes shelf card information; as items are received, update each record. Such steps will greatly speed eventual entry into an online catalog and/or circulation system.

If feasible, include staff members and patrons in software decisions. Encourage discussion and curiosity about the new system.

Plan the physical space for the computer. If your library does not contain a telephone, have one installed where the computer will be (this is essential). If you are going to use a modem, the telephone line cannot go through a switchboard. Check electrical systems; make sure wiring is adequate and grounded outlets are available.

Decide exactly what you want the computer to do.
Think ahead. Decide where you would like your library to be in five years, and work back. Don't try to do everything at once; buy a system that enables you to start small and build as you gain experience and knowledge.

Make a detailed shopping list.

Write down all your *must haves* and *would likes,* for both software and hardware. Develop matrices for comparing systems. If you are looking for a complex system, such as one that includes consideration, ordering, acquisitions, and cataloging, make a separate matrix for each module in order to evaluate them more effectively in terms of your needs.

Quantify your needs. How many records will you have initially? How many will you add over the next few years? Do you need multi-user capabilities? How many different kinds of programs do you expect to use?

Shop around.

Compare packages, hardware systems, and vendors. Get names of current users and talk to them. Get price quotations on the total system — cables, interfaces, surge protection, service, etc. Is installation included? Is local service available? Get written guarantees about software compatibility, record handling, etc. Don't be charmed by vaporware. Buy a system that you know is up and running for someone else, unless you are prepared to be a test site.

If the system is complex and multifunctional, go over all functions in detail with the vendor so there is no misunderstanding about what the system can or can't do. (To be safe, have the vendor sign your written checklist.) And remember, if at all possible, choose the software first.

Don't forget to check on insurance policies to protect your investment.

Take your time.

You will be living with this system for a long time. Don't let anyone rush you into a decision.

IMPLEMENTATION CHECKLIST

Become familiar with the system.

Designate one or two primary computer person(s) who will be responsible for this phase. They should learn how to connect the hardware correctly, turn everything on and off, load the printer, use the operating system, and install the applications software. If the system includes a modem, they should practice sending and receiving information with the modem. They should go through disk and/or manual tutorials, and experiment with the applications software.

Start a journal.

Include backup procedures and logs, software and hardware use policies, details on data entry methods and formats, detailed descriptions of problems, support calls, diagnostic test results, and user comments.

Develop written computer policies.

This includes policies on the loaning and use of equipment and software, backup procedures, use of games, etc. All users should be aware of these policies and sign agreements to abide by them.

Plan your retrospective conversion.

The transition process should be gradual, and may take months or even years. Weed before you start, or as you go, to cut down on unnecessary data entry. Even if you are not implementing a catalog or circulation system right away, you should consider it as a future possibility, and adapt your manual procedures accordingly.

Develop a training program for staff and patrons.

Everyone who will use the computer must go through at least an orientation program. Training is especially important for data entry people and online searchers. Also, staff members who will be working with patrons must be trained to assist them properly. Be sure to include "free" practice and familiarization time for anyone who will be working a lot with the computer.

Make a contingency plan.

Know what you will do if the hardware should go down, or if your main computer person should leave. Develop and enforce consistent backup policies. Know what your insurance covers, and keep it current.

Maintain your equilibrium, sense of humor, curiosity, and enthusiasm.

Anyone who works with computers experiences frustration, especially during the initial stages. But the same could be said of any job, including, of course, yours. If you have a clear purpose for your system, have done your homework, and have made careful choices, the rewards of your computer system should more than equal the frustration, and you will eventually be able to say "I don't know how we ever did without it."

Smooth implementation is a matter of planning, patience, and realistic expectations. Ideally, you have purchased a system from a local vendor who will be able to help you through the initial get-acquainted process and deal with any bugs or unusual problems that come up. You are paying for this service, so take advantage of it — but don't abuse it. In summary, think ahead, take your time, involve others, and have fun!

FURTHER READINGS

Planning

Anglin, Richard. "Computer Commandments — Cooperate and Plan before You Buy Anything." *Library Journal* 109, no. 10 (1 October 1984): 1821-22.

Beiser, Karl. "Getting There from Here." *Small Computers in Libraries* 5, no. 9 (October 1985): 9-13.
Discusses "moving data between computer systems or between programs on the same system. . . ."

Bills, Linda G. "Making Decisions about Automation for Small Libraries." *Library Resources and Technical Services* (April/June 1985): 161-71.

Boss, Richard. "Microcomputers in Libraries: The Quiet Revolution." *Wilson Library Bulletin* 59, no. 10 (June 1985): 653-60.
"Planning ensures that one doesn't take steps that will move the library in the wrong direction."

Collins, Gayle. "From Catalog to Database: Preliminary Steps." *School Library Journal* 31, no. 7 (March 1985): 123.
Discusses how to prepare for future computerization of catalog.

"Cutting through the Hidden Costs of Computing." *Personal Computing* 8, no. 10 (October 1984): 122-29.
"Forewarned users with a plan can defuse spending—turning it into an investment in productivity."

Friedman, Rich. "When Consultants Clash." *Popular Computing* 2, no. 6 (April 1983): 96-102.
"Computer consultants should be seen as givers of advice, not wizards or shamans."

Hlava, Majorie. "When Should I Computerize?" *Information Today* 2, no. 9 (October 1985): 13, 30.
"Keeping your data generic means you can move it from system to system."

King, Judith. "Improved Efficiency through an Alternate Check-out Procedure." *School Library Media Quarterly* 10, no. 2 (Winter 1982): 190-92.
Changing your manual circulation procedures may be the most effective preparation for future computerization.

Markuson, Carolyn. "How Do I Decide . . ." *School Library Media Quarterly* 14, no. 1 (Fall 1985): 28-29.

Matthews, Joseph R., and Joan Frye Williams. "Oh, If I'd Only Known . . ." *American Libraries* 14, no. 6 (June 1983): 408-12.
"Ten things you can do today to prepare for library automation tomorrow."

Micossi, Anita. "Ergonomics Is Good Business." *PC World* 1, no. 10 (December 1983): 300-307.

Roblyer, M. D. "Do Schools Need Outside Consultants?" *Educational Computer Magazine* 3, no. 5 (September 1983): 28, 88.

Rowley, Jennifer E. "Concise AACR2: A Review and Evaluation." *Special Libraries* 75, no. 4 (October 1984): 319-28.

"Strategic Planning: A Change in Mind Set Toward Automation." *ONLINE Libraries and Microcomputers* 2, no. 5 (May 1984): 1-2.

Stronge, James. "Avoiding the Pitfalls." *Electronic Education* 4, no. 6 (March/April 1985): 8-9, 22.
In same issue see also "Computer Purchasing Comparison Table Simplifies" by R. Hermelin, p. 19.

"What Not to Computerize." *Small Computers in Libraries* 5, no. 3 (March 1985): 8-9.

Selection

Burke, Robert L. "Selecting Micros for Schools." *Electronic Education* 3, no. 7 (April 1984): 18, 23.

Crawford, Walt. "Commonsense System Pricing; or, How Much Will That Really Cost?" *Library HiTech* (Issue 6) 2, no. 2 (2nd quarter 1984): 27-32.

Hamilton, John F. "Buy It YOUR Way." *Industry Week* (30 September 1985): 67-68.
"You don't have to accept an equipment vendor's 'standard contract' . . . Get it in writing."

McGonagle, John J., Jr., and Larry McCain. "Negotiating Computer Contracts—Knowing What to Ask for Is the Key." *Popular Computing* 2, no. 5 (March 1983): 126-30.

"Shortcuts!" (productivity column). *Personal Computing* 9, no. 12 (December 1985): 58-65.
"Knowing how to cut corners can help you get quicker results from your software or hardware."

Spokony-Smith, Marion, and Richard Smith. "Getting the Best Software Support." *Electronic Education* 3, no. 6 (March 1984): 23-50.

Taylor, James B. "Integrated Systems and Vendor Survival." *Library Journal* 110, no. 16 (1 October 1985): 50-51.
Includes vendor information to consider when involved in selecting a large integrated system.

Thompson, James C. "How Not to Choose a Lemon—Advice for the Automated-system Buyer." *American Libraries* 16, no. 10 (November 1985): 690-93.

Implementation

Barden, William, Jr. "Can Software Break?" *Popular Computing* 2, no. 5 (March 1983): 52, 54-55, 58.

Cole, David. "Your New Library IBM Microcomputer: Unpleasant Surprises." *M300 and PC Report* 2, no. 10 (November 1985): 1-3.
    Includes: "Diskcopy Surprise"; "Database Surprise"; "Sorting Surprise"; "Telecommunications Surprise"; "Printer Surprise"; "Hard Disk Surprise"; "Preparing for Surprises."

Levy, Steven. "Getting Help—Finding an Answer to a Specific Problem." *Popular Computing* 3, no. 9 (July 1984): 70, 75-78.

Malinconico, Michael. "To Eat an Elephant." *Library Journal* 110, no. 8 (1 May 1985): 38-39.
    "One bite at a time! This is sound advice for anyone confronting a large, complex undertaking."

Meilach, Dona Z. "The Agony and the Ecstacy of a New Computer Owner." *Interface Age* 7, no. 1 (January 1982): 98-99.

Miller, Gloria. "No One Said It Was Easy!" *School Library Journal* 31, no. 3 (November 1984): 62-66.

Milone, Michael N., Jr. "Disk Crashes: They Can't Happen to Us!" *Classroom Computer Learning* 6, no. 2 (October 1985): 13.
    "Best way to deal with the loss of data is through rigorous backup policies and procedures."

Needle, David. "The Smart Way To Learn Computing." *Personal Computing* 9, no. 6 (June 1985): 101-6.
    "For most of us, becoming an expert is not the primary goal in computing; it is developing enough understanding to get the job done."

Quint, Barbara. "Protecting Your Micro and Its Data: Locking the Barn Door First." *Small Computers in Libraries* 5, no. 9 (October 1985): 5-8.
    "Failing to backup data probably causes more damage to micro owners than any other error."

Tannenbaum, Michael, and Larry McCain. "The Pains of Implementation." *Popular Computing* 2, no. 5 (March 1983): 38-44.
    "Your system works best when you anticipate the worst."

Online Catalogs

Arret, Linda. "Can Online Catalogs Be Too Easy?" *American Libraries* 16, no. 2 (February 1985): 118-20.

_____. "Of Catalogs and Kitchen Sinks." *American Libraries* 14, no. 7 (July/August 1983): 482.

Cochrane, Pauline Atherton. "Modern Subject Access in the Online Age." *American Libraries* 15, nos. 2-7 (February 1984 through July/August 1984). No pages available.
"American Libraries' first continuing education course." These articles provide information about an important issue today: "[a] majority of online catalog users — in all types of libraries — are doing subject searching; but often they cannot find related subject terms and cannot easily reduce or increase their search results."

Epstein, Susan Baerg. "Automated Authority Control: A Hidden Timebomb? Part 1." *Library Journal* 110, no. 18 (1 November 1985): 36-37.
Librarians looking at online cataloging systems often ask about the "authority file." "But what does authority control really mean in an online environment?"

Hudson, Judith. "Bibliographic Record Maintenance in the Online Environment." *Information Technology and Libraries* 3, no. 4 (December 1984): 388-93.

Malinconico, S. Michael. "Catalogs and Cataloging." *Library Journal* 109, no. 11 (15 June 1984): 1210-13.

Price, Bennett J. "Printing and the Online Catalog." *Information Technology and Libraries* 3, no. 1 (March 1984): 15-20.
"What is to be printed and how it can best be done are questions that have hardly begun to be faced."

Data Entry and/or Retrospective Conversion

Attig, John C. "The Concept of a MARC Format." *Information Technology and Libraries* 2, no. 1 (March 1983): 7-16.

Bocher, Robert. "MITINET: Catalog Conversion to a MARC Database." *School Library Journal* (March 1985): 109-112.

Boss, Richard. "Retrospective Conversion: Investing in the Future." *Wilson Library Bulletin* 59, no. 3 (November 1984): 173-78, 238.

"Converting to CDs and Downloading Data." *American Libraries* 16, no. 11 (December 1985): 768.

Coyle, Karen. "Record Matching: A Discussion." *Information Technology and Libraries* 4, no. 1 (March 1985): 57-58.

Dalehite, Michele I. "MARC Format on Tape: A Tutorial." *Library HiTech* (Issue 5) 2, no. 1 (1st quarter 1984): 17-22.
This is an excerpt from a chapter of *From Tape to Product,* to be published by Pierian Press.

Kruger, Kathleen Joyce. "MARC Tags and Retrospective Conversion: The Editing Process." *Information Technology and Libraries* 4, no. 1 (March 1985): 53-58.

Ludy, Lorene E., and Sally A. Rodgers. "Authority Control in the Online Environment." *Information Technology and Libraries* 3, no. 3 (September 1984): 262-66.

"Special Section: Retrospective Conversion." *Information Technology and Libraries* 3, no. 3 (September 1984): 267-92.
Includes information about MITINET, MITINET/marc, Electronic Keyboarding, Inc., OCLC, REMARC, and "authority control in the retrospective conversion process."

Watkins, Deane. "Record Conversion at Oregon State." *Wilson Library Bulletin* 60, no. 4 (December 1985): 31-33.
Includes other recommended reading.

Miscellaneous

Beiser, Karl. "256 Kilobytes and a MULE." *Library Journal/School Library Journal* (library computing supplement) 110, no. 8, p. 117; 31, no. 9 (May 1985): 147.

Carlson, David H. "The Perils of Personals: Microcomputers in Libraries?" *Library Journal* 110, no. 2 (1 February 1985): 50-55.

"Confusion." *ONLINE Libraries and Microcomputers* 1, no. 3 (November 1983): 9-10.
"READ—READ—READ!! That is the best precaution and advice to avoid confusion about microcomputers. 'Read-up' on basic knowledge and then 'keep posted' by reading current periodical literature—especially that geared to your own interests and applications. Communications is the name of the game—and your own kind of people—are the best resources available."

Epstein, Susan Baerg. "Libraries and Systems." *Library Journal.*
See especially columns on: "Problems of Integration" (1 September 1985); "Testing: Did You Get What You Bought" (1 May 1985); "Testing and More Testing" (July 1985).

Freedman, Mary, and Larry Carlin. "The Mary and Larry Show." *Library Journal.*
See columns: "A Micro for Warminster." (1 January 1985); "An Interview

in Four Voices." (1 May 1985); ". . . And Now Press ⟨ENTER⟩" (August 1985); "The Computer as Scapegoat." (July 1985).

Freedman, Maurice J. "Automation and the Future of Technical Services." *Library Journal* 109, no. 11 (15 June 1984): 1197-1203.

Graham, Judy. "Automated Library System." *CMC News* 3, no. 3 (Spring 1983): 2-4.
Describes the automated library system piloted by Graham and now available from the Foundation for Library Research. Originally developed on TRS-80 Model III with hard disk, now also available on IBM PC.

Hegarty, Kevin. "Myths of Library Automation." *Library Journal* 110, no. 16 (1 October 1985): 43-49.
Although the author is director of a large public library, his opinions regarding automation will be helpful to any library, large or small, looking at automation.

Jay, Hilda. "Administering the Microcomputer Program — Assessing for Direction and Policy: A Checklist." *School Learning Resources* (June 1983): 6-9.
Covers hardware, organizing a work station, scheduling, managing equipment use, preservation of data, student instruction, and supplies.

Knoop, Lynn. "Steps to Automation, the Curriculum Materials Center." *Apple LUG Newsletter* 3, no. 3 (July 1985): 39-43.

Mason, Robert M. "Mason on Micros." *Library Journal.*
See columns on: "What Good Are Microcomputers, Anyway?" (15 January 1983); "Human Resources and the Micro System" (15 March 1985); "The Challenge of the Micro Revolution" (15 June 1984).

Matthews, Joseph R. "Unrelenting Change: The 1984 Automated Library System Marketplace." *Library Journal* 110, no. 6 (1 April 1985): 31-40.
"In this annual review article, the progress made and pitfalls encountered by the automated library system marketplace during calendar year 1984 are examined." Includes a list of library automation vendors, both large and small.

"RECON Roundup — News and Resources in Retrospective Record Conversion." *American Libraries* 16, no. 10 (November 1985): 700.

Sloan, Bernard G. "Micromania: A Manager's Perspective." *Library Journal* 110, no. 12 (July 1985): 30-31.

8 Computer Ethics: Tough Questions in a Changing World

In addition to technical and logistical challenges, the growing role of computers in our society presents libraries with serious ethical challenges as well. The two largest issues for libraries are software piracy and the difficulties presented by online searches. Intertwined with these is the need for teaching and modeling ethical computer use.

SOFT WARS: THE PROBLEM OF PIRACY

"Piracy" is the unauthorized copying of computer software. Unauthorized copying covers a wide range of sins and sinners, from the executive who breaks a copy protection scheme to install a newly purchased program on a hard disk, to the corporation that copies a program and manual for distribution to five or five hundred employees, to the "hacker" who obtains an as-yet-unreleased program through a bulletin board, to the teacher who boots ten computers off the same Logo disk. Under federal copyright law, the first person is probably within his rights; the others are clearly in violation. Consequences of such actions vary: the executive may come up against a "worm" that destroys the original program when he tries to make a copy; the corporation may find itself the object of an investigation that ends in an expensive out-of-court settlement; the unreleased program may never make it to market; the teacher may complain about the lack of quality educational software.

End users argue that the software companies have committed a few ethical violations of their own in attempts to protect themselves against theft and gather large returns on their investments. They use elaborate copy protection schemes that cause legitimate users endless inconvenience and frustration. They impose unilateral "contracts," in the form of "shrink-wrapped licenses," which state that by the act of removing the wrapper from a piece of software, a user agrees to the terms of the license. For the most part, shrink-wrapped licenses claim exorbitant rights for the software producers while giving no rights at all to users. Many of the licenses even take away rights given to users under federal copyright law, such as the right to make a backup copy or to use the software on different computers at different times (that is, not simultaneously). The licenses also expressly remove the warranty which is assumed by law to be provided with other types of products, such as refrigerators and radios. Software manufacturers rarely allow potential users to preview a package in order to decide if it is appropriate for their purposes. For these unwarrantied and possibly inappropriate products, buyers are expected to plunk down large sums of nonrefundable money.

It is also true that computer programs, like books and films, take time, expertise, and considerable money to produce. Computer programming is very complex, as you can discover by taking even an introductory programming course. Try to write a program that successfully computes the square roots of a list of variables, or alphabetizes a list of names, and you begin to appreciate the effort involved in developing a program that acts as a chess partner or prints an itemized inventory for a small business. In addition, software manufacturers are shooting at a moving target; even when a product is released, it is not finished. Frequent hardware and operating system changes, as well as the intense competition, drive software producers to continually work on upgrading previous versions.

Another argument in defense of software manufacturers is that, at least in the case of vertical, or specific applications, software (including educational programs), they are selling to limited markets, some with very specific and complicated needs. They must also deal with the tremendous expense and headaches of providing postsale support. It is expensive to maintain those phone lines, and more expensive to have qualified people manning them. Another major problem is that software is unpredictable. It is impossible to anticipate every possible situation that may occur and what a program will do in response to it. Bugs may crop up even after years of trouble-free use. This is why companies are so reluctant to warranty their products. Unfortunately, most of them take the position of being unwilling to guarantee that a program will do even what they say it will do.

One of the most reasonable shrink-wrapped licenses exhorts the buyer to "treat this like a book." Only one person may read a book at a time; to copy and distribute the book to an entire class or company is both illegal and wrong. A book, however, differs in that it may be loaned freely, used by any number of different people in succession, and used in any number of places. You may look at a book before buying it, and even the most expensive books (except for encyclopedias) cost less than all but the cheapest software. However, you do not need to have the publisher tell you how to read a book, and a book does not have the kind of potential power to wreak havoc with your business records that an accounting or database management package does.

As you can see, the situation is far from clear-cut. The unfortunate consequences are distrust and resentment on both sides, and a vicious circle wherein the producers try ever harder to foil the copiers, who regard each new release as a challenge. And as long as software producers are perceived by many people to be unreasonable, software piracy will continue (though not, we trust, in your library). Meanwhile, of course, the expenses of the battle are passed on to paying customers, and a number of software companies go out of business or cease producing good but unprofitable programs.

What can you do, then, to support legal and effective ways of finding a solution that is equitable for both sides? First, you are legally and morally obligated to uphold the provisions of federal copyright law. (Whether you are legally and morally obligated to live by the terms of one-sided license "agreements" is not so clear. The next few years will probably see some heated battles, in court and out, before a solution is reached.) In 1983, the International Council for Computers in Education developed a policy statement regarding the multiple copy and network use of software, which is reproduced at the end of this chapter. We have also included portions of a paper prepared by ALA attorney Mary Hutchings Reed and associate Debra Stanek, offering legal guidelines for library and classroom use of computer software. A large number of school systems throughout the country have already adopted such policies. We strongly suggest developing a similar, *written* policy, and insisting that anyone who uses your library's software, whether staff members, teachers, or patrons, should sign an agreement to uphold its terms. Among other things, this provides your library with legal protection in the event that software is copied without your knowledge or consent.

Besides upholding the law, there are things you can do to help improve the situation. One approach that is especially effective for volume users such as schools, corporations, and libraries seeking to increase loanable software is site licensing. Site licenses are negotiated agreements which allow the user to make and use multiple copies of a package legally. The terms of such agreements vary widely, usually involving a flat fee that amounts to a volume discount and should include updates and support. More and more software companies are proving open to such agreements, but they will generally not open the negotiations—you have to ask. Site licenses offer advantages for both sides, and keep the whole transaction within the law. If you are considering any kind of volume use of a software package, you should explore this alternative thoroughly. If the software company is unwilling to issue a site license, or unwilling to negotiate a fair agreement, buy a different package.

Know your rights and obligations—and your power—as a consumer. Encourage software companies to provide a backup or, better yet, to forgo copy protection. Many people are refusing to buy copy protected software, with the result that a number of companies have removed protection, preferring to generate good will among their paying customers. Similarly, you should insist on the right to preview packages. Form an evaluation committee and include patrons and volunteers, or students and teachers for a school library. If you decide not to buy a package, let the manufacturer know why, in detail. If a package is too expensive, say so. If it does not meet your needs, explain what your needs are. *And play fair!* Do not keep copies of a package you return. Besides providing valuable feedback for manufacturers, this policy sets a good example of a legal approach to a serious problem.

When planning your computer purchases, especially if you are buying several machines for public access or school use, be sure to allow ample funds for purchasing software. This will ensure that you don't find yourself in the unfortunate position of having a large collection of hardware that is useless because you can't afford any software for it. Also, as we mentioned in chapter 2, don't neglect to investigate the availability of public domain programs for the equipment you have or intend to buy. The assortment and quality of programs you can obtain for next to nothing may amaze you. (For information on resources for public domain software, see appendix B.)

Finally, advocate legislative action that seeks an equitable solution to the problem. As of this writing, shrink-wrapped licenses have not been tested in court. Many believe they will not hold up, but at least two states have passed laws saying they are enforceable. Computer consumers need to seek legislative protection, and to work for laws that are fair to all.

As time goes on and more companies produce more software, prices will probably fall just as have hardware prices. If people refuse to buy from companies with unreasonable policies, those companies will either change their policies or go out of business. If users let software companies know they are willing to pay a fair price for quality products, the companies that expect to stay in business will meet them halfway. If both producers and users feel they are getting a fair deal, the piracy problem may eventually solve itself.

PROBLEMS OF ONLINE SEARCHES

In chapter 6, we talked about providing patrons with access to information through searches of online databases. "Information brokering" is becoming a business in itself, and libraries who undertake this role will find themselves dealing with problems not presented by manual searches. The information available online is vast and varied, so much so that without special skills and knowledge, searchers may spend a great deal of time and money without locating the specific information they are seeking. If you are going to provide such services, you must make sure that you do so responsibly.

First, it is vital that the staff members who will be doing the searches receive thorough training in methods for developing effective strategies, and that they become familiar with the particular online services they will be using. Equally important is the ability to conduct patron interviews, in order to ensure that the question being answered is the same question that was asked. This part of the process is critical. If the question relates to a subject in which the searcher has little background, the patron and the searcher should work out the search strategy together; it might even be helpful to have the patron present during the search.

Searchers must also be aware of the limitations of the databases they use, and pass this information on to patrons. Because of the nature of online searches, the patron is likely to feel that you have "searched the world," and thus believe he has received the final word on his subject. In order for the information to be useful, it must be presented honestly.

TEACHING AND MODELING
ETHICAL COMPUTER BEHAVIOR

New technology always seems to bring with it a certain amount of social upheaval, and computers are not excepted from these changes. The library's role as a computer resource center carries with it a responsibility to model ethical computer behavior. This includes, at the least, the establishment and enforcement of policies regarding software use and copying. Other important aspects include the encouragement of participation by patrons in software selection and evaluation, and responsibility and accountability in conducting online searches.

In addition to serving as a role model for ethical behavior, you may also wish to include in your collection materials on computer ethics, addressing such issues as the new technology's effects on employment, computer crime, and "quality of life," as well as on personal ethics of computer use. If you are involved in computer literacy classes for students and/or patrons, ethics should be an important part of the curriculum.

Properly applied, computer technology has the capability to change our society for the better in many ways. Libraries can and must play an important part in ensuring that computers play a positive role in our future.

****

ICCE POLICY STATEMENT ON NETWORK AND MULTIPLE MACHINE SOFTWARE*

Just as there has been shared responsibility in the development of this policy, so should there be shared responsibility for resolution of the problems inherent in providing and securing good educational software. Educators have a valid need for quality software and reasonable prices. Hardware developers and/or vendors also must share in the effort to enable educators to make maximum cost-effective use of that equipment. Software authors, developers and vendors are entitled to a fair return on their investment.

Educators' Responsibilities

Educators need to face the legal and ethical issues involved in copyright laws and publisher license agreements and must accept the responsibility for enforcing adherence to these laws and agreements. Budget constraints do not excuse illegal use of software.

Educators should be prepared to provide software developers or their agents with a district-level approved written policy statement including as a minimum:

1. A clear statement that copyright laws and publisher license agreements be observed;

2. A statement making teachers who use school equipment responsible for taking all reasonable precautions to prevent copying or the use of unauthorized copies on school equipment;

3. An explanation of the steps taken to prevent unauthorized copying or the use of unauthorized copies on school equipment;

---

*Reprinted with the permission of the International Council for Computers in Education.

4. A designation of who is authorized to sign software license agreements for the school (or district);

5. A designation at the school site level of who is responsible for enforcing the terms of the district policy and terms of licensing agreements;

6. A statement indicating teacher responsibility for educating students about the legal, ethical and practical problems caused by illegal use of software.

Hardware Vendors' Responsibilities

Hardware vendors should assist educators in making maximum cost effective use of the hardware and help in enforcing software copyright laws and license agreements. They should as a minimum:

1. Make efforts to see that illegal copies of programs are not being distributed by their employees and agents;

2. Work cooperatively with interested software developers to provide an encryption process which avoids inflexibility but discourages theft.

Software Developers'/Vendors' Responsibilities

Software developers and their agents can share responsibility for helping educators observe copyright laws and publishers' license agreements by developing sales and pricing policies. Software developers and vendors should as a minimum:

1. Provide for all software a backup copy to be used for archival purposes, to be included with every purchase;

2. Provide for on-approval purchases to allow schools to preview the software to ensure that it meets the needs and expectations of the educational institution. Additionally, software developers are encouraged to provide regional or area centers with software for demonstration purposes. The ICCE encourages educators to develop regional centers for this purpose;

3. Work in cooperation with hardware vendors to provide an encryption process which avoids inflexibility but discourages theft;

4. Provide for, and note in advertisements, multiple-copy pricing for school sites with several machines and recognize that multiple copies do not necessarily call for multiple documentation;

5. Provide for, and note in advertisements, network-compatible versions of software with pricing structures that recognize the extra costs of

development to secure compatibility and recognize the buyer's need for only a single copy of the software.

The Board of Directors of The International Council for Computers in Education approved this policy statement, with attachments, June 5, 1983.

The committee that drafted this policy included:

Jenny Better, Director of Curriculum, Cupertino Union
    Elementary District
LeRoy Finkel, San Mateo County Office of Education
Pennie Gallant, Apple Computer, Inc.
John Hazelwood/Jeffrey Armstrong, Corvus Systems, Inc.
Marion B. Kenworthy, Saratoga High School
Richard R. Monnard, Addison-Wesley Publishing Co.
Henry Vigil/Cliff Godwin, Cybertronics International
William Wagner, Santa Clara County Office of Education

ATTACHMENT 1
Suggested District Policy on Software Copyright

It is the intent of_____to adhere to the provisions of copyright laws in the area of microcomputer programs. Though there continues to be controversy regarding interpretation of those copyright laws, the following procedures represent a sincere effort to operate legally. We recognize that computer software piracy is a major problem for the industry and that violations of computer copyright laws contribute to higher costs and greater efforts to prevent copies and/or lessen incentives for the development of good educational software. All of these results are detrimental to the development of effective educational uses of microcomputers. Therefore, in an effort to discourage violation of copyright laws and to prevent such illegal activities:

1. The ethical and practical problems caused by software piracy will be taught in all schools in the District.

2. District employees will be expected to adhere to the provisions of Public Law 96-517, Section 7(b) which amends Section 117 of Title 17 of the United States Code to allow for the making of a back-up copy of computer programs. This states that ". . . it is not an infringement for the owner of a copy of a computer program to make or authorize the making of another copy or adaptation of that computer program provided:

    a. that such a new copy or adaptation is created as an essential step in the utilization of the computer program in conjunction with a machine and that it is used in no other manner, or

    b. that such a new copy and adaptation is for archival purposes only and that all archival copies are destroyed in the event that continued possession of the computer program should cease to be rightful."

3. When software is to be used on a disk sharing system, efforts will be made to secure this software from copying.

4. Illegal copies of copyrighted programs may not be made or used on school equipment.

5. The legal or insurance protection of the District will not be extended to employees who violate copyright laws.

6. _____of this school district is designated as the only individual who may sign license agreements for software for schools in the district. (Each school using the software also should have a signature on a copy of software agreement for local control.)

7. The principal of each school site is responsible for establishing practices which will enforce this policy at the school level.

ATTACHMENT 2
Sample Software Policy of a Community College with a Large Microcomputer Lab

It is the policy of this college that no person shall use or cause to be used in the college's microcomputer laboratories any software which does not fall into one of the following categories:

1 . It is in the public domain.

2. It is covered by a licensing agreement with the software author, authors, vendor or developer, whichever is applicable.

3. It has been donated to the college and a written record of a bona fide contribution exists.

4. It has been purchased by the college and a record of a bona fide purchase exists.

5. It has been purchased by the user and a record of a bona fide purchase exists and can be produced by the user upon demand.

6. It is being reviewed or demonstrated by the users in order to reach a decision about possible future purchase or request for contribution or licensing.

7. It has been written or developed by_____ (college employee) for the specific purpose of being used in the _____(college) microcomputer laboratory.

It is also the policy of the college that there be no copying of copyrighted or proprietary programs on computers belonging to the college.

Source: De Anza College, Cupertino, California.

ATTACHMENT 3
Suggested Format of Software Licenses

1. Designated on a per site, district-wide or other geographic basis.

2. Requires the signature of a responsible school employee.

3. Includes provisions for a single copy purchase (with archival back-up copy) at full price.

4. Multiple-machine pricing:
   Includes provisions for a quantity discount for subsequent purchases of the same software provided:

   a. the purchase discount applies to a single purchase order.
   b. the purchase order is noncumulative.
   c. the software is for the same computer type.

   i.e.: Radio Shack presently offers a 50% discount for purchases of 10 or more sets of the same software; Gregg/McGraw-Hill offers a discount schedule with incremental increases—buy 2, pay 10% less; 3—20% less; 4—30% less; 5 or more, 40% less.

5. Network Pricing:

   May be offered as per school site or with quantity discount for school districts with multiple sites.

   Provide for a flat license fee for network-compatible versions of the software.

   - flat fee provision is preferred over any variable rate based on number of computers or number of student users.

   - network-compatibility, not just an unlocked version of the software, is required to eliminate the need for local reprogramming of copyrighted and licensed software.

   Include provision for purchase of multiple copies of documentation and accompanying materials.

   i.e.: A flat fee of two times the single copy retail price is offered to network users of Random House software.

ATTACHMENT 4
Some Technical Notes on Software Encryption for
Software/Hardware Vendors

1. Single Machine Encryption

Explanation:
The purchased disk is not copiable by ordinary means. The software cannot be transferred to a network system or used on several computers at once. This scheme is the most common, especially for inexpensive software.

Technical notes:
The protected disk is usually formatted in a non-standard way which will defeat standard disk copy programs such as COPYA on the Apple or TRSDOS BACKUP on the TRS-80. Alternatively, the publisher may write special information on the disk in places which the standard disk copy programs do not check. The copy program proceeds to completion, but the special information is not transferred to the duplicate disk. When the duplicate is used, the software checks for the special information, fails to find it, and stops.

Implications:
Schools will need to purchase many copies of the same program and should expect significant volume discounts. The customer is entitled to an archival backup and should expect the publisher to include a backup disk with every purchase.

Manufacturers of network systems should recognize that single machine encryption (which is incompatible with their products) will remain the software industry standard unless they actively support software protection on their systems.

2. Single Site Encryption

Explanation:
A single product can serve all the machines at a site. This scheme applies to VisiCalc™ and Logo.

Technical Notes:
Software which loads initially into memory and subsequently interacts only with data disks is de facto "single site encrypted," even though the program may be uncopiable. A single program disk can be used to initialize all the computers in a room, after which each user operates with his or her own data disks. VisiCalc™ and Logo operate in this way.

A functionally equivalent alternative is referred to as "master and slave" or "lock and key" encryption. This scheme is common where a program is too large to fit in memory all at once. Frequent disk access is needed as different parts of the software are brought into play.

In the "lock and key" scheme, the program modules which are routinely needed can be freely copied. A "slave" disk containing these modules is duplicated for each computer (or even for each student). The slave will not operate, however, unless the computer has been cold started with the (uncopiable) master disk.

Implications:
Since the "master" disk is uncopiable, the publisher still bears the burden of providing an archival backup. The protection on the "master" disk normally makes the software incompatible with network systems, so the above comments again apply.

Single site encryption reduces the dependence on volume discounts to facilitate multiple machine use. However, volume discounts should still be made available at the district level to encourage district level adoption of software.

3. Hard Disk/Network Compatible Versions of Software

Explanation:
Floppy disks containing network compatible software must be copiable since the software is copied as it is transferred onto the network. The problem of protecting network compatible software is how to allow this legitimate copying while preventing illegal copying.

One solution is to abandon software protection altogether and to rely on license agreements to prevent illegal use of the program(s). The problem with this solution is that freely copiable software may be freely copied.

Other solutions rely on publishing special versions of the software for the various network systems available. These versions do not run on stand-alone computers.

A publisher can also take steps to discourage people from installing the network software at sites other than the intended site.

Technical Notes:
A publisher can prevent network software from running on a stand-alone computer by using a device check. The software senses whether it is running on a network system and stops if it is not. The device check is specific to the network system involved. Software with a device check could be installed at many network sites, not just the one for which it was licensed.

To discourage use at non-licensed sites, the publisher can embed the name of the licensee in the software. This requires that the publisher customize each network-compatible version sold. Although such customization discourages porting the software to another network site, it does not physically prevent it.

To prevent porting of the software to another network, the publisher might implement what is essentially single machine encryption on the network level. This protection scheme would work by checking the serial number or other unique identifier in the network hardware. If the software encountered a change in identifier, it would fail to operate. This has the disadvantages that a licensee would have to be a single network installation and that normal activities such as replacing or upgrading one's network system would disable the software.

Implications:
Use of a device check or serial number check requires a publisher to maintain a separate inventory item for each device to be supported. The time required for a publisher to embed the customer's name in each product sold for use on networks can become prohibitive.

These protection schemes may prove economically unfeasible for inexpensive software.

These protection schemes require close working relationships and sharing of information between publishers and network system manufacturers.

****

LIBRARY AND CLASSROOM USE
OF COPYRIGHTED VIDEOTAPES AND
COMPUTER SOFTWARE*

By Mary Hutchings Reed and Debra Stanek

Mary Hutchings Reed is a partner in the law firm of Sidley & Austin, Chicago, and counsel to the American Library Association. Debra Stanek will graduate in June from the University of Chicago Law School.

After receiving numerous queries regarding library use of copyrighted videotapes and computer programs, I asked ALA attorney Mary Hutchings Reed to prepare a paper that would address the issues that librarians had brought to my attention and offer some guidance. The result is the following which we've published as an insert so that it can be removed and posted for ready access. A longer, more detailed article by Debra Stanek, "Videotapes, Computer Programs and the Library," will appear in the March 1986 issue of *Information Technology and Libraries*. These papers express the opinion of

*Reprinted by permission of the American Library Association. First published in *American Libraries,* February 1986, copyright ©1986 by ALA.

ALA's legal counsel; individuals and institutions deeply involved in copyright matters should consult their own attorneys. *Donna Kitta, Administrator, ALA Office of Copyright, Rights & Permissions*

COMPUTER SOFTWARE

**A.   Purchase
     Conditions
     Generally**

Most computer software purports to be licensed rather than sold. Frequently the package containing the software is wrapped in clear plastic through which legends similar to the following appear:

> You should carefully read the following terms and conditions before opening this diskette package. Opening this diskette package indicates your acceptance of these terms and conditions. If you do not agree with them you should promptly return the package unopened and your money will be refunded.

OR

> Read this agreement carefully. Use of this product constitutes your acceptance of the terms and conditions of this agreement.

OR

> This program is licensed on the condition that you agree to the terms and conditions of this license agreement. If you do not agree to them, return the package with the diskette still sealed and your purchase price will be refunded. Opening this diskette package indicates your acceptance of these terms and conditions.

While there is at present no caselaw concerning the validity of such agreements (which are unilaterally imposed by producers), in the absence of authority to the contrary, one should assume that such licenses are in fact binding contracts. Therefore by opening and using the software the library or classroom may become contractually bound by the terms of the agreement wholly apart from the rights granted the copyright owner under the copyright laws.

Following such legends are the terms and conditions of the license agreement. The terms vary greatly between software producers and sometimes between programs produced by the same producer. Many explicitly prohibit rental or lending; some limit the program to use on one identified computer or to one user's personal use.

B. Avoiding License Restrictions

Loans of software may violate the standard license terms imposed by the copyright owner. To avoid the inconsistencies between sale to a library and the standard license restriction, libraries should note on their purchase orders the intended use of software meant to circulate. Such a legend should read:

PURCHASE IS ORDERED FOR LIBRARY
CIRCULATION AND PATRON USE

Then, if the order is filled, the library is in a good position to argue that its terms, rather than the standard license restrictions, apply.

C. Loaning Software

1. Copyright notice placed on a software label should not be obscured.
2. License terms, if any, should be circulated with the software package.
3. An additional notice may be added by the library to assist copyright owners in preventing theft. It might read: SOFTWARE PROTECTED BY COPYRIGHT, 17 U.S.C. § 101. UNAUTHORIZED COPYING IS PROHIBITED BY LAW.
4. Libraries generally will not be liable for infringement committed by borrowers.

D. Archival Copies

1. Libraries may lawfully make one archival copy of a copyrighted program under the following conditions

   a) one copy is made;
   b) the archival copy is stored;
   c) if possession of the original ceases to be lawful, the archival copy must be destroyed or transferred along with the original program;
   d) copyright notice should appear on the copy.

2. The original may be kept for archival purposes and the "archival copy" circulated. Only one copy—either the original or the archival—may be used or circulated at any given time.
3. If the circulating copy is destroyed, another "archival" copy may be made.

4.   If the circulating copy is stolen, the copyright owner should be consulted before circulating or using the "archival" copy.

E.   In-library and   1.   License restrictions, if any, should be observed.
In-classroom Use

2.   If only one program is owned under license, ordinarily it may only be used on one machine at a time.

3.   Most licenses do not permit a single program to be loaded into a computer which can be accessed by several different terminals or into several computers for simultaneous use.

4.   If the machine is capable of being used by a patron to make a copy of a program, a warning should be posted on the machine, such as: MANY COMPUTER PROGRAMS ARE PROTECTED BY COPYRIGHT, 17 U.S.C. § 101. UNAUTHORIZED COPYING MAY BE PROHIBITED BY LAW.

EXAMPLES

. . . .

12. A book about the Apple IIe computer contains a diskette with a program for the computer. May the software be loaned with the book?

If the software is not subject to a license agreement it may be freely loaned like any other copyrighted work. If it is licensed, the agreement may or may not prohibit lending. A careful reading of the license is in order. If the license appears to prohibit any ordinary library uses the software producer should be contacted, and the agreement amended in writing. If this is not possible, the library should be able to return the package for a refund, as the seller, by selling to a library, may be on notice of ordinary library uses.

13. A math teacher uses one diskette to load a computer program into several terminals for use by students.

This use would violate copyright laws as well as most license agreements. It violates § 117 of the Copyright Act, which authorizes the making of *one* copy if necessary in order to use the program, because it creates copies of the program in several terminals. Further, many license agreements prohibit use of the software on more than one terminal at a time, as well as prohibiting networking or any system which enables more than one person to use the software at a time.

14. A math teacher puts a copy of "Visicalc" on reserve in the school library. The disk bears no copyright notice. May the library circulate it?

The disk ought to bear the copyright notice, but whether it is the library's legal duty to require one or to affix it is unclear. Individual library reserve policies may govern this situation—it's probably a good idea to require that the appropriate notices be affixed prior to putting the copy on reserve. Further, the lack of copyright notices may put the library on notice that this is a copy rather than the original program. If the original is retained by the teacher as an archival copy (i.e., not used) there is no problem. If not, then the reserve copy is an unauthorized copy and its use would violate the copyright laws and most license agreements. While the library might not be legally liable in this situation it would be wise to establish a policy for placing materials on reserve which prevents this.

15. May the library make an archival copy of the "Visicalc" program on its reserve shelf?

Usually yes. Section 117 permits the owner of the software to make or authorize the making of one archival copy. If the teacher who put the program on reserve has not made one, she or he may permit the library to do so. Remember, most licensing agreements and the copyright laws permit the making of *one* archival copy.

16. Same as 15, except the reserve copy is damaged. May the library make another copy (assuming it has the archival copy) for circulation?

Yes, the purpose of an archival copy is for use as a back-up in case of damage or destruction. The library may then make another archival copy to store while circulating the other.

17. Same as 16, except the reserve copy is stolen.

Perhaps. It is not clear whether the purpose of a back-up copy includes replacement in the event of theft but arguably it does. However, § 108 (c) permits reproduction of audiovisual works (which includes many computer programs) in the event of damage, loss, or theft *only* if a replacement may not be obtained at a fair price. Further, some license agreements require that archival copies be destroyed when possession (not ownership) of the original ceases. Therefore a replacement copy may need to be purchased. A safe course is to consult the software vendor.

18. When the teacher retrieves his or her copy of the program may the library retain the archival copy?

No. When possession of the original ceases, the archival copy must be transferred with the original or destroyed. If it is returned with the original, the teacher would not be permitted to make additional copies—he or she would have an original and the archival copy. Most license agreements contain similar provisions.

19. A librarian learns that a patron is copying copyrighted software on the library's public access computers.

There is a duty to notify the patron that the software is subject to the copyright laws. The computers should have notices similar to those on unsupervised photocopiers.

FURTHER READINGS

Class/Workshop Materials

"Ethical Issues in Computer Use."
Materials for teaching computer ethics, available from ICCE, University of Oregon, 1787 Agate Street, Eugene, OR 97403. Write for information.

Periodicals

Becker, Gary. "A Question of Copyright." *Electronic Education* (September 1985): 36.
Is it "permissible to . . . load into several machines?"

_____. "A Question of Copyright." *Electronic Education* 5, no. 2 (October 1985): 9.
"When is one more too many?"

Burroughs, Robert. "Editor's Note: Caveat Vendor." *Electronic Learning* 4, no. 3 (November/December 1985): 4.
Discusses two letters—one from an educational software publisher and one from an educator. An introduction to the feature of the issue "Untangling Copyright Issues."

Demas, Samuel. "Microcomputer Software Collections." *Special Libraries* 76, no. 1 (Winter 1985): 17-23.
Discusses considerations in developing software collections, including cataloging practices, loan procedures, and policies regarding copyright.

Elias, Steve. "Copy-Rights Law." *A+ Magazine* 2, no. 11 (November 1984): 35-38.

Finkel, LeRoy. "Software Copyright Interpretation." *The Computing Teacher* 12, no. 6 (March 1985): 10.
An up-to-date interpretation as it applies to schools and school-related problems, including backup copies, multiple machine licensing, and network licenses.

Pattie, Kenton. "Copyright Abuse: No Need for Lawsuits." *Tech Trends* 30, no. 7 (October 1985): 39, 40.
The International Communications Industries Association (ICIA) "decided to intensify its campaign to inform software users about their responsibilities. . . ."

Planton, Stanley. "Hacking at the Apple Tree." *Library Journal/School Library Journal* 110, no. 18, pp. 156-59; 32, no. 3 (November 1985): 144-47.

Rubin, Charles. "Site Licensing: What's in It for Users." *InfoWorld* 7, no. 30 (29 July 1985): 32-37.
Discusses site licensing for corporations, providing some background for comparison with problems in the educational market.

Shaver, D., N. S. Hewison, and L. W. Wykoff. "Ethics for Online Intermediates." *Special Libraries* 76, no. 4 (Fall 1985): 238-45.
"Issues explored include searcher competence, search bias, inaccurate search results, misuse of search results by the client, and privacy and confidentiality. A model for ethical decision making is presented and a list of guidelines for ethical conduct is suggested."

"Software Piracy Survey Completed." *The Computing Teacher* 12, no. 7 (April 1985): 8.

Talab, Rosemary S. "Copyright and Database Downloading." *Library Journal/School Library Journal* 110, no. 18, pp. 144-47; 32, no. 3 (November 1985): 132-35.

Williams, Christopher, and the editors of *EL*. "Untangling Copyright Issues." *Electronic Learning* 4, no. 3 (November/December 1985): 46-51, 78.
"Confused about networked software, multiple-loading, and archive copies? This survey of 39 publishers' policies will answer your questions."

9 "Micro Conversion": Three Case Studies

Having a computer professional in the family has meant that computers have had a slightly more than average impact on my life.* Until about 1977, however, that impact consisted mostly of late night phone calls and interrupted vacations due to various computer crises. When the first microcomputer kits came out in the mid-1970s, we naturally had one in our basement. Within a year the original kit was replaced by a more complex and capable machine, but computers had not yet captured my interest.

During that period, the district where I worked as a library media specialist had acquired a mainframe computer. One of its functions was to computerize building inventory records. Unfortunately, the system took several years to get into working order, during which time teachers and administrators at building level had to deal with its growing pains. The printout lists we received came in no definable order. One cassette recorder might appear on page 1 and another on page 15. Other items appeared more than once, with different identification numbers and different descriptions. Further, the printouts were organized differently every year.

I was becoming increasingly frustrated trying to reconcile the district lists with my own inventory reports, until I thought of a practical use for my husband's grown-up toy. At my request, he wrote a program that allowed me to store my equipment inventory records and retrieve them in multiple ways. Instead of writing and organizing file cards, I was bringing home records and entering them into the computer using a fill-in screen. Once entered, the inventory items could be retrieved by any field and printed out in easy-to-follow lists. The success of what was a relatively simple program had a radical effect on my ideas both about computers and about library management.

In the fall of 1980 I became library media specialist at a brand new elementary school, under a principal who was eager to incorporate microcomputers into the library from the beginning. Our objectives were twofold: first, to make library resources readily available to both staff and students, and second, to give every student an opportunity to actually use a computer and learn to regard it as a useful tool. The method we chose was ambitious—more so than we realized at the time. Rather than purchasing a traditional card catalog system, we elected to put our library's catalog on a microcomputer.

Putting a collection of more than two or three thousand items on floppy disks was just not feasible. At that time, however, hard disks had just come onto the market, and increased storage availability made a microcomputer

---

*The first part of this chapter is Betty Costa's personal story.

catalog a real possibility. The school district had already purchased several Apple computers, which meant we were in the position of finding software to fit our existing hardware. An exhaustive search, however, did not turn up anyone who had written a catalog program for an Apple or any other micro. Since the district did not have an in-house programming staff, we decided to use Software Acquisition Method Number Two, and find someone to write a custom program to our specifications.

Fired by dreams of an accessible, easy-to-use, and always-current catalog, I wrote out the functional specifications, with technical assistance from my "in-house" consultant-husband. The proposal was put out for bid and awarded to a local computer dealer who hired a leading Apple programmer to write the catalog. Although it was a custom program, the dealer recognized its marketing possibilities, and proposed a contract giving us the software at a volume price if we would agree to serve as a test site. The software was to be written, delivered, and tested in several phases.

What followed was one of the most intensely frustrating, exciting, and rewarding periods of my library career. Though being a test site meant dealing with all the inevitable bugs, delays, and difficulties, it also meant being part of the discovery and development of something totally new and different and exciting. The major obstacles I had encountered in my ten years as a library media specialist were the lack of time left over from routine clerical and management duties, and the reluctance of students and staff members to acquire and use library skills. Therefore, I found the idea of an accessible, easy, and even fun-to-use system exhilarating enough to boost me through the difficulties of implementing it.

We received the first portion of the program, for manual data entry, that October, and my aide and I began entering our collection, typing information from shelf cards into a fill-in screen on the computer and storing the data on floppy disks (see figure 9.1). (A second data entry phase arrived later in the fall, which enabled us to transfer information directly from the district OCLC catalog to our own.) At that time my only experience with microcomputers had been using the equipment inventory program, plus a ten-hour dealer-taught course on how to use the Apple; my aide had no computer experience at all. Both of us were average typists; we found we could enter about 50 records an hour.

During that first semester we did not have a card catalog. Few new schools do, since setting up a traditional card catalog, with the large amounts of filing involved, is also a lengthy process. By December, the "look-up" portion of the program had arrived. We transferred our floppy disk data to the hard disk, and when the students returned to school after Christmas we introduced them to our "card catalog," which by then had been christened "Computer Cat."

Although the catalog was new to the students, the computer was not. During that first semester everyone was introduced to the computer and had an opportunity to use it. We labeled all of the components (and left them labeled), for example, monitor, keyboard, disk drive, etc. Two copies of *The Computer Alphabet Book,* by Elizabeth Wall, taken apart and laminated, became giant flash cards for teaching computer vocabulary. Each student learned how to

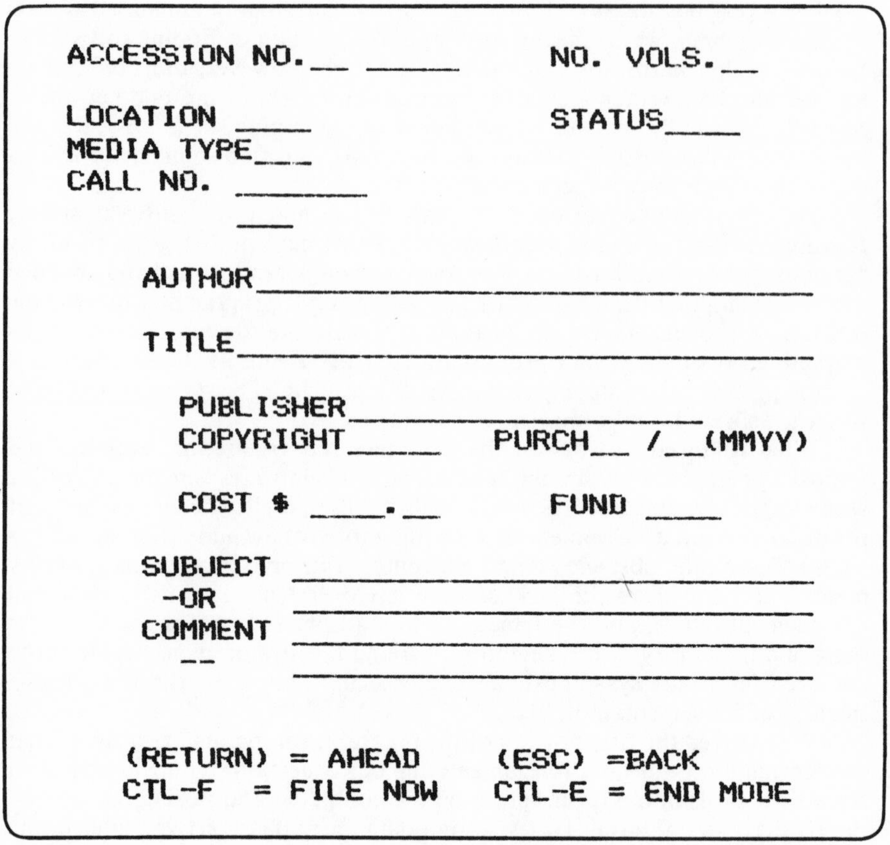

```
ACCESSION NO.__  _____        NO. VOLS.__

LOCATION _____               STATUS_____
MEDIA TYPE___
CALL NO. _____
        ___

    AUTHOR_____

    TITLE_____

        PUBLISHER_____
        COPYRIGHT_____    PURCH__ /__(MMYY)

        COST $ _____.__        FUND _____

        SUBJECT  _____
        -OR      _____
        COMMENT  _____
        --       _____


    (RETURN) = AHEAD      (ESC) =BACK
    CTL-F  = FILE NOW     CTL-E = END MODE
```

Fig. 9.1. The data entry screen from Computer Cat (early version).

turn on the computer and monitor and boot a disk, and how to do two simple programs, writing either his or her own or a teacher's name across the screen in different ways (see figure 9.2.A-D). Little "Apple reminders" posted behind the computer reminded students that < HOME > clears the screen, < NEW > clears the computer for a new program, < PR#6 > boots a disk, and so on, and cautioned them to "Hold the disk by the label" and "Read directions first."

The children went through the computer introduction by the peer-tutoring method. Each class sent two students who went through the flash cards and sample programs with me; the first two taught the next two, who taught the next two, and so on until everyone had the opportunity to type something into the computer and see it on the screen. The entire school, from first through sixth grades, went through the mini course, including learning disabled children.

```
10 PRINT "" MICROS ARE IN ""

20 GOTO 10

RUN
```

Fig. 9.2.A.

Fig. 9.2. A-D. Two simple programs and the resulting screens. Note the difference made by adding a semicolon to the PRINT command.

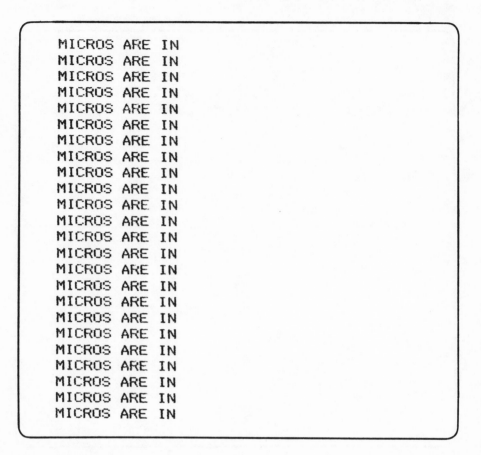

Fig. 9.2.B.

```
10 PRINT '' MICROS ARE IN '' ;

20 GOTO 10

RUN
```

Fig. 9.2.C.

```
MICROS ARE IN  MICROS ARE IN  MICROS ARE
N  MICROS ARE IN  MICROS ARE IN  MICROS
 IN  MICROS ARE IN  MICROS ARE IN  MICRO
RE IN  MICROS ARE IN  MICROS ARE IN  MIC
 ARE IN  MICROS ARE IN  MICROS ARE IN  M
OS ARE IN  MICROS ARE IN  MICROS ARE IN
CROS ARE IN  MICROS ARE IN  MICROS ARE I
MICROS ARE IN  MICROS ARE IN  MICROS ARE
N  MICROS ARE IN  MICROS ARE IN  MICROS
 IN  MICROS ARE IN  MICROS ARE IN  MICRO
RE IN  MICROS ARE IN  MICROS ARE IN  MIC
 ARE IN  MICROS ARE IN  MICROS ARE IN  M
OS ARE IN  MICROS ARE IN  MICROS ARE IN
CROS ARE IN  MICROS ARE IN  MICROS ARE I
MICROS ARE IN  MICROS ARE IN  MICROS ARE
N  MICROS ARE IN  MICROS ARE IN  MICROS
 IN  MICROS ARE IN  MICROS ARE IN  MICRO
RE IN  MICROS ARE IN  MICROS ARE IN  MIC
 ARE IN  MICROS ARE IN  MICROS ARE IN  M
OS ARE IN  MICROS ARE IN  MICROS ARE IN
CROS ARE IN  MICROS ARE IN  MICROS ARE I
MICROS ARE IN  MICROS ARE IN  MICROS ARE
N  MICROS ARE IN  MICROS ARE IN  MICROS
 IN  MICROS ARE IN  MICROS ARE IN  MICRO
```

Fig. 9.2.D.

Even though we had not finished entering the entire collection, everyone was encouraged to use the computer catalog when school resumed after the holidays. For orientation, the computer was hooked up to a 19-inch television monitor and the students sat on the floor and watched as each classmate searched on the computer, wrote down a call number, and went to the shelves to find the corresponding item (see figures 9.3 and 9.4). The fact that data entry was incomplete actually turned out to be an advantage, since it acquainted students with an important part of the system—"I don't find anything on. . . . Please ask your librarian." The resulting student and staff input has proven immensely valuable in building the cross-reference, *see,* and *see also* section of the catalog.

The summer and fall of 1981 were spent adding nonprint media, vertical file items, and a collection of leased media to the catalog. A Computer Cat search on a given subject therefore turns up not only all applicable books, but filmstrips, records, and vertical file items as well. The catalog may even be expanded to include community resources. One district that later purchased the program, for example, added locally available speakers on given subjects. For small neighboring schools and/or public libraries, multiple collection catalogs with location codes could facilitate interlibrary loans.

Computer Cat has features that make it especially suitable for use by elementary students who are just developing spelling and alphabetizing skills. The program will conduct a search on an entry as brief as one letter, so anyone who is unsure about spelling can type in only as much of the word as he or she knows, for example, DINO for dinosaurs, and receive a response. Students who are unfamiliar with the keyboard are encouraged to find the first three letters of the word before starting to type. Besides reinforcing basic skills, the program seems to encourage students to read subject headings more closely.

Even during the first semester it was in use, Computer Cat produced some unexpected benefits. For example, the program reinforces the concepts of subject, author, and title, which are ordinarily difficult for students to grasp. A student typing in "Seuss" for a subject search discovers that the computer cannot find any books under that subject and that he or she should consult the librarian, who will explain that "Seuss" is an author and not a subject heading. In the same way, a search for books by "Beverly Cleary" instead of "Cleary, Beverly" would lead back to the librarian and the realization that an author search is conducted using the last name first (see figure 9.5).

Among the more helpful services a library may provide are bibliographies on various topics. In the past this meant manually compiling, typing, and running off dittoed lists—a painstaking and time-consuming process. Also, although bibliographies could be recycled from year to year, it was difficult or impossible to keep them current. With Computer Cat, obtaining a complete and current bibliography on any subject requires nothing more than doing a quick subject search and having the program print the results. This makes it possible for teachers to obtain printed bibliographies on as little as a day's notice for subject units or special class projects. The bibliographies can be distributed for research projects, and/or kept in teachers' unit files for annotation and year-to-year updates. In addition, bibliographies on most-requested subjects may be printed and kept available in the library for patron use.

```
LOOKING FOR SUBJECT PETS


A #PET STORIES
B PETS &...
C HAMSTERS...
D CAPYBOPPY


   _ _ _ _ _ _ _ _ _ _
   _____



S PETS-VF (636,)
T #HAMSTER WHO HID, THE

PUSH THE LETTER OF THE ITEM YOU
WOULD LIKE TO SEE OR (SPACE)
TO KEEP LOOKING
```

Fig. 9.3. An option screen from Computer Cat (early version). Selecting option "D" results in the display shown in the screen opposite.

```
ITEM D


599.3        CAPYBOPPY
PEE
             BY PEET, BILL

             PUBLISHER HOUGHTON MIFFLIN

             COPYRIGHT 1966


SUBJECTS
             CAPYBARAS
             PETS

(SPACE) SEE THE LIST AGAIN
ANY LETTER A TO T SEE THAT ITEM
(CTRL) AND P TO PRINT THIS
(ESC) START OVER
```

Fig. 9.4. An onscreen "catalog card" from Computer Cat (early version).

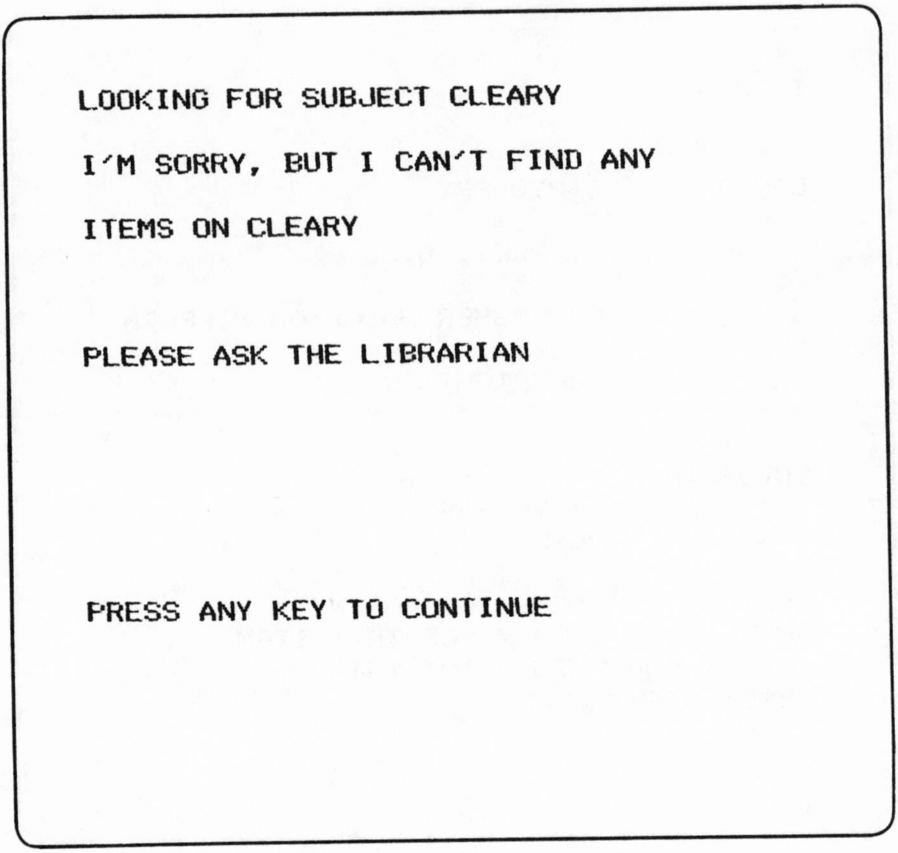

LOOKING FOR SUBJECT CLEARY

I'M SORRY, BUT I CAN'T FIND ANY

ITEMS ON CLEARY

PLEASE ASK THE LIBRARIAN

PRESS ANY KEY TO CONTINUE

Fig. 9.5. An unsuccessful subject search in Computer Cat (early version) leads to the librarian.

Computer Cat can be used to print other types of "bibliographies" as well, for ordering and inventory purposes. Information on items can be retrieved by any field, including publisher, copyright date, and price (see figure 9.6). This feature makes the system marvelous for preventing duplications and weeding out obsolete items. In addition, the library need not close down for inventory, since items may also be listed in shelf order. We set up a continuous inventory system, section by section—the 600s in January, 700s in February, and so on. A printed shelflist may be easily checked against shelves and charge tray without any interruption in service. (The only exception to this is easy fiction,

```
                    EXECUTIVE MODE
    LOCATION                    STATUS
    MEDIA TYPE
    CALL NO      599.3
                 PEE

    AUTHOR     PEET,BILL
    TITLE      CAPYBOPPY
    PUBLISHER  HOUGHTON MIFFLIN
    COPYRIGHT  66      PURCH 6/81
    ACCESSION #81-171  COST $ 7.20

    SUBJECTS:

        CAPYBARAS
        PETS



    C)CHANGE    D)DELETE   P)PRINT
```

Fig. 9.6. A Computer Cat (early version) record shown in the "executive mode." Note the additional fields, as opposed to the standard "catalog card" shown in figure 9.4.

where the turnover is very great; this section is best done the last week or two of school.)

Another service I always wanted to provide and never seemed to have time for is an extensive cross-reference system. The first cross-reference to go on Computer Cat was of course "CARS—See subject AUTOMOBILE" (see figure 9.7).

The number of cross-reference entries grew steadily in response to student and staff requests. Computer Cat also allows data to be entered in such a way that a given item may be retrieved by several subject headings, so we were able to introduce some nontraditional categories into our catalog. The new subject headings included such topics as "Newberry — 19____," "Caldecott —

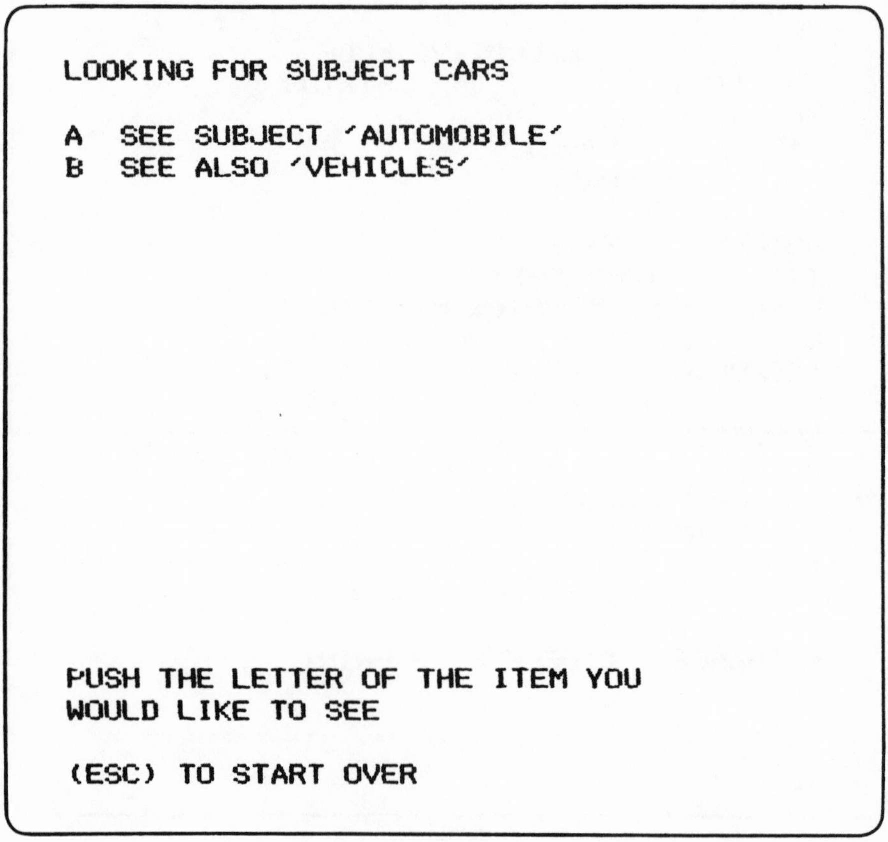

```
LOOKING FOR SUBJECT CARS

A   SEE SUBJECT 'AUTOMOBILE'
B   SEE ALSO 'VEHICLES'

















PUSH THE LETTER OF THE ITEM YOU
WOULD LIKE TO SEE

(ESC) TO START OVER
```

Fig. 9.7. A *see, see also* screen from Computer Cat (early version).

19____," "Encyclopedia Brown Series," "Raggedy Ann Series," and "The Chronicles of Narnia." When we received a series of books for our professional collection for art instruction, cataloged under the single subject heading of "Handicrafts," we added the second heading of "Art" to each book entry, since "Art" is the heading most teachers would use to look up that type of book. Similarly, "Guidance," which is not a preferred Sears heading, was incorporated into records for items cataloged under headings like "Emotions," "Feelings," or "Behavior." Other subject headings were added to help students as teachers taught various units. If a teacher wanted a certain book listed when a student looked up "Environment," for example, "Environment" was added as a heading for that book. Making such additions to Computer Cat takes seconds. A single modification to one record has the same effect as pulling and changing an entire series of catalog cards.

I received a graphic lesson in the literal mindedness of computers after we had entered about 4,000 items. We had entered authors' names without spaces between the comma and the first name (e.g., "Cleary,Beverly"). The OCLC formatted entries, however, inserted a space after the comma. The result was that a search by "Cleary,Beverly" missed all the OCLC entries, and one by "Cleary, Beverly" missed the manual entries. We also entered "Mys and Detective Stories" where OCLC used "Mystery and Detective Stories," with similar results. Consistency is *very* important when working with computers, and the only way for humans with their fickle memories to practice consistency is to *document*—abbreviations, identification numbering sequences, dates, problems, everything. This becomes even more important when there is a staff turnover, in order to save newcomers from starting over from scratch.

Computer Cat is still growing. A circulation component was added in 1984 which allows the use of a bar code system. Also, as other libraries purchase and implement the system, they are finding new ways to use it. Though the format of the program is fixed, it is wonderfully flexible, since it may be used for any type of media, as well as other resources and even equipment inventory. It is also possible to add a networking peripheral to the hard disk drive so that it may be used with several microcomputers simultaneously. The multi-user system allows one or more patrons to use the "look-up" feature while a staff member edits, does data entry, or prints lists for ordering, inventory, or bibliographies.

Both students and staff members have become more informed about and intrigued by computers. A second Apple was added during the first year for instructional purposes, and a number of teachers checked it out regularly for classroom use. During the second year the catalog was in use (1981-1982), the students renamed it "Kitten on the Keys." The name inspired the assistant principal, who was taking a programming class, to write a program that used an animated kitten to lead students through the three search methods—subject, author, and title. We now use her program to instruct new students in the use of our catalog.

My knowledge and experience are increasing as well. Many of my frustrations that first year came from ignorance about computers—the sort of ignorance we have tried to dispel in this book. Programs will appear to "hang" for a variety of reasons, most of which are simple to detect and solve,

providing you know what to look for. Static electricity, power problems, a
printer not being available when the computer is ready for it—these are all
minor problems once they are understood. I have experienced some intensely
frustrating times attempting to "unhang" a computer that was spewing garbage
across the screen or onto a printout for no apparent reason. But I have also
had the intense satisfaction of seeing children eager for a turn at the catalog, of
watching students simply "browse" until they find something new that catches
their interest, of handing teachers bibliographies on every conceivable subject.
Through the conception, testing, and success of Computer Cat I have realized
many facets of my "dream library," and become aware of other possibilities I
had not even considered. I have come to regard computers not as cold, imper-
sonal, and incomprehensible machines, but as marvelously capable and flexible tools that can be used to realize human goals.

In 1983 I retired from my position as media specialist and became a
freelance consultant. Since that time I have shared in the microcomputer experiences of many librarians around the United States and Canada. I continue
to marvel at the changes in technology and the opportunities offered by

Betty Costa demonstrates Computer Cat for two pupils.

microcomputers, particularly as costs go down. The changes in Computer Cat exemplify the changes in the industry as a whole. When we first implemented the system in 1980, it ran on an Apple II+ with 48K of memory, two floppy disk drives, a 10-megabyte Corvus hard disk (one of the first available, at a cost of $4900), and a dot matrix printer (cost $900), and was strictly a one-station catalog system. While it still runs on the Apple II+ or IIe computers, Computer Cat now can use one of the newer Omnidrives with up to 45-megabyte capacity, can use Omninet for multiple stations (each with its own printer), and has added a circulation component—all available for less than the cost of the original system.

Microcomputers continue to gain momentum throughout the library community. In 1985, AASL and the Follett Software Company instituted two awards to recognize and honor library media specialists "who have demonstrated an innovative approach to microcomputer application in-the library media center." The following text of the acceptance talks given by the first two recipients of these awards at the ceremony on July 7, 1985 provide a glimpse of two other "micro conversion" experiences.

Accepting the award for the 1985 Microcomputer in the Media Center Award in the category of "The Microcomputer as a Management Tool" was Raymond W. Barber, library media specialist at the William Penn Charter School in Philadelphia, Pennsylvania. Ray said, in part:

> First of all, thank you. I wish to thank the Follett Software Company and AASL for giving this award. It arrives when we have reached the end of the first phase of our computerization and acts as a seal of approval on what we have done as well as a goad to move forward. I wish to thank them on behalf of all school librarians, for I feel that with the computer we have a tool enabling us to increase our services.
>
> A special word of thanks is due to numerous other people. To the College of Information Studies at Drexel University for setting out to be a leading force in the utilization of microcomputers in libraries. To Guy Garrison, Jacqueline Mancall, and Chris Swisher for all the encouragement they provided. To Frank Innes, John Harvey, and Seth Horowitz, students at Drexel, who suffered with me as I learned to use the computer and survived to become my friends and technical advisors. To the faculty and staff at Penn Charter, especially Earl J. Ball, Headmaster, and the library staff: Doug Uhlmann, Liz Lutz, Suzi Gerber, and Linda Leube.
>
> I was in hope that when the award was given this morning, I would learn what impressed the committee about our program. Not hearing this from them, I would like to say why I would like to think we were given the award.
>
> Sharing. We have shared what we have learned. During the past fifteen months, over fifty librarians have come to observe our use of computers. Some have come several times as they progressed toward their goal. We have candidly shared our failures as well as our successes. The administration could have discouraged this use of our time but remained faithful to the school's Quaker heritage of generosity and hospitality.
>
> Students. We have involved students. Students like Hunter Allen, who developed the program we use to accession and one we use to update subject headings. Or Adam Koppel, who is always ready to demonstrate his latest program. Or Jason Wells, who made all our periodical labels. Or Joe

Livezey, who sat and watched us and in a bemused manner said, "What will you find next to run into the ground?"

Creativity. Jack Luskay told me this morning that there were schools who applied for the award who did certain administrative routines better than we do, but that there was no school who did as many things well as we. This is due to a great extent to the fact that I have the fortune to having as my assistant Doug Uhlmann, one of the most creative young librarians in the country today. This award belongs as much to him as to me.

Earlier, I mentioned that through the handling of repetitive tasks, the computer enables us to channel more of our resources into serving students and teachers. While this is important, it is not the greatest benefit. Using a computer to administer a library enables one to recapture the essence of learning which we all possessed as children, but not adults.

Creativity. Software is a tool. Tools can be used for many jobs. Don't be limited by what a program says it can do. We use our catalog program for ordering, our subject heading program to create labels for microfiche.

Cooperation. Meaningful learning is often cooperative. A whole network of librarians using the computer has developed. Each excitedly calls others to say what he or she has discovered and then in an hour or so receives a return call saying, "Have you tried . . .?" We build on what each has found.

Mistakes. Mistakes are not failures, but answers that don't fit the solution. Be prepared to make a great many errors. We have often found that the mistakes we have made in our explorations of computerization have turned out to be answers to other problems. On the other hand, we have learned that the first time we attempt anything it takes four or five times longer than expected.

Play. Two years ago in September I expected to purchase a computer at once, since the money had been allocated. January came and there was no computer. When I asked the headmaster why the purchase had not been approved, he said, "I know how you people work, and when you get a computer all you are going to do is play." Two weeks ago when we received notification of the award, Doug Uhlmann asked if I had told the headmaster. I said, "No." Doug asked to tell him and says he said, "See what happens when people play."

Judy Logan, library media specialist at Hamilton Heights Elementary School, Arcadia, Indiana, is the 1985 recipient in the category of "The Microcomputer as an Educational Tool." In accepting the award, she made the following remarks:

I want to express my thanks to the Follett Software Company, the American Association of School Librarians, and the selection committee for presenting me with the Microcomputer in the Media Center Award.

Though the award is presented to me personally, the efforts of many working together are what make our program special. Thanks to my media center staff; my administrators—Principal Mr. Joe Bellman, Superintendent Dr. Bob Carnal, and especially, Assistant Superintendent Dr. Thomas Rose for his vision and determination. I've saved the best for last—a big THANK YOU goes to the fifty teachers at Hamilton Heights Elementary School. They have forged ahead to become aware of what wonderful tools microcomputers can be. They've taken advantage of in-service opportunities and computer classes. They've learned from each other, without a computer teacher in residence. My role with computers and microcomputer software has been the same as my role with books and audiovisual materials.

Two years ago it was decided that the elementary computer lab would be located in our media center. Physical space in our school of 1,100 was at a premium. There really wasn't any other alternative. I must admit, I had some major concerns: How would the lab affect the media program? Would the extra traffic and confusion be detrimental? How much of our already busy schedule would be taken up by the computers and software?

Luckily, the media center is large, and we were able to accommodate a lab of fifteen microcomputers and still have space for three other classes to use the media center. The lab was installed in November 1983. It wasn't long until I *knew* that I would fight to keep the computer lab if other space ever became available. My initial concerns were unfounded. The lab doesn't affect our program; rather, the lab is an integral part of our program. The extra traffic promotes use of other media services, and the media center is large enough to handle the added activity. Yes, the computers have created additional work, but they've provided us with additional benefits as well.

Probably many of you in this audience know much more about computers than I. I'm not a programmer and I may never be! One thing I'm sure of though — there are so many ways to use microcomputers that don't require a knowledge of programming. If we, as media specialists, can get our teachers excited about what they can do using a word processing package, a grade management program, or a prescriptive program to accompany the basal reading series, we'll be well on our way to having microcomputer software accepted as "just another form of media." As teachers get more comfortable with computers, they find more ways to incorporate them into all facets of the curriculum. When this happens, microcomputers become a sophisticated information tool, and it is clear that microcomputers belong in the domain of media services.

To quote Dr. Joseph Rogus:
"One who believes she is finished is finished.
When you think you've arrived, you've lost your way.
When you think you've achieved your goal, you missed it."

I'm thrilled to accept this award, and our use of microcomputers is just beginning!

Reprinted by permission of the American Library Association, "Raymond W. Barber and Judy Logan Accept 1985 Microcomputer in the Media Center Award" in "AASL News," *School Library Media Quarterly,* Fall 1985, pp. 6-7; copyright © 1985 by ALA.

APPENDICES

Appendix A: Glossary

acoustic coupler — a modem that works by converting digital data into sound waves for transmission over ordinary telephone lines.

address — (noun) the location of information in a register, internal memory, or external storage device, usually identified by a label or a number; (verb) to directly access data in memory.

algorithm — a process for carrying out a complex operation by breaking it down into a hierarchical sequence of simpler operations; e.g., multiplying 67 times 308 by performing a series of additions: 308 + 308 = 616, 616 + 308 = 924, 924 + 308 = 1232, etc. All computer operations are carried out using algorithms.

alphanumeric character — a character that is machine processable; includes alphabetic upper- and lowercase letters A through Z, digits 0 through 9, and special characters such as =, /, ⟨ ⟩, #, etc.

AppleDOS — disk operating system for the Apple II family of microcomputers.

applications software — programs written to perform specific functions, e.g., inventory control, word processing, etc.

arithmetic logic unit — the portion of the CPU that performs arithmetic and logic operations.

ASCII code — American Standard Code for Information Interchange, developed by the National Standards Institute for transmitting information between computers and computer components; consists of 8 binary characters, a 7-bit character code and a parity bit. There are 128 codes, 96 of which represent "printable characters"; the remainder represent control functions.

assembler — a program that converts nonmachine language programs to machine language so that they may be used by a computer.

assembly language — a low-level programming language resembling machine language that uses mnemonic rather than numeric instructions.

asynchronous transmission — data transmission in which the time interval between characters varies according to the speed at which they are sent; uses start and stop elements to identify individual characters.

authoring language — a programming language used for designing instructional (CAI) programs using English commands.

217

✓ **authority control**—the use of established headings within both an authority file and bibliographic files such as card catalogs.

auto-answer—a device, usually part of a modem, that automatically answers a phone and establishes a data communications link with the caller.

auto-dial—a device, usually part of a modem, that can automatically dial a preprogrammed telephone number.

backup—a procedure for copying a data file or software in order to have a reserve copy in case the original is lost or destroyed; also procedures and/or equipment to use in the event of power loss or other equipment failure.

band—referring to data communications, a range of frequencies.

bandwidth—the difference, in hertz, between the highest and lowest frequencies in a band.

bar code—a system for automatic identification of items, such as books in a library or grocery items in a supermarket, by means of printed bars of different widths which represent numbers. The code is read by a light-sensitive peripheral device similar to a light pen.

BASIC—Beginner's All-purpose Symbolic Instruction Code: a high-level, relatively simple-to-use algebraic programming language, which is widely used for all types of computers, especially micros.

batch processing—a method for collecting and executing programs in groups, or batches, then returning the results to users; usually performed in a computer center to which the users have no direct access.

baud rate—the rate at which signals change from one frequency to another; one baud equals one signal change per second.

BDOS, BDOS error—basic disk operating system, the disk-handling component of the CP/M operating system; it is standard for all microcomputers using CP/M. A "BDOS error" is any error arising when the computer cannot read or write to a disk; causes may range from a drive door being open to a disk being full to a data wipeout.

bells and whistles—enhancements to software or hardware that are mainly aesthetic rather than functional, as in the use of color graphics for an accounting program.

beta test—a final test phase by one or more actual end users before a software or hardware product is released.

bibliographic utility—a network consisting of a large union bibliographic database, accessible online to time-sharing members. The network may also provide a variety of other services such as cataloging. OCLC, RLIN, WLN, and UTLAS are all bibliographic utilities.

binary code—the basic code used by computers. In binary arithmetic, there are only two digits, 1 and 0. Therefore, the equivalent of 2 in base 10 (decimal) would be 10 in base 2 (binary), decimal 4 would be binary 110, 5 would be 101, and so on. In binary code, all data are broken down into bits, which are represented by either 1 or 0.

BIOS — basic input output system, that part of the firmware or operating system which controls low-level input and output functions such as displaying characters on the screen or sending them to the printer.

bit — abbreviation for binary digit (1 or 0); also used to refer to the signals sent between computers, or between computer components. Generally, 8 bits equals 1 byte.

block — in word processing, a user-defined section of text, ranging in size from part of a word to an entire file, which may be manipulated as a single unit.

board — a card that plugs into a computer's bus structure and that contains the circuitry for one or more functions, such as interfacing with a peripheral device or substituting a different CPU for the built-in microprocessor.

bomb — a dramatic program failure; as when an operator accidentally presses the wrong control character while entering data and the screen fills up with garbage. Good programs should be well protected against this possibility.

book catalog — a catalog in book rather than card form.

Boolean algebra — a system of symbolic logic similar in form to algebra but dealing with logical rather than numeric relationships. Named for its creator, George Boole.

Boolean search — a search method using logical delimiters to specify the search object; e.g., all scientists who were born before 1920 AND were women who worked in either medicine OR physics. Using AND in a search restricts the possibilities (the object must satisfy both criteria); using OR expands them (the object may satisfy either criteria).

bootstrap — the process by which an operating system is loaded into the computer's RAM from a disk, usually abbreviated to "boot."

bps — bits per second. The rate at which data are transmitted between computer components, or between computers via cables or modems and telephone lines; often confused with baud rate.

buffer — a temporary storage area for data that are being transmitted between devices with different operating speeds; e.g., a printer that cannot input and use data as rapidly as a computer can send them.

bug — a mistake or malfunction in computer software or hardware.

bundled software — software which is included with a hardware system as part of a total package.

byte — a group of binary digits, or bits, that are treated as a single unit by a computer; usually a byte consists of 8 bits. Also used to designate a group of bits which represent a single coded character.

C — a popular and highly sophisticated applications programming language used by professional programmers.

CAD — computer-aided design, programs which do drawing and/or technical drafting.

CAE — computer-aided engineering, programs which include formulas and data for engineering of offices, buildings, cars, etc., as well as technical drafting.

CAI—computer-assisted instruction, individualized instruction using a computer to provide a preprogrammed sequence of instruction, which a student may follow at his or her own rate, and which is interactive and responsive to a user's individual needs.

CD ROM—compact disk read only memory. A 4¾-inch diameter CD ROM has a storage capacity comparable to 1500 floppy disks (over 600 million characters).

character—a letter, digit, punctuation mark or symbol which may be stored and/or processed by a computer or its peripherals.

character string—a connected sequence of characters which is treated as a single data unit.

chip—a very small piece of silicon containing integrated circuitry, including transistors, diodes, and resistors, with electrical paths consisting of thin layers of gold or aluminum.

CIP—cataloging in publication, a Library of Congress program that makes partial cataloging information (distributed as MARC records) available for items before they are published.

COBOL—COmmon Business Oriented Language, a high-level language used mainly for business applications.

cold boot—the process by which the operating system is loaded into the computer's memory by turning the power switch on. Cf. warm boot.

COM—computer output microform, catalog information produced by a computer and stored on microfilm rather than on a card or online catalog.

command—a coded instruction that causes a computer to do something.

command-driven—requiring the operator to input commands rather than choosing options from a menu (see also menu-driven).

compatibility—the ability of a computer to run software and/or use peripherals designed for another computer.

compiler—a program that translates the source code for a program into object code all at once, before the program is run. Cf. interpreter.

computer literacy—nontechnical, use-oriented knowledge of computers and their role in society.

concurrency—the ability of a system to appear to perform two or more tasks "simultaneously" by switching rapidly between them.

CONTROL key—usually abbreviated CTRL on the keyboard; often indicated by ‹CTRL› in users' guides; used in conjunction with other keys to input commands for applications programs.

control unit—the portion of the CPU that interprets program commands stored in RAM and ROM and coordinates their execution.

courseware—instructional software, which includes instructor materials such as teaching objectives, course outlines, lesson plans, related activities, etc.

CP/M—Control Program for Microcomputers, the de facto standard disk operating system for 8-bit computers using 8080 and Z80 microprocessors.

CPU—central processing unit, consisting of a control unit, an arithmetic logic unit, and several registers; the computer component that interprets and executes program commands. In a microcomputer, the CPU circuitry is etched on a microprocessor chip.

cursor—a marker that indicates positions on the CRT screen, varying in appearance from a line to a small rectangle; may or may not "flash."

daisy wheel printer—a printer that uses a rotating flower-shaped print element containing characters on the ends of the spokes, or "petals"; when the proper character is aligned with the paper, a small hammer strikes it, pressing it against a ribbon to imprint the character image on the paper.

data—information.

database—a collection of data used or produced by a computer program; also a collection of related information, in machine-readable format, which may be numeric, bibliographic, factual, etc.

database service—a service providing remote, online access via dedicated terminals and/or microcomputers and modems to a variety of databases.

debug—to eliminate bugs (i.e., mistakes or malfunctions) in computer software or hardware.

dedicated circuit—wiring system which reserves an entire circuit for the computer system(s), not serving any other electrical devices.

default—in data entry, information a program enters in a field automatically unless the operator enters something different; in computer operations, the conditions or operating mode which is used unless the operator specifies a different condition. For example, the default mode for a printer may be "draft quality." Unless the operator specifies "near-letter quality" when giving a print command, the document will be printed in draft mode.

density—a measurement of how closely data may be "packed" on a storage surface such as one side of a floppy disk.

descender—a character image that is displayed on a CRT screen or by a printer so that any "tail' (e.g., of a "y" or "g") extends below the base line.

dial-up access—use of a dial or push-button telephone to initiate a station-to-station telephone call, as between a library's microcomputer and modem and a database service computer.

DIF—data interchange format. A standardized ASCII format used primarily for database and spreadsheet files. DIF files may be used by a variety of software programs.

DIP switches—small switches on printers, interfaces, and other devices for setting operating modes or default conditions.

directory — 1) a list of files on a floppy or hard disk; 2) a logical division of a hard disk.

disk controller — the interface between a computer and a disk drive.

documentation — the technical information, manuals, user's guides, and accompanying instructions included with hardware or software.

DOS — disk operating system, an operating system that is loaded into the computer from a floppy or hard disk.

dot matrix printer — a printer that forms characters consisting of close patterns of small dots by means of a head containing several fine wires that act as individual print hammers.

download — to transfer information from one system to a different type of system, as from a remote mainframe to a local microcomputer.

dumb terminal — a terminal without independent computing capabilities, for communicating online with a computer at another location.

dump — to copy information from one storage medium to another.

electrical noise — small power variations caused by such devices as small appliances, hand tools, powerline switching equipment, etc.

electronic mail — a method for sending messages via computer, usually through a network that uses a mini or mainframe computer accessed via modems or direct lines by either intelligent terminals (including microcomputers) or dumb terminals.

end user — the person(s) or organization who uses an applications program and the hardware needed to run it.

ergonomics — the physical relationship between people and machines.

expandability — the ability to add memory, peripheral devices, or capabilities to an existing system using plug-in interfaces.

expert system — a software program that simulates human expertise by using-a specialized database and heuristics for solving problems and making decisions.

field — in database management systems, a single data item within a record.

file — an organized collection of related data stored and processed as a unit.

firmware — program instructions or data that are permanently stored in the ROM of a computer.

fixed field — a field which always contains the same number of characters (including spaces), regardless of its contents. Cf. variable field.

fixed length record — a record which always requires the same amount of storage space, regardless of how much actual information it contains. In a file of such records, all records are the same length.

flag—a method for marking a record or file for later attention, e.g., errors detected by a spelling check program within a word processing file.

floppy disk—a flexible magnetic disk used for secondary or auxiliary storage of data; provides fairly high capacity and easy access to information at low cost.

font—a set of print characters of a specific style and size; may be hardware or software determined or both.

form feed—the automatic progression of a continuous sheet of paper through a printer so that the next line of print will begin on a new page.

format—1) the logical arrangement of data inside a file; 2) the physical arrangement of data on a storage medium such as a floppy or hard disk; 3) the physical arrangement of data on a screen or printed document.

FORTRAN—FORmula TRANslator, a high-level language used mainly for scientific, mathematical, and engineering applications.

front-end software—a program that assists a searcher to "talk to" and interpret the information from an online retrieval service.

full duplex—able to transmit and receive information simultaneously.

function key—a key on a keyboard that acts as a single-stroke command for applications software.

garbage—meaningless characters or information.

gateway—a sophisticated version of a front-end program that "blends" various online services so that they appear uniform to a user.

generation (computer)—a way of classifying computers according to technological development. First generation computers used vacuum tubes, were bulky, slow and unreliable; second generation computers used transistors and were somewhat faster, etc.

GIGO—garbage in, garbage out; i.e., if the input data are wrong ("bad"), the output data will also be wrong.

glitch—originally used to indicate a short, low-magnitude electrical disturbance; has come to mean any unexpected and inexplicable problem.

half duplex—able to both transmit and receive information, but not at the same time.

handshake—an exchange of information between a CPU and a peripheral device that verifies that communications have been established before actual data transfer begins.

hang—to cease to respond to keystrokes or other input.

hard copy—a printed copy of output data.

hard disk—a rigid, as opposed to flexible, storage disk, which provides higher capacity and faster access speed, but at a greater cost, than floppy disks.

hard-sector — a method for making floppy disks into sections by means of punched holes to indicate the sectors.

hardware — the physical components of a computer system.

hertz — in measuring signal frequency, the number of cycles per second.

heuristics — rules of thumb used to solve problems or make decisions.

hexadecimal — a number system using base 16; numbers greater than 9 are indicated by the letters A through F, e.g., decimal 168 is equivalent to hexadecimal A8.

high-level language — a machine-independent, procedure- or problem-oriented programming language, usually with English-based commands and syntax.

hit — a successful match during a file or database search. Each record that meets the search criteria is a "hit." The "hit rate" is the number or percentage of matches found.

Hollerith card — a punched card with 80 columns and 12 rows; characters are represented by holes punched in specific column/row positions according to a special code, which is also named after Herman Hollerith, inventor of the punched-card tabulator.

icon — a pictorial symbol for an object or action. For example, an icon for "draw" might be a pencil.

initialize — in the case of a disk, to prepare it to receive data according to a specific computer's format.

input — introduction of data via a peripheral device into a computer's internal memory.

integrated software — related packages with separate functions. Integrated packages may exchange data without file conversions, and usually have similar commands and procedures.

intelligent terminal — a terminal with built-in computer processing capabilities.

interactive — in an interactive system each input entry elicits a response, as in games or instructional programming.

interface — the connection between two components that converts the signals from one so that they may be "understood" by the other.

interpreter — a program which converts source code to object code, one instruction at a time as the program is running. Cf. compiler.

I/O — input/output, including devices, techniques, and processes.

ISAM — indexed sequential access method, for retrieving data stored by a database management system, according to a user-specified key or keys.

ISBN — International Standard Book Number. A ten-digit number assigned by a publisher to identify a specific book.

ISDN — integrated services digital network. An invisible rebuilding of local and long-distance telephone networks to allow simultaneous high-speed digital voice and data transmission over a standard pair of telephone wires.

ISSN — International Standard Serial Number. An eight-digit number assigned by a publisher to identify a specific serial.

joy stick — an input device, often used with graphics (as in games), with a stick that is manipulated by the operator to control input.

justification — alignment of characters, as in word processing, where margins may be flush on both sides of the text; or as in database management or a spreadsheet application, where one character may be flush with either the leftmost or rightmost position in a field.

K — kilobyte, or 1,024 bytes of data.

key — in database management, a field used to identify a record or sort the records in a file (see also search key).

LC-MARC — see MARC II.

light pen — an input device resembling a pen which is used to "write" directly onto a CRT screen or to "read" predefined patterns from the screen.

log on — to initiate a terminal or computer session, either by turning on the computer and loading a program, or by establishing contact with a remote computer, as for a database search.

logged disk drive — the disk drive currently in use by the computer.

LSI — large-scale integration, placing many (over 100) integrated circuits on a single silicon chip; very large-scale integration places 1,000 or more circuits on a single chip.

machine language — the most basic programming language; it can be "understood" and used by the computer without further interpretation.

MARC — machine readable catalog records which conform to a national standard for communication of bibliographic information, established and used by the Library of Congress.

MARC II — overall record structure designed by the Library of Congress in 1968; also applies to all the MARC formats. Replaced by USMARC in 1983.

menu-driven — using a list of command options called a "menu" that appears on the terminal screen. The operator indicates his/her choice by pressing the appropriate key, and the command is executed.

microprocessor — a "computer on a chip," which may serve, alternatively, as the CPU in a microcomputer, or as a preprogrammed control device for an appliance, traffic signal, business machine, etc.

mode — an operating condition or method.

modem — modulator-demodulator, a communications device that converts computer signals (bits) into tones that can be transmitted over telephone lines (modulation) and also converts incoming frequencies received over a telephone into signals the computer can use (demodulation).

monitor — a video display unit or CRT; alternatively, a control program usually built into the ROM of a computer.

motherboard — the assembly inside the computer that connects all the circuitry, interface cards, etc.

mouse — an input device which the user rolls around on a desktop as its movements are duplicated on the screen; the user chooses menu options and performs other tasks by "clicking" a button on the mouse.

MS-DOS — Microsoft disk operating system; the de facto standard (as of 1986) for 16-bit microcomputers.

multi-tasking — able to perform two or more tasks simultaneously.

multi-user — enabling users at multiple terminals, each of which may or may not have its own CPU and/or secondary storage, to share a common CPU and/or bus configuration.

network — a system which facilitates the exchange of information, programs, and resources among computers, with or without dumb terminals.

object code — the machine-language version of a program.

OCLC MARC — USMARC with extensions defined and generated by OCLC.

OCR — optical character recognition, the process of converting human readable data to a form suitable for computer input by means of a device that recognizes light reflected from printed characters.

OEM — original equipment manufacturer; now mostly replaced by VADs and VARs.

online — in direct communication with the CPU of a computer, either through a physically connected peripheral device or through remote access using a modem or a dumb terminal.

OPAC — online public access catalog, an automated catalog with subject, title, and author search options, directly available to patrons.

open architectural system — a hardware or software system whose technical specifications are made available to third parties, free or for a fee, by the manufacturer.

operating system — a type of systems software that serves as a controller for all the operations of a computer.

output — transfer of data from a computer's internal memory to a peripheral device for display or transmission.

parallel input/output — simultaneous transmission of bits using individual, parallel wires.

parity bit — an extra bit added to the group of bits composing a character, word, or byte to ensure that the number of bits is always either odd or even; parity bits thus establish a consistent bit pattern within the system and make it possible to detect errors and loss of bits.

Pascal—a general purpose, high-level language used on both large computer systems and micros.

peripheral devices—input/output (I/O) and secondary storage devices (e.g., disk drives and terminals) connected with the CPU by circuitry and/or cables.

pin-feed printer—a type of printer with pins for feeding paper affixed to the platen; it is capable of accepting only one width of paper, as opposed to an adjustable tractor feed printer.

pixels—the "dots" of light that make up an image on a CRT screen.

platen—on a printer, a roller or other backing against which the paper rests as the print head strikes it to form a character impression.

plotter—an output device for graphing data with an automatically controlled pen; the two main types are drum plotters and flatbed plotters.

port—an input/output channel through which a peripheral device can communicate with a computer.

powerline conditioner—a device that acts as an electrical shock absorber to suppress voltage spikes and electrical noise which may cause system damage or loss of data.

ProDOS—the upgraded version of AppleDOS, designed for use with Apple II family microcomputers using hard disks.

program—a sequence of instructions that cause a computer to perform a specific task; programming is the process of designing, writing, and testing such instructions.

prompt—a message indicating that the software or operating system is ready to receive an instruction, command, or data. For example, in MS-DOS, "C›" (read "C-prompt") means the operating system is waiting for you to enter a command.

proprietary system—a hardware or software system for which the technical specifications are kept secret by the manufacturer.

protocol—a set of rules or procedures, usually software-defined, for governing the exchange of information (via interfaces and ports) between computer equipment.

public domain software—software which is not copyrighted by the owner and thus is freely available for use by anyone.

RAM—see random access memory.

random access memory—the portion of a computer's internal memory that may be either read to or written to and is therefore changeable; it is usually volatile. Random access means that the time needed to read or write a piece of data is not dependent on its location within the memory. Abbreviated RAM.

read only memory—the portion of a computer's internal memory that is permanently programmed and may be read but not changed; such programming is called firmware. Abbreviated ROM.

record—in database management, a collection of related data items, or fields, which are treated as a single unit; comparable to a record in a manually kept file.

register—a device within the CPU used for temporary storage of data during processing.

resolution—the quality, in regard to clarity, sharpness, and density, of a video screen display.

RFP—request for proposal. A set of specifications issued to potential vendors or consultants for bidding, which describes the services needed and the format of the proposal, along with deadlines and other requirements for submissions.

ROM—see read only memory.

save—to store data in a secondary storage medium, such as a floppy disk, rather than in the computer's internal memory.

scroll—the vertical or horizontal movement of a screen display, such as word processing text or a spreadsheet, in either direction.

search—in database management, to examine a data file for those records meeting a specific set of criteria.

search and replace—in word processing, the ability to locate a given character string anywhere it appears in a file and replace it with a different, operator-specified character string, e.g., replacing every use of "John Jones" with "Stan Smith."

search key—data to be compared with specific items within records in order to locate desired records during a search.

sector—on a floppy disk, a section of a track.

sequential access—in a search, function in which each record is read or scanned in sequence.

serial input/output—transmission of data bits one at a time over a single wire.

silicon chip—see chip.

simulation—a type of program that simulates a physical or biological situation on a computer, e.g., an educational game that simulates the consequences of various decisions in the operation of a rocket.

soft return—in word processing, a return (line ending) that is not kept when text is reformatted.

soft-sector—a method for marking floppy disk sections using information written on the disk as opposed to hard-sector disks, which use physical holes.

software—the sets of instructions, or programs, that cause hardware to perform specific functions; also includes related documentation.

sort—to rearrange the records in a file according to a specific, logical order, e.g., alphabetically.

source code—the high-level language instructions for a program.

spike—a brief but sharp surge in a power supply.

spooling – the process of storing data temporarily in a buffer until an input/output device is ready to use them.

standalone – a self-contained, single-purpose system, such as a dedicated word processor or circulation system.

synchronous transmission – data transmission in which signals are sent at a fixed rate that is controlled by clock signals in the transmitter and receiver.

systems software – programs that act as monitors to enable a computer's various components to function, or which cause the computer to run more efficiently; e.g., operating systems.

tag – one or more characters (three in MARC records) used to identify an element of data or a field. In a MARC record, for example "100" is the tag for the author field.

terminal – a peripheral device that includes a keyboard, video display monitor, and a video generator; alternatively, an input/output device that is online to a computer in another location.

throughput – the amount of processing performed within a given period of time by a computer or one of its components.

timeshare – a system that allows a number of users to share access to the same computer facility; although to the users it appears that they are all using the computer simultaneously, they are actually being serviced in sequence at very high speed.

toggle – having two stable states, only one of which may be in effect at any given time, e.g., dynamic insert mode in word processing.

track – a continuous path on a floppy disk or other medium such as magnetic tape, along which data are recorded. On a disk, the tracks are divided into sectors.

tractor feed printer – a printer that has pins for feeding paper on adjustable tractors so that it is capable of handling paper of different widths.

transistor – a semiconductor device for controlling the flow of electrical current.

tree – a hierarchal structure used for storing records or files. For example, the hard disk file structure for MS-DOS consists of a "root directory" which contains any number of secondary directories, each of which may contain subdirectories; also, a network configuration in which stations are linked along "branches" leading to the host computer.

truncate – to cut off information in a field because its length exceeds the proscribed field length; also, to terminate a process at a predetermined point.

turnkey system – a packaged system, including both hardware and software, designed for a specific purpose; it is intended to be operated by persons with little or no knowledge of computer programming, systems, or operations.

upward compatibility – the ability of an operating system or computer to run programs written for its earlier versions.

user friendliness – description of a computer system in regard to ease of use and interactivity.

USMARC — current term for machine-readable cataloging format used in the United States. Previous names were LC MARC, LC/MARC, MARC II, or MARC.

VAD — value added distributor. A manufacturer who buys equipment and/or software produced by another company, adds "value" to it in the form of additional software and/or hardware, then resells it to retailers.

VAR — value added retailer. A manufacturer who buys equipment and/or software produced by another company, adds "value" to it in the form of additional software and/or hardware, then resells it to end users.

variable field — a field which varies in length according to its contents. Cf. fixed field.

variable length record — a record which varies in length according to its contents, so that records within a file may be different in length. Cf. fixed length record.

video display unit — an output device that displays data on a CRT screen.

video generator — a device contained in a computer or terminal that generates the signals that control the CRT screen display.

volatile memory — memory that loses its contents if the system's power is turned off or lost.

voltage regulator — a circuit that controls voltage output so that it remains consistent regardless of changes in the voltage passing through it.

volume — a logical subdivision of a hard or floppy disk.

warm boot — the process by which the operating system is reloaded into memory by pressing a reset switch or combination of keys, without turning off the power. Cf. cold boot.

wildcard — in searching or selecting, a character (usually an asterisk or a question mark) that tells the computer to "accept anything in this position," e.g., in conducting a search for a name when unsure of the spelling ("Smith" or "Smythe"), typing "Sm?th?".

Winchester drive — a hard disk unit in which the disk and the read/write assembly are encased in a hermetically sealed chamber to protect them against damage and/or data loss due to smoke or other types of particles.

window — a secondary screen display that overlays all or part of the main screen. Windows are used for entering or displaying supplemental information, such as "Help" text.

word wrap — in word processing, the ability to start a new line automatically whenever a word is typed that is too long to fit inside the margins.

write-protect — a method for protecting a disk against inadvertent recording of data (and simultaneous erasing of data already present); on a floppy disk it is accomplished by a notch in the protective sleeve, which is either covered or uncovered depending on the individual computer system.

Appendix B:
Resources

The following represents a selection of available resources on microcomputers, libraries, and education. As large as this selection is, it is not comprehensive; new resources are appearing almost literally every day. Still, the publications, organizations, individuals, and products listed here should provide any media specialist with a wide range of information and assistance in his or her microcomputer venture. Please note, however, that inclusion in this list does *not* constitute a recommendation unless specifically noted, as we were not able to examine each item.

The resources are organized by format (reference books, periodicals, newsletters, etc.) and further broken down by subject (library management, special education, etc.), with annotations and/or review sources, contact names, and price information (when available).

We want to thank the many people who took the time to answer our inquiries concerning their activities with microcomputers. The research for this section was most rewarding.

Please note when writing individuals and organizations, particularly nonprofit organizations such as libraries, it is a good idea to enclose a self-addressed, stamped envelope and/or postage with your request.

REFERENCE WORKS
Bibliographies

Monographs

Adler, Anne G., et al., comps. *Automation in Libraries, 1978-1982: A LITA Bibliography*. Ann Arbor, Mich.: Pierian Press. n.d. unpaged. $18.95.

Bewsey, Julia J. *Microcomputers and Libraries*. Brooklyn, N.Y.: Vantage Information Consultants, 1985. 63p. $15.00. (Vantage Information Consultants, 298 State St., Brooklyn, NY 11201).
This title in the CompuBibs series of annotated paperback bibliographies on current topics "lists books, bibliographies, and articles on library applications of microcomputers, with sections devoted to academic, public, school, and special libraries." Many of the articles listed are available through document delivery service.

Computer Books for Children. By Cuyahoga County (Ohio) Public Library. n.p. n.d. unpaged. Free. (Children's Services Dept., 4510 Memphis Ave., Cleveland, OH 44144. Enclose SASE).

Lists fifty basic computer books for children arranged by author, with annotations and indications for grade level.

Library Applications of Microcomputers: A Bibliography. By Missouri Library Association. n.p. n.d. 59p. $6.00. (Missouri Library Association, Parkard Plaza, Suite 9, Columbia, MO 65203).
Lists materials published between 1982 and 1984; also contains citations for articles on some hardware and on evaluating and circulating software.

Periodicals

AASL Committee. "Microcomputer Software and Hardware—an Annotated Source List." *School Library Media Quarterly* 12, no.2 (Winter 1984): 107-19.
  Includes "How to Obtain"; "How to Evaluate"; "How to Catalog"; and "How to Standardize."

Burke, Barbara, and Linda McNamara. "Electronic Bulletin Boards: An Annotated Bibliography." *Small Computers in Libraries* (June-December, 1985). No pages available.
Part I (June 1985), software available to set up a BBS; part II (July/August 1985), bulletin board directories; part III (September 1985), general publications that cover all aspects of bulletin boards; part IV (October 1985), guide to publications describing specific BBSs; part V (November 1985), information about accessing the boards; part VI (December 1985), information about setting up local bulletin boards.

Dewey, Patrick R. "Microcomputers and Telecommunications: A Checklist of Books and Journals." *American Libraries* 15, 9 (October 1984): 631-32, 649.
Dewey pioneered in library-based, electronic community bulletin boards, and has devoted a chapter to this subject in his book *Public Access Microcomputers: A Handbook for Librarians.*

Hanley, Karen Stang. "Best Computer Books for Kids." *Classroom Computer Learning* 4, no. 4 (November/December 1983): 34-35.

Haworth, Carol. "Telecommunications Policy: A Selective List of Periodicals." *Library HiTech* (Issue 5) 2, no. 1 (1st quarter 1984): 67-71.
These periodicals were "selected for their value in tracking current regulatory and industry developments in the United States."

La Faille, Eugene. "Sources Which Offer Guidelines or Other Advice in the Evaluation of Microcomputer Software." *Apple Library Users' Group Newsletter* 3, no. 4 (October 1985): 23-25.

Lyon, Sally. "End-User Searching of Online Databases: Selective Annotated Bibliography." *Library HiTech* (Issue 6) 2, no. 2 (2nd quarter 1984): 47-50.

Smith, Stephen C. "Search Strategy Index." *Library HiTech* (Issue 5) 2, no. 1 (1st quarter 1984): 77-82.
Includes "for the online searcher . . . citations to articles containing useful hints on search procedures, record structure and contents, and new database developments."

Dictionaries

Monographs

Naiman, Arthur. *Computer Dictionary for Beginners.* New York: Ballantine Books.
n.d. 150p. $6.95.
Reviewed in *Personal Computing* (January 1984): 231.

Sippl, Charles J., and Roger J. Sippl. *Computer Dictionary and Handbook.*
Indianapolis, Ind.: Howard W. Sams, 1908. unpaged. $34.95.
Reviewed in *The Computing Teacher* 8 (December 1980): 52-53.

Wall, Elizabeth, and Alexander C. Wall. *The Beginners Computer Dictionary.* New
York: Avon Camelot, 1984. unpaged. Price not given.
Reviewed and compared to two others in *The Computing Teacher* (April 1985):
58-59. Elizabeth Wall also authored the *Computer Alphabet Book.*

Periodicals

Dewey, Patrick R. "Microcomputer Dictionaries—Buzzwords, Lexicons and
Glossaries: Definitions You Can Byte Into." *Library Journal* 110, no. 2 (1 February
1985): 59-61.
Provides brief description of dictionaries available followed by brief reviews of
over 30 various types of computer dictionaries.

Directories and Guides

Online Services

Database Directory Service. White Plains, N.Y.: Knowledge Industry Publications, Inc.
Available through BRS. Also available in print (see page 234).

Educational Technologies Database Project. Cambridge, Mass.: Harvard University
Graduate School of Education, Monroe C. Gutman Library, annual.
The source of earlier directories on "uses of microcomputers in educational set-
tings," this directory will first be published electronically and offered online on Compu-
Serve with plans to update the information annually. Print directories will also be
available at a later date. For information, contact Mary Grace Smith, Project Director,
Harvard University Graduate School of Education, Monroe C. Gutman Library, Ap-
pian Way, Cambridge, MA 02138.

Monographs

Bowers, Richard A., comp. *CD-ROM Guide.* Carmel, Calif.: Information Arts, 1986.
unpaged. $20.00. (Information Arts, P.O. Box 1032, Carmel Valley, CA 93924
(408) 659-5235).
This "comprehensive guide to the growing number of CD-ROM and related write-
once CD-ROM publications, videodisc format publications, hardware, peripherals, and
services dealing with the new media . . . includes explanatory information about the
technology." It is aimed at the library and information center market. Contact Richard
Bowers at Information Arts for further information.

Bowker's 1985 Complete Sourcebook of Personal Computing. New York: Bowker, 1985. 1050p. $19.95.

Reviewed: *Wilson Library Bulletin* (March 1985): 499; *Library Journal/School Library Journal* (library computing supplement) (May 1985): 7.

Brand, Stewart, ed. *Whole Earth Software Catalog.* New York: Quantum Press/Doubleday, 1984. 208p. $17.50.

Reviewed: *Special Libraries* (Spring 1985): 161; *Library Journal/School Library Journal* (library computing supplement) (May 1985): 8.

Burwell, Helen P. *Directory of Fee-Based Information Services.* Houston, Tex.: Burwell Enterprises, annual. Price not given. (Burwell Enterprises, 106 F.M. 1960a W. Suite 349, Houston, TX 77069 (713) 537-9051).

Includes company names, individuals' names, subjects, services indexes.

Closing the Gap 1985 Resource Directory. Henderson, Minn.: Closing the Gap, 1985. $7.95. (Closing the Gap, P.O. Box 68, Henderson, MN 56044).

Lists microcomputer resources for special education and rehabilitation. Contains sections on software, hardware, and other resources, as well as a glossary of terms.

Communications Software Directory. Norcross, Ga.: Hayes Microcomputer Products, 1983. unpaged. Price not given. (Hayes Microcomputer Products, Inc., 5923 Peachtree Industrial Blvd., Norcross, GA 30092 (404) 449-8791).

Lists and describes communications software compatible with Hayes modems. Contact Hayes for information about latest version.

Database Directory. 2d ed. By American Society for Information Science (ASIS). White Plains, N.Y.: Knowledge Industry Publications, n.d. unpaged.

The two semiannual editions, updated monthly by the newsletter *Database Alert,* contain information on an estimated 2750 online databases. Also available online via BRS. Reviewed: *Library Journal* (1 May 1985): 42.

Directory of Microcomputers in Hospital Libraries (1985). n.p., n.d. unpaged. $11.50 members/$16.50 nonmembers. (Nancy Fazzone, Library Director, Salem Hospital, 81 Highland Avenue, Salem, MA 01970).

Directory of Public Domain and User-supported Programs for IBM PC. n.p., n.d. unpaged. $4.95. (PC Software Interest Group (PC-SIG), 1556 Halford Ave., Suite #130JQ, Santa Clara, CA 95051).

Ferrarini, Elizabeth. *Infomania: The Guide to Essential Electronic Services.* Boston, Mass.: Houghton-Mifflin Co., 1985. unpaged. $14.95.

Provides an overview of over 250 electronic data services. Major sections cover communications software and modems, steps for going online, selected professional databases, news services, search services, and bulletin boards. Recommended by John C. Dvorak ("Inside Track"), *InfoWorld* (14 February 1986).

Information Sources 1986. Washington, D.C.: Information Industry Association (IIA), 1986. 504p. $59.95.

"Covers more than 400 information companies [including] database publishers and distributors, electronic and print publishers, financial information services, telecommunications firms, information brokers and retailers, abstracting and indexing services, computer hardware and software, and videotex providers."

Matthews, Joseph R. *Directory of Automated Library Systems.* New York: Neal-Schuman, n.d. 217p. $34.95.
Reviewed: *Library Journal* (15 October 1985): 56.

McAffee, Michael, ed. *Apple Access: User's Guide to Apple Computer Related Periodical Literature.* Petaluma, Calif.: Stony Point Publications, biannual. $19.95. (Stony Point Publications, P.O. Box 4467, Petaluma, CA 94953).
Reviewed: *Apple LUG Newsletter* (January 1985): 28.

Microcomputer Directory: Applications in Educational Settings. Cambridge, Mass.: Harvard University, Monroe C. Gutman Library, annual. $15.00. (Harvard University Graduate School of Education, Appian Way, Cambridge, MA 01238. Prepaid orders add $1.00 for postage and handling, purchase orders add $2.50.)
This is an excellent source of information about educational applications. The directory is indexed by subject area (libraries/media centers, administration, special education, etc.) and by state. Each entry includes a brief description of the application, the equipment used, funding, contact person, and address.

National Directory of Bulletin Board Systems. Westport, Conn.: Meckler Publishing, 1985. unpaged. $9.95 prepaid or $16.95 when billed.
Will be updated annually.

1984 Directory of Resources for Technology in Education. By Far West Laboratory for Education Research and Development. n.p., n.d. unpaged. $12.95. (Far West Laboratory for Education Research and Development, 1855 Folsom St., San Francisco, CA 94103 (415) 565-3000).
"Intended as an annual publication, the Directory includes national and state associations, resource organizations, computer camps, summer institutes, periodicals, databases, funding sources, etc., in the technology-in-education field."

Nolan, Jeanne M., ed. *Micro Software Evaluations.* Westport, Conn.: Meckler Publishing, n.d. unpaged. Price not given.
Reviewed: *Information Technology and Libraries* (September 1984): 320-21.

_____. *Micro Software Report, Library Edition.* Westport, Conn.: Meckler Publishing, n.d. unpaged. (Vols. I, II, and III). Price not given.
Reviews: *Small Computers in Libraries* (October 1982): 1-2; *Information Technology and Libraries* (September 1984): 320-21; *Technicalities* (February 1985): 9, 14. Volume I covers programs that appeared in literature from July 1981-July 1982; volume II covers July 1982-July 1983; volume III covers 1984-1985. A three-year cumulative index for all three volumes is available from Meckler.

PLA Library Microcomputer Users Database Directory. By PLA Technology in Public Libraries Committee, Carol F.L. Liu, chair. n.p., n.d. unpaged. Price not given. (Queens Borough Public Library, 89-11 Merrick Blvd., Jamaica, NY 11432).

Described in *American Libraries* (December 1985): 824. A library micro users' directory with information on microcomputer use in over 380 libraries of all types. May order regional directories or the entire directory for United States and Canada.

Shirinian, George. *Microcomputing Periodicals: Annotated Directory,* 11th ed. New York: Garland Publishing, 1985. unpaged. $24.95.

This is a regularly updated bibliography divided into three sections. The first details publications that provide indexing to various periodicals, the second provides a list of all periodicals on microcomputers currently in print, and the third gives information on those periodicals that have ceased publication or changed their name. Includes indexes by subject and country of origin.

Software Encyclopedia. New York: Bowker, 1985. unpaged. $95.00.

Reviewed: *Wilson Library Bulletin* (December 1985): 67.

SpecialWare Directory. By LINC Associates, Inc. Phoenix, Ariz.: Oryx Press, 1984. 98p. Price not given.

Lists companies that produce over 200 programs and software or courseware products suitable for special education. Arranged by company with ordering information and product descriptions, including curriculum areas, grade levels, hardware requirements, format, handicapping condition for which appropriate, and instructional design or approach. Reviewed: *The Computing Teacher* (March 1985): 66-67.

Swift's Educational Software Directory for Corvus Networks—Apple Edition. Austin, Tex.: Sterling Swift, 1984. 219p. Price not given. (Sterling Swift Publishing Co., 7901 South 1H-35, Austin, TX 78744).

TESS: The Educational Software Selector. By the EPIE Institute. New York: Teachers College Press, 1984. unpaged. $49.95.

Reviewed: *The Computing Teacher* (May 1984): 38. Also available online.

Walton, Robert A. *Directory of Microcomputer Software for Libraries.* Austin, Tex.: Texas State Library, 1985. 183p. Price not given. (Texas State Library, Library Development Division, Texas Archives and Library Building, Box 12927-Capitol Station, Austin, TX 78711).

Profiles of library software packages include, for each program: purpose, microcomputer resources required for operation, and price. Also includes useful indexes: title, subject, Apple software, IBM software, CP/M software, and Tandy/Radio Shack software.

Periodicals

Tenopir, Carol. "Database Directories: The Rest." *Library Journal* 110, no. 15 (15 September 1985): 56-57.

Discussion of database directories which includes lists of selected directories in three categories: comprehensive directories, directories for end users, and specialty directories.

Indexes

Microcomputer Index. Palo Alto, Calif.: Microcomputer Index. Bimonthly.
(Microcomputer Index, P.O. Box 50545, Palo Alto, CA 94303 (415) 961-2880).
Includes annual cumulations, micro reviews on disk. Online as Dialog File 233.
Abstracts and citations of articles, hardware and software, and book reviews, as well as
new product announcements. Coverage since 1981 of about 70 microcomputer
magazines.

SCIL Four-Year Cumulative Index (April 1981-December 1984). Westport, Conn.:
Meckler Publishing, n.d. unpaged. $25.00.

Yearbooks

Miller, Elwood R., and Mary Louise Mosley, eds. *Educational Media and Technology
Yearbook.* Vol. 11-. Littleton, Colo.: Libraries Unlimited. 1985-. Annual. $47.50.
Formerly *Educational Media Yearbook.* It offers essays on an annual topic plus
sections on "Organizations and Associations"; "Graduate Programs"; "Funding
Sources"; "Media Resources."

MONOGRAPHS

Artificial Intelligence

Feugenbaum, E., and P. McCorduck. *Fifth Generation: Artificial Intelligence and
Japan's Computer Challenge.* Reading, Mass.: Addison-Wesley, 1983. 275p.
$14.95.
Reviewed: *Popular Computing* (October 1983): 253-54.

Gloess, Paul. *Understanding Artificial Intelligence.* Sherman Oaks, Calif.: Alfred
Publishing Co., Inc., 1981. unpaged. Price not given.
Recommended in "Marooned on a Desert Island with a Micro—Ten Books to Take
Along." *The Computing Teacher* (November 1983): 54.

Litterick, Ian. *Robots and Intelligent Machines.* New York: Franklin Watts, Inc.,
1984. 47p. illus. Price not given.
Reviewed: *CMC News* (Spring 1985): 12. For upper elementary and junior high
readers. Includes a history of robotics, an overview of how computers are being used in
society today, and a section on the moral issues involved in developing intelligent
machines.

Schrank, Roger C., with Peter G. Childers. *Cognitive Computer: On Language,
Learning and Artificial Intelligence.* Reading, Mass.: Addison-Wesley, n.d. 269p.
$17.95.
Reviewed: *Personal Computing* (August 1985): 134.

Computers in Education

Alper, Lynne, and Meg Holmberg. *Parents, Kids, and Computers.* Berkeley, Calif.:
Sybex, Inc., 1984. 145p. Price not given.
Reviewed: *CMC News* (Spring 1985): 12. "Excellent book for students to check out
and share with their parents. . . . strong support for parents working cooperatively with
teachers and schools."

Bitter, Gary G., and Ruth A. Camuse. *Using a Microcomputer in the Classroom.*
Reston, Va.: Reston Publishing, n.d. 339p. $15.95.
Reviewed: *Personal Computing* (April 1984): 196-97; *Electronic Education*
(January 1984): 44; *The Computing Teacher* (October 1984): 41.

Coburn, Peter, et al. *Practical Guide to Computers in Education.* Reading, Mass.:
Addison-Wesley, 1982. unpaged. $10.95.
Reviewed: *Popular Computing* (February 1983): 167-70. Recommended by Ann
Lathrop in *Educational Computer* (July/August 1982): 16.

D'Ignazio, Fred. *Computing Together: A Parents' and Teachers' Guide for Using
Computers with Young Children.* Greensboro, N.C.: Compute! Publications,
1984. 312p. $12.95.
Reviewed: *Popular Computing* (January 1985): 172.

Doerr, Christine. *Microcomputers and the 3R's: A Guide for Teachers.* Rochelle Park,
N.J.: Hayden Book Co., 1979. unpaged. $7.95.
Reviewed: *Electronic Education* (November 1981): 30; *The Computing Teacher* 8
(November 1980): 59; *OnComputing* (Spring 1981): 40.

Goldberg, Kenneth P., and Robert D. Sherwood. *Microcomputers: A Parents' Guide.*
New York: John Wiley and Sons, 1983. 196p. $8.95.
Reviewed: *The Computing Teacher* (March 1984): 60-61.

Hunter, Beverly. *My Students Use Computers.* Englewood Cliffs, N.J.: Prentice-Hall,
1984. unpaged. $24.95.
Also available in paperback ($17.95). Reviewed: "My Favorite Computer Books"
by Gerald W. Bracey, *Electronic Learning* (November/December 1985): 64 and
(November/December 1983): 104-5.

Joiner, Lee M., et al. *Microcomputers in Education, a Nontechnical Guide to
Instructional School Management Applications.* Holmes Beach, Fla.: Learning
Publications, Inc., 1982. unpaged. $24.95 plus $1.50 shipping/handling. (Learning
Publications, Inc., P.O. Box 1326, Holmes Beach, FL 33059).
This is a nontechnical language guidebook for educators describing recent ac-
complishments with microcomputers in schools, including both management and in-
structional applications.

O'Shea, Tim, and John Self. *Learning and Teaching with Computers: Artificial
Intelligence in Education.* Englewood Cliffs, N.J.: Prentice-Hall, Inc., 1984. 307p.
$12.95.
Reviewed: *Personal Computing* (June 1984): 233.

Papert, Seymour. *Mindstorms: Children, Computers and Powerful Ideas.* New York: Basic Books, 1980. 230p. $6.95.

Background for the use of LOGO. Reviewed: *The Computing Teacher* 8 (March 1981): 52-53; *Classroom Computer News* (March 1981): 26; *80 Microcomputing* (February 1981): 14. Included in "An Elite Microdozen," *Library Journal/School Library Journal* (library computing supplement) (May 1985): 8. "Guaranteed to be useful past the next few computer model changes."

Peterson, Dale. *Intelligent Schoolhouse: Readings on Computers and Learning.* Reston, Va.: Reston Publishing, 1984. 321p. $14.95.

Reviewed: *Popular Computing* (November 1984): 190; *School Library Journal* (November 1984): 42.

School Library Media Annual, 1985. Edited by Shirley L. Aaron and Pat R. Scales. Littleton, Colo.: Libraries Unlimited, 1985. 525p. (Vol. 3). $40.00.

Includes: "Additions to Your Core Collection of Microcomputer Software"; "Microcomputers in School Library Media Centers: Utilization and Research"; "Telecommunications and the School Media Program"; "Using Microcomputers in Elementary School Library Media Programs"; "Ethical Concerns in an Age of Technology"; "Elementary/Secondary Schools and School Systems Using OCLC."

Tashner, John H., ed. *Educational Microcomputing Annual.* Phoenix, Ariz.: Oryx Press, 1985. 184p. (Vol. 1). $24.50.

Contains 33 nontechnical articles covering general trends in educational microcomputing, hardware trends, software development and computer language issues, micros in the curriculum, and training of personnel. Also includes bibliographies, resource lists, a glossary, and an index.

_____. *Improving Instruction with Microcomputers: Readings and Resources.* Phoenix, Ariz.: Oryx Press, 1984. 255p. $24.50.

Reviewed: *School Library Media Quarterly* (Spring 1985): 147; *School Library Journal* (November 1984): 42.

Taylor, Robert, ed. *The Computer in the School: Tutor, Tool, Tutee.* New York: Teacher's College Press, 1980. unpaged. $14.95.

Reviewed: *The Computing Teacher* (February 1981): 36; *The Computing Teacher* (February 1982): 49-50; *Creative Computing* (October 1981): 266-67.

Troutner, Joanne. *The Media Specialist, the Microcomputer, and the Curriculum.* Littleton, Colo.: Libraries Unlimited, 1983. 197p. $19.50.

Reviewed: *The Book Report* (September/October 1984): 46; *Electronic Education* (March/April 1985): 62; *School Library Journal* (November 1984): 44.

Computers in Special Education

Computers and the Handicapped in Special Education and Rehabilitation. Eugene, Oreg.: University of Oregon, 1983. unpaged. $7.00. (ICCE, University of Oregon, 135 Education, Eugene, OR 97403 (505) 686-4414).

This resource guide with over 180 annotated citations focuses on computer-assisted and computer-managed instruction in both educational and client settings.

Goldenberg, Paul E. *Special Technology for Special Children.* Baltimore, Md.: University Park Press, 1979. 200p. Price not given.
Reviewed: *The Computing Teacher* (April 1984): 38-40.

Goldenberg, Paul E., et al. *Computers, Education, and Special Needs.* Reading, Mass.: Addison-Wesley, 1984. unpaged. $13.95.
Reviewed: *Electronic Learning* (February 1984): 86; *Electronic Education* (February 1985): 44.

Hagen, Dolores. *Microcomputer Resource Book for Special Education.* Reston, Va.: Reston Publishing Co., 1984. 224p. $15.95.
Reviewed: *The Computing Teacher* (April 1984): 41; *Electronic Learning* (February 1984): 86; *Electronic Education* (February 1985): 44; *School Library Journal* (November 1984): 44.

McWilliams, Peter. *Personal Computers and the Disabled.* New York: Quantum Press/Doubleday, 1984. 416p. $9.95
Reviewed: *Popular Computing* (November 1984): 190; *Electronic Education* (February 1984): 44.

Tabor, Florence M. *Microcomputers in Special Education.* Reston, Va.: Council for Exceptional Children, 1983. 112p. $7.95. (ERIC, 1920 Association Dr., Reston, VA 22091).
Reviewed: *The Computing Teacher* (May 1984): 38-39.

Computer History

Asimov, Isaac. *How Did We Find Out about Computers?* New York: Walker and Company, 1984. 54p. Price not given.
Reviewed: *CMC News* (Spring 1985): 12. "History of computers from the abacus to the attempt today to create artificial intelligence . . . manages to transform a dull subject into interesting reading material."

Augarten, Stan. *Computer History for Everyone.* New York: Ticknor and Fields, n.d. 324p. $17.95.
Reviewed: *Personal Computing* (August 1985): 136.

Freiberger, Paul, and Michael Swaine. *Fire in the Valley.* Berkeley, Calif.: Osborne/McGraw-Hill, n.d. unpaged. $9.95.
Presents history of the Apple computer.

Levy, Steven. *Hackers: Heroes of the Computer Revolution.* New York: Doubleday, 1984. 446p. $17.95.
Reviewed: *Popular Computing* (December 1984): 203-4.

Lukoff, Herman. *From Dits to Bits: A Personal History of the Electronic Computer.* Forest Grove, Oreg.: Robotics Press, 1979. unpaged. $12.95. (Robotics Press, P.O. Box 555, Forest Grove, OR 97116).

This autobiography of the director of technical operations at Sperry Univac, one of the first people to become involved with computers, recounts his experiences with five of the first computers, beginning with ENIAC. Reviewed: *Creative Computing* 6 (November 1980): 188; *Interface Age* 5 (July 1980): 22.

Osborne, Adam. *Running Wild, the Next Industrial Revolution.* New York: McGraw-Hill, 1979. unpaged. Price not given.

This insider's look at computers in the 1980s provides insight into the future impact of computers on our lives.

Stern, Nancy. *From ENIAC to UNIVAC: An Appraisal of the Eckert-Mauchly Computers.* North Billerica, Mass.: Digital Press, 1981. unpaged. $25.00.

Reviewed: *Kilobaud Microcomputing* 5, no. 12 (December 1981): 233-34. "Interesting, informative and well-written account. . . ."

Computers in Libraries

Adle, Anne G., and Elizabeth A. Baber, eds. *Retrospective Conversion: From Cards to Computer.* Ann Arbor, Mich.: Pierian Press, 1984. 312p. (Library HiTech Series). $39.50.

Reviewed: *Library Journal* (1 November 1985): 41. Includes a paper describing an affordable means of record conversion for school and small public libraries.

Chen, Ching-Chih, ed. *Microcomputers in Libraries.* New York: Neal-Schuman, 1982. unpaged. Price not given.

Clark, Philip. *Microcomputer Spreadsheet Models for Libraries.* Chicago: ALA Publishing, 1985. unpaged. $24.95.

Includes models for activity reports, financial records, budgets, statistics, projections, etc. Also included are guidelines for when and how to use spreadsheets and comparisons of several of the most popular spreadsheets.

Corbin, John. *Managing the Library Automation Project.* Phoenix, Ariz. Oryx Press, 1985. 274p. Price not given.
Reviewed: *Wilson Library Bulletin* (February 1986): 56.

Dewey, Patrick R. *Public Access Microcomputers: A Handbook for Librarians.* White Plains, N.Y.: Knowledge Industry Publications, Inc., 1984. 151p. $27.50.

Reviewed: *Information Today* (December 1985). "Different from most . . . Instead of explaining what microcomputers can do for libraries, it shows how librarians can use microcomputers to help their patrons"; *Information and Technology* (December 1984): 425-26; *International Journal of Reviews* (1985): 32.

Dodd, Sue, and Ann Sandberg Fox. *Cataloging Microcomputer Files.* Chicago: ALA Publishing, 1985. 272p. $37.50.
Reviewed: *Wilson Library Bulletin* (February 1986): 56.

Dowlin, Kenneth. *The Electronic Library*. New York: Neal-Schuman, 1984. 199p.
   Price not given.
   Dowlin is director of Pikes Peak Library District in Colorado Springs, Col-
orado—the home of "Maggie's Place." Reviewed: *Information Technology and
Libraries* (December 1984): 426-27; *Wilson Library Bulletin* (May 1984): 671.

Essential Guide to the Library IBM PC. Westport, Conn.: Meckler Publishing,
   n.d. unpaged. Price not given.
   Series of five volumes announced in March 1985. For information contact
Meckler.

Falk, Howard. *Personal Computers for Libraries*. Medford, N.J.: Learned
   Information, Inc., 1985. 174p. $18.95.
   Reviewed: *Information Today* (October 1985): 15.

Fayen, Emily Gallup. *Online Catalog: Improving Public Access to Library Materials*.
   White Plains, N.Y.: Knowledge Industry Publications, 1983. unpaged. Price not
   given.

Hunter, Eric J. *Computerized Cataloging*. London: Britain's Clive Bingley, Ltd.,
   distr.; Hamden, Conn.: Shoe String Press, 1985. 215p. $19.50.
   Reviewed: *Library Journal* (1 February 1986): 64.

Lein Ho, May. *Appleworks for School Librarians*. Fayetteville, Ark.: Hi Willow
   Research and Publishing, 1985. 129p. $20.00. (Hi Willow Research and Publishing,
   P.O. Box 1801, Fayetteville, AR 72702).
   First copy to any address includes a template disk. Multiple copies to the same ad-
dress without the template disks are $10.00 each. Includes a section on collection map-
ping technique by David Loertscher.

Markey, Karen. *Subject Searching in Library Catalogs*. Dublin, Ohio: Online Library
   Computer Center (OCLC), 1984. unpaged. Price not given. (Online Computer
   Library Center, Inc., 6505 Franz Road, Dublin, OH 43017).

Miliot, Jim. *Micros at Work: Case Studies of Microcomputers in Libraries*. White
   Plains, N.Y.: Knowledge Industry Publications, 1985. 140p. $28.50.
   Reviewed: *Library Journal* (1 October 1985): 78. "Valuable resource for any
librarian who is contemplating the use of a microcomputer." Thirty case studies profile
public, special, and academic library microcomputer applications . . . with emphasis on
public use of microcomputers.

Miller, Inabeth. *Microcomputers in School Library Media Centers*. New York: Neal-
   Schuman, 1984. 165p. $19.95.
   Reviewed: *School Library Media Quarterly* (Winter 1985): 77-78; *The Book Report*
(September/October 1984): 46.

Naumer, Janet Noll. *Media Center Management with an Apple II*. Littleton, Colo.:
   Libraries Unlimited, 1984. 250p. $19.50.
   This is a step-by-step guide to using general applications software for library tasks.
Includes more than 50 sample templates. Includes sources for similar software available

for other microcomputers. Reviewed: *Library Journal* (1 October 1985): 78. "Valuable resource for any librarian who is contemplating the use of a microcomputer."

Palmer, Roger C. *dBase II and dBase III: An Introduction for Information Services.* 2d ed. Studio City, Calif.: Pacific Information, Inc., 1984. unpaged. $25.00. (Pacific Information, Inc., 11684 Ventura Blvd., Suite 295, Studio City, CA 91604 (818) 797-7654).
"Designed for users in a library setting."

Polly, Jean Armour, ed. *Essential Guide to Apple Computers in Libraries.* Westport, Conn.: Meckler Publishing, 1986—. unpaged (five volumes). $19.95/vol.
This is a series of five volumes on using Apple II and MacIntosh computers in your library. First volume available in early 1986.

Pope, Nolan F. *Microcomputers for Library Circulation Control.* Indianapolis, Ind.: Indiana Cooperative Library Services Authority (INCOLSA), 1984. unpaged. Price not given. (INCOLSA, 1100 West 42nd St., Indianapolis, IN 46208 (317) 926-3361).
Aims "to provide guidelines to help you compare systems."

Post, William E., and Peter G. Watson. *Online Catalog, the Inside Story: A Planning and Implementation Guide.* Chico, Calif.: Ryan Research International, 1983. 158p. $14.95 pa.

Rice, James. *Introduction to Library Automation.* Littleton, Colo.: Libraries Unlimited, 1984. 223p. $28.50; $18.50 pa.

Rorvig, Mark. *Microcomputers and Libraries, a Guide to Technology, Products and Applications.* White Plains, N.Y.: Knowledge Industry Publications, 1981. unpaged. $27.50.
Reviewed: *Small Computers in Libraries* (February 1982): 6-7; *ACCESS: Microcomputers in Libraries* (January 1982): 12.

Rush, James E. *Microcomputers for Libraries.* James E. Rush Associates, 1983. Looseleaf. Price not given. (James E. Rush Associates, 2223 Carriage Road, Powell, OH 43065-9703).
Reviewed: *Wilson Library Bulletin* (April 1984): 591; *Library HiTech* (Issue 6): 83-86—compared with *Librarian's Guide to Microcomputer Technology and Applications* by Larry A. Woods and Nolan F. Pope.

Saffady, William. *Introduction to Automation for Librarians.* Chicago: ALA Publishing, 1983. unpaged. Price not given.

Tarrish, Laura. *Apple Computer Clubs' Activities Handbook.* Englewood Cliffs, N.J.: Prentice-Hall, n.d. 244p. $14.95.
Official Apple Computer Clubs' series. Reviewed: *School Library Journal* (August 1985): 26.

Thomason, Nevada Wallis. *Circulation Systems for School Library Media Centers.* Littleton, Colo.: Libraries Unlimited, 1984. 184p. $23.50.
Reviewed: *School Library Journal* (January 1986): 32.

Walton, Robert A. *Microcomputers: A Planning and Implementation Guide for Librarians.* Phoenix, Ariz.: Oryx Press, 1983. 96p. $18.50.
Reviewed: *Technicalities* (May 1984): 15; *School Library Media Quarterly* (Spring 1985): 152-53; *Information Technology and Libraries* (June 1984): 217-20.

Woods, Larry A., and Nolan F. Pope. *Librarian's Guide to Microcomputer Technology and Applications.* White Plains, N.Y.: Knowledge Industry Publishing, 1983. 209p. $27.50.
Reviewed: *Library HiTech* (Issue 6): 83-88. In this issue it is compared to *Microcomputers for Libraries* by James E. Rush Associates (see page 243).

Woolls, Blanche, and David Loertscher. *Microcomputer: Educational Technology Application for School Library.* Chicago: ALA Publishing, 1984. unpaged. Price not given.

Computer Literacy

Ball, Marian J., and Sylvia Charp. *Be a Computer Literate.* Morristown, N.J.: Creative Computing, 1977. unpaged. $3.95.
Reviewed: *The Computing Teacher* 8 (December 1980): 51.

Barden, William, Jr. *What Do You Do After You Plug It In?* Indianapolis, Ind.: Howard W. Sams and Co., Inc., 1984. unpaged. $10.95.
"Covers practical computer problems with hardware, software, languages, operating systems, and data communications."

Berner, Jeff. *Overcoming Computer Fear—"Confronting Technophobia."* Berkeley, Calif.: Sybex, n.d. 92p. $3.95.
Reviewed: *Personal Computing* 8, no. 4 (April 1984): 196.

Billing, Karen, and David Moursund. *Are You Computer Literate?* Beaverton, Oreg.: Dilithium Press, 1979. unpaged. $9.95.
"Covers everyday use of computers, their parts, history and programming; self-quizzes in each chapter increase interest and allow reader to check his or her progress."
Reviewed: *Personal Computing* 6 (October 1980): 186.

Bitter, Gary G. *Exploring with Computers.* New York: Messner, 1981. unpaged. $7.95.
Reviewed: *Popular Computing* (March 1982): 127; *Educational Technology* (February 1982): 54; *Kilobaud Microcomputing* (December 1981): 232-33.

Covvey, H. Dominic, and Neil H. McAlister. *Computer Consciousness: Surveying the Automated 80's.* Reading, Mass.: Addison-Wesley, 1980. unpaged. $6.95.
"Pulls together a wide range of 'buzz words', describes them in context and explains much of the current technology. Excellent for one just starting to work in the

area"—from *Small Computers in Libraries* (October 1981): 7. Reviewed: *The Computing Teacher* 8 (January 1981): 36-37; *Desktop Computing* 2 (March 1982): 85; *Kilobaud Microcomputing* (April 1981): 224.

Danzer, Paul M. *A Young Person's Guide to Computers.* Milford, Conn.: Scelbi Publications, n.d. unpaged. $7.95.
"A computer primer that will hold even the most active child's rapt attention"—from *Popular Computing* (March 1982): 125-26. Reviewed: *Interface Age* (March 1982): 134.

Ericson, Robert. *Appleworks: Tips and Techniques.* Berkeley, Calif.: Sybex, 1985. 373p. Price not given.
An expanded version of Robert Ericson's "Notes for Appleworks." Contains useful information for the intermediate or advanced AppleWorks user.

Evans, Christopher. *The Micro Millenium.* New York: Viking Press, 1980. unpaged. $10.95.
Reviewed: *The Computing Teacher* (September 1981): 36; *Creative Computing* (July 1981): 219; *Interface Age* (August 1981): 142; *Popular Computing* (February 1982): 103-4; *Kilobaud Microcomputing* (June 1981): 235-37.

Freedman, Alan. *Computer Glossary: It's Not Just a Glossary.* Englewood Cliffs, N.J.: Prentice-Hall, 1983. 298p. $14.95.
Reviewed: *The Computing Teacher* (February 1984): 57-58.

Heller, Rachelle S., and C. Dianne Martin. *Bits 'N Bytes about Computing: A Computer Literacy Primer.* Rockville, Md.: Computer Science Press, n.d. 174p. $17.95 (Computer Science Press, 11 Taft Court, Rockville, MD 20850).
Reviewed: *The Computing Teacher* (May 1983): 69-70.

Luehrmann, Arthur, and Herbert Peckham. *Computer Literacy: A Hands-On Approach.* New York: McGraw-Hill, 1983. 370p. Price not given.
Includes teacher's guide and diskette. Pupil edition and workbook available.
Reviewed: *The Computing Teacher* (November 1983): 51-52; *Electronic Learning* (September 1983): 144-45; *Classroom Computer News* (May/June 1983): 79; *Popular Computing* (January 1984): 227-30.

MacBook: The Indispensable Guide to MacIntosh Hardware and Software. Hasbrouck Heights, N.J.: Hayden, 1985. unpaged. $14.95.
Reviewed: *Wired Librarian's* (November 1985): 3. "Has more neat stuff on the Mac than even I can deal with. A must for Mac attacks."

Rice, Jean, and Marien Haley. *My Computer Picture Dictionary.* Minneapolis, Minn.: T. S. Denison and Co., 1981. unpaged. $3.00. (T. S. Denison and Co., Inc., 9601 Newton Avenue South, Suite 8223, Minneapolis, MN 55431).
Reviewed: *The Computing Teacher* (March 1982): 37-38.

Roth, Judith Paris. *Essential Guide to CD-ROM.* Westport, Conn.: Meckler
    Publishing, 1985. unpaged. $49.95.
    "An overview of CD-ROM technology as it relates to information storage and
retrieval [and a] survey of CD-ROM organizations."

Spencer, Donald D. *Introduction to Computers: Developing Computer Literacy.*
    Columbus, Ohio: Charles E. Merrill, 1983. 655p. $18.95 (Charles E. Merrill,
    1300 Alum Creek Dr., Columbus, OH 43216).
    Reviewed *The Computing Teacher* (November 1983): 50.

Vies, Joseph M. *Computer Fundamentals for Nonspecialists.* New York: AMACOM,
    1981. unpaged. $14.95.
    Reviewed: *Popular Computing* (May 1982): 110.

Wall, Elizabeth S. *Computer Alphabet Book.* Nokomis, Fla.: Bayshore Books, 1979.
    unpaged. $9.95. (Avon paperback $2.25). (Bayshore Books, P.O. Box 848,
    Nokomis, FL 33555).
    Provides simple definitions of computer parts and terms, useful at the beginning of
any computer literacy program. Good for all ages.

Wolverton, Van. *Running MS DOS.* Bellevue, Wash.: Microsoft Press,1985. 408p.
    $21.95. (Microsoft Corp., 10700 Northrup Way, Box 97200, Bellevue, WA 98009).
    This is the second edition of this popular book, updated and expanded to include
all MS-DOS versions through 3.1.

Worth, Don, and Peter Lechner. *Beneath Apple DOS/Apple ProDOS.* Chatsworth,
    Calif.: Quality Software, n.d. unpaged. Price not given.

Information Retrieval, Online Searching, Networking, Communications

Boss, Richard W. *Telecommunications for Library Management.* White Plains, N.Y.:
    Knowledge Industry Publications, 1985. 180p. $36.50.
    Reviewed: *Wilson Library Bulletin* (November 1985): 55; *Library Journal* (1
February 1986): 64.

Bowen, Charles, and David Peyton. *How to Get the Most Out of CompuServe.* New
    York: Bantam Books, 1985. unpaged. Price not given.
    Reviewed: *Booklist* (1 January 1985): 615-16.

_____. *How to Get the Most Out of The Source.* New York: Bantam Books, 1985.
    unpaged. Price not given.

Electronic Bulletin Boards. New York: Franklin Watts, 1985. unpaged. $9.40.
    This is part of the Computer Awareness series, for junior high and up. Reviewed:
School Library Journal (August 1985): 27.

Gengle, Dean. *Netweaver's Sourcebook, A Guide to Micro-Networking and Communications.* Reading, Mass.: Addison-Wesley, 1984. 326p. $14.95.
Reviewed: *Popular Computing* (August 1985): 116.

Glossbrenner, Alfred. *Complete Handbook of Personal Computer Communications.* New York: St. Martin's Press, 1983. 325p. $14.95.
Reviewed: *The Computing Teacher* (November 1984): 45-46; *Wilson Library Bulletin* (March 1985): 477; *Booklist* (1 June 1983): 125. "Cutting On-Line Costs" by Steven Levy in *Popular Computing* (December 1983): 71-79, includes a reaction to Glossbrenner's book.

Hansen, Carol. *Microcomputer Users' Guide to Information Online.* Hasbrouck Heights, N.J.: Hayden, 1984. unpaged. $14.95.
Reviewed: *Wilson Library Bulletin* (March 1985): 477.

Kenney, Brigette L., ed. *Cable for Information Delivery.* White Plains, N.Y.: Knowledge Industry Publications, 1984. 172p. $27.50.
Reviewed: *Information Technology and Libraries* (March 1985): 77; *Journal of ASIS* (March 1985). No pages available. *Special Libraries* (October 1985). No pages available.

Lee, Joann H., ed. *Online Searching: The Basics, Settings, and Management.* Littleton, Colo.: Libraries Unlimited, 1984. 174p. $23.50.
Reviewed: *Special Libraries* (Fall 1985): 302-3: "Introductory reading [concerning] problems involved in incorporating online sources in . . . collections."

Software Sources and Evaluation Aids

Chartrand, Marilyn, and Constance D. Williams, comps., for Corporate Monitor, Inc. *Educational Software Directory: A Subject Guide to Microcomputer Software.* Littleton, Colo.: Libraries Unlimited, 1982. 292p. $27.50.

Glossbrenner, Alfred. *How to Get Free Software: The Master Guide for Every Brand.* New York: St. Martin's Press, 1984. 436p. $14.95.
Reviewed: *The Computing Teacher* (April 1985): 46-47; *Popular Computing* (December 1984): 204.

Guide to Free Computer Materials. Randolph, Wis.: Educators Progress Service, annual. Price not given. (EPS Guides, Dept. CT, 214 Center St., Randolph, WI 53956).
Described in *The Computing Teacher* (April 1985): 46.

Lathrop, Ann, and Bobby Goodson. *Courseware in the Classroom: Selecting, Organizing, and Using Educational Software.* Menlo Park, Calif.: Addison-Wesley, 1983. 187p. $9.95.
Reviewed: *The Computing Teacher* (May 1983): 68; *Electronic Learning* (January 1984): 98-99; *Electronic Education* (January 1985): 44; *Teaching, Learning, Computing* (January 1984): 92-93.

Mason, Robert M., ed. *Micro Consumer: Library Software (A Guide to Selection)*. Atlanta, Ga.: Metrics Research Corporation, n.d. 127p. Price not given. (Metrics Research Corporation, 130 West Wieuca Road, Suite 200, Atlanta, GA 30342 (404) 255-1976).

Edited by the author of *Library Journal* column "Mason On Micros," this work includes a brief introduction to library software, scope of reviews, and how to compare programs. Also has appendices with guidelines for locating and purchasing the appropriate software. Reviews include editorial descriptions and excerpts from published reviews. Other selection guides and library publications available from MRC. Reviewed: *Library Journal* (August 1985): 71.

Selecting . . . for the IBM PC. Berkeley, Calif.: Sybex, n.d. unpaged. $6.95/vol.

This series of books aims to help with software purchasing: "the right data base," "right spreadsheet," "word processing."

Truett, Carol, and Lori Gillespie. *Choosing Educational Software: A Buyer's Guide*. Littleton, Colo.: Libraries Unlimited, 1984. 216p. $18.50.

Reviewed: *School Library Media Quarterly* (Spring 1985): 152; *Electronic Education* (January 1985): 44.

SELECTED JOURNAL ARTICLES
Selecting Computer Books

Albertson, Chris. "Building Your Apple Bookshelf." *A+ Magazine* 3, no. 2 (February 1985): 43ff.

Describes a core collection of Apple books for your library.

Bracey, Gerald W. "My Favorite Computer Books." *Electronic Learning* 4, no. 3 (November/December 1985): 64-65.

Discusses the following: *Discovering Computers* (Gledhill); *My Students Use Computers* (Hunter); *Microcomputer Applications in the Classroom* (Hofmesiter); *Elements of Computer Education* (MT); *Mindstorms* (Papert); *Electronic Cottage* (Deken); *Little Book of Basic Style* (Nevison); *Micro Millenium* (Evans); *Communications Revolution* (Williams); *Evaluation of Microcomputer Courseware,* 2d ed. (Ragsdale).

Herb, Betty. "Books about Computer Technology." *School Library Journal* 31, no. 3 (November 1984): 38-48.

This is an annotated bibliography in "Computer Technology and Libraries" supplement.

Kesselman, Martin. "Online Update Column." *Wilson Library Bulletin* 59, no. 7 (March 1985): 477-78.

Reviews several books "aimed directly at the home end-user market (although librarians will find them useful too)."

Novy, Sister Helen Jean, H.M. "Marooned on a Desert Island with a Micro—Ten Books to Take Along." *The Computing Teacher* 11, no. 4 (November 1983): 54-55.

Price, Robert. "On the Order of FREE." *The Computing Teacher* 12, no. 9 (June 1985): 7.
Provides brief reviews of "guide books which provide information on free and inexpensive software."

Roberts, Justine. "An Elite Microdozen." *Library Journal/School Library Journal* 110, no. 8, pp. 99-100; 31, no. 9 (May 1985): 129-30.
"Everything you wanted to know about personal computers in 12 books or less."

Troutner, Joanne. "How to Develop a Computer Book Collection." *School Library Journal* 31, no. 3 (November 1984): 31-32.

PERIODICALS

Use library stationery (with letterhead) to write publishers for current subscription prices and to request sample issues.

A + Magazine, the Independent Guide for Apple Computing. New York: Ziff-Davis Publishing Co. Monthly.

American Libraries. Chicago: American Library Association. Monthly.
Columns such as "The Source," "Action Exchange," and "Software Showcase" contain product news and helpful suggestions.

Bar Code News. Peterborough, N.H.: North American Technology. Bimonthly. (North American Technology, 174 Concord St., Peterborough, NH 03458).
"Distributed free to qualified U.S. subscribers who request a subscription in writing and fill out the *Bar Code News* reader qualification form." Applications can be requested from North American by calling (603) 924-7136. Some back issues are available. Recommend ordering copy of January/February 1986 issue which contains complete index for 1981-1985.

BOOKLIST. Chicago: American Library Association. Semimonthly.
This is a review publication.

Bulletin Board Systems. Westport, Conn.: Meckler Publishing. 8/yr.
Covers electronic bulletin boards and computer telecommunications.

Business Software. San Diego, Calif.: Business Software. Monthly. (Business Software, P.O. Box 27975, San Diego, CA 92128).
Includes articles and reviews of interest to business which are also applicable to any management use of microcomputers. Indexed in *Microcomputer Index.*

BYTE. The Small Systems Journal. Martinsville, N.J.: McGraw-Hill. Monthly.
Includes a catalog of ads, serves as a source for information concerning new products. The articles are generally aimed at those with some technical background, not the novice. Indexed in *Microcomputer Index.*

Call—A.P.P.L.E. Renton, Wash.: Apple Puget Sound Program Library Exchange. Monthly. (Apple Puget Sound Program Library Exchange, 290 S.W. 43rd St., Renton, WA 98055).

Membership in A.P.P.L.E. Co-op, plus one-time application fee, includes magazine subscription. Popular magazine with Apple owners; contains a great deal of programming information for all levels of programmers. A special section of The SOURCE is open only to members who may download. Indexed in *Microcomputer Index*.

Classroom Computer Learning. Dayton, Ohio: Peter Li, Inc. Monthly except June, July, August, December. (Peter Li, Inc., 2451 E. River Rd., Dayton, OH 45439).

Departments include software reviews, classroom activities, Q & A, "Technology Update," "Administrator's Eye," "Newsline," "Product News," "Dates & Events."

Commodore Microcomputers. West Chester, Pa.: Contemporary Marketing, Inc. Bimonthly. (Contemporary Marketing, Inc., 1200 Wilson Drive, West Chester, PA 19380).

Computer Software/Hardware Index. Haledon, N.J.: Computer Software/Hardware Index. (Computer Software/Hardware Index, P.O. Box 7991, Haledon, NJ 07538).

This looseleaf service is cumulated annually; includes short descriptive and evaluative reviews. Reviewed: *Library Journal* (1 February 1986): 66.

Computers in the Schools. New York: Haworth Press.

For free sample copy request on library letterhead.

The Computing Teacher. Eugene, Oreg.: The International Council for Computers in Education (ICCE). 9/yr. (ICCE, University of Oregon, 1787 Agate St., Eugene, OR 97403 (503) 686-4414).

This is one of the oldest educational computer magazines. Information for teachers using computers and/or teaching about computers; articles addressing educational issues related to computers; book reviews, software reviews, film reviews, and articles concerning applications for computers in a wide range of curriculum areas. Includes regular column "The Computing Librarian," edited by Carol Truett. Indexed in *Microcomputer Index*. ICCE also publishes a number of booklets, etc. Write for information.

Database. Weston, Conn.: Online, Inc. 6/yr. (Online, Inc., Dept. B385, 11 Tannery La., Weston, CT 06883).

"Covers ONLY databases, with lengthy in-depth articles on database usages, and comparisons and evaluations."

Database End-User. Westport, Conn.: Meckler Publishing. Monthly.

"For the profesional online searcher, the searching professional, or any librarian desiring to keep current with online/database news . . . articles, tips and techniques, and reviews."

Digest of Software Reviews: Education. Fresno, Calif.: Digest of Software Reviews: Education. Monthly. (Digest of Software Reviews: Education, 301 West Mesa, Fresno, CA 93704).

Includes cumulative indexes by title, subject, publisher, and computer. "1000 + review extracts from 150 education and educational computing journals."

Drexel Library Quarterly. Philadelphia: College of Information Studies, Drexel University. (College of Information Studies, Drexel University, Philadelphia, PA 19104 (215) 895-2483).

Has several issues which address microcomputers in libraries. Write for list of available back issues and ordering information.

Educational Technology. Englewood Cliffs, N.J.: Educational Technology. Monthly.

Covers more than computers—all media, plus instructional design and development, systems, etc. Back issues are available. Indexed in *Microcomputer Index.*

80 Microcomputing. Peterborough, N.H.: 80 Microcomputing. Monthly (80 Microcomputing, 80 Pine St., Peterborough, NH 03458).

Specializes in covering the TRS-80 microcomputers. Good source for BASIC program listings, ads for TRS-80 products, reviews. Indexed in *Microcomputer Index.*

Electronic Education. Tallahassee, Fla.: Electronic Communications, Inc. 9/yr. (Electronic Communications, Inc., Attn: Electronic Education, P.O. Box 20221, Tallahassee, FL 32316).

Free to qualified educators. Articles address issues in the educational use of computers; departments include "Almost-on-Line," "A Question of Copyright," "Up-to-Data," "New Software," "New Products," "Book Reviews," "Around the Circuit," etc. First issue was September 1981.

Family Computing. New York: Scholastic, Inc. Monthly.

This is a good general interest magazine.

InfoWorld, The Newspaper for the Microcomputing Community. Southeastern, Pa.: InfoWorld. Weekly. (InfoWorld, P.O. Box 1018, Southeastern, PA 19398 (800) 544-3712).

Gives news of what's happening in the industry. Departments cover news, trends, reviews, products, resources (events, user groups), and regular columns such as "Tech Street," "A User's View," "First Look," and "Inside Track." As with all publications you will also want to read "Letters."

Library HiTech. Ann Arbor, Mich.: Pierian Press. Quarterly.

"Provides in-depth coverage of the new technologies having applications within libraries and information centers." Also publishes the monthly *Library HiTech News,* with "timely and late-breaking news about all aspects of technology related to library operations."

Library Journal/School Library Journal. Riverton, N.J.: R. R. Bowker/Reed Publishing. 20/yr.; 10/yr.

Includes regular articles and reviews. *Library Journal* columns, including "Public Libraries Online," "Computers for the Public," "Online Databases," and "Mason on Micros," provide excellent source of up-to-date information. Read the letters, question/answer, and idea exchange columns regularly for current happenings and helpful suggestions.

Library Software Review. Westport, Conn.: Meckler Publishing. Bimonthly.
    Contains articles and reviews on library related software. Indexed in *Microcomputer Index.*

M300 and PC Report. Westport, Conn.: Meckler Publishing. Monthly.
    This is an independent guide to uses of OCLC's M300 Workstations and IBM personal computers in libraries. Indexed in *Microcomputer Index.*

Media & Methods. Philadelphia: Media & Methods. 10/yr. (Media & Methods, 1511 Walnut St., Philadelphia, PA 19102).

Microcomputers for Information Management. Norwood, N.J.: Ablex Publishing Corp. Quarterly.
    "Devoted exclusively to the innovative application of microcomputers for information management and processing in all types of libraries and information centers." Editor-in-chief, Ching-Chih Chen.

OCLC Micro. Dublin, Ohio: Online Computer Library Center, Inc. (OCLC). Semimonthly. (OCLC, 6565 Frantz Road, Dublin, OH 43017).
    Published by OCLC for users of its M300 Workstation and the IBM PC, but helpful to other library microcomputer users as well. Features articles on how to use microcomputers more effectively with the OCLC system, plus user comments, hardware and software reviews, article abstracts, and articles on other popular micros. Regular columns include "DOS-tips," "Eric (not ERIC)," "Re: Views." Some issues are accompanied by diskettes. First issue reviewed in *Library HiTech News* (August 1985).

ONLINE. Weston, Conn.: Online, Inc. Semimonthly. (Online, Inc., Dept. B385, 11 Tannery La., Weston, CT 06883).
    "Coverage is general, ranging from information management to short descriptive articles on databases."

PC World. San Francisco, Calif.: PC World Communications. Monthly. (PC World Communications, 555 De Haro St., San Francisco, CA 94107).

Personal Computing. Hasbrouck Heights, N.J.: Hayden Publishing. Monthly.
    This is one of the remaining general interest multilevel magazines. Topics include: productivity, performance, corporate/business, leisure, buyers guides, product reviews and listings, and the always helpful letters and answers columns.

School Library Media Quarterly. Chicago: AASL/ALA. Quarterly.
    Includes regular "Software Review" column by Joanne Troutner. In the fall 1985 issue Carolyn Markuson ("Readers' Queries") discusses the selection of library management software.

Small Computers in Libraries. Westport, Conn.: Meckler Publishing. 11/yr.

Founding editor, Allan D. Pratt (1981). This is an excellent source of information about microcomputer products, user groups, and articles of interest to libraries. Indexed in *Microcomputer Index.*

Software Reviews on File. New York: Facts on File Publications. Monthly.

"Publisher promises a type of *Book Review Digest* for about 500 new programs a year." Reviewed: *Library Journal* (1 February 1986): 66.

Special Libraries. Washington, D.C.: Special Libraries Association. Quarterly. (Special Libraries Association, 1700 18th St., NW, Washington, DC 20009 (203) 234-4700). Annual index in fall issue.

Tech Trends. Washington, D.C.: Association for Educational Communications Technology. Monthly. (AECT, 1126 Sixteenth St., N.W., Washington, DC 20036).

This is the AECT official publication (replaces *Instructional Innovator).* Monthly or with AECT membership. Selected back issues available. Indexed in *Microcomputer Index.* "Instructional Resources" dept. includes information about ERIC documents/bibliographies, etc.

T.H.E. Journal (Technological Horizons in Education). Santa Ana, Calif.: Information Synergy, Inc. 8/yr. (Information Synergy, Inc., 2922 S. Daimler St., Santa Ana, CA 92705).

Free to qualified educators.

Videodisc and Optical Disk. Westport, Conn.: Meckler Publishing. Bimonthly.

Includes articles on developments and uses of interactive videodisc, digital optical disk, and CD ROM.

Wilson Library Bulletin. Bronx, N.Y.: H.W. Wilson. 10/yr.

Includes regular columns related to library use of microcomputers, such as "School Library Technology" (Patricia Berglund); "Microcomputing" (Karl Beiser); "Software for Libraries" (Patrick Dewey); and "Online Update" (Martin Kesselman).

NEWSLETTERS

Apple Education News—An Information Service for Educators and Trainers. Cupertino, Calif.: Apple Education News. Quarterly. Free. (Apple Education News, Mail Stop 18-C, Apple Computer, Inc., 20525 Mariani Ave., Cupertino, CA 95014).

Features new software and hardware announcements, plus in-depth stories about training, funding, and schools that are creating exciting computer literacy programs. Write to be added to mailing list.

Apple Library Users Group Newsletter (ALUG). Cupertino, Calif.: Library and Information Services. Quarterly. Free. (Monica Ertel, Apple Computer Library and Information Services, 32AJ, 20740 Valley Green Drive, Cupertino, CA 95014).

Designed for people interested in using Apple computers in libraries or information centers. Written contributions are encouraged and welcomed. Address correspondence to Monica Ertel or via DIALMAIL.

Closing the Gap. Henderson, Minn.: Closing the Gap. 6/yr. (Closing the Gap, P.O. Box 68, Henderson, MN 56044 (612) 248-3294).

Newspaper includes news, reviews, and updates on the use of microcomputers for the handicapped. Hands-on training and consultation are provided at CTG's Training and Resource Center, and national conferences on computer technology for the handicapped are held annually. Proceedings from these conferences are available.

CMC NEWS (Computers and the Media Center). Cannon Falls, Minn.: CMC News. 4/yr. (CMC News, 515 Oak Street North, Cannon Falls, MN 55009 (507) 263-3711).

Edited by Jim Deacon. "Providing a forum for information on microcomputers and library programs since 1979." *CMC News* features articles on microcomputer applications in libraries, listings of available commercial library software, and listings of libraries across the United States and Canada and how they are using microcomputers. Back issues available. Every school library should subscribe.

Computer Data Report. Potomac, Md.: U.S.A. Computer Data Services. Monthly. (U.S.A. Computer Data Services, 12400 Beall Mt. Rd., Potomac, MD 20854 (301) 983-8220).

Reviewed: "Finding Database Bargains," *Popular Computing* (May 1984): 30, 32. The review describes the newsletter as identifying free and low-cost data sources for business, research, or personal information needs. Write for more information and a sample copy of "The Data Informer."

C.U.E. Newsletter. San Jose, Calif.: Computer-Using Educators, Inc. 6/yr. (Computer-Using Educators, Inc., P.O. Box 18547, San Jose, CA 95158 (408) 244-2559).

This newsletter is a benefit of membership in Computer-Using Educators, Inc., and a good source of information. As the group's name implies, the newsletter concerns educational happenings with computers: reviews of products, software, hardware, and books; reports about and from educational conferences; and update information about SOFTSWAP, a public domain software project. It also serves as a vehicle for the exchange of ideas related to computer issues in education. Columns include "Computer Labs," "Electric Librarian," "Logo Corner," "Networking," "Special Deliveries," and "Telecommunications."

DLA Bulletin. Berkeley, Calif.: University of California, Division of Automation. Irregular. Free. (University of California, Division of Automation, 186 University Hall, Berkeley, CA 94720 (415) 642-9485).

Provides a variety of information about library automation, particularly at the University of California. Includes a glossary for each issue. Write to be added to mailing list.

DragonSmoke. Menlo Park, Calif.: DragonQuest. Bimonthly. Free. (DragonQuest, P.O. Box 7627, Menlo Park, CA 94026 (415) 854-1548. Include SASE).

Edited by Bob Albrecht and George Firedrake, "for families who want to "Play Together, Learn Together" using computers. [Includes] news about our projects, books, articles, computer software . . . mainly explore[s] the use of three home computers . . . Radio Shack Color Computer, IBM PC Jr., Apple MacIntosh." Published by Bob Albrecht, founder/president of DragonQuest, a California communications corporation that develops written materials, software, and video programs relating to computers for home use. Albrecht writes regularly for several computer publications and has co-authored several books. He was a co-founder (with Ramon Zamora) of ComputerTown, USA! a community computer literacy project. Write for more information.

Follett's Library Automation News (formerly *Book Trak News*). Crystal Lake, Ill.: Follett Software Company. Irregular. (Follett Software Company, 4506 Northwest Highway, Crystal Lake, IL 60014 (800) 435-6170).
Write to have your name added to mailing list for this well-done, informative newsletter edited by Betty Furrie. Also write to receive your complimentary copy of *The Primer of Library Microcomputing* by Eric S. Anderson — product #JY69611. Everyone should read this! Additional copies are available (10/package) #JY69611P — $10.00.

Hot Off the Computer: Microcomputer Newsletter. Elmsford, N.Y.: Westchester Library System. 10/yr. (Westchester Library System, 8 Westchester Plaza, Cross Westchester Executive PkC, Elmsford, NY 10523).
Provides practical information on uses of microcomputers in libraries around the country. Included are software reviews and new releases.

Information Today: The Newspaper for Users and Producers of Electronic Information Services. Medford, N.J.: Learned Information Inc. 11/yr. (Learned Information Inc., 143 Old Marlton Pike, Medford, NJ 08055).
Includes articles and reviews about the latest developments in hardware and software for the "information industry."

Library Currents. Grass Valley, Calif.: Practical Perspectives, Inc. (Practical Perspectives, Inc., P.O. Box 1796, 256 Buena Vista St., Suite 100, Grass Valley, CA 95945).
"We review and summarize library and management literature on a regular basis, to provide library managers with useful and timely information." Issue topics may include: automation, cataloging, micros, online catalog, online searching, technology, etc.

Library Systems Newsletter. Chicago: American Library Association. (Library Technology Reports, ALA, 50 E. Huron St., Chicago, IL 60611).

The LITA Newsletter. Chicago: Library and Information Technology Association/ American Library Association. Quarterly. (LITA/ALA, 50 E. Huron St., Chicago, IL 60611).
Only available with membership in LITA. For more information contact Donald P. Hammer, executive director.

MECC NETWORK. St. Paul, Minn.: Minnesota Educational Computing Corp. (MECC). Quarterly. Free. (MECC, 3490 Lexington Avenue No., St. Paul, MN 55126 (612) 481-3606).
Write to be added to mailing list.

National LOGO Exchange/The International LOGO Exchange. Charlottesville, Va.:
  National LOGO Exchange/The International LOGO Exchange. (National LOGO
  Exchange/The International LOGO Exchange, P.O. Box 5341, Charlottesville,
  VA 22905).
  Contains practical suggestions for implementing LOGO in the classroom. National
exchange (monthly, September through May) is now in its fourth year of publication.
The international newsletter (bimonthly) features reports by LOGO field editors
representing each continent, to give the reader a global LOGO perspective. Write for
more information.

ONLINE Libraries and Microcomputers. Phoenix, Ariz.: Information Intelligence
  Inc. Monthly. (Information Intelligence Inc., P.O. Box 31098, Phoenix, AZ 85046
  (602) 996-2283).
  This is a monthly edition of the database available on the ONLINE HOTLINE
news service.

Print Shop User's Newsletter—The Showcase for Print Shop Ideas and Tips. Rich-
  mond, Calif.: Pixellite Computer Products, Inc. (Pixellite Computer Products,
  Inc., 5221 Central Avenue, Suite 205, Richmond, CA 94804).
  This is a free newsletter for owners of The Print Shop.

Research in Word Processing Newsletter. Rapid City, S.D.: South Dakota School
  of Mines and Technology. (South Dakota School of Mines and Technology, Rapid
  City, SD 57701).
  This is an 11-page newsletter. Limited back issues available. Described in *The
Computing Teacher* (December/January 1984-85): 7.

Technicalities. Phoenix, Ariz.: Oryx Press. Monthly.
  Newsletter concerned with "exploring the technical side of library and information
systems and management. . . . *Technicalities* offers a spirit of dialog, a discussion of
alternatives ranging from philosophical concerns to pragmatic how-to-do-it
articles"—from first issue, December 1980.

The Wired Librarian's Newsletter. Sioux City, Iowa: Micro Libraries. Monthly. (Micro
  Libraries, 20 Congress Ave., Sioux City, IA 51104).
  Described in *Library Automation News:* "There is none other like it for 'Library
Micro News and Views': the real inside scoop," and by John C. Dvorak of *InfoWorld*:
"The infamous 'Wired Librarian's Newsletter' rates an honorable mention: it really raps
bad products." While readers may not agree with the viewpoints expressed by the
"Wired Librarian," Eric S. Anderson, he does keep up with library micro "happenings"
and brings up points others may not have considered. Eric Anderson writes articles and
reviews for a variety of publications including *Booklist, The Book Report,* and *OCLC
Micro,* and has written a booklet, *The Primer of Library Microcomputing,* available
free from Follett.

WUG Newsletter. Caledonia, Minn.: Winnebago Software Co. Irregular. (Winnebago
  Software Co., WUG Newsletter, 121 S. Marshall, P.O. Box 430, Caledonia, MN
  55921).

This is a newsletter for Winnebago products (which include LCS I, II, and III, Catalog Card Maker, and Computer Cat) users. Several local users' groups have been organized and meet at state conferences. Write for more information.

BOOKLETS, REPRINTS, AND REPORTS OF STUDIES AND SURVEYS

Bausser, Jaye. *Online Catalogs: Issues and Concerns.* Syracuse, N.Y.: ERIC, 1984. 40p. Price not given. (ERIC Clearinghouse on Information Resources, Syracuse University, School of Education, Syracuse, NY 13210)
This is an information analysis product.

Carter, Yvonne. *Role of Libraries in Creating and Providing Viewtext Information Service.* Washington, D.C.: U.S. Department of Education, n.d. unpaged. Price not given. (Yvonne Carter, Project Officer, U.S. Dept. of Education, Library, Education, Research and Resources Branch, Division of Library Programs, 400 Maryland Ave., S.W., Washington, DC 20202).
This report contains information on the use of videotext, teletext, online retrieval of bibliographic information, videodisc, and cable and satellite television.

Comparative Profile of Integrated Online Library Systems. Pascagoula, Miss.: Jackson-George Regional Library, n.d. unpaged. $4.00. (Jackson-George Regional Library, 3214 Pascagoula Street, Pascagoula, MS 39567 (601) 769-3059).
Data for this publication were collected over a nine-month period beginning September 1984. Although the systems surveyed are for large installations, the comparison formats and planning timelines would be helpful for any library planning automation. Systems included in the survey are: CLASSIC, CLSI, DATAPHASE, DATA RESEARCH, DYNIX, GEAC, OCLC, SIRSI, and VTLS.

The DPMA Secondary Curriculum on Information Technology and Computer Information Systems. Park Ridge, Ill.: The Data Processing Management Association, n.d. unpaged. Free. (DPMA, 505 Bussee Highway, Park Ridge, IL 60068).
Booklet briefly describes four courses: computer literacy for grades 7-8; a "career-related indoctrination to computers and their applications" for grades 8-9; an honors-type course for grades 11-12; and practical training for grades 11-12.

Hutchinson, R. Anthony. *Computer Eye-Strain; How to Avoid It, How to Alleviate It.* New York: M. Evans and Co., n.d. 85p. Price not given. (M. Evans and Co., 216 E. 49th St., New York, NY 10017).
Written by an optometrist, this booklet "describes ways to improve the work station and lighting conditions." Includes information on children and VDT viewing.

1984 Educational Software Preview Guide. Eugene, Oreg.: Educational Software Evaluation Consortium, n.d. unpaged. $5.00 (ICCE, Preview Guide, University of Oregon, 1787 Agate St., Eugene, OR 97403).
Based on critical evaluations at the 1984 California Software Evaluation Forum.

Reed-Scott, Jutta. *Issues in Retrospective Conversion.* Washington, D.C.: Council on Library Resources, 1984. 57p. $3.00 (prepaid). (Council on Library Resources, 1785 Masachusetts Ave., NW, Washington, DC 20036).

Reviewed in *Information Technology and Libraries* (March 1985); recommended for purchase with companion report edited by Dorothy Gregor for $6.00 (prepaid).

Remmes, Harold. *Computers: New Opportunities for the Disabled.* Babylon, N.Y.: Pilot Books, n.d. 32p. $3.50.

Includes advice on purchasing, basic glossary, and supplemental reading list.

Role of Fees in Supporting Library and Information Services. Washington, D.C.: National Committee on Libraries/Information Sciences, n.d. unpaged. Price not given. (NCLIS, GSA Bldg., Suite 3122, 7th and D Streets, S.W., Washington, DC 20024).

Contact for more information about obtaining copy of this study.

Selection of Microcomputer Systems (S/N 003-003-02553-4). Washington, D.C.: National Bureau of Standards. n.d. unpaged. $1.50. (Superintendent of Documents, Dept. 36-FZ, Washington, DC 20402).

This useful publication was described in *School Library Media Quarterly* (Fall 1984): 367, along with *Microcomputers: Introduction to Features and Uses* (S/N 003-003-02560-7), $4.25).

Software Reviews. Redwood City, Calif.: SMERC Library Microcomputer Center, n.d. unpaged. $10.00 (SMERC Library Microcomputer Center, San Mateo County Office of Education, 333 Main Street, Redwood City, CA 94063).

Described in *The Computing Teacher* (March 1984): 9. Contains 50 reviews by the California Library Media Consortium for classroom evaluation of microcomputer courseware. Send orders (prepaid only) to SMERC. Some copies of earlier editions may also be available at $10.00 each.

Publishers of Multiple Reports

American Association of School Librarians (AASL). (AASL/ALA, 50 E. Huron St., Chicago, IL 60611).

Publications include *Microcomputer Software and Hardware—An Annotated Source List* and *Guidelines for Processing and Cataloging Computer Software for Schools and Area Educational Agencies.* Write for catalog of latest offerings.

The Center for Social Organization of Schools. (Johns Hopkins University, 3503 N. Charles St., Baltimore, MD 21218).

The center has published many reports on studies in education, including a six-part series called "School Uses of Microcomputers." This report is based on a national survey and more are in progress. Write for more information.

ERIC—Information Analysis. (ERIC Clearinghouse on Information Resources, Syracuse University, School of Education, Syracuse, NY 13210).

Booklets include *Direct Use of Online Bibliographic Information Systems by*

Untrained End Users: A Review of Research, by Michael Eisenberg and *How to Prepare for a Computer Search of ERIC: A Non-Technical Approach,* by Marilyn R. Laubacher. Write for information about current offerings and ask to be added to newsletter mailing list.

ICCE Publications. International Council for Computers in Education. (ICCE, University of Oregon, 1787 Agate St., Eugene, OR 97403).

ICCE publishes a variety of booklets, monographs, and class/workshop packets. Titles include *The Computer Coordinator, Evaluator's Guide for Microcomputer-Based Instructional Packages, LOGO in the Classroom,* parents' guide and teachers' guides (for various levels), *Ethical Issues,* etc. Write for latest catalog.

Top of the News Reprints. ALSC/YASD. (Top of the News, 50 E. Huron St., Chicago, IL 60611).

Reprints available include "Microcomputers and Library Services to Children and Young Adults." Write for list.

⚔ SOURCES FOR LIBRARY APPLICATIONS SOFTWARE

We strongly recommend that, when considering any software, you contact one or more users if at all possible. Often you may do this through the many computer user groups and/or organizations, if not through the original distributor.

Addison Public Library. 235 North Kennedy Drive, Addison, IL 60101. (312) 543-3617

Source of *CARDS.* For Apple, Alpha Micro, IBM. Reviewed: *Book Report* (January/February 1985): 64; *Wired Librarian's Newsletter* (January 1985): 1.

Alpine Data Services. 695 E. Main, Montrose, CO 81401

Source of *BOOKPATH,* an interlibrary loan being used in several library systems in Colorado; runs under MS-DOS.

Andent, Inc. 1000 North Avenue, Waukegan, IL 60085

Variety of database programs for Apple.

Apple Computer, Inc. 20525 Mariana Ave., Cupertino, CA 95014. (408) 996-1010

Automated Micro Solutions. 6943 Haskell Ave., Van Nuys, CA 91406. (808) 780-8884

Source of *Library Master* (formerly *MicroPAC/CIRC*), a complete library management system for the IBM PC/XT/AT and compatibles; multi-user and networking capabilities for larger schools. Implemented in several school districts. Contact for user names. May also contact Ron Evans, Automated Micro Solutions, 1534 Cherokee Trail, Plano, TX 75023, (214) 423-6001.

A.V. Systems, Inc. P.O. Box 49210, Los Angeles, CA 90049

Source of *Tapit: Apple Periodicals.*

Bits & Bytes. Rt. 1, Box 165, Newburg, MO 65550. (417) 458-4470
Source of *C.C. Writer* (card program) for Apple. Reviewed: *CMC News* (Spring 1985): 9.

Blackwell Library Systems. 202 East Main Street, Suite 105, Huntington, NY 11743. (800) 645-5395
Designer and marketer of the *PERLINE* and *BOOKLINE* serials and acquisitions software.

Tom Brinck. 3900 N.E. 59th Street, Gladstone, MO 64119. (816) 455-0205
Source of catalog card program for the Apple.

Brodart. P.O. Box 3037, 1609 Memorial Ave., Williamsport, PA 17705

Wm. L. Brown. 8781 Lee Rd., Brighton, MI 48116
Source of *Date Due Library Circulation Program* for the Commodore.

CALICO (Computer Assisted Library Instruction Co., Inc.). P.O. Box 15916, St. Louis, MO 63411
Source of series of self-instruction programs for the Apple, prepared as guides for using periodical indexes, almanacs, *Bartlett's Quotations, Current Biography,* and poetry indexes. Demo disk ("The Sampler") available. Other Apple programs include *Call Number Order, The Library Catalog,* and *Fiction Finder.* Reviewed: *Educational Computer* (January/February 1982); *Booklist* (1 November 1982); *Wilson Library Bulletin* (November 1984); *School Library Journal* (November 1984): 68-73; *Library Journal* (1 April 1985): 31-40. In 1985 CALICO announced a program for a public access catalog, the *LION* (Library Information ONline).

Capital Systems Group, Inc. 11301 Rockville Pike, Kensington, MD 20895. (301) 881-9400
Source of *Newsdex* and *Bookdex*—generate book and periodical indexes. Described in *American Libraries* (November 1984): 746.

Center for the Study of Rural Librarianship. College of Library Science, Clarion University of Pennsylvania, Clarion, PA 16214
Source of *OUTPUTM*—a statistical program for public libraries (IBM PC/XT). Described in *American Libraries* (December 1984): 830.

CLASS. 1415 Koll Circle, Suite 101, San Jose, CA 95112. (408) 289-1756
A membership-based public agency that provides cooperative services to libraries and technical information centers. Distributor of *CHECKMATE,* serials control software for the IBM PC/XT; a demo disk is available. *CHECKMATE* is also available from CSG (Capital Systems Group, Inc.), EBSCO Industries, Inc., F.W. Faxton Co., and Gaylord Bros., Inc.

Colorado Computer West. P.O. Box 206, Kremmling, CO 80459. (303) 724-9364
Source of *Library Monitor,* a library circulation program for small libraries. Also other management programs for small school districts.

Combase. Suite 890, 333 Sibley Street, St. Paul, MN 55101
Source of a variety of library skills/management programs designed by Ruth Sather, which include *Elementary Library Media Skills, Elementary Literacy,* and *Using the Index to Periodicals.*

D and H Software. 703 Country-Aire Ct., Waunakee, WI 53597
Source of a program to handle audiovisual inventory records on the Apple. Described in *Small Computers in Libraries* (March 1983): 3. For more information, call David Hineline after 6:00 p.m. CST at (608) 849-5507.

Dalton Computer Services, Inc. P.O. Box 2469, Dalton, GA 30720. (404) 259-3327
Source of *MediaTrak,* library circulation and catalog system for the IBM XT/AT, Texas Instruments Professional Computer, and TI Minicomputers.

Delmar Software. 107 N. 4th, RR2, Pierceton, IN 46562
Source of *Cataloging by Computer.* Reviewed: *Book Report* (January/February 1985): 63.

Christine M. Dowd. 14 Bright Oaks Drive, Rochester, NY 14546
Source of *Card Catalog I and II* (program written in Apple PILOT).

DTI Data Trek. 121 West E. Street, Encinitas, CA 92024. (619) 436-5055
Source of a variety of library management programs for CP/M and MS-DOS, including acquisitions, circulation, online catalog, serials control, av-handler.

Dynix, Inc. 1455 West 820 North, Provo, UT 84601. (801) 375-2770
Dynix has a number of minicomputer installations in academic and public libraries. They demonstrated a version for the IBM PC/XT/AT at ALA 1985, to be available when marketing plans are completed.

Educational Activities. P.O. Box 392, Freeport, NY 11520
Source for a variety of library programs including those developed and used by the Pinellas County schools.

Educational Associates. P.O. Box 35221, Phoenix, AZ 85069
Source of *Educational Sourcedisk,* plus a variety of other library and educational software.

Educational Courseware. 67 A Willard Street, Hartford, CT 06105
Source of *School Inventory Program.* Reviewed: *CMC News* (Fall 1984): 2.

EDUCOMP Library Processes System. 919 West Canadian St., Vinita, OK 74301
Source of a card printing program designed for TRS-80 two-disk systems, with a minimum of 48K, and a heavy duty tractor feed printer. Available for models I, II, and III. Write for descriptive flyer.

Embar Information Consultants. 1234 Folkstone Court, Wheaton, IL 60187
Source of *COMPULOG,* an online catalog by Indrani Embar. Described in *Small Computers in Libraries* (June 1984): 5-6. Runs under CP/M or MS-DOS.

ERIC Clearinghouse. 030 Huntington Hall, Syracuse University, Syracuse, NY 13210
Source for ERIC MICROsearch software.

E.T.S. Center. P.O. Box 651, 35026-A Turtle Trail, Willoughby, OH 44094
Source of *Lablmkr-2*.

ETT Library Automations Inc. 9201 Drake Avenue, Suite 103, Evanston, IL 60203.
(312) 677-7704
Source of acquisitions system for Apple. Reviewed: *Wired Librarian's Newsletter*
(January 1986): 2.

EXSYS. 2728 23rd St., Greeley, CO 80631. (303) 330-8021
Source of programs to teach/simulate telecommunications for grades 3-12 +, e.g.,
The Electronic Mailbag, The Electronic Village, Ethics Online.

Eyring Research Institute, Utah. Pikes Peak Library District, Box 1579, Colorado
Springs, CO 80901
Eyring Library System PAC, Circulation and Bibliographic Maintenance. Producer of the system used by CARL (Colorado Alliance of Research Libraries) and Maggie III, the new system at Pikes Peak Library, Colorado Springs, Colorado. Videotape
"The Resource Connection" focuses on the present and future capabilities of Maggie
and is available through interlibrary loan; catalog number is 021.28 R434.

Facts on File, Inc. 460 Park Ave. S., New York, NY 10016
Source of public domain software. Review: *Wilson Library Bulletin* (December
1985): 59.

Fayette County Junior High School. Martie Courington, Fayetteville, GA 30214
Source of *Video Tape Tracker*. Reviewed: *CMC News* (Winter 1986): 6.

Follett Software Company. 4506 Northwest Highway, Crystal Lake, IL 60014
(800) 435-6170
Distributes a large variety of library management software programs. Acquired all
the programs of The Library Software Company in 1985, including *Circulation Plus,
Overdue Writer, Bibliography Writer,* etc. Publishes an informative newsletter.

Gaylord Brothers, Inc. P.O. Box 4901, Syracuse, NY 13221. (800) 448-6160
Distributes a variety of library management and skills programs including the DTI
DataTrek programs, *Checkmate,* and *Telemarc III.* Order catalog for more
information.

Geoglobal Systems, Inc. Marketing Division, 5296 Butternut, Columbus, OH 43229.
(614) 431-0660
Source of *Library Mate* (formerly LIBRARIAN), a database management system
for libraries. Demo available.

J. L. Hammett Co. P.O. Box 545, Braintree, MA 02184. (800) 225-5467
Source of *BOOKWORM,* library overdue program. Reviewed: *Booklist*

(1 November 1983): 436; *School Library Journal* (March 1985): 128; *School Library Journal* (August 1982): 28; *Apple Library Users Group Newsletter* (July 1985): 22-23.

T.A. Highum. 561 Parkview Drive, New Richmond, WI 54017
Source of a library circulation record keeping system. Reviewed: *CMC News* (Winter 1984): 12.

John Horemans. 2588 Inlake Ct., Mississauga, Ontario, Canada L5N 2A7
Source of PET *Computer Library Card Maker.* Reviewed: *Small Computers in Libraries* (February 1983): 5.

Information Access Company. 11 Davis Drive, Belmont, CA 94002. (800) 227-8431
Source of *Search Helper.* Provides simpler access to bibliographic databases.

Information Management Consultants, Inc. Librarian, 333 N. Broadway, Jericho, NY 11753
Source of integrated modules for the IBM PC/XT/AT, including *LiAcquire,* acquisitions and accounting; *LiCat,* cataloging; *LiCirculate,* circulation control; and *LiSerial,* serials control.

Information Transform, Inc. 502 Leonard Street, Madison, WI 53711. (608) 255-4800

INMAGIC. 238 Broadway, Cambridge, MA 02139. (617) 661-8124
Source of a program for creating online catalogs; runs on IBM PC/XT/AT. Also runs as a multi-user system on DECs, PDP.VAX, H.P. 3000. Reviewed: *Special Libraries* (Winter 1986): 57.

ISI (Institute for Scientific Information). 3501 Market Street, University City Science Center, Philadelphia, PA 19104. (215) 386-0100
Source of *Sci-Mate, Universal Online Searcher,* and *Sci-Mate Personal Data Manager.*

JMC Computer Service, Inc. 1005 West Elm Street, Lake City, MN 55041
Source of *Library Usage Skills,* developed by Jim Deacon for the students at Cannon Falls, Minnesota school system.

K-12 Micro Media. 172 Broadway, Woodcliff Lake, NJ 07675
Distributes a variety of library programs.

LBI (Library Bureau of Investigation). 1920 Monument Blvd., Suite 540, Concord, CA 94520. (415) 945-7268
Source of programs designed by Bob Skapura (formerly of The Library Software Co.), using an Apple computer, to "create and print individualized exercises for library instruction. [The] exercises refer to books and authors from your library with call numbers consistent with the way you catalog."

Learnco, Inc. 128 High St., Greenland, NH 03840
Source of *Answering Questions Library Style.*

Learning Technology and Libraries, Inc. P.O. Box 3096, Carbondale, IL 62902
Source of *Cardprep.*

Learning Well. Dept. A 200 South Service Road, Rosalyn Heights, NY 11577
Source of *Library Adventure.*

The Library Corp. P.O. Box 40035, Washington, DC 20016. (800) 624-0559

The Library System. 240 H Street #113, Blaine, WA 98230. (604) 926-7222
Source of *BCA* (bar code applications) and *The Library System,* library circulation
and cataloging for the IBM XT/AT.

MacNeal Memorial Hospital. Health Sciences Resource Center, F.I.L.L.S., 3249 S.
Oak Park Ave., Berwyn, IL 60402
Source of F.I.L.L.S. (fast interlibrary loan and statistics) program. Described in
American Libraries (June 1984): 454. Reviewed: *Small Computers in Libraries* (October
1984): 7; *Technicalities* (January 1985): 2, 6.

Madeira City Schools. Jon Mauch and Sharyn Van Epps, 7465 Loannes Drive,
Cincinnati, OH 45243
Source of *Catalog Card Assembler.* Reviewed: *CMC News* (Winter 1984): 12;
Booklist (1 January 1984): 689.

Marketing Data Research. 8103 104th St., S.W., Tacoma, WA 98498
Source of *Master Tab,* analyzes library surveys. Described in *American Libraries*
(January 1985): 69.

Master Software. Box 101, Brighton, MI 48116
Source of *OVERDUE Master* (formerly *Date Due*). Runs on the PET/CBM,
SUPERPET, Commodore 64. Reviewed. *Small Computers in Libraries* (October 1983):
4-5.

Media Center Factory. P.O. Box 13536, Greensboro, NC 27405. (919) 274-5653
Source of several library management programs for the Apple and TRS-80.

Media Flex, Inc. P.O. Box 1107, Champlain, NY 12919. (518) 298-2970
Also: **Bibliofiches.** 1557, Rue Begin, St. Laurent, Quebec, H4R 1W9.
(514) 336-4340
Distributor for *The Mandarin System,* an integrated library management system
for the IBM PC and compatibles.

Micro Power and Light. 12820 Hillcrest Rd., Suite 219, Dallas, TX 75230
Source of a variety of programs, including a readability program described in
American Libraries (October 1984): 667. Others described in "Micro Software for

Library Skills Instruction," by Jane E. Ross in *School Library Journal* (November 1984): 68-72.

Microcomputers in Education. 4148 Winetka Ave., North Minneapolis, MN 55427
Source of *Bookshelf.*

Microdex. 3000 Pemberly Court, Suite 3, West Lafayette, IN 47906
Source for customized reference statistics programs described in *American Libraries* (March 1984): 179.

MicroEd., Inc. 8108 Eden Road, Eden Prairie, MN 55344
Source of several library skills programs described in "Micro Software for Library Skills Instruction," by Jane E. Ross, *School Library Journal* (November 1984): 68-72.

Microhouse, Inc. 4379 William Penn Highway, Bethlehem, PA 18017. (800) 523-9511
Source of *Research Reporter,* custom designed for the efficient filing and analysis of research questionnaire responses.

MicroSolutions. 587 W. 77th St., Indianapolis, IN 46260. (317) 253-9353
Source of *Circulation Manager* program. Demo available. Reviewed: *Wired Librarian's Newsletter* (October 1985): 2.

Micro-Systems Software, Inc. 4301-18 Oak Circle, Boca Raton, FL 33431. (305) 391-5077
Distributes software for setting up electronic bulletin board with IBM micros.

Midwest Library Service. 11443 St. Charles Rock Road, Bridgeton, MO 63044. (800) 325-8833
Source of *MATSS* (Midwest Automated Technical Services System), which includes a communication interface (for OCLC, RLIN, WLN), ordering, fund accounting, catalog cards, spine and pocket labels. For PC/MS-DOS.

Minnesota Computer. 1854 Graydon Ave., Brainerd, MN 56401. (218) 829-0548
Source of *Library Overdue Material Record.* Reviewed: *Small Computers in Libraries* (June 1983): 6.

MSC ComputerStore. 1455 South State Street, Orem, UT 84058. (801) 224-1169
Source for *Circa II Library System.* This system handles basic circulation functions, including checkout, check-in, patron file, overdue notices, and statistics. Originally an Apple system, now available only for the IBM PC/XT or the IBM PC with a hard disk expansion unit. It uses an Intermec light pen and CODABAR bar codes.

New Dimensions Software. Box 327, 1505 Maple Street, Northfield, MN 55057
Source for *Disk Catalog System.*

Nichols Advanced Technologies, Inc. 400 Bentall Bldg., 10180-102 St., Edmonton, Canada, T5J 0W5. (403) 424-0091
Source for *MOLLI,* automated searching, cataloging and indexing. PC/MS-DOS. Demo disk available. Described in *American Libraries* (September 1985): 597.

Ocelot Library System. ABALL Software, Inc., 461 Osler St., Reginia, Sask., Canada, S4P 1W8. (306) 569-2180
U.S. Distributor: Tescor Inc., 461 Carlisle Dr., Hemdon, VI 22070. (703) 435-9501
Includes catalog module, circulation module, purchase for the IBM. Reviewed: *Wired Librarian's Newsletter* (January 1985): 4. *Canadian Library Journal* (June 1985): 155-56.

OCLC (Online Computer Library Center). 6565 Frantz Road, Dublin, OH 43017 (614) 764-6000
Distributes a variety of library management programs for the IBM.

Orchard Systems. 207 East Third St., Waunakee, WI 53597. (608) 849-5727
Source for *Orchard System Circulation Management System* (for Apple). Demo available. Reviewed: *CMC News* (Spring 1984): 6.

PERCON. 2190 West 11th Street, Eugene, OR 97402. (503) 344-1189
A manufacturer of bar code scanning equipment, Percon has program to print bar code labels that runs on IBM/compatible. Described in *Small Computers in Libraries* (February 1985): 10.

Personal Bibliographic Software, Inc. P.O. Box 4250, Ann Arbor, MI 48106
Described in *American Libraries* (January 1984). Reviewed: *Booklist* (1 January 1984): 690.

Phi Delta Kappa. University of Maryland, College of Education, College Park, MD 20742
Source for *Library Skills*. Reviewed: *The Computing Teacher* (February 1984): 33.

Pinellas County Schools. Library/Media Microcomputer Pilot Project, Carlton E. Hoffman, Director of Media Services, Hope R. Bottebusch, AV/TV Supervisor, 1960 E. Druid Road, Clearwater, FL 33546. (813) 442-1171
The Pinellas County School District has implemented an in-house project that uses microcomputers for library/media skills and management tasks. As of November 1985, six programs have been developed and are available for purchase. The pilot library/media centers began using the programs in the first semester of the 1982-1983 school year. Today, the project numbers 48 microcomputers and printers. Programs for the project are on TRS-80 format; however, Apple formats are available for purchase. Programs available include *Audiovisual Equipment Inventory; Audiovisual Equipment Scheduling; Audiovisual Materials Inventory; Audiovisual Materials Scheduling; Film Manager; Star Library Skills*. Programs are distributed through Educational Activities, Inc.

Professional Software. 21 Forest Ave., Glen Ridge, NJ 07028. (201) 748-7658
Source of serials control system for IBM PC. Demo disk available.

PRO-SEARCH.
PRO-SEARCH, online searching software products, acquired by Personal Bibliographic Software, Inc. (Spring 1986).

Reference Press. Box 1141, Postal Station F, Toronto, Ontario, Canada, M4Y 2TB
Source of *Authex.*

Richmond Software Corporation. P.O. Box 5587, San Mateo, CA 94402.
(800) 222-6063
Robert Stevens, original developer of *Book Trak Systems,* is now marketing and
supporting these library management programs for the Apple.

Right On Programs. P.O. Box 977, Huntington, NY 11743
Distributes a variety of library skill and management programs for the Apple,
Commodore, and IBM. Some described in "Micro Software for Library Skills Instruc-
tion," by Jane E. Ross in *School Library Journal* (November 1984): 68-72.

Richard K. Riley. P.O. Box 2227, Augusta, ME 04330
Source of *Riley's Catalog Cards.* Reviewed: *The Book Report* (January/February
1985): 64; *Wired Librarian's Newsletter* (April 1985): 3.

Ringgold Management Systems, Inc. Box 368, Beaverton, OR 97075. (503) 645-3502
Has library management programs for circulation and acquisitions; for CP/M,
MP/M, MS-DOS, PC-DOS, TRSDOS, UNIX, XENIX.

RTI (Research Technology International). 4700 Chase Avenue, Lincolnwood, IL
60646. (800) 323-7520
Source of AMI film booking system.

Sarte Systems. 8110 Manitoba St. #202, Playa del Rey, CA 90293
Source for Atari-based *School Library Circ System* described in *American
Libraries* (April 1985): 270.

Scarecrow Press. 52 Liberty St., Box 656, Metuchen, NJ 08840. (201) 548-8600
Source for *The Librarian's Helper.*

Scientific Software Products, Inc. 5720 West 71st, Indianapolis, IN 46278.
(317) 293-9270
Source for *BIBLIOTEK,* a program not written to handle complete bibliographic
data but intended for the cataloging of private collections of scientific reprints. It could,
however, be useful in small technical libraries which have needs similar to individual
scientists and researchers. Contact for user names.

Scribe Software, Inc. Kurt Parks, president, 4435 No. Saddlebag Trail, Suite #1,
Saddlebag Trail Plaza, Scottsdale, AZ 85251. (602) 990-3384
Source for *Innovation-45 Plus: School Library Management System,* integrated
library management system designed to operate on IBM PC/XT/AT, Compaq
Deskpro, or Altos 586. System offers acquisitions, circulation, public access catalog, in-
ventory control, patron information, and library management reports.

Sensible Software. 210 S. Woodward, Suite 229, Birmingham, MI 48011
Source of *Bookends.*

Serials-Acquisitions
Contact large magazine subscription agencies for information about microcomputer-based ordering systems, e.g., EBSCO Industries, Inc., P.O. Box 1943, Birmingham, AL 35201, (205) 991-6600, and F.W. Faxton Co., 2112-B Gallows Road, Vienna, VA 22180, (703) 893-3190.

Small Library Computing. 48 Lawrence Avenue, Holbrook, NY 11741. (516) 588-1387
Has programs that support the full MARC format for the IBM PC/XT/AT and compatibles: retrospective conversion (using the LC MARC database on CD ROM), acquisitions (with fund accounting), card production, and MARC record transfer. Demo disks and manuals available.

Southern Micro Systems. 716 E. Davis St., Burlington, NC 27215. (800) 334-5521
Source for *Library Helper* "Overdues" program for Apple II (48K). Also has a variety of programs for school psychologists, special services directors, L.D./E.M.R. teachers, and speech pathologists.

Southwestern Oregon Community College. Learning Resource Center, Coos Bay, OR 97420
Source for *Shelving Books the LC Way.*

Speak Softly, Inc. 303 Calvert Ave., Clinton, SC 29325
Source of *CALM—Card and Label Manager.*

Hugh Starke. RFD #1, River Road, Peru, NY 12972
Source for *CARDPRO,* for Apple family with Microsoft MBasic; TRS-80 Model III and Model 4. Reviewed: *School Library Journal* (March 1985): 129.

Sunburst. 39 Washington Ave., Pleasantville, NY 10570. (800) 431-1934
Distributes *How Can I Find It If I Don't Know What I'm Looking For?* designed by Ann Lathrop.

Swan Software. P.O. Box 206, Lititz, PA 17543. (717) 627-1911
Source for *Reserve Power*™, a film reservation program for Apple or IBM. Demo available.

Sydney Dataproducts, Inc. Suite 100-11075 Santa Monica Blvd., Los Angeles, CA 90025. (800) 992-9778
Produces micro library system in five modules: cataloging/inquiry, acquisitions, circulation control, serials, and MARC-record interface.

E. F. Tennen and Associates. 757 Creekmont Court, Ventura, CA 93003
Source for *AV Handler* for CP/M, PC/MS-DOS.

Vertical Software Systems, Ltd. 118 Song Meadoway, Willowdale, Ontario, Canada, M2H 2T7
Source of *MEDIA,* a cataloging/booking program under CP/M.

Winnebago Software Company. 121 S. Marshall, P.O. Box 430, Caledonia, MN 55921. (800) 533-5430

Source for Apple programs, including: *Library Circulation System I and II,* floppy disk circulation; *Library Circulation III,* hard disk circulation system; *Computer Cat* (acquired in late 1984), online catalog; *Catalog Card Maker III.*

ℱ SOFTWARE REVIEW CITATIONS

Sources are indicated in parentheses after program name. Refer to previous section for source information.

Acquisitions

Online Acquisition System. (Brodart).
"Brodart's Online Acquisition System," by Lucille Wilson. *CMC NEWS* (Fall 1984): 13.

AV Management

Audiovisual Equipment Inventory. (Educational Activities).
School Library Journal (March 1985): 127.

Audiovisual Equipment Scheduling. (Educational Activities).
School Library Journal (March 1985): 127.

The A-V Catalog Writer. (Follett Software Company).
CMC News (Fall 1984): 10-11; *Booklist* (1 June 1983): 1287-88; *The Computing Teacher* (October 1983): 45-46.

Bibliography Programs

Bibliography Writer. (Follett Software Company).
Booklist (1 September 1983): 104; *Access: Microcomputers in Libraries* (Spring 1983): 14; *CMC News* (Fall 1983): 7; *School Library Journal* (March 1985): 128.

Bookends, the Reference Management System. (Sensible Software).
Softalk (August 1983): 164-66; *The Journal of Computers in Mathematics and Science Teaching* (Summer 1983): 36-37; *Instructor* (November/December 1983): 96; *inCider* (January 1984): 168-69; *New England Journal of Medicine* (12 January 1984): 134; *Microcomputing* (May 1984): 144; *Booklist* (1 September 1984): 82; *Wilson Library Bulletin* (June 1985): 701. Enhanced *Bookends* reviewed in *Wired Librarian's Newsletter* (January 1986). No pages available.

Professional Bibliographic System. (Personal Bibliographic Software, Inc.).
Small Computers in Libraries (November 1983). No pages available; *Booklist* (1 January 1984). No pages available; *Information Technology and Libraries* (June 1983): 184-87; *Media and Methods* (December 1983): 39; *Technicalities* (January 1984); *RQ*

(Fall 1983): 95-96; *Small Computers in Libraries* (November 1984): 4; *Information Technology and Libraries* (December 1985): 372-74.

Card and Label Production

Program Comparisons

Anderson, Eric S. "Catalog Cards by Computer: A Look at the Offerings." *The Book Report* (January/February 1985): 63-64.

Specific Programs

Book Trak Card Printing Program. (Richmond Software).
    Apple LUG Newsletter (September 1984): 8; *Apple LUG Newsletter* (January 1985): 23-34; *Book Report* (January/February 1985). No pages available.

CALM — Card and Label Manager. (Speak Softly, Inc.).
    Described in *American Libraries* (September 1984): 603. Reviewed: *CMC News* (Spring 1985): 8-9; *Book Report* (January/February 1985): 64; *School Library Journal* (March 1985): 128; *Booklist* (1 May 1985): 1268; *Wired Librarian's Newsletter* (March 1985): 1.

Card Printing Program (Right On). (Right On Programs).
    Apple LUG Newsletter (September 1984): 8. Includes cost comparisons.

Cardprep. (Learning Technology and Libraries, Inc.).
    Described in *American Libraries* (June 1985): 450. Reviewed: *Apple LUG Newsletter* (January 1985): 25-27; *School Library Journal* (January/February 1985): 64; *Book Report* (January/February 1985): 64; *Wired Librarian's Newsletter* (March 1985): 1.

Catalog Card and Label Writer. (K-12 Micro Media).
    Small Computers in Libraries (July 1982): 1; *Small Computers in Libraries* (October 1982): 4; *Booklist* (1 November 1982): 90; *Small Computers in Libraries* (October 1984): 3; *CMC News* (Spring 1983): 3-6; *Book Report* (January/February 1985): 63.

Catalog Card Maker. (Winnebago Software).
    CMC News (Spring 1984): 7; (Fall 1984): 13.

Label Maker II. (Winnebago Software).
    CMC News (Winter 1984): 11.

LABLMKR-2 (for the TRS-80 Model II). (E.T.S. Center).
    CMC News (Winter 1984): 10.

The Librarian's Helper (for IBM PC, CP/M, CP/M-86). (Scarecrow Press).
    Described in *American Libraries* (October 1985): 669. Reviewed: *Wilson Library Bulletin* (October 1985): 61; *Library Journal* (15 September 1985): 6ff; *Small Computers in Libraries* (October 1984): 5-6; *Wired Librarian's Newsletter* (October 1985): 1.

Quick Card. (Follett Software Company).
    Apple LUG Newsletter (April 1985): 33-34; *The Book Report* (January/February 1985): 64.

Telemarc Catalog Card Program. (Gaylord Brothers, Inc.).
   Small Computers in Libraries (July 1982): 1. *Small Computers in Libraries* (March 1983). No pages available.

Ultracard. (Small Library Computing).
   Small Computers in Libraries (November 1983): 3; *Library Software Review* (Fall 1984): 394-98.

Circulation

Program Comparisons

Berglund, Patricia. "School Library Technology." *Wilson Library Bulletin* (February 1984): 427.
   Experiences of librarians with several circulation systems including *Overdue Writer, Book Trak,* and student programs.

"Circulation Software: Comparison of *Book Trak* and *LCS.*" *The Book Report* (March/April 1985): 23-25.

Specific Programs

Book Trak Circulation System. (Richmond Software).
   "*BOOKTRAK:* Advantages and Disadvantages," by Jim Crook in *BCTLA Bookmark* (March 1985). No pages available. "Outlines the steps in setting up the collection to use the program, gives recommendations to anyone considering automated circulation and assesses cost factors" — from *Apple LUG Newsletter* (October 1985): 64. Reviewed: *Booklist* (1 November 1983): 436; *CMC News* (Fall 1983): 8-9; *School Library Journal* (November 1984): 85-86; *Emergency Librarian* (March/April 1985): 41; *The Book Report* (March/April 1985). No pages available.

Card Datalog Circulation Module. (DTI Data Trek).
   Reviewed: *Online* (March 1983): 20-22.

Library Circulation System II. (Winnebago Software).
   CMC News (Winter 1984): 8-9.

Overdue Writer, Overdue Collector, Overnight Writer. (Follett Software Company).
   Classroom Computer News (March 1983): 73-74; *Electronic Learning* (April 1983): 80-81. *CMC News* (Winter 1983): 9; *Technicalities* (May 1984): 13-14. Described by developer in *School Library Media Quarterly* (Summer 1982): 347-50. *Overdue Writer* described in *American Libraries* (May 1984): 340.

Periodical Management

AUTHEX — Periodical Indexing System. (Reference Press).
   Wilson Library Bulletin (December 1985): 58.

Book Trak Magazine Control System. (Richmond Software).
   CMC News (Fall 1984): 11; *Technicalities* (May 1984): 13-14; *Booklist* (1 April

1983): 1047-48; *School Library Journal* (November 1984): 85-86; *CMC News* (Spring 1983): 9-11; *The Computing Teacher* (September 1983): 58-59.

Tapit: Apple Periodicals. (A.V. Systems, Inc.).
    CMC News (Fall 1984): 14. "A unique periodical index system."

Online Catalogs

General Articles

Perry, William B. "Micro−O.P.A.C.: The U.T.L.A.S.−Brookfield Experiment." *CMC News* (Fall 1984): 8-10.
Describes pilot online catalog project at Brookfield High School in Ottawa.

Specific Programs

Card Datalog Catalog Module. (DTI Data Trek).
    Online (March 1983): 20-22.

Computer Cat. (Winnebago Software).
    Electronic Learning (February 1983): 70; *Classroom Computer News* (March 1983): 73-74; *Wilson Library Bulletin* (January 1985): 336ff. See also further readings at the end of chapter 9.

INMAGIC. (INMAGIC).
    Program for creating online catalogs. Reviewed: *Special Libraries* (Winter 1986): 57.

Retrospective Conversion

BiblioFile. (Library Corp.).
    "BiblioFile for Retrospective Conversion," by Norma Desmarais, *Small Computers in Libraries* (December 1985): 24-28.

MITINET/marc. (Information Transform, Inc.).
    Wired Librarian's Newsletter (January 1986): 1. "Micro-based utility to create fully formatted MARC records on a micro computer."

Search Software

Program Comparisons

"Software for Online Searching." *Library Journal.* (15 October 1985): 52-53.
    Three types of "front-end package database access packages" reviewed, including *Searchware, PRO-SEARCH, Biblio-Line,* and *PBS.*

Specific Programs

Biblio-Link (for use with Personal Bibliographic System). (Personal Bibliographic Software, Inc.).
    Small Computers in Libraries (November 1984): 4.

In-Search. (See Pro-Search).

Personal Software (June 1984): 47; *Personal Computing* (June 1984): 52-53; *Library Journal* (1 October 1984): 1828-29; *Popular Computing* (November 1984): 149-52; *Business Software* (September 1984): 71.

MICROsearch by ERIC. (ERIC Clearinghouse).

Runs under AppleDOS 3.3; IBM version available in 1986. *Apple LUG Newsletter* (January 1985): 20-22; more information about *MICROsearch* in *The Computing Teacher* (March 1985): 62-63. Reviewed: *RQ* (Summer 1983): 417-18; *CMC News* (Winter 1985): 7; *Wired Librarian's Newsletter* (January 1985): 2; *Library Software Review* 3, no. 4; *Booklist* (1 June 1985): 1414.

PRO-SEARCH. (Personal Bibliographic Software, Inc.).

For computer communications and online searching. *Information Technology and Libraries* (December 1985): 374-82.

Search Helper. (Information Access Company).

RQ (Fall 1983): 96-97; *Library Journal* (1 June 1984): 1104-1105; *Apple LUG Newsletter* (April 1985): 27-31.

Skills/Instructional Programs

Program Comparisons

Anderson, Eric S. "Library Skills Software." *Apple LUG Newsletter* (April 1985): 49-54.

Brief reviews of eight library skills programs.

Hamilton, Donald, and Sandra Nelson. "Where Is It?" *Wilson Library Bulletin* (November 1985): 57.

Margo, Roberta. "School Inventory." *CMC News* (Fall 1984): 12.

Discusses educational courseware.

Specific Programs

Answering Questions Library Style. (Learnco, Inc.).

Booklist (1 September 1984): 81-82; *Apple LUG Newsletter* (April 1985): 25-26.

Bookshelf. (Microcomputers in Education).

Booklist (1 September 1982): 58. Described in "Micro Software for Library Skills Instruction," by Jane E. Ross, *School Library Journal* (November 1984): 68-72.

CALICO Library Skills Series. (CALICO).

Booklist (1 November 1982): 389-90; *American Libraries* (April 1984): 264. Discussed in "Micro Software for Library Skills Instruction," by Jane E. Ross, *School Library Journal* (November 1984): 68-72.

Electronic Bookshelf. (Richmond Software).

A computer-managed reading program. Reviewed: Apple LUG Newsletter (April 1985): 53-54; *Wired Librarian's Newsletter* (February 1985): 1 and (January 1986): 1.

Elementary Library Media Skills. (Combase).

Booklist (1 May 1984): 1263; *Electronic Learning* (May/June 1984): 94-95; *CMC News* (Spring 1984): 5-6; *School Library Media Quarterly* (Winter 1985): 80; *Apple LUG Newsletter* (April 1985): 50.

How Can I Find It If I Don't Know What I'm Looking For? (Sunburst).

Library skills software; lab pack available. Reviewed: *Electronic Learning* (November/December 1985): 61-62; *CMC News* (Winter 1986): 7; *School Library Media Quarterly* (Fall 1985): 44.

Library Adventure. (Learning Well).

Apple LUG Newsletter (October 1985): 18.

Library Skills Programs (Right On). (Right On Programs).

Educational Technology (June 1982): 38.

Library Usage Skills. (JMC Computer Service).

Developed and used by Jim Deacon. Reviewed: *CMC News* (Fall 1983): 6-7; *Apple LUG Newsletter* (April 1985): 50.

Shelving Books the LC Way. (Southwestern Oregon Community College).

Booklist (1 May 1985): 270; *Wired Librarian's* (February 1985): 1; *Apple LUG Newsletter* (January 1986): 23.

Skills Maker. (Follett Software Company).

CMC News (Winter 1985): 8; *Apple LUG Newsletter* (April 1985): 52; *Booklist* (1 May 1985): 1270; *Wired Librarian's Newsletter* (January 1985): 1.

Using an Index to Periodicals (Levels I and II). (Combase).

Apple LUG Newsletter (April 1985): 32; *Booklist* (1 May 1985): 1271; *School Library Media Quarterly* (Spring 1985): 155.

Miscellaneous

Program Comparisons

Dewey, Patrick. "Software for Libraries." *Wilson Library Bulletin* (January 1985): 353; (February 1985): 418.

The January issue discusses a group of programs for small libraries, including *Overdue Writer, Overdue Collector, Bibliography Writer* and *A-V Catalog Writer*. The February issue reviews *Catalogit!!!* and *Overdue Books* from Right On Programs.

"Peoples' Message System—Bulletin Board Software." *Wilson Library Bulletin* (April 1985): 554.

Specific Programs

Appleworks. (Apple Computer, Inc.).
↙ *The Computing Teacher* (October 1984): 34-35; *CMC News* (Winter 1985): 9-10; *The Book Report* (September/October 1984): 28, 67. Eric Anderson reviews *Appleworks* library applications.

Book Trak System (all five programs). (Richmond Software).
Electronic Learning (February 1984): 82; *School Library Journal* (November 1984): 85-86; *Apple LUG Newsletter* (September 1984): 8 and (January 1985): 23-24.

Disk Catalog System. (New Dimensions Software).
CMC News (Spring 1985): 10. "Quickly set up the database for the programs in a software collection . . . can print labels for each diskette. Makes the task of producing catalogs of your school's software easier."

Educational Sourcedisk. (Educational Associates).
Database of available educational software. Reviewed: *CMC News* (Spring 1984): 8.

Fiction Finder. (CALICO).
Booklist (1 September 1984): 82; *Wilson Library Bulletin* (November 1984): 222.

MEDIA AND MEDIA SOURCES

General

Monographs

Training for Microcomputers: A Directory of Diskette-Based and Video Training Packages. Studio City, Calif.: n.p., n.d. 70p. $20.00. (Pacific Information, Inc., 11684 Ventura Blvd., Suite 295, Studio City, CA 91604).
Lists 257 instructional guides covering all aspects of hardware, software, and programming. Includes an index by subject and a directory of producers and distributors.

Articles

Bardes, D'Ellen. "Video Technology: Conveying Information Visually." *Wilson Library Bulletin* (April 1985): 523-26.
"Video is changing the marketing, management, and design of technical information products. [There are] four distinct classifications: Marketing, Informational, End-product, Demonstrational." Many vendors have video programs available which may be very helpful in your planning, evaluation, and selection processes.

Elberfeld, John K. "Preparing Slide Presentations on Computers." *The Computing Teacher* (October 1982): 34-35.
"Fewer than ten people can comfortably watch a video monitor, but several hundred can watch a slide show at the same time."

Computer Literacy

This list contains a number of sources for good films to use in computer literacy classes. As these resources are constantly changing, you will want to write and have your library added to the mailing lists, in order to receive information about the current film holdings and their costs.

Allis Chalmers Film Library. 4431 West North Avenue, Milwaukee, WI 53208.

AVC Media Library, Audio-Visual Center. University of Iowa, Iowa City, IA 52240.

Brigham Young University, Educational Media Services. 290 Herald R. Clark Building, Provo, UT 84602. ·

British Broadcasting Corporation. 55 Bloor Street West, No. 1220, Toronto, ON, Canada M4W 1A5.

Business Education Films. 7820 Twentieth Avenue, Brooklyn, NY 11214.

Changing Times Education Service, EMC Corporation. 180 East Sixth Street, St. Paul, MN 55101.

Children's TV International. Suite 1207, Skyline Place, 5265 Leesburg Pike, Falls Church, VA 22041.
Has produced *Adventures of the Mind,* six 15-minute videocassettes; they are available for preview. This series has been shown on some PBS television stations.

Contemporary/McGraw-Hill Films, Film Rental Library. McGraw-Hill Book Company, P.O. Box 590, Highstoron, NJ 08520.

Control Data Corporation, Photo Library. HQN11U, P.O. Box O, Minneapolis, MN 55401.

Coronet Films. 65 E. South Water Street, Chicago, IL 60601.
Write for list of computer-related films. Some, such as *Data Processing: An Introduction* (reviewed in *The Computing Teacher* 8 [February 1981]), are available from film libraries.

CRM McGraw-Hill Films. 110 Fifteenth Street, Del Mar, CA 92104.

Digital Equipment Corp., Film Library – Public Relations Department. 146 Main Street, Maynard, MA 01754.

Educator's Guide to Free 16mm Films, Educators Progress Service, Inc. Randolph, WI 53956.
Annual publication.

Encyclopaedia Britannica Educational Corp. 425 North Michigan Avenue, Dept. 10A, Chicago, IL 60611.

Film Fair Communications. 10900 Ventura Boulevard, Studio City, CA 91604.
Source for computer-related films such as *The Computer*.

Films, Inc. 8124 North Central Park Avenue, Skokie, IL 60076.

Films Incorporated. 1213 Wilmette Avenue, Wilmette, IL 60091, (800) 323-4222.
Source for computer-related films such as *The Silicon Factor: So What's It All About,* reviewed in *The Computing Teacher* 10 (December 1982): 20. Other films include *Making the Most of the Micro* (Computer Literacy Unit from the BBC); *The Computer Programme; The Computer Programme Inservice Workshop.* Contact for more information.

General Electric Corp., Educational Films. Corporation Park, Scotia, NY 12303.

Guidance Associates. Communications Park, P.O. Box 300, White Plains, NY 10602.
Source for computer-related media such as *Computers: From Pebbles to Program.*

IBM Corporation. Old Orchard Road, Armonk, NY 10504.

Indiana University, Audiovisual Center. Bloomington, IN 47401.

Journal Films. 909 West Diversey Parkway, Chicago, IL 60614.

Kent State University, AV Services. Kent, OH 44242.

Library Video Network. 1811 Woodlawn Drive, Baltimore, MD 21207, (301) 265-6983.
Has a series of videotapes created for library staff training. These are available for either rental or purchase and "on a limited, time available basis" for previews. Contact for more information.

MacMillan Films, Inc. 34 MacQuestern Parkway, South, Mt. Vernon, NY 10550.

MECC (Minnesota Educational Computer Consortium). 2520 Broadway Drive, St. Paul, MN 55113-5199, (612) 638-0627.
Using the Computer in the Classroom Training Materials. Materials developed by MECC for teaching an introductory course in instructional computing for educators using the Apple are available from MECC. An Atari version will be released soon. For more information see description in *The Computing Teacher* 10 (December 1982): 6, or contact MECC.

Metrics Research Corp. 130 W. Wieuca Rd., Suite 200, Atlanta, GA 30342.
"Computer literacy is the goal of *Understanding Personal Computers,* a series of videotapes. Topics covered include hardware, software, printers, word processing, and 'starting out right.' " Tapes available in different formats. Contact Metrics for more information.

Modern Talking Pictures, Film Scheduling Center. 2323 New Hyde Park Road, New Hyde Park, NY 11040.

National Audio-Visual Center, General Services Administration Order Section/BB. Washington, DC 20409.

Northwestern Bell Telephone Co. (or local Bell office), Program Service. 224 South Fifth Street, Room 1335, Minneapolis, MN 55402.

Pacific Telephone Film Libraries. 1145 North McCadden Place, Los Angeles, CA 90038.

You can also contact your local phone company for a list of computer-related films such as *The Thinking ??? Machines,* reviewed in *The Computing Teacher* 8 (November 1980): 43.

Remington Rand Division of Sperry Rand Corp. 1290 Avenue of the Americas, New York, NY 10011.

Sandia Laboratories, Division 3153. Albuquerque, NM 87185.

SFFL (Santa Fe Film Library). 80 East Jackson Boulevard, Chicago, IL 60604.

Sperry-Univac. P.O. Box 500, Blue Bell, PA 19422.

Martha Stuart Communications, Inc. POB 246B, Hillsdale, NY 12529.

Powersharing: The Microcomputer is a 50-minute videotape explaining and demonstrating five types of microcomputer applications: electronic spreadsheets, business graphics, word processing, online searching, and database management. For sale or rent.

Syracuse University, Film Rental Library. 1455 East Colvin Street, Syracuse, NY 13210.

Time-Life Films, 16mm Dept. 43 West Sixteenth Street, New York, NY 10011.

TRW Systems Group. One Spack Park, Redondo Beach, CA 90278.

University of Florida Foundation. University of Florida, Gainesville, FL 32611, (904) 392-0342.

Has a program to train OCLC users. Described in *American Libraries* (November 1985): 749.

ELECTRONIC SERVICES

Bibliographic Utilities and Informational Databases

Articles

Schultz, Lois. "Bibliographic Utilities in the 1980's." *Library HiTech* (Winter 1983): 83-86.

"Select bibliography provides a synopsis of what is happening in the world of bibliographic utilities . . . (defined as) an organization that maintains large online bibliographic databases and provides products and services related to these bases and to its members. . . . excludes profit-making organizations, since they have customers rather than members. Articles are from 1980-June 1983 and subdivided by utility: OCLC, RLG/RLIN, UTLAS, WLN, General (about more than one utility.)"

Utilities and Databases

American People Link. 3215 North Frontage Road, Suite 1505, Arlington Heights, IL 60004, (312) 870-4260.

Provides home service similar to CompuServe, The Source, and Delphi. Described by Russ Lockwood in his "Telecommunications" column, *A + Magazine* (June 1985): 80-81.

BRS (Bibliographic Retrieval Services, Inc.). BRS/BRS After Dark, 1200 Route 7, Latham, NY 12110, (518) 783-1161.

Operates national network which includes access to SPIN, the School Practices Information Network. Includes a database of commercial curriculum materials including the entire Curriculum Development Library produced by Fearon-Pitman publishers. See "Databases of Microcomputer Software: An Overview," *Library Journal/School Library Journal* (May 1985): 101-4; 131-34. BRS After Dark, available evenings/weekends, is described in "Online Update" column by Martin Kesselman in *Wilson Library Bulletin* (June 1985): 652-53, 687.

CompuServe Information Service. 5000 Arlington Centre Boulevard, Columbus, OH 43220, (614) 457-8600.

CompuServe offers online access to electronic mail, news, and a variety of information of interest to the home computer owner. Schools are using this service also, particularly for the current access to news. See *The Computing Teacher* (February 1982): 18. Also see "Databases of Microcomputer Software: An Overview," *Library Journal/School Library Journal* (May 1985): 101-4; 131-34.

Delphi (Information Service). General Videotex Corp., 3 Blackstone Street, Cambridge, MA 02139, (800) 544-4005.

Provides such services as: E-Mail, electronic banking, shop-at-home services, current news and wire services, tutorials and games, plus 200 databases providing multidisciplinary research services.

Dialog Information Services, Inc. 3460 Hillview Avenue, Palo Alto, CA 94394, (800) 544-4005.

With over 300 databases, Dialog is the largest vendor. Has three services: the regular Dialog service; Knowledge Index, the evening/weekend service to about 25 databases; and Online Training and Practice, for classroom instructional purposes. See "Databases of Microcomputer Software: An Overview," *Library Journal/School Library Journal* (May 1985): 101-4; 131-34.

EduNet. P.O. Box 364, Princeton, NJ 08540, (609) 734-1878.

MDC (Mead Data Central, division of Mead Corp.). 9393 Springboro Pike, P.O. Box 933, Dayton, OH 45401, (800) 543-6862.

OCLC (Online Computer Library Center). OCLC, Inc., 6565 Frantz Road, Dublin, OH 43017.

Operates international network used by libraries to acquire and catalog library materials, arrange interlibrary loans, and maintain location information. As of October 1985, OCLC had over 12 million bibliographic records. Various microcomputer packages and software are available. OCLC also publishes *OCLC MICRO,* a bimonthly magazine. Membership: several levels of participation; regional network brokers provide contracts, training, and support.

RLIN (Research Libraries Information Network). Research Libraries Group (RLG), Stanford University, Stanford, CA 94305, (415) 497-0015.

This bibliographic utility, originally called BALLOTS and sponsored by Stanford University, joined with the Research Libraries Group (RLG) to form the RLIN network. Although a variety of libraries have membership, the emphasis is on its research libraries members.

SDC, Information Services, Orbit Search Service. System Development Corporation, 2525 Colorado Avenue, Santa Monica, CA 90406, (213) 820-4111; (800) 421-7229 (outside CA); (800) 352-6689 (in CA).

Eighty databases online are available through the Orbit Information Retrieval System in the major subject areas: patents, chemistry, engineering, and energy.

The Source. 1616 Anderson Road, McLean, VA 22102, (703) 734-7500.

Offers online access to electronic mail, news, and a variety of information of interest to the home computer owner. Schools are also using this service. See "Databases of Microcomputer Software: An Overview," *Library Journal/School Library Journal* (May 1985): 101-4; 131-34.

TECHCENTRAL. AECT—Electronic Network, 1126 Sixteenth Street, NW, Washington, DC 20036.

This international electronic mail system links AECT membership as well as serving as the network for other professional associations such as the American Association for Colleges and Universities and the Chamber of Commerce.

TESS On Line—The Electronic Software Selector maintained by EPIE Institute. EPIE Institute, Box 839, Watermill, NY 11976, (516) 283-4922.

Available through CompuServe. Database contains references to reviews, recommended lists. Described in *Electronic Education* (October 1985): 10. Print version reviewed in *The Computing Teacher* (May 1984): 38.

UTLAS, Inc. (University of Toronto Library Automated System). 80 Bloor Street West, 2nd floor, Toronto, ON, Canada, M5S 2V1, (416) 923-0890.

Other offices: 701 Westchester Ave., Suite 308W, White Plains, NY 10604, (914) 997-1495/6; 2150 Shattuck Ave., Berkeley, CA 94704, (415) 841-9442.

This is a bibliographic utility; membership made up of various types of libraries.

WILSONLINE. H.W. Wilson Co., Wilsonline, 950 University Avenue, Bronx, NY 10452, (212) 588-8400.

Read "Wilsonline—A Look at H. W. Wilson's Offerings for Online Access to Its Indexes a Year after WILSONLINE's Debut," by Danuta A. Nitecki in *American Libraries* (December 1985): 804-9. Described in "Databases and Dialogues," by Russ Lockwood, *A + Magazine* (June 1985): 79-80.

WLN (Western Library Network). Washington State Library, Olympia, WA 98504, (206) 753-5595.
This is a bibliographic utility; membership consists of various types of libraries in the Pacific Northwest region.

Cataloging and/or Retrospective Conversion Services

Companies that provide online catalog data entry, retrospective conversion, and tape record conversion services or programs. Contact for more information.

Auto-graphics, Inc. 751 Monterey Pass Road, Monterey Park, CA 91754, (213) 269-9451.

BIBLIOFILE, The Library Corporation. P.O. Box 40035, Washington, DC 20016, (800) 624-0559.

Brodart Co. 500 Arch St., Williamsport, PA 17701, (717) 326-2461, ext. 640 in the East, or 10983 Via Frontera, San Diego, CA 92127 (619) 451-0250 in the West.
MicroCheck retrospective conversion system—described in *American Libraries* (February 1985): 133.

The Computer Company. 1905 Westmoreland Street, Richmond, VA 23230, (804) 358-2171.

Electronic Keyboarding, Inc. 140 Weldon Parkway, Maryland Heights, MO 63043, (314) 567-1780.
See "Retrocon for LCS in Academic Libraries," by Doris R. Brown, *Information Technology and Libraries* (September 1984): 274-76.

Information Transform. Hank Epstein, 502 Leonard Street, Madison, WI 53711, (608) 255-4800.
MITINET described in *American Libraries* (February 1984): 113-14 and *Information Technology and Libraries* (June 1983): 166-73. "MITINET Retro in Wisconsin Libraries," by Robert Bocher in *School Library Journal* (March 1985): 109-10; *Information Technology and Libraries* (September 1984): 267-74; *Wired Librarian's Newsletter* (January 1986). No pages available. New program available, "micro-based utility to create fully formatted MARC records on a microcomputer."

Inforonics, Inc. 550 Newtown Road, Littleton, MA 01460, (617) 486-9876.
See "Company Profile: Inforonics—'Can Do' Outlook Guides Small Entrepreneur," by Bev Smith, *Information Today* (November 1985): 17-19.

Library of Congress. Customer Services Section, Cataloging Distribution Service, Washington, DC 20541, (202) 287-6171.

LSSI (Library Systems and Services, Inc.). MiniMarc and MicroMARC, 1395 Piccard Drive, Suite 100, Rockville, MD 20850, (800) 638-8725.

MARCIVE, Inc. P.O. Box 47508, San Antonio, TX 78265, (512) 646-6161.

OCLC (Online Computer Library Center, Inc.). 6565 Frantz Road, Dublin, OH 43017, (614) 764-6000.

REMARC. Carrollton Press, 1911 Fort Myer Drive, Arlington, VA 22209, (800) 368-3008.
See "Retrospective Conversion with REMARC at Johns Hopkins University," by Virginia Drake and Mary Paige Smith, *Information Technology and Libraries* (September 1984): 282-86.

Small Library Computing. 48 Lawrence Avenue, Holbrook, NY 11741, (516) 588-1387.
Software that supports full MARC format for the IBM PC/XT/AT and PC compatibles includes: Retrospective Conversion—"using the LC MARC database on CD ROM optical disks" and MARC Record Transfer—"MARC tape to PC disk and PC disk to MARC tape." Manuals and demo disks available.

ORGANIZATIONS AND SAMPLE USER GROUPS
General Articles

"Computer Clubs to the Rescue." *Popular Computing* (April 1983): 152-53.

Mace, Scott. "Users Groups Reach Out." *InfoWorld* (17 September 1984): 20-24.
"New computer buyers find services and support."

Powledge, Fred. "The Power of Users' Groups." *Popular Computing* (December 1984): 95-102.

Skapura, Robert. Apple Library Users Group. "Apple Template Exchange." *Apple Library Users Group Newsletter* (October 1985 and January 1986): 4-5; 4-6. For more information contact: Robert Skapura, 1920 Monument Blvd., Suite 540, Concord, CA 94520.

"Where to Find User Groups." *Popular Computing* (September 1983): 175-78.

Organizations and User Groups

ADAPSO. 1300 North Seventeenth Street, Arlington, VA 22209, (703) 522-5055.
This is the computer software and services industry trade association. A free pamphlet on copyright and software is available upon request.

American Society for Information Science (ASIS). 1424 Sixteenth St., NW, Washington, DC 20036, (202) 462-1000.

This is a new address as of 24 August 1985. "The ASIS Umbrella," an editorial by John Berry in *Library Journal* (15 November 1985): 4, describes his perception of this organization.

Apple "User Group Evangelist." Ellen Petry Leanse, Apple Computer Inc., 20525
   Mariani Ave., Mail Stop 23G, Cupertino, CA 95014.
   Leanse is the Apple contact person for user group support.

Association for Development of Computer-Based Instructional Systems (ADCIS).
   ADCIS International Hdqtrs., Computer Center, Western Washington University,
   Bellingham, WA 98225.
   Write for information about membership and current publications.

Association for Special Education Technology (ASET). UMC 68, Utah State
   University, Logan, UT 84322, (801) 750-1999.
   ASET co-publishes the *Journal of Special Education Technology*.

Association of Computer Users. P.O. Box 9003, Boulder, CO 80301, (303) 443-3600.
   This is an independent nonprofit association offering comparisons of the most popular small computers, software reviews, a monthly journal, and consumer guides. Write for more information.

Atari, Inc., User Group Support Program. P.O. Box 50047, San Jose, CA 95150.
   Atari maintains a list of user groups around the country. Write for a copy.

Central Illinois Libraries Microcomputer Users' Group. Randy Wilson, director,
   Parlin-Ingersoll Library, 205 West Chestnut, Canton, IL 61520.
   Has a newsletter and a union list directory for 47 contributing libraries in seven Illinois systems which provides an annotated software list, a directory of libraries listing hardware, and contact person. Directory is available for $4.00. For more information contact Randy Wilson.

Committee on Personal Computers for the Handicapped (COPH-2). 2030 Irving Park
   Rd., Chicago, IL 60618.
   Membership $8.00/yr. "Purpose . . . to disseminate information about micro-computers to the disabled . . . publishes a quarterly newspaper discussing hardware developments, provides technical help, and makes modifications to hardware so that the disabled can use it. The equipment is then offered to members at low prices."

Commodore User Groups. Commodore Business Machines, Attn: New User Group or
   Input/Output, 1200 Wilson Drive, West Chester, PA 19838.
   The September/October 1985 issue of *Commodore Microcomputers* contains a listing of Commodore user groups by state. Commodore has a new program to support user groups—groups receive meeting posters and membership cards, and are sent *Input/Output* newsletter. "FOR user groups BY user groups supported by Commodore without advertisements." Write for more information.

Computer Coaching Interest Group. Frank Downing, 202 W. Mitchell Avenue, State
  College, PA 16803, (814) 237-6401.
  An example of the many special interest user groups. For $5.00/yr. membership
dues the members receive six or eight copies of the *C.I.G. Newsletter.*

Ed-Line, Nationwide Electronic Telecommunications Network for Educators. National
  School Public Relations Association, 1801 N. Moore Street, Arlington, VA 22209.
  Has developed "RuraLine," a special network for rural schools, available through
The Source. Write for more information.

Educational Software Evaluation Consortium. TECC Software Library and
  Clearinghouse, San Mateo Office of Education, 333 Main Street, Redwood City,
  CA 94063.
  Organized in 1982 as a TECC project, this national consortium has been expanded
to include representatives from Canada and Australia in addition to those 27 software
evaluation centers throughout the United States. Membership includes ICCE, EPIE,
MicroSIFT, a number of state education departments, and several large regional software evaluation projects. The consortium meets once a year to select about 500 titles for
the annual *Educational Software Preview Guide,* a list of favorably reviewed instructional software programs for the computers most popular in K-12 schools. Each annual
guide is annotated and arranged by subject, indicates instructional modes and suggested
grade levels. The consortium was organized by Ann Lathrop, the current chair and
editor. Copies of the guide and a list of consortium members are available from the
TECC Software Library and Clearinghouse.

EPIE Institute, Educational Projects Information Exchange. P.O. Box 839, Water
  Mill, NY 11976, (516) 283-4922.
  Offers three monthly newsletters, each designed to address various aspects of
education: *EPIEgram Materials, EPIEgram Equipment,* and *MICROgram,* as well as
Micro PRO/FILES. The Educational Software Selector (TESS) is published jointly by
EPIE and Teachers College Press, Columbia University. Read about services in "School
Library Technology" column by Patricia Berglund, *Wilson Library Bulletin*
(November 1985): 36-37 and/or write for more information.

ERIC Clearinghouse on Information Resources. 030 Huntington Hall, Syracuse
  University, Syracuse, NY 13210.
  ERIC has a wealth of information available — booklets, bibliographies, etc. — much
of it available for SASE. Write for brochures describing latest offerings, read columns
describing materials in journals such as *Tech Trends* and *School Library Media
Quarterly,* and write to have name added to mailing list for periodic newsletter.

IBM PC Users Group. Kathryn A. Crawford, Group Chair, Library, University of
  Texas at Dallas, P.O. Box 830643, MC33, Dallas, TX 75080-0643, (214) 690-2963
  or Rebecca Bills, Library, West Virginia School of Graduate Studies, Institute, WV
  25112, (304) 768-9711, ext. 229.
  First meeting held at ALA July 1985. Write for more information.

Information Industry Association. 316 Pennslvania Ave., SE, Suite 400, Washington,
  DC 20003.

International Association for Computing in Education (IACE) (formerly called (AEDS). 1201 Sixteenth Street, N.W., Washington, DC 20036.

Designed for educators and data processing professionals at all levels of education. Primarily concerned with administrative information systems, it has branched out to include microcomputers and instructional applications. Write for more information about publications and regional meetings.

Library Microcomputer Template Clearinghouse. 20 Congress Avenue, Sioux City, IA 51104.

Write for current catalog of library templates for DB Master, Visicalc, and Appleworks (enclose SASE).

Michigan Association for Computer Users in Learning (MACUL). Larry R. Smith, MACUL, Communications Secretary, P.O. Box 628, Westland, MI 48185.

A nonprofit organization which publishes a newsletter and journal and sponsors regional, statewide, and national conventions. Membership is $5.00 (U.S.). No purchase orders.

MicroSIFT, a project of the Northwest Regional Educational Laboratory. Northwest Regional Educational Laboratory, 300 S.W. Sixth Avenue, Portland, OR 97204, (503) 248-6800.

This is a clearinghouse for information about educational software and computer applications. The courseware reviews produced by this project are distributed through various state and local educational agencies, as well as through some periodicals. The information is also retrievable from the Resources in Computer Education (RICE) database through BRS (Bibliographic Retrieval Services) Information Technologies. Write to NWREL for further information.

Modem Users' Group. 132 Gazza Boulevard, Farmingdale, NY 11735.

"Users group for MODEM users designed to HELP you get more for your telecommunications dollar." Membership includes six issues of *Modem-Lines* with articles, tips, tutorials, and reviews. Send $2.00 for a sample issue and a membership application.

New England Microcomputer Users Group (NEMICRO). Ching-chih Chen, Professor and Associate Dean, Graduate School of Library/Information Science, Simmons College, 300 The Fenway, Boston, MA 02115.

Publishes a quarterly newsletter.

OCLC Microcomputer Program Exchange (OMPX). OMPX, OCLC, 6565 Frantz Road, Dublin, OH 43017.

An exchange program for IBM PC and M300 workstation microcomputer programs, this is the successor to the exchange program started by Allan Pratt at the University of Arizona. Contains three general types of material: contributed programs from IBM PC and M300 users, written in BASIC and other languages; command files and templates for use with commercially available programs; and data files, such as the names/addresses of library schools, library periodicals, etc. Write for more information.

PLA — Technology in Public Libraries Committee. Carol F. L. Liu, Chair, Queens Borough Public Library, 89-11 Merrick Blvd., Jamaica, NY 11432. (718) 990-0752.

See *American Libraries* (December 1985): 824 for complete description and copy of application form in this book. The first edition of this library micro users' directory has information on microcomputer use in over 380 libraries of all types. You may order regional directories or the entire directory for the United States and Canada. The committee is exploring the possibility of making the directory available online. Do fill out an application and participate, for the benefit of all.

SOFTSWAP. Computer Using Educators (CUE), P.O. Box 2087, Menlo Park, CA 94026.

The Microcomputer Center was organized through the cooperation of CUE (Computer-Using Educators) and the San Mateo County Office of Education. A variety of microcomputers are housed here and a number of commercial software programs are available for preview. The center is the home of SOFTSWAP, a large library of public domain software for Apple, Atari, Commodore, IBM, and TRS-80 computers which volunteers have previewed and enhanced. These programs are available free to those bringing their own disks to the center or by mail for a nominal fee. NOTE: As of 1 July 1986, SOFTSWAP is no longer distributed through the San Mateo County Office of Education. As of April 1986, no distribution site had been chosen. For information, contact CUE at the above address.

Special Education Software Center. Phyllis Carder Baker, LINC Resources Inc., 3857 North High Street, Columbus, OH 43214, (614) 263-5462.

Described in *The Computing Teacher* (December/January 1984-85): 7.

SpecialNet — National Association of State Directors of Special Education. 2021 K St. NW, Suite 315, Washington, DC 20006, (202) 296-1800.

This is the largest education oriented computer-based communication network in the United States, designed to provide up-to-the-minute information and instant communication for persons concerned with educational programs for handicapped students.

Young People's Logo Association. 1208 Hillsdale Drive, Richardson, TX 75081.

Turtle News has gone electronic. It is now "The Logo Forum" on CompuServe. For more information contact Jim Muller (214) 783-7548; on CompuServe: 76703,3005, and The Logo Forum, GO EDU-21.

INDIVIDUALS

Anderson, Eric S. Micro Libraries, 20 Congress Avenue, Sioux City, IA 50312.

Editor of *Wired Librarian's Newsletter*. Librarian, writer, and consultant.

Costa, Betty. Think Small Computers, Inc., 405 Meadow Brook Court, P.O. Drawer JJ, Hayden, CO 81639, (303) 276-4345.

Speaker, workshop presenter/trainer, and library media consultant with emphasis on library applications using microcomputers.

Dewey, Patrick R. Director of the Maywood Public Library, 121 South 5th Avenue, Maywood, IL 60153, (312) 343-1847.

Author of *Public Access Microcomputers: A Handbook for Librarians;* regular columnist for *Wilson Library Bulletin* and *Library Software Review;* editor of new Meckler publication, *Public Computing,* devoted to libraries and public access microcomputers. If you are considering this type of activity, read his book and watch for his numerous articles and conference presentations. For a user's guide and other information, send him a 9x12 SASE.

Fiebert, Elyse Evans. Head Librarian, Radnor High School, 130 King of Prussia Road, Radnor, PA 19087, (215) 293-0855.

Online bibliographic instruction via DIALOG is an integrated part of the regular ninth-grade library skills curriculum which is taught within the English classes at Radnor High. More advanced online instructional units are designed to meet the needs of individual classroom teachers as requested.

Konopatzkie, Pat. Elmira High School, 24936 Fir Grove Lane, Elmira, OR 97437.

Konopatzkie's early work is described in "Computers and the Media Center: A Principal's Perception," by Gary Zosel, *The Computing Teacher* (March 1982): 34-37. She is currently using a variety of library management software, has added a computer lab to the computers available for teacher/student use in the media center, and is planning for the addition of student online database searching.

Lathrop, Ann. Library Coordinator, SMERC Library and Microcomputer Center, San Mateo County Office of Education, 333 Main Street, Redwood City, CA 94063.

Lathrop's background includes work as a teacher and a librarian in both elementary and secondary schools. She is founder of the SOFTSWAP, an exchange of public domain microcomputer software. She designed *How Can I Find It?* reference search (Sunburst), and is editor of the *Digest of Software Reviews: Education and Software Reviews on File.* She chairs the national Educational Software Evaluation Consortium. Lathrop is also working on a doctoral dissertation at the University of Oregon on the use of online information databases in school libraries and would like to hear of any first-hand experience librarians are having with their students.

Lord, Mort. San Juan College, 4601 College Boulevard, Farmington, NM 87401, (505) 326-3311.

President of the former Corvus National End-Users Group and editor of their publication *The Educational Networker.* Lord and his staff have tested a large number of software programs on the Corvus hardware/software. Some back issues of the *Networker,* containing helpful information for those interested in networking, may still be available. Send SASE for information.

Matlock, Lois. Tandy/Radio Shack, Education Division, 1400 One Tandy Center, Fort Worth, TX 76102, (817) 390-3091.

Contact Matlock for information about current products, services, and names of local representatives for Tandy/Radio Shack.

Murphy, Catherine. District Department Head of Educational Media, Stamford Public Schools, 381 High Ridge Road, Stamford, CT 06906, (203) 358-4112.

OPAC (Online Patron Access Catalog) researcher. Dissertation in progress is an "investigation into the bibliographic practices and attitudes of school library media specialists who are implementing OPACs."

Sather, Ruth. Project Manager, Combase, Inc., Suite 890, 333 Sibley Street, St. Paul, MN 55101, (612) 221-0214.

Speaker, workshop presenter, writer. Sather, a former teacher and library media specialist, has designed several software programs including *Elementary Computer Literacy, Elementary Library Media Skills,* and *Using an Index to Periodicals.*

Skapura, Robert. 1920 Monument Boulevard, Suite 540, Concord, CA 94520, (415) 945-7268.

Librarian, speaker. High school librarian with extensive experience using microcomputers to facilitate the management and instructional tasks in libraries. Formerly with The Library Software Company.

Smith, Janice. Supervisor of Media Services, Adams County School District No. 12, District Media Center, 10291 North Huron Street, Denver, CO 80221, (303) 451-8889.

Smith's media center is using a film management system developed by Research Technology, Inc., using an ADDS Multivision II microcomputer with a Centronics printer. The system correlates teaching objectives with the film collection. In addition, the district media staff is using a wide variety of commercial software for management and processing. The first Computer Cat site (1980-1981) is in District #12.

Yanow, Arlene M. Educational Marketing Manager, Corvus Systems, Inc., 2100 Corvus Drive, San Jose, CA 95124, (408) 559-7000.

Yanow is a responsive source for information about Corvus Systems. Another number to use if you are considering the installation of a Corvus System is Corvus Customer Service Administration, (408) 559-5229.

Appendix C:
Caring for Your Computer

Computers have acquired an unfortunate reputation for being unreliable, and the earlier computers actually did spend as much or more time "down" as up and running. Microcomputers, in addition to advances in speed and capacity, also offer considerably more reliability and durability than their predecessors. They are, however, vulnerable to carelessness, mishandling, power quirks, and ignorance. Properly treated, your computer should give years of faithful and reliable service. Following are a few basic rules for keeping your computer system "up." We also highly recommend adding to your library a comprehensive guide to computer care such as *DON'T! or How to Care for Your Computer* by Rodney Zaks, published by Sybex, Inc.

1) *Read the manual* — at the very least read the section on care and cautions. Many components or systems have individual quirks which dictate certain procedures. Certain types of hard disks, for example, must be powered up only *after* the computer itself is turned on. Reversing the order could mean losing a whole disk's worth of data. Some systems may be powered up with disks in the disk drives; to do so with other systems can mean lost data. Know your system's special needs before you start to use it.

Your dealer should show you how to set up your system, such as what plugs in where and how (remember, it is possible to plug things in the wrong way). He or she may also show you some basic care procedures, such as cleaning a disk drive. You should also be familiar with the utilities on your operating system disk that are used for testing various parts of the system.

2) Keep it clean. Computer components themselves, and especially storage media such as disks and tapes, are very vulnerable to dirt and dust, fingerprints, and even hair. And NEVER, NEVER eat, drink, or smoke while using (or in the vicinity of) the computer.

3) Use antistatic mats or sprays if you have a lot of static electricity in the library. A shock can be as "painful" to a computer and its memory as to a person. If your school power supply is erratic or you live in an area that is subject to thunderstorms or power failures, invest in a voltage regulator, powerline filter, or backup power supply.

4) We've said it before, we'll say it again. **BACK UP** — every time you add or change data. Also, keep backup copies of all programs. Backup copies should be kept in a safe place separate from working copies. DO NOT SKIP THIS STEP — EVER. The exact method used for backup will depend on the type of storage medium and

the operating system you are using. Consult your manual, and/or have your vendor show you the technique(s) for backing up data with your system.

When you are doing frequent data entry, such as for an online catalog or a circulation system, use a rotating backup system. NEVER backup on your most recent backup. A good method is to use a different disk for each day of the week, and back up on the next-to-last day's disk. For example, Wednesday's data would be backed up on Monday's disk, Thursday's data on Tuesday's disk, and so on. That way any major or minor catastrophe would result in only one day's work being lost. It is also a good idea to make daily printed reports, just in case.

5) Caring for floppy disks: Floppies are a wonderfully convenient way to store data. They are also terribly vulnerable to:

Dirt — including dust, fingerprints, smoke, soft drinks, hair, eraser or pencil lead particles, and food. When not in use, even for a few minutes, disks should be kept in their protective sleeves. Never touch the exposed portions of a disk. of a disk.

Magnets — including those found in telephone receivers and color television tubes. Also suspect metal objects such as screwdrivers, keys, and paper clips.

Extreme temperatures — window sills, cars, and radiators are not safe storage areas.

Pressure — especially direct pressure such as that caused by writing on the disk with a pencil or ballpoint pen. Labels should be written before you attach them to the disk. If you must write on an already labeled disk, use a felt tip pen. Also, disks should never be laid down where other objects might be placed on top of them. Store disks vertically in a safe place when not in use, and don't try to cram too many into one box.

Bending, creasing, and folding — will keep your disk from making proper contact with the read/write head in the drive.

Forcing or jamming into a drive — always make sure that the disk is facing the right way (know your system) and be *gentle*.

Gobbling — various minor or major events that cause a computer to "eat" the disk and destroy the data on it. The only protection against this is frequent *backup*.

6) Caring for a hard disk: Like floppies, hard disks are vulnerable to dirt, smoke, and liquids. In fact, since the distance between the read/write head and the disk is so small, a particle of cigarette smoke is enough to cause a head crash, i.e., allow the read/write assembly to come into contact with the disk itself. At the least a head crash will destroy your data, and at the most it will destroy your disk. Winchester drives, because the disk and read/write assemblies are in a hermetically sealed chamber, are fairly well protected. They can, however, be "wiped" by a ringing telephone, by improper use (such as powering up or down in the wrong order), by physical damage such as dropping, and by power irregularities. Among other things, hard disks should not share outlets with other appliances such as coffee makers or vacuum cleaners — in fact, you should avoid using any other powerful device while the hard disk is running. And always *back up* to tape or floppies.

7) Plan your computer area. Make sure that all the components are placed where they are both stable and easy to reach. Printers, especially, can vibrate a good deal. Also make sure that cables are tucked out of the way where they can't be

tripped over or accidentally unplugged. The computer system should, if at all possible, use a dedicated circuit to avoid power interferences.

8)   Educate the users. A list of disk do's and don'ts plus reminders prohibiting food or drinks and encouraging gentleness could be posted at each computer station. Also, each user should be required to go through an orientation session before being allowed to use the computer.

9)   Keep a journal. Make this a habit from the first day you acquire your system. Keep track of all procedures, including backups, with dates and descriptions. It is especially important to note any unusual events or problems with either hardware or software. Describe what the operator did and what happened. This can be enormously useful when you or by-the-hour service personnel are hunting down hardware or software bugs.

10) What to check before calling the service department: First, try the operation again. If it doesn't work the second time, turn everything off, then turn it all back on and try once more. If the problem persists, suspect the software first. Try a backup copy of the software. If you still can't get it to work, then you can begin to suspect a hardware malfunction. Check all the tables and circuit boards to be sure they are plugged in properly. If you have duplicate components, you can try substitutions — such as a different CRT.

When you must have a service person call, try to be present while the problem is being corrected. If it is something simple, such as a blown fuse, you may be able to fix it yourself next time. However, unless you feel very confident that you know what you are doing, *don't* open the equipment and start trying do-it-yourself diagnosis and repair. At the least, you may invalidate the warranty.

FURTHER READINGS
Monographs

Beechold, H. F. *Plain English Maintenance and Repair Guide for IBM Personal Computer.* New York: Simon and Schuster, 1985. unpaged. $14.95.
  "Reference all IBM hobbyists need." — *The Computing Teacher* (June 1985): 47.

Brenner, Robert C. *Apple II Plus/IIe Troubleshooting Guide and Repair Guide.* Indianapolis, Ind.: Howard W. Sams, n.d. unpaged. $19.95.
  Recommended in *Personal Computing* (July 1985): 216.

Microcomputer Equipment Security — A Handbook for Schools. By the Wisconsin Educational Media Association. Manitowoc, Wis.: WEMA, n.d. unpaged. $8.00.
  (WEMA, c/o Don Jorgensen, 1010 Huron Street, Manitowoc, WI 54220).
  "Practical guide to procedures and commercial items designed to improve microcomputing security."

Rafferty, Robert. *Care and Feeding of Your Personal Computer.* New York: Holt, Rinehart and Winston, n.d. 199p. $9.95.

"A 'no-nonsense guide' containing tips on choosing applications, setting up a workspace, preventative maintenance and repairs, organizing disks and files, where to go for help, and other problems confronting new micro owners." Includes a glossary.

Zaks, Rodnay. *DON'T or How to Care for Your Computer.* Berkeley, Calif.: Sybex, 1981. unpaged. $11.95.
    Reviewed: *Popular Computing* (April 1982): 119-20. "DON'T is cheap insurance," *Educational Computer Magazine* (March/April 1983): 44.

Articles

Allswang, John M. "Maintaining Your Computer System." *Interface Age* 9, no. 7 (July 1984): 26-31.
    "Getting a computer fixed can be almost as challenging as buying it, but these guidelines can simplify the process."

"Coping with Static Electricity." *Popular Computing* 3, no. 3 (January 1984): 150, 155.

Doll, Carol A. "Care and Handling of Micro Disks." *School Library Journal* 32, no. 3 (November 1985): 43.

Epstein, Susan Baerg. "Maintenance of Automated Library Systems." *Library Journal* 108 (15 December 1983): 2312-13.

Foster, Edward. "Computer Insurance—Are You Protected?" *Personal Computing* 9, no. 8 (August 1985): 65, 67.
    "Personal computers are vulnerable to a variety of evils, and insuring your hardware and software isn't a simple matter."

Glidewell, Richard. "Service Contract Strategy." *Popular Computing* 4, no. 12 (October 1985): 27-30.

"In Case of Emergency." *Teaching and Computers* (September 1985): 11.
    Includes customer service information for Apple (800) 538-9696; Atari (408) 745-4851; Commodore (800)247-9000; IBM (800) 428-2569; Tandy/Radio Shack (817) 338-2394; and Texas Instruments.

"Insuring Your Micro." *Small Computers in Libraries* 4, no. 10 (November 1984): 1.

Jackson, Phil, and LeRoy Finkel. "When It Breaks . . ." and "Before It Breaks." *CUE (Computer Using Educators) Newsletter.* 8, no. 4 (February/March 1986): 8-9, 10, 13.
    Pair of articles with good advice for addressing computer repair problems. Includes information about handling, Apple, IBM, Commodore, and Tandy/Radio Shack repairs.

Keough, Jim. "How To Keep Your System Running." *Personal Computing.* 8, no. 4 (April 1984): 114-20.
    "It takes more than tender loving care to prevent a computer 'crash'."

LaPier, Cynthia. "Care and Maintenance of an Apple Orchard." *Reference Librarian* (Fall/Winter 1982): 51-56.
Discusses service issues, security problems, accessing DIALOG and staff training at the Elmira College Learning Center.

Levin, James A., Naomi Miyake, and Jerry Olivas. "Computer Rx." *Electronic Learning* 4, no. 1 (September 1985): 55-57.

Littlefield, Patti. "What to Try BEFORE Taking Your Microcomputer into the Repair Department." *Educational Computer Magazine* 3, no. 3 (May/June 1983): 73.

Matthews, Joseph R. "Security and Automated Library Systems: A Ticking Time Bomb?" *Information Technology and Libraries* 2, no. 3 (September 1983): 265-71.
Includes an "Automated Library System Security Checklist."

Nadelman, Michael K., and Chip Carman. "First Aid for Disk Drives," Parts I and II. *A + Magazine* 3, nos. 3 and 4 (March and April 1985): No pages available.

Netizke, Curt. "The Library Tinker's Tool Kit." *Technicalities* 4, no. 10 (October 1984): 14-15.
"A checklist of the equipment you need to maintain AV and computer hardware."

O'Malley, Christopher. "Taking Care Of Your Computer." *Personal Computing* 9, no. 5 (May 1985): 63-71.
"Requires a little extra time and effort . . . pay off big in averted repair bills."

"Power Surges Second Largest Reason for Computer Loss." *Library HiTech News* 1, no. 3 (March 1984): 4.

Price, Robert. "Care and Feeding of the Micro." *Electronic Education* 4, no. 6 (March/April 1985): 10-11, 60.

Scarola, Robert. "When the Chips Are Down." *Popular Computing* 4, no. 9 (July 1985): 73-74, 136-37.
"Beat the high cost and headaches of repair by fixing most problems yourself."

Scott, Patricia B., and Richard D. Howel. "Troubleshooting: Dealing with a Misbehaving Apple." *The Computing Teacher* 11, no. 6 (February 1984): 29-30.

Shawkey, Bruce. "Computer Owner's Guide to Insurance." *Popular Computing* 2, no. 5 (March 1983): 144.

Warshaw, Robin. "Keeping It Clean for Best Performance." *Popular Computing* 3, no. 6 (April 1984): 152, 155.

Appendix D: No Computer in the Budget? Alternative Funding Possibilities

There are a number of sources outside regular budget allotments that might be used to introduce or supplement computer applications in school and public libraries. These sources include federal and state block grants, district funds, a wide list of foundations, local community groups (including parent organizations, student groups, Friends of the Library, etc.), and computer companies themselves. Locating these sources and then persuading them to fund projects involving computers will take research, creativity, and persistence, but even in these days of higher costs and lower budgets, money is available to those who know whom and how to ask for it.

With the possible exception of student groups (such as school computer clubs), any potential funding source will require some form of written and/or oral proposal that explains clearly and specifically the goals, objectives, and methods of the proposed project(s). Although the art of grant writing is outside the scope of this book, there are numerous resources available to anyone seeking to learn it, including books, magazine articles, and even courses at adult education and university extension centers. The main points to remember are these:

1) You must be able to state exactly why you are seeking the funds and what you intend to do with them. The proposal must document clearly the need for and benefits of the proposed project, along with its goals, objectives, and expected outcomes.

Most of the special funding for libraries has had an instructional slant, primarily toward the teaching of library skills, although some grants have been made for the purpose of making library management more time and cost effective. The objective in the latter cases has been to free the library staff to provide more and better patron services. However, it is also important to note that the media center is a logical place to base computer activities for an entire school (see chapter 5, "The Library as a Computer Resource Center"). Therefore, the media specialist will probably be deeply involved in selecting, funding, and implementing computer-oriented projects that go beyond the library.

2) Know your potential sources. Both government and foundation funds tend to have very specific requirements for recipients. These requirements range from geographic and demographic restrictions to the specific types of projects that are eligible. Most agencies will provide guidelines upon request, listing restrictions and requirements for submitting proposals, so there is no need to waste time and effort

preparing a proposal for a program for which you may not be qualified. Once you have decided where to submit your proposal, research the organization to determine your best approach, including the way to format the proposal. This will depend on such factors as the organization's main interests and areas of priority, its familiarity with your specialty, and the attitudes of the selection committee. Some organizations demand a formal, by-the-rules grant proposal; others prefer a straightforward, "plain talk" statement. Find out what your target organization wants.

3) Include specific methodology, time frame, and budgetary requirements in the proposal, as well as the credentials of the person or persons who will actually be carrying out the project. You will also need to include the method(s) to be used for evaluating the success of the project and determining whether and how well your objectives have been met. Your project, after all, represents an investment by the funding organization, and they will want to know if the investment was worthwhile.

4) Timing is important. It can be anywhere from six weeks to six months or even longer between the submission of a proposal and notification of action upon it. Also, many organizations will only accept proposals at specific times of the year. Preparing a proposal is a long-term project in itself.

SOURCES OF FUNDS

Block Grants. The Reconciliation Act of 1981 consolidated over 33 formerly discretionary programs for elementary and secondary education. Under Chapter II of the revised block grants program, local education agencies ("LEA's," i.e., school districts) will now be receiving about $5 to $10 per student to be distributed by the districts themselves. Chapter II is divided into four subchapters, three of which might include monies for library media programs: subchapter A, Basic Skills Development; subchapter B, Educational Improvement and Support Services; and subchapter C, Special Projects. Funds are distributed by state education agencies to the districts according to a formula similar to the one used for the old ESEA-Title B program (from which the majority of the block grant funds come). In order for an LEA to receive funds, it must submit to the state an application that includes a description of the planned allocation of funds. Therefore any library media projects to be funded out of block grants must be included in the LEA's original application.

In most cases, district level funding recommendations will be made by the superintendent of schools in conjunction with a committee of teachers, administrators, and parents. You should make sure that the committee includes at least one library media specialist. Library programs are more likely to receive funds if their proponents can show how the programs will benefit programs in other areas as well. Criteria will vary from district to district, but a well-thought-out and well-presented proposal could result in the purchase of computers for individual schools, or possibly a district level cooperative project.

For further information on the block grant program, particularly in regard to educational technology, contact: AMP Block Grant Center for Media and Technology, Attn: Anne Cullather, 1101 Connecticut NW, Washington, DC

20036, (202) 857-1195. Though intended primarily for companies marketing products to grant recipients, the services of the center are available to educators as well.

Computer companies. Three of the largest microcomputer manufacturers have established formal grant programs for distributing hardware, software, and money for worthwhile and *innovative* educational projects. Several other companies, though they do not have grant programs as such, are not averse to hearing from individuals and institutions with good ideas for using their equipment. Whether seen as a philanthropic commitment to education or as industry competition for the very large educational market, these programs represent tremendous benefits for educators and students. Although each company has its own criteria for choosing recipients, there are some common factors to keep in mind. First, you must know something about computers, or team up with someone who does. The grants are not being made for the purpose of teaching basics, or for repeating work that has already been done. Rather, they are aimed at funding creative, original projects on any scale, including anything from development of a marketable software package to special school or community computer programs. Whatever the type of project, your chances are better with a single, carefully thought-out idea than with a shotgun approach. For information on current possibilities for funding and/or hardware or software grants, contact major manufacturers, such as Apple, IBM, Tandy/Radio Shack, and Commodore.

District funds. Each district has its own methods for determining budget allotments. Often budget decisions are made almost out of habit, or based on "tradition." Administrators at district level might be interested to learn that a library can be equipped with a good quality microcomputer system, serving the entire student body, at a cost less than that of a wrestling mat, which serves only a small proportion of students.

Foundations and government grants. There are a number of foundations, both public and private, that delight in funding worthy educational projects. Although only a minority of the grants are specifically earmarked for technology-related programs (see below), a proposal for a creative project that *includes* one or more microcomputers could very well qualify for funding. One foundation that has shown a particularly strong interest in innovative projects for education is the General Mills Foundation. (Contact: W. R. Humphries, Jr., Executive Director, General Mills Foundation, P.O. Box 1113, Minneapolis, MN 55440.) To find out about other possibilities, check a nearby large library or one of 60 regional collections affiliated with the Foundation Center in New York. Contact the center at 888 Seventh Avenue, New York, NY 10106, (212) 975-1120 or toll free (800) 424-9836, for the location of the collection nearest you. The center has also published a directory, which is available in most public libraries. The following is a list of other publications that can be helpful to grant seekers. Many of them are available at public libraries and/or from district professional collections:

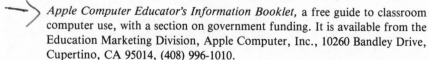

Apple Computer Educator's Information Booklet, a free guide to classroom computer use, with a section on government funding. It is available from the Education Marketing Division, Apple Computer, Inc., 10260 Bandley Drive, Cupertino, CA 95014, (408) 996-1010.

The AV Connection: The Guide to Federal Funds for Audio-Visual Programs, an annually updated guide published by the National Audio-Visual Association (NAVA), which includes information on federal programs which make funds available for audiovisual equipment, materials, and services (including computers). It is available from NAVA, 3150 Spring Street, Fairfax, VA 22031 (703) 273-7200.

The Catalog of Federal Domestic Assistance, a comprehensive listing of funds available through federal agencies, and two daily publications, *The Federal Register* and *The Commerce Business Daily,* all published by the U.S. Superintendent of Documents, U.S. Government Printing Office, Publications Dept., Washington, DC 20402.

Foundation Center Source Book Profiles and *About Foundations: How to Find the Facts You Need to Get a Grant,* both from the Foundation Center, 888 Seventh Avenue, New York, NY 10106.

Foundations Reports, a bimonthly magazine that provides listings of foundation grants, cross-referenced by state, subject area, and receiving institution.

Grants—How to Find Out about Them and What to Do Next, Plenum Press, 227 West Seventeenth Street, New York, NY 10011.

The Grants Register, St. Martins Press, 175 Fifth Avenue, New York, NY 10010. An annually updated directory of funding organizations, with grants indexed by subject.

ICIA Directory of Foundations. By International Communications Industries Association. Fairfax, Va.: ICIA, n.d. unpaged. $19.95 + $1.50 postage & handling (ICIA, 3150 Spring Street, Fairfax, VA 22031). Lists foundations that make grants to educational institutions, including public and private schools, libraries, media centers, and museums.

In addition, a number of the periodicals mentioned in appendix B, particularly those aimed at educators, publish frequent articles on obtaining funds for microcomputer-related projects.

School and/or community fund-raising. Local fund-raising ideas range from bake sales to full-scale community fund drives. In order to launch a successful fund-raising project, you will need to have specific goals, first in terms of what you want to obtain—five new computers for classroom use, special software, a new printer?—and then in terms of monetary requirements. Then you will need a dedicated and energetic committee, preferably including students, teachers, parents, and community business leaders, to carry out the campaign. Get as much publicity as possible, through open houses and PTA presentations—particularly effective if you already have micros that can be used for hands-on demonstrations—local newspaper coverage, handouts and newsletters, and so on. Local business leaders are often willing to support educational projects, perhaps in the form of matching donations, and local service organizations may be willing to help as well. Set a time frame for achieving your goals and be persistent.

Another way to raise money for computer projects is to earn it, using computers. This is particularly true in schools and communities with active computer clubs.

One high school club in California, for example, raised money by working with the school athletic department during a "Lift-a-thon" fund drive. The club computerized the pledge list, printing and mailing statements to people who had pledged money for the Lift-a-thon, in return for 10% of the proceeds. Besides making money, club members got to carry out a challenging project. Such ideas are limited only by club and committee members' imaginations and energy.

Coin-operated computers are also becoming popular for public library use. They are available through several vendors, or you may wish to devise your own system, perhaps charging a fee for software use as well.

Public interest in and support for computer-related education is growing at a tremendous rate. Parents want their children to be exposed to computers, and in fact, often would not mind a little exposure themselves. Take advantage of this interest to enlist their support, as well as the support of the students themselves. If your library is a public one, you are in a position to offer computer services to the community as a whole. Ask the community to help make those services available. Everyone will benefit.

FURTHER READINGS

Monographs

35 Ways to Take a 'Byte' Out of Software Costs . . . Fund Raising Ideas. Wentworth, N.H.: COMPress, Division of Wadsworth, Inc., n.d. unpaged. Free (COMPress, P.O. Box 102, Wentworth, NH 03282, (603) 764-5225).
Write for this free and helpful booket.

Articles

Stronge, James H. "Funding Computer-Related Technology in the Public Schools." *The Computing Teacher* (August 1983): 13-15.
Though not the most recent article it may lead you to an avenue not explored.

Swartz, Theodore F. "Finding Funding for Your Computer Project." *Classroom Computer Learning* (March 1984): 36-41.
Includes: "Identifying Major Funding Sources"; "Researching Successfully Funded Projects"; "Getting Support from Parents and Civic Groups"; "Tapping the Business Community"; "Resources to the Rescue." This article has been adapted from "How to Fund a Computer Project," a chapter in *Educator's Complete Guide to Computers*, by Theodore F. Swartz, Stephen M. Shuller, and Fred B. Chernow (Parker Publishing Co., 1984).

Appendix E:
Sample Comparison
and Evaluation Charts

Included in this section are several sample forms which might be used to evaluate potential computer purchases. The exact nature of your charts will, of course, depend on the specific needs of your particular library, but these examples should give you a good starting point for developing your own evaluation methods.

Chart 1 is a comparative analysis of the different methods of acquiring software, as discussed in chapter 2; charts 2-5 represent some different methods of software evaluation; and chart 6 is a sample comparison chart for evaluating hardware systems.

We are grateful to those who have allowed us to reprint their work here.

FEATURE	IN-HOUSE DEVELOPMENT	CUSTOM DEVELOPMENT	PURCHASED SOFTWARE	PURCHASED SERVICES
Development Cost	Very high development cost.	Design and programming costs higher than in-house; but total cost could be less.	Package cost estimated at 20 to 50% or less of in-house development. Implementation costs may exceed in-house.	No development cost unless tailoring modifications are required. Implementation cost will vary with amount of internal system modification required.
Development Lead Time	Long lead time due to system design, programming and testing.	Lead time shorter than in-house, but still lengthy.	Shorter lead time than in-house. Will require time for system familiarization and installation.	Minimum lead time. Support usually provided by service bureau to speed implementation.
Development Risk	Risk high due to the many variables involved.	Lower risk than in-house, but is relative to the capabilities of the vendor and system complexities.	Low risk is relative to the level of package use and complexity of requirements.	Low risk relative to experience and quality of the service bureau.

Chart 1. Comparative analysis of software systems. Reprinted by permission of McDonnell Douglas Automation Company.

FEATURE	IN-HOUSE DEVELOPMENT	CUSTOM DEVELOPMENT	PURCHASED SOFTWARE	PURCHASED SERVICES
Company Acceptance	Should receive wide and easy acceptance if user heavily involved in requirements definition and development.	Should be accepted if user has been involved in selection, requirements definition and development.	Some resistance; can be overcome by planning and user commitment, beginning with involvement in selection.	Some resistance; user may accept external processed system if involved in selection and is convinced of strong, continuing vendor support.
System Quality	Some errors will be latent in most development efforts; general quality will be as good as staff capabilities.	Quality will be as good as vendor ability; level of errors is reduced by vendor specialized skills.	Quality of base packages should be superior to in-house software; modification to method of operation and enhancements may have an effect on quality.	Because the system is in use, the quality should be superior to in-house; no operation quality factors should impact user since service bureau operates the system.
System Flexibility	Will be as good as that which was planned for; high initial cost will reduce the chance of enhancements soon.	Level of flexibility should exceed in-house.	System flexibility will be higher than in-house; designed for broad market and usually has numerous features included. Enhancements will be somewhat tied to the vendor ability to change and update the package.	System flexibility will be high; systems should have dynamic characteristics as service bureau should continually enhance the system to meet new requirements and improved hardware.

Chart 1—*Continued*

FEATURE	IN-HOUSE DEVELOPMENT	CUSTOM DEVELOPMENT	PURCHASED SOFTWARE	PURCHASED SERVICES
Implementation Support	Level of support controlled by staff availability and skill.	Level of support will be consistent with contract terms; in-house support will have to be developed to augment vendor support.	Support is usually limited to software installation and initial user training. Prime effort of vendor is directed toward package sale.	Support is directed toward rapid, successful implementation since revenue is primarily related to the amount of processing after implementation.
Documentation	Generally lower quality than other sources; usually the last area of system development to be completed.	Documentation should be better than in-house if the vendor has people skilled in preparing it.	Documentation level and quality vary; quality can be quite good but initial appearance may not properly reflect the true quality.	Documentation quality tends to be highest among all sources since attention is directed towards helping the user process with minimal problems; quality varies among vendors.
System Operation	Generally will run efficiently on current equipment; changes in equipment may cause operating inefficiencies.	Should operate more efficiently than in-house because of broader knowledge gained in designing for a variety of hardware shops; care must be taken to assure that operation and user ease of operation has been fully considered.	Generally designed to operate efficiently only on the machine for which it was initially designed; user operations characteristics may not be consistent with your standards, and may require noticeable effort to "fine tune".	Usually designed to meet user needs in an efficient manner and well tuned to run efficiently in the service bureau's environment.

Chart 1 — *Continued*

FEATURE	IN-HOUSE DEVELOPMENT	CUSTOM DEVELOPMENT	PURCHASED SOFTWARE	PURCHASED SERVICES
Maintenance	Total maintenance must be performed by user.	Maintenance may be performed by user after acceptance; time must be allocated to learn system.	Maintenance costs may be reduced substantially if maintenance contracts are available.	Maintenance is included in the service; no effort is required by user.
Enhancements	Growth to meet future needs dependent on the skill with which the initial design was developed and on staff availability.	Enhancements done by the vendor can be expensive if his original staff is not available. The alternative will require learning time by in-house programmers to become familiar with design techniques.	Vendor personnel may be available to make modifications; otherwise, your programming staff will have to become familiar with programs and make changes, possibly voiding warranties and maintenance contracts.	Systems tend to be most flexible with periodic system enhancements; service bureau will usually make changes for clients since programming support staff is available.
User Support	Require continued training and allocation of personnel familiar with manufacturing systems.	Must be provided in-house following the acceptance of the working system.	Initial user training may be provided by the vendor; subsequent support will be the users' responsibility.	On-going support with manufacturing and DP background will usually be available to assist users.

Chart 1—*Continued*

RATING: Circle the letter abbreviation which best reflects your judgment.

IMPORTANCE: Circle the letter which reflects your judgment of the relative importance of the item in this evaluation.

	RATING	IMPORTANCE	
	SA–Strongly Agree A–Agree D–Disagree SD-Strongly Disagree NA–Not Applicable	H–HIGH L–LOW	
CONTENT	SA A D SD NA	H L	Content is accurate
	SA A D SD NA	H L	Content is organized in a clear, concise way
	SA A D SD NA	H L	Content is free of race, ethnic, sex or other stereotypes.
	SA A D SD NA	H L	Student is allowed to build on skills
	SA A D SD NA	H L	Graphics/color/sound are used for appropriate instructional purposes
	SA A D SD NA	H L	Learner controls the rate and sequence of presentation and review
	SA A D SD NA	H L	Program is relevant to the curriculum
INSTRUCTIONAL QUALITY	SA A D SD NA	H L	Flexibility in skill leveling is allowed
			Principles of learning are employed:
	SA A D SD NA	H L	Retention
	SA A D SD NA	H L	Motivation
	SA A D SD NA	H L	Transfer
	SA A D SD NA	H L	Reinforcement
	SA A D SD NA	H L	Teaches to one objective
	SA A D SD NA	H L	Bloom's Taxonomy is employed beyond the knowledge level
	SA A D SD NA	H L	Students are allowed to exit from program
	SA A D SD NA	H L	Directions are easy to use
	SA A D SD NA	H L	Program is well documented
TECHNICAL QUALITY	SA A D SD NA	H L	Intended users can easily and independently operate the program
	SA A D SD NA	H L	Program is free from errors
	SA A D SD NA	H L	Visual display is readable
	SA A D SD NA	H L	User support materials are comprehensive

Chart 2. Software evaluation. Reprinted by permission of School District No. 12, Adams County, Colorado.

SOFTWARE EVALUATION

Courseware Description	Technical Information

Courseware Description

Program Title _____

Call Number _____

Developer/Publisher Names_____

_____

Release Date _____ Cost _____

Vendor _____

Subject Area _____

With which instructional objectives does this software correlate?

_____

Copyright Privileges No _____ Yes _____

    If allowed, restrictions? _____

Estimated time for student interaction with the program to achieve the objectives. (Can be stated as total time or time per day)

_____

Type of Program:

    Computer-Assisted Instruction (Please check all applicable descriptions)

    Drill and Practice _____   Problem Solving _____

    Tutorial _____   Informational Retrieval _____

    Game _____   Other _____

    Simulation _____

    User Grade Level:

    1 2 3 4 5 6 7 8 9 10 11 12

    Reading Level _____

Computer Managed Instruction

    Learning Management _____

    Diagnosis _____

    Prescription _____

Administrative

    Data Base Management _____

    Text Editing _____

    Turnkey System Yes _____ No _____

    Best used by _____

Technical Information

Computer Company _____

Computer Model_____

Memory Capacity _____

DOS: 3.2 _____ 3.3 _____ Other, specify_____

_____

Number of Disk Drives _____

Required Hardware:

    Color Monitor _____   Paddles _____

    B/W Monitor _____   Wand _____

    Printer _____   Graphics Table _____

Special Requirements (hardware, application, software)

_____

_____

Language _____

Storage Media:

    Cassette _____   Cartridge _____

    Disk _____   Other, specify _____

    _____

    Floppy Disk _____   Sectors

        13 _____ 16 _____

    Hard Disk _____   Type _____

(PLEASE COMPLETE EVALUATION ON REVERSE)

Reviewer's Name _____   School _____

Date of Review _____   (If owned by school): Program location in school _____

Authorized as available for sharing Yes _____ No _____   Comments _____

_____

School District No. 12, Adams County
11285 Highline Drive
Northglenn, Colorado 80233

© Copyright applied for
Form N-1730/Jul 82

Chart 2—*Continued*

NOTE: Please copy this form and use it to contribute reviews to the SOFTSWAP file. Send your reviews to: Ann Lathrop, San Mateo County Office of Education, 333 Main Street, Redwood City, CA 94063.

CALIFORNIA LIBRARY MEDIA CONSORTIUM FOR

CLASSROOM EVALUATION OF MICROCOMPUTER COURSEWARE

FOLD HERE AND STAPLE TO RETURN (ADDRESS ON REVERSE)

- -

Program title_____

Disk/tape/package title (if different)_____

Microcomputer brand, model_____ ___K memory needed

Language __BASIC (or_____) Publisher_____ Cost_____

Peripherals needed_____ __Disk __Tape __Cartridge __Other(_____)

Supplemental materials/equipment needed_____ Backup possible?_____

*   *   *   *   *   *   *   *   *   *   *   *   *   *   *

Reviewed by_____ grade level/subject_____

School/District_____ Phone (   )_____

Address_____

May we use your name in the published review?_____

THANK YOU FOR YOUR HELP. PLEASE RETURN IMMEDIATELY TO THE ADDRESS ON THE BACK.

Chart 3. Classroom evaluation of microcomputer courseware. Reprinted by permission of California Library Media Consortium, San Mateo County Office of Education.

CHECKLIST OF EVALUATION CRITERIA

YES NO N/A

GENERAL:

___ ___ ___ 1. Is this an effective/appropriate use of the computer?

___ ___ ___ 2. Are the objectives/purpose of the program well defined?

___ ___ ___ 3. Does the program achieve its objectives/purpose?

___ ___ ___ 4. Is the program technically sound, free of programming errors, easy to operate?

___ ___ ___ 5. Does it provide a useful summary or report of student performance?

___ ___ ___ 6. Is the program free of excessive competition and violence?

___ ___ ___ 7. Is it free of racial, sex, and ethnic stereotypes?

___ ___ ___ 8. Is the documentation sufficient?

CONTENT:

___ ___ ___ 1. Is the content factually correct?

___ ___ ___ 2. Is the presentation logical, well organized, with internal consistency?

___ ___ ___ 3. Can the instructor modify the program (word lists, data, speed, etc.)?

___ ___ ___ 4. Are the interest level, difficulty level and vocabulary level compatible?

INSTRUCTIONS (available within the program)

___ ___ ___ 1. Are they clear, complete and concise?

___ ___ ___ 2. Can user skip them and return to them as needed (HELP)?

___ ___ ___ 3. Is user told how to end program? start over? reenter where user left?

___ ___ ___ 4. Can user control speed and sequence of paging?

___ ___ ___ 5. Is there a menu to allow user to access specific parts of the program?

INPUT:

___ ___ ___ 1. Is input consistent, using common conventions and symbols?

___ ___ ___ 2. Can user correct input if necessary before continuing program?

___ ___ ___ 3. Is there a cursor or other indicator to show where input is to go?

___ ___ ___ 4. Does the computer give a helpful response to input errors?

___ ___ ___ 5. Is the amount of typing required appropriate to the grade level?

SCREEN OUTPUT:

___ ___ ___ 1. Is the screen format neat and uncluttered?

___ ___ ___ 2. Are punctuation and grammar correct?

___ ___ ___ 3. Is the correct answer, or appropriate help, given after a reasonable time or after a given number of errors?

___ ___ ___ 4. Does the program branch to easier or harder material in response to user input?

___ ___ ___ 5. Are responses to errors non-judgmental, free of harsh or demeaning comment?

___ ___ ___ 6. Is the positive feedback for correct response more interesting/enjoyable/exciting than is the response to errors/failure?

___ ___ ___ 7. Does the program use motivational devices effectively? CIRCLE those used. STAR (*) ones used effectively to enhance the program.

__timing __scoring __game format __personalization __color __sound

1/82   __graphics for instruction __graphics for reward __random order

Chart 3—*Continued*

GRADE LEVEL(S) (circle) k 1 2 3 4 5 6 7 8 9 10 11 12 college teacher use

SUBJECT AREA(S)_____

SCOPE

__single concept program
__program is one part of a
   larger instructional series
__complete instructional unit

GROUP SIZE

__individual use
__small group (2 to 5)
__large group/class

DOCUMENTATION

__in program
__guide/manual
__student materials
__none

TYPE OF PROGRAM

__simulation (a model of a portion of the real world)
__educational game
__game
__drill and practice
__tutorial (presents new material for student to learn)
__problem solving
__testing
__authoring system (allows teacher to develop a program)
__classroom management
__other _____

BRIEF DESCRIPTION OF THE PROGRAM

Objectives_____

_____

Content_____

_____

Classroom uses_____

_____

Strengths/weaknesses_____

_____

STUDENT RESPONSE

Did your students like the program?_____

Did they want to use the program repeatedly, or share it with friends?_____

Did they learn from it?_____

PLEASE USE ANOTHER SHEET IF YOU HAVE ADDITIONAL COMMENTS

OVERALL OPINION ***** OVERALL OPINION ***** OVERALL OPINION ***** OVERALL OPINION

     __Great program! I recommend it highly!
     __Pretty good/useful -- consider purchase.
     __OK, but you might wait for something better.
     __Not useful. I don't recommend purchase.

Chart 3—*Continued*

The Computing Teacher

FIGURE 1
SOFTWARE EVALUATION FORM & CHECKLIST
(Permission to reprint is granted)

DATE:_____   EVALUATOR: _____

PROGRAM NAME _____   WRITTEN FOR _____ COMPUTER

VENDOR-AUTHOR_____   IN _____ LANGUAGE

ADDRESS _____

CITY, ST., ZIP _____

PHONE _____

COST $_____

PROGRAM CLASS (Check one or more boxes)   **SYSTEM REQUIRED** (Check one or more boxes)

☐ Computer assisted instruction   ☐ 16K   ☐ 32K   ☐ 48K COMPUTER

☐ Computer managed instruction   ☐ DISK DRIVE

☐ Administrative   ☐ TAPE

☐ (Other)_____   ☐ PRINTER   ☐ W/GRAPHICS

_____   ☐ PLOTTER

INTENDED USER (Check one or more boxes)

☐ Teachers

☐ Students _____ Grade Level

☐ Other _____

_____

PROGRAM MODE ** (Check one or more boxes)

☐ Drill & Practice*   ☐ Test Construction or Analysis*

☐ Instructional Game*   ☐ Tutorial Instruction*

☐ Instructional Management*   ☐ Programming Utility

☐ Instructional Support*   ☐ Information

☐ Problem Solving or Research*   ☐ Other (please specify) _____

☐ Simulation*   _____

GENERAL DESCRIPTION OR PURPOSE OF PROGRAM

**The definitions of the eight starred modes of educational applications of computers have been the focus of five years of work by Dr. J. Richard Dennis of the University of Illinois at Urbana/Champaign, and are available through Dr. Bob Kansky, Science/Math Teaching Center, Box 3992- University Station, Laramie, Wyoming 82071.

Chart 4. Software evaluation form and checklist. Reprinted by permission of *The Computing Teacher*.

The Computing Teacher

FIGURE 1a

OVERVIEW OF PROGRAM CHARACTERISTICS

	LITTLE	SOME	MUCH
A. DOCUMENTATION AVAILABLE	☐	☐	☐
B. INSTRUCTOR ORIENTATION NEEDED	☐	☐	☐
C. USER ORIENTATION NEEDED	☐	☐	☐
1. Directions (Verbal)	☐	☐	☐
2. Directions (Written)	☐	☐	☐
3. Systems Errors Handled?	☐	☐	☐
4. Keyboard Input by User	☐	☐	☐
5. Dependence on Background or Prior Knowledge	☐	☐	☐

D. USER TARGET(S)

☐ Individual

☐ Group

E. INTERACTION

☐ Cooperation

☐ Competition

CHARACTERISTICS OF TEACHING STRATEGY/MOTIVATION

☐ Games   ☐ Audio   ☐ Student Control

☐ Color   ☐ Graphics   ☐ Ancillary Materials & Worksheets

SOUNDNESS OF CONTENT IS —

☐ Mathematically and Computationally Correct

☐ Conceptually Correct and Contemporary

☐ Compatible with Other Instructional Material in Use

☐ Instructionally Significant

ALL OVER GENERAL RATING

☐ Poor   ☐ Fair   ☐ Good   ☐ Excellent   ☐ Superior

OTHER COMMENTS

_____

_____

_____

_____

_____

FORM DESIGN: BOB HILGENFELD, SCHOOL DISTRICT #1, ROCK SPRINGS, WYOMING

Chart 4—*Continued*

Reviewer's Name _____Date _____

Subject/Grade Level Taught _____

Name of Program _____Source_____

Author's Name_____ Machine Used_____

1. What were the Objectives for this program?

2. Subject Area(s)_____

3. Instructional level(s)_____

4. Pre-requisite skills:_____

5. Type of Activity: Drill & Practice_____Tutorial_____
   Remediation_____Enrichment_____Problem Solving_____
   Simulation_____Strategy Game_____Video Game_____

6. Is this activity a good application for computers?_____

7. Is there documentation? (Instructions, Teacher's Guide, Methods of implementing changes, references to other resources.)_____

8. Does this program contain a "Title Page" with author & Source?___

9. Does the program allow the following functions?
   Possibility of student quitting?_____
   Teacher lock up so student must complete program?_____
   Clear instructions with ability to return to them at will?_____
   Student control of screen page changes?_____
   Personalized interaction?_____
   Encouraging positive reinforcement?_____ Varied?_____
   Gentle means of negative reinforcement? _____Varied?_____
   Does the program give answers?_____After how many tries?____
   Can the answers be locked?_____Retrieved?_____
   Does the student know how many problems he is to do?_____
   Does the program tell the student how many have been done?_____
   Is the program randomized or is it the same each time it is run?___
   How many choices of format?_____
   Can the program be easily changed to accept teacher data?_____
   Is this by file or by data changes?_____

Chart 5. Software review and rating form.

Does the program require students to record data or plan action on paper?_____

Is the program timed?_____In what way?_____

Does the program reward the child by providing a game or graphics display for problems correct?_____

Is a score board given?_____Does it include:
Time to complete program?_____Number of correct responses?_____
% correct?_____Listing of problems that gave the student trouble?_____
Does the program give the option of reviewing the problems missed with a tutorial presentation?_____

At the end, does the student get to try the program again or is the program terminated automatically?_____

Was the program easy to follow and to understand what the student was to do?_____

Did the program use interesting graphics?_____Was there variety?_____

Did the program have animation?_____

Did the program follow a sequence or did it allow branching if a student responded correctly?_____

10. If a simulation, or problem solution does the event follow actual dates, events, places, etc. accurately?_____Is the simulation as close to reality as possible?_____ Does it use the computer's ability for animation?_____ Does it require the student to record data, plan action and pose solutions on paper?_____ Does it give the student clues as to wrong choices or is the student "bombed"?_____Does it require good interaction?_____

SUMMARY EVALUATION: Rate each category. A=Excellent B, C, D, F=Terrible

Level of interest._____   Educational Value._____ Program polish

(amateurish, incomplete, bugs, ease of use, etc.)_____ Quality of

documentation._____ Use of graphics and/or animation?_____

Response to knowledgeable student?_____Use of computer as a unique

instructional tool?_____ Positive, personalized interaction?_____

Summary of student performance?_____Ease of adaptation by teacher?____

OVERALL VALUE: A   B   C   D   F   (A=Every school should have one.)
                                     (F=Not worth the effort to load & view.)

Please write a short summary of the program including strengths and

weaknesses, functions listed in item 9 and a personal reaction to the

value of the program for your classroom.

Chart 5—*Continued*

DESIRED SOFTWARE APPLICATIONS IN ORDER OF IMPORTANCE:

    1. Word processing

    2. Accounting, fund

    3. Database management/file
       management

    4. Spreadsheet/statistical
       analysis

    5. Special Applications

	Computer A	Computer B	Computer C
1.Established stand alone single application package	1,4	2,3	1,2, 3,4
(one package that meets needs of first application priority)			
2. Compatible software pkgs available:	1,4	2,3	1,4
(packages from one developer which will interface and meet the needs of more than one application on your priority list)			
3.Operating Systems:			
Standard	CP/M	CP/M86	(?)DOS
Others		UNIX	CP/M
4.Memory:			
RAM	48K	128K	64K
ROM	NA	20K	12K
Expandable to	64K	512K	NA
5. Programming Languages available:			
Standard	MBASIC	MBASIC	(?)BASIC

Chart 6. Hardware comparison chart.

Others	FORTRAN -Pascal	"C" Pascal	Pascal
6. Keyboard:			
Attached	yes		
Detached		yes	yes
Numeric pad			yes
Cursor keys		yes	
Function keys		yes	yes
7. Video display:		amber	
Color(b/w,amber...)	green b/w	green b/w	green b/w
Attached	yes		
Detached		yes	yes
Adjustable		yes	
Graphics	yes	yes	yes
Pixels Horizontal, Vertical (number of "dots" in pattern)	180,90	400,360	240,160
8. Character display (40,54,72,80)	54	80	40
Expandable		120	80
9. Lower Case	no	yes	
Expandable			yes
10. Graphics	no	yes	yes
11. Color possible			yes
12. Sound possible			yes

Chart 6—*Continued*

13. Interfaces:

# of serial(RS-232C)		3	2
# of parallel	1	1	1
Expandable			

14. Printer

Dot Matrix	X		X
Daisywheel		X	X
Graphics	X		
# of columns	80	132	80

15. Vendor:

Reliable/Established

Will train/hand-hold

Service/warranty

16. COST

CPU/Keyboard

Video display Unit

Drive(s)

    Floppy

    Hard

Printer

Cables & interfaces

Other

     BE SURE HARDWARE MATCHES SOFTWARE REQUIREMENTS!

Chart 6—*Continued*

Index

Micro conversion. *See* Case studies on
micro conversion
Microcomputers, 7-9, 11, 71, 32-33, 36, 41,
60(fig.). *See also* Computers
auxiliary devices, 37, 45-55
care and maintenance, 289-93
conversion case studies, 196-213
defined, 33
for networking, 133, 135
standardization, 20-21, 59
user policies, 167
Microperf paper, 54
Microprocessors, 6, 11, 17-18, 35, 52
Microsoft (software manufacturer), 18
Microsoft DOS (MS-DOS), 11, 18, 20, 23,
34, 42, 45, 100, 134
Minicomputers, 6-7, 11, 32-33, 71
for networking, 91, 133, 135
Minnesota Educational Media Organization,
118
Modems, 33, 45, 57-58, 91, 133, 137-38,
163, 169
compatibility, 55-56
for networking, 88, 135
MOdulator-DEModulator. *See* Modems
Monitors, 33, 35, 47-49. *See also* Cathode-
ray tubes; Screens
Monochrome monitors, 48
Monographs, 237-48
Mouse (input device), 19, 47
MS-DOS. *See* Microsoft DOS

Napier, John, 3, 10
National Cash Register (NCR), 5
National Commission on Libraries and Infor-
mation Science, 140
National networks, 136
NCR. *See* National Cash Register
Near-letter-quality printers, 50-51
Nebraska, 135
Networking and networks, 125, 133-36
computerization, 156, 158
policies on software use, 180, 182-89
resources, 246-47
New Jersey, 135
New York, 135
Newsletters, 253-57
Nonimpact printers, 51-52
Nonprint materials. *See* Audiovisual formats
NTSC monitors, 48

Object code, 15
OCLC. *See* Online Computer Library Center
OCR. *See* Optical character recognition
Ohio, 135
Ohio College Library Center (OCLC), 7. *See
also* Online Computer Library Center

Online bulletin boards. *See* Bulletin board
services
Online catalogs, 106, 109, 135. *See also*
Card catalogs: conversion to computerized catalog
and circulation system combined, 93, 100,
103, 134, 165, 168
patron-accessed, 89-92
resources, 272
Online Computer Library Center (OCLC), 7,
89, 91, 135-36, 138, 209
Online databases, 44, 55, 109, 117, 134-40.
See also Electronic services; Online
searching
Online searching, 81, 90, 109, 138-39. *See
also* Online databases
ethics, 181
resources, 246-47
On-screen formatting for word processing, 75
Open architecture policy, 17, 19, 35
Operating systems, 42, 45, 52, 62, 72-73, 134.
See also Apple DOS/ProDOS; Con-
trol program for microcomputers;
Microsoft DOS
definition and types, 15-20
software requirements, 24-25, 33-36, 179
Optical character recognition (OCR), 47
Optical disks (CD ROM), 6, 11, 44, 89
Orientation for patrons. *See* Patrons: orient-
ing to computer system
Originate-answer modems, 56
Originate-only modems, 56
Oughtred, William, 3-4, 10
Output devices, 33, 47-55
Overdue systems, 100, 103, 106

Paddles (input devices), 47
Page numbering for word processing, 75
Paper for printers, 53-54, 163
Paperless society, 137
Parallel interfaces, 52-53, 58
Pascal, Blaise, 4, 10
Pascal (programming language), 15
Patrons
identification numbers, 101-2
keyboards for, 46
online catalogs for, 89-92
orienting to computer system, 166-67,
171, 197-98, 203, 291
printers for, 52
publicizing new system, 152-59, 164-66
Patterson, John, 10
Peer-tutoring, 165, 198
Pennsylvania, 135
Periodicals. *See* Journals and periodicals;
Serials control